Mike Rein
Aug. 20, 2
New Ulm, .

M000187537

The Quest for the Lost Roman Legions

Discovering the Varus Battlefield

Tony Clunn

The Quest for the
Lost Roman Legions

Discovering the Varus Battlefield

Best Wishes
Tony Clunn

Savas Beatie
New York

SPELLMOUNT
Staplehurst, UK

Cataloging-in-Publication Data is available from the Library of Congress.

Published in the United States by Savas Beatie in 2005
First edition, first printing. ISBN 1-932714-08-1

Savas Beatie LLC
521 Fifth Avenue, Suite 3400
New York, NY 10175
Phone: 610-853-9131
sales@savasbeatie.com
www.savasbeatie.com

_____

British Library Cataloguing in Publication Data:
A catalogue record for this book is available
from the British Library

Also published in the UK by Spellmount Limited in 2005
ISBN 1-86227-316-2

Spellmount Limited
The Village Centre
Staplehurst
Kent TN12 0BJ

Tel: 01580 893730
Fax: 01580 893731
E-mail: enquiries@spellmount.com
Website: www.spellmount.com

Printed in the United States of America.

This book is dedicated to the people of Kalkriese for the peace and tranquility of their homes, for their friendship, and for their invaluable assistance over the years.

To my dear friend and colleague
Professor Dr Wolfgang Schlüter

To good friends
Paul and Ursula, Bissendorf,
Karl and Maria, Berlin,
Willy Dräger, Hannover,
Denny Warta, USA,
Wolfgang Prauss, Berlin.
Ron & Margaret, UK

And to Sean, Tanya, and Erika

Also in special memory of *Gisela*, who walked over the Kalkriese fields so many times and who passed away to greener fields in February 1997.

With much love to Anna and our children,
Jana, Mark Anthony, and Josephine Louise.

The Mask. Originally covered in silver, this iron face was part of a soldier's helmet. The author excavated it from the central battlefield at Kalkriese.

Author's Collection

Contents

PART I

Contents (continued)

PART II

Maps and Photographs

A gallery of photos can be found after page 150.

In addition to many other sources, this book is primarily based upon the records and diaries I kept of nine years of involvement with the archaeological excavations in Kalkriese, near Osnabrück, in Germany. It was there, in 9 AD, that three Roman legions (the Seventeenth, Eighteenth and Nineteenth) under command of Quinctilius Varus, Consul of Rome, and Governor of the province of Germania, some twenty thousand men in all, were slaughtered in a running battle by German tribesmen under the command of Arminius. The stunning defeat was one of the most important military engagements in Western civilization's history, though where it took place remained a mystery for almost 2,000 years.

My good friend and Osnabrück archaeologist, Professor Wolfgang Schlüter, and I spent many years searching for the truth about the disappearance of the Varus legions in the highlands of the Teutoburger Wald, and the bloody battle that finally destroyed them at Kalkriese. The records kept throughout allowed me to provide an accurate account of the long, exhilaring, and often frustrating journey to document where Varus and his men met their end. This modern-day archaeological detective story comprises one of the two primary storylines in *The Quest for the Lost Roman Legions*.

In order to more fully and completely appreciate and come to grips with what happened in 9 AD, I decided to include a parallel story based upon my understanding of Rome and its army, the terrain of northern Germany, and artifacts uncovered during my quest for the battlefield and the truth of Varus' demise. What was happening inside the Roman column during the march toward the Rhine? What was it like to be a member of a Roman legion stationed in Germany during the reign of Augustus? How did Arminius plan and execute one of the most devastating ambushes in military history? How did the Romans react when they realized they were under attack and how did the battle unfold from that point to the final bloody confrontation? Although this portion of the book is historical fiction, it is firmly grounded on accepted historical sources, among them Tacitus, Cassius Dio, and Florus, archaeological evidence, and a firm grasp of the topography in this portion of Germany. Of course, we will never know exactly what was said and who did what, but I believe the liberties taken help provide readers with a richer understanding of what these people were experiencing as the book alternates between the 20th Century and the time of Augustus. For example, we know a Roman solder named Marcus Aius was present with Varus and killed in the bloody melee, because a bronze clasp bearing his name has been unearthed. Although his exact rank is unknown, I elevated Aius to Senior Tribune and Second-in-Command of the legions under Varus, and use him in a historically accurate sense to convey to readers the responsibilities and actions expected from an officer of such high rank. Virtually everyone else—Varus, Arminius, Segestes, his daughter Thusnelda, and many others—actually lived and died during this early period of Germany's history.

The *Varusschlacht* (Varus Battle) spun history, and thus Western civilization, in a different direction. *The Quest for the Lost Roman Legions* is not the final word on that watershed event. Out in the fields, there is much more waiting to be discovered.

Acknowledgements

I would like to thank all those who have helped me in the writing of this book, those who have encouraged me, and those who have become friends and colleagues.

For editing the original diaries: Greg Payne, *Treasure Hunting Monthly*, and my daughter Tanya.

For professional advice and guidance: Professor Dr. Wolfgang Schlüter, Osnabrück; Professor Dr. Siegmar von Schnurbein, Frankfurt; Professor Müller, Hamburg; Dr. Frank Berger, formerly of Hannover and now Frankfurt; Dr. Susanne Wilbers-Rost, Osnabrück; Dr. Gebers, Denkmalpflege Hannover; Dr. Johann-Sebastian Kühlborn, Münster; Dr. Erhard Cosack, Hannover; Dr. Joachim Harnecker, Osnabrück; Dr. Georgia Franzius, Osnabrück; Dr. Achim Rost, Osnabrück; Dr. Hermann Queckenstedt, formerly Landschaftsverband Osnabrück; Lt-Col. Ken Martin, Royal Army Medical Corps.

For friendship and assistance in Kalkriese: Herr Christian Jaletske, (Director Museum and Park Kalkriese); Dr. Heidrun Derks, (Curator and Manager Kalkriese Museum); Dr. Sabine Düring, Frau Gisela Söeger, Katharina von Kurzynski, MA; Herr Baron and Christoph von Bar; Frau Fisse-Niewedde; Herr and Frau Sommerfrüchte; Herr and Frau Meyer Holtkamp and family; Herr and Frau Dröge; Herr Sonderman; Herr and Frau Wilfried Fisse; Herr and Frau Wischmeyer; Herr Dusterberg; Herr Finke; Herr Eberhard Niewedde; Frau Barbara Bigalke; Herr Jürgen Conze; Herr Schumacher; Herr Macke; Herr Eggemann; Herr Brünning; Herr Mügge; Klaus Fehrs; and the late Gisela Hornung.

I would also like that thank Landrat Manfred Hugo, President of the Landshaftsverband Osnabrück; Herr Heinz-Eberhard Holl, Oberkreis-director Osnabrück; Kreisrat Dr. Joseph Rottman, Geschaftsführer Osnabrück; The Bürgermeisters of Bramsche and Kalkriese; Herr Wilhelm Held and Herr Peter Wilmering, Schwagstorf; Herr Mathias Brorman, Felsenfeld;

Frau Yankofski, Barkhausen; Frau Beckmann, Borgwedde; Herr Horst Brüggeman and Frau Henpel-Stüve, Engter; Herr Sigurd Hauff, Bürgermeister of Spandau, Berlin; Erik Christensen, Connecticut (USA); my publisher and editor, Theodore P. Savas of Savas Beatie LLC, California and New York (USA), and Sarah Stephan, marketing director at Savas Beatie; Jim Lewellen, California (USA); Jim Corless, New Jersey (USA); Bill Whitman, USA; John Castle–"Joan Allen" Biggin Hill, UK; Alan Golbourn, UK; Rolf Bökemeier, Germany.

And a very special thank you for someone who actively encouraged Anglo-German friendship, and immense support for Kalkriese from the beginning: Herr Hans-Jürgen Fip

Oberbürgermeister of Osnabrück, Vice-President of the Landschaftsverband Osnabrück.

Tony Clunn
December 2004

Foreword

When Lieutenant Clunn, a British army officer with the Rhine Army stationed in Osnabrück, called on me at the Department for Preservation of Archaeological Monuments (DPAM) in March 1987, I had no idea of the consequences of the meeting. Consequences not only for scientific research of Roman–German conflict in the decades around Christ's birth, but for cultural understanding and tourism in the Osnabrück area and for all those persons who are today associated with the Kalkriese project.

I was not really opposed to Lieutenant Clunn's request to search for Roman artifacts in the Osnabrück area with the use of a metal detector. The fact he had actually asked permission before conducting the work spoke for him. However, I was very skeptical regarding the success of such a mission. It was his inspiration and optimism that compelled me to certify Lieutenant Clunn as an honorary member of the DPAM and to hand him notes on the discovery of Roman findings in the Osnabrück area. I was convinced if he found anything, it would be only Roman coins relating to the so-called *Wiehengebirgshorizon* dating from the second half of the fourth century and the early part of the fifth century. The alleged findings of Roman coins from Barenau, Venne, Kalkriese and Engter, which led Theodor Mommsen to conclude in 1885 that the gap between the Kalkriese Berg and the Great Moor must have been the location of the Varus battle in 9 AD, was met with deep misgivings by myself and the rest of the archaeological world. Apparently, many gold and silver coins from the Roman republic and the time of Augustus were found here between the end of the seventeenth and early nineteenth century, but these coins no longer existed, and except for the discovery of a denarius in 1963, no further finds had been reported for nearly eighty years.

However, I did not reckon with the persistence, ingenuity, and natural curiosity of Tony Clunn. In order to plot a possible target area for coins in the Kalkriese–Niewedde Bowl, he first traced—unbeknownst to the DPAM—the man who discovered the 1963 denarius. He was shown the site, and it was there, near the Lutter crossroads on the edge of the Great Moor, that Tony Clunn found one hundred and five additional denarii, part of a ploughed hoard, on the 5th and 12th of July, 1987.

These coins (and an additional fifty denarii unearthed during other excavations organized by the DPAM), were not the beginning of the Kalkriese project; these finds were not of any more importance than those that led Mommsen to express his thesis. The main criticism of Mommsen's theory was that there was no real evidence, bar an insignificant number of gold and silver coins, to suggest a sizeable conflict like the Varus battle had taken place in the area.

In the following months, Tony Clunn was essentially left to his own devices in his search for Roman treasures in the Kalkriese–Niewedde Bowl, and his persistence paid dividends. More denarii were found on the perimeter of the Great Moor and on the foot of the Kalkriese Berg. The significant breakthrough occurred in the summer of 1988: on a single weekend he found lead slingshot (from catapult slings) in three separate locations. Supporting forces commonly used such weapons and were mostly recruited by the Romans in the Mediterranean region. The discovery of these slingshots in the Kalkriese–Niewedde Bowl led to the conclusion that Roman troops—in whatever shape or form—must have been in the area, and that the coins found to date were connected to that event and not a result of some Roman–German trading or Germanic sacrificial ceremony.

Tony Clunn's persistence and his tireless dedication bore real fruit in the autumn of 1988, when the DPAM began a systematic search of the bowl. The results after one year of investigation formed the basis for the first successful excavation on the Oberesch field (the center of the battlefield). The Landschaftsverband (Land Council Association) then agreed to sponsor the project in November 1989.

Today, after some seventeen years of intensive archaeological research in the Kalkriese–Niewedde Bowl, the southeast area and toward Schwagstorf and Ostercappeln, there is no longer any doubt that three Roman legions, the seventeenth, eighteenth, and nineteenth, mounted squadrons, and six regiments of the Roman forces under the command of P. Quinctilius Varus, were defeated by Western Germanic clans under the leadership of the Cheruscian Arminius. Much information exists today on the Varus battle, the battle tactics of the Germans, the composition and equipment of the Roman army, and indeed the landscape of the area in the period around Christ's birth. But several questions remain unanswered. It will probably take years, and perhaps decades, until the outstanding questions on the battle are resolved.

From the beginning, Tony Clunn has supported the project from its early days of scientific research in the Kalkriese–Niewedde Bowl, and continued to do so while stationed in Hannover, London, Berlin, and Rheindahlen. He is directly accountable for many finds on the Felsener field near Schwagstorf, others close to Ostercappeln, and all of the discoveries on the northwest slope of the Kalkriese Berg. He is directly responsible for increasing the size of the excavation area within this period.

Tony Clunn has since left military service and settled in the Osnabrück area—where else but on the battlefield! In 1996, Major Clunn was appointed a Member of the Most Excellent Order of the British Empire by Her Majesty, Queen Elizabeth II, in recognition of his services to Anglo-German relations. In 1997, he became the first recipient of a special award from the Landschaftsverband Osnabrück in recognition of his honorary services and dedication to date. In June 1999, he was presented with the Landkreis Medal of Honor, the highest award for services to the community.

In *The Quest for the Lost Roman Legions: Discovering the Varus Battlefield*, Major Clunn describes in his own words his experiences, deliberations, discoveries, contact with the locals, and his work with the archaeologists. The research value of his book cannot be praised enough. He also describes the events in 9 AD as they might have occurred. An attempt to describe the history leading up to and including the Varus battle to readers is nothing new. What is new and unique, however, is the combination of historically-based fiction and facts: facts relating to the precise location of the German victory, facts on artifacts lost and found on the battlefield, and facts about the battle itself based on evidence revealed to date.

Prof. Dr. Wolfgang Schlüter

Resident Archaeologist for Osnabrücker *Land*

The Lost Legions Found

This is a book about the discovery of a battlefield. It is an important and an enthralling book for two reasons. First, the event itself. Known in English as the Battle of the Teutoburg Forest—and to the Romans as the Varian Disaster—it was fought in northwestern Germany during the autumn of 9 AD. Three legions and supporting units under the command of P. Quintillius Varus were ambushed and destroyed by Germanic resistance fighters led by Arminius, a German prince and renegade officer in the Roman auxiliary army. The defeat ended Augustus' dream of conquering Germany, and all attempts to add that country to the empire permanently ceased.

The significance for Europe's future is beyond reckoning. Henceforward the Rhine became the imperial frontier and would remain so for four centuries. West of it the provinces were Romanized and their speech Latinized. East of it, the Germans stayed defiantly German. And so an existing division was perpetuated, with Europe growing from two racial roots and branching into two linguistic groups. Like most who write about history's fatal encounters, Maj. Gen. J. F. C. Fuller included the Teutoburg Battle in his "Decisive Battles of the Western World." Here is General Fuller's attempt to calculate the incalculable: "Had Germany been for four centuries thoroughly Romanized, one culture, not two would have dominated the western world. There would have been no Franco-German problem, no Charlemagne, no Louis XIV, no Napoleon, no Kaiser Wilhelm II and no Hitler."

The Teutoburg Battle still holds the Germans in thrall. It was the first great expression of their nationality and birthplace of their nation—much like Bannockburn is to the Scots or a combination of Hastings and Runnymede is to the English. But these British locations are known and provide a focus for patriotic sentiment.

Which brings us to the second reason for this book's importance. All trace of the Teutoburg battlefield had been lost, forgotten even in folklore. Small wonder the urge to return it to the nation became an obsession. During the late 19th century, it seemed every schoolmaster, every country clergyman, and every retired general was poking among pinewoods, Tacitus in hand. Theories swarmed like bees: almost 700 of them, with perhaps thirty of them deserving serious attention. The search concentrated around the areas through which the route from Varus' summer headquarters was likely to have passed. Indeed, during the 1870s a giant monument to Hermann (Arminius) was erected on a hilltop near Detmold. It stands there still, eighty-eight feet to the top of the uplifted sword, a national shrine.

With hindsight, the most promising theory was that of Theodor Mommsen, greatest of all Romanists. By plotting Augustan coin finds, he concluded they radiated from a point nearly fifty miles northwest of the statue beyond today's Osnabrück. However, his critics pointed to other reasons for the presence of Roman coins, such as trade. In the absence of military evidence, Mommsen's proposal languished.

Almost a century passed. Then, in 1987, a British officer of the Osnabrück garrison, armed only with a metal detector, the suppositions of Mommsen, and the accounts of Roman historians, set out on weekends to explore the ground just north of the forest some ten miles north by northeast of the city. Clunn was rewarded by coin discoveries on agricultural land at Kalkriese, beneath the northern slopes of the Wiehen Ridge, final outlier of the Teutoburg Forest region.

Once again, however, coins alone were not enough. But the next season began to yield objects of unmistakable military provenance.

Intensive excavations followed, and today these fields are the setting for a multi-million dollar park and museum with a 120 foot viewing tower.

The Quest For the Lost Roman Legions: Discovering the Varus Battlefield is written by that officer, Tony Clunn MBE, Royal Army Medical Corps. He tells his story in two parallel strands. First an archaeological diary and personal narrative, recounting the solitary search leading to the crucial finds, followed by the extensive digs that would win ample corroboration from the soil. The other strand takes the form of an imaginative reconstruction, in dramatic and semi-fictional terms, of the sinister events of the ninth year of our era.

Kalkriese was made for ambush. Where hills meet plain, a sandy corridor had provided a prehistoric track between forest and the notorious marshes that covered much of the flat lands. The difficulty of locating the battle outside the forest had always been the insistence of classical historians, especially Cassius Dio, that the fighting had been in densely wooded upland.

This has been proved both true and untrue. Major Clunn's proposal is that Varus, returning to the Rhine with his army before the onset of winter, was duped by German treachery into a more northerly course, across a corner of the forest. What followed was a three day running fight in exactly the circumstances Dio described. However, it is now evident the Romans, though badly mauled, broke out onto the plain, then swung westward along the sandy strip. At its narrowest point, where the Kalkriese Hill meets the plain, a mighty ambush awaited. Here many thousands would die and with them Roman hopes for Central Europe.

This is a book from an amateur pen—in the best sense of sincerity and enthusiasm. Clunn's discovery and remarkable book remind us that antiquity does not belong to professional archaeologists and lifetime academics. The discovery it describes is as meaningful for Northern Europe as the disclosure of older cultures in distant lands, announced by pioneers like Petrie, Evans, and Wooley. Yet its abiding image, for this reader at least, is human and personal: a soldier, alone in a field, listening to the click of some tiny metallic object, dropped by another soldier in the last moments of life, trampled in the struggle of desperate men, when Jesus was still a boy in Nazareth.

Derek Williams

Historical Roman Characters

Nero Claudius Drusus, stepson of Augustus, was born January 13, 38 BC. Youngest son of Tiberius Claudius Nero and Livia Drusilla, brother of Emperor Tiberius, and father of Emperor Claudius. In 13 BC, Drusus became the Governor of the Province of Galilee and was later appointed the Governor of the upper Rhine. He launched offensives into the German heartland from Vecht and Ijssel in Holland, where he had built the Drusus Canal, and from Herven, where he built the Drusus Dam. He was also involved in Neus, Basel, and Zurich. In 12 BC, he foraged forward to the Weser, and the following year crossed the Weser and engaged the Chatti and Sugambrer tribes. Drusus re-crossed the Rhine in 9 BC and fought four additional campaigns in Germany. He erected the line of fortresses on the Lippe and established a German province from the Rhine to the Elbe. He died in 9 BC after suffering a riding injury during his return from the Elbe to the Rhine.

Gaius Julius Caesar Germanicus was born on May 24, 15 BC, in Rome. Son of Drusus, and adopted by Augustus in AD 4. Married

Agrippina. Accompanied Tiberius in seven campaigns in Pannonien. Fought in Germany from 11-14 AD, and led the Army of the Rhine in Germany from 14-16 AD. With eight legions, he fought against the Chatten, Brukterer, Marser, and Cherusker, until Tiberius ordered that no further incursions be made into Germany, essentially establishing the Rhine as the eastern flank of the Roman Empire in Northern Europe. Germanicus returned to Rome in triumph in 17 AD. He remained Pro-Consul of the Eastern Border until his early death on October 10, 19 AD at Antichia. Germanicus may have been poisoned by Piso, the Roman Governor of Syria (see Tiberius, below).

Tiberius Julius Caesar was born November 16, 42 BC, in Rome. Second stepson of Augustus from 38 BC. Son of Livia Drusilla. In 13 BC and 7 BC he acted as Consul, and from 6 BC appointed as Tribune for five years. Between 12 and 9 BC, Tiberius mounted expeditions to Pannonia, and Dalmater and Daker from 8 to 7 BC, and an expedition to the Elbe in Germany from 6 to 2 BC. On his return, he remained in private life in Rhodes until the death of the grandson of Augustus in 4 AD, after which he was adopted by the Emperor. Tiberius fought in Germany from 4-6 AD, and then waged extensive campaigns in Pannonia, after which he was appointed Imperium Proconsular Maius from 6-9 AD. The following year, Tiberius was again involved in campaigns in Germany, particularly after the defeat of the Varus Legions in 9 AD. He succeeded Augustus as Emperor in 14 AD. Tiberius curtailed the emergence of Germanicus as a favorite in Rome and maintained the Roman position on the Rhine as the eastern flank of the Roman Empire in Europe. He died March 16, 37 AD, in Misenum.

Augustus Caesar was born Gaius Octavius on September 23, 63 BC. Known as Gaius Julius Caesar after his adoption by Julius Caesar. The secondary name of Octavius was later discarded. His recognized name of Augustus was bestowed on him in 27 BC by the Senate. After the death of Julius Caesar in 44 BC, Octavius fought against Mark Antony (Antonius), but in 43 BC formed a second Triumvirate with Antony and Lepidus. With Antony, he then fought against Brutus and Cassius at Phillippi in Macedonia. In 40 BC, Octavius assumed control of the Western portion of the Roman Empire, and Antony the East. After his defeat of Antony and Cleopatra at the Battle of Aktium in 31 BC, Octavius effectively installed himself as Emperor. He outlined his ideas for the definitive borders of the Roman Empire and ordered the establishment of a Roman province in

Germany from the Rhine to the Elbe. He was both admired and respected as Emperor. Augustus died on August 19, 14 AD, in Nola.

Publius Quinctilius Varus was born in 46 BC. He was the husband of Augustus' grandniece. In 13 BC, Varus was appointed Pro-Consul for Africa, 4-6 AD as Governor of Syria, and then appointed Consul for Germania east of the Rhine in 7 AD. With three legions, three *alen*, and six cohorts, he was defeated by Arminius at the *Varusschlacht* in September of 9 AD.

Gaius and Lucius Caesar were the sons of Marcus Agrippa, a commoner and first-rate soldier chosen by Augustus as his son-in-law. Adopted into the imperial family as nephews to Augustus Caesar, both died early under separate but suspicious circumstances.

Gaius Numonius Vala was one of the legion commanders at the *Varusschlacht*.

Fabricius was a century commander in one of Varus' legions.

Marcus Aius was a soldier whose bronze shoulder clasps were excavated at the site of the battle. His clasps (engraved with his name) identified him as a legionary in the first cohort in the century commanded by Fabricius. I have taken him from history and made him Varus' second in command. (See also the separate entry in Appendix XX).

Aius Caecina Severus was a Roman commander under Germanicus.

Lucius Apronius was a Roman commander under Germanicus.

Fictional Roman Characters

Gaius Claudius Suebus was created to help explain the role of Centurion during the days of the legions of Varus.

Brutus Maximus was a standard-bearer (Signifier), and later bearer of the Seventeenth Eagle.

The Germans

Arminius was born in 18 or 16 BC. He was the son of the Cherusci chieftain Segimer and became chief of the Cherusci tribe. He is also known as Herman the Cherusker. In 8 BC, Arminius was taken to Rome with his brother, Flavius, where he was made a Roman knight by Tiberius in 4 AD. He accompanied Tiberius back to Germany for his campaigns to 6 AD, and the following year joined Varus during his Consulship of Germany. With the German tribes of the Chatten, Brukterer, Marser, and Cherusker, he defeated Varus at the *Varusschlacht* in September, 9 AD. Thereafter, Arminius fought the German Wars against Germanicus from 14-16 AD. He was never defeated in the field. He died circa 21 AD, possibly poisoned by members of his own family.

Thusnelda was Arminius' wife. She was originally engaged to a friend of her father.

Segestes was Thusnelda's father. He looked upon the Romans as friends. As a senior chieftain of the Cherusci, Segestes opposed Arminius.

Segimerus was the brother of Segestes.

Segimundus was the son of Segimerus. He was present at the *Varusschlacht* and assisted in the defiling of Varus' corpse.

Marobodus was a leading German chieftain who initially fought against Roman imperialism in Bohemia. He established a defence of Saxony and Silesia before coming to terms with the Romans and becoming their ally.

Flavus was Arminius's brother. He served with the Roman legions at the battle of Idistaviso in 16 AD, where Arminius fought Germanicus.

Fictional German Characters

Dagan is the fiancé of Thusnelda.
Roden is Wodenicus' brother.
Wodenicus is Arminius' lifelong friend.

German Tribes

Cherusci: The tribe that produced Arminius held territory extending from the Weser almost to the Elbe. In 4 AD, the Cherusci were given the privileged position of a federated state within the Roman Empire.

Chatten: This tribe was situated on the Upper Weser.

Marser: This tribe was situated between the Lippe–Ruhr area.

Brukterer: This tribe was situated between the Lippe and the Ems.

Marcomanni: Led by Marobodus, this tribe was situated in the Bohemia-Czech Republic-Slovakia area. In 5 AD, Marobodus led his tribe on a migration from Germany into free Bohemia and established authority over the German tribes of Saxony and Silesia. The Roman government decided to put a stop to this expansionism and launched a three-pronged invasion with a trio of legions under the command of Tiberius in 6 AD. When a large revolt in what was the former Yugoslavia broke out, the Romans were forced to leave the Marcomanni under Marobodus and put down the uprising. The Romans and Marcomanni came to terms, and Marobodus and his tribe became Roman allies.

The History of the Times

Through the dank, swirling early morning mist, a lone warrior strode slowly through the forest. His legs brushed aside the sodden under growth as he moved purposely towards the smoking fires scattered about the small hill. In his left hand he carried a short bloodied sword, and in his right a human head. As the warrior neared the knoll where sacrificial altars had been erected, he heard the groans and sobs of the vanquished invaders of his land. They were now being punished terribly for their defeat.

The chief of the Cherusci, Arminius, gazed down dispassionately at a Roman legionary tied down before him on a rack. Roden, brother of Wodenicus, brother in arms to Arminius from many years of campaigns and battles, stood close by. The prostrated Roman, the standard-bearer of the Seventeenth Legion of Rome, lay grievously wounded about the head and face from close-quarter battle. He had been unable or unwilling to reveal the information Arminius sought: the whereabouts of Marcus Aius, Senior Tribune and second in command of Varus' legion. He was fast slipping away into death.

Arminius felt the presence of the approaching warrior and looked up. He recognized the tribesman as Segimundus, the son of Segimerus, another of his close allies and compatriots in the struggle against the Romans. Segimundus raised his sword in salute and held the bloody head high in his other hand.

"Arminius, here is the head of Varus, the great Roman commander. He was dead, killed by his own hand! He was no warrior—he was a coward! His men were trying to burn his remains when we came across them and sent them to their gods. We have thrown his body to the carrion crows, so the spirit of Varus has died with him. What would you have me do with his head?"

Arminius considered the question for a few seconds. "Let us send it to Marobodus. Let him see the might of our warriors. When he sees the head of the great Varus, he will join us in battle against the Roman invaders, these cowards who take their own lives rather than fight us in battle. I should throw his head to the dogs, for he is not worthy of our attention. This one at least fought us bravely. Now he joins his false gods." With a powerful sweep of his sword, Arminius slew the legionary stretched out before him.

With a grim look on his face he looked about him and shouted, "This was Brutus Maximus of Rome, Signifer of the Seventeenth Legion. His Eagle is missing! Let this place be marked for all to know that Rome and her Eagles are no more than carrion against the Cherusci. Let this place be remembered as the place of Rome's defeat. Let it be remembered as the place where her Eagles died! Her centurions and soldiers were warriors, but her generals and tribunes were not. Rome will forever be vanquished in these lands, for it is our land, and Romans shall never take it from us! Mark the place well! Leave the bodies where they lie, and hang the heads high. All men must know this place. Mark it well!"

Roden bent down and recovered the long red cloak that had been tied around the neck of the dead legionary and raised it aloft, saying, "I think this a fitting blanket for my woman to lie on tonight when we celebrate this great battle. What do you say, Arminius?"

"No," replied Arminius, as he picked up and studied one of the bronze clasps that had fallen from the cloak onto the rack. "I think not, my friend. There is something strange here. I know this cloak clasp belonged to Marcus Aius. It had been his father's, and yet it was worn by this Signifer, Brutus Maximus, who was the standard-bearer and carrier of the

Seventeenth Eagle. Why should he be wearing Marcus Aius' cloak? And where is the cursed Marcus Aius? I have seen nothing of the remains of Varus' second in command. I saw him sorely wounded not so long ago during this day's battle. His head would be a fitting tribute to our victory. As for his cloak, wrap up the head of Varus within its folds and send it to Marobodus." Arminius paused before continuing. *"Bring up another prisoner, Roden—one with a suitable cloak, if you so choose, and let us see if anyone can remember the whereabouts of Marcus Aius. Send out more men to look for the missing Eagle of the Seventeenth. We have found the Eighteenth and Nineteenth golden birds, and I want the glory of taking all three from the mighty Augustus!"*

*   *   *

Arminius presided over his great victory during late summer, September, of the year 9 AD in the upper reaches of the Teutoburger range of hills and forests of northern Germany at a place called Kalkriese. There, some 20,000 legionaries and perhaps 2,000 auxiliaries were either slaughtered or captured and executed by the German tribesmen. It was the greatest defeat ever suffered by Rome. But when Marobodus, a powerful prince with the Marcomanni tribe, received the head of Varus, he refused to support Arminius, believing instead it wiser to stand by his recent treaty with Rome. The head was forwarded to Augustus Caesar, who performed the funeral rites for his defeated general.

Augustus unwrapped from the soiled red cloak the putrid head of his former commander and placed it on an altar illuminated by candles. His words still echo two centuries later: *"Quinctilius Varus, give me back my legions!"*

*   *   *

The soil was black, peat-like, and still very moist considering the time of year. I moved my metal detector over the small hole I had dug. Again I heard the sharp, double-toned signal ringing in my headset indicating a round solid object. There appeared nothing obvious in the hole, so I carefully lifted a small amount of soil in my hand and again moved the machine over the hole. Nothing. Whatever it was lay in the earth gathered in the palm of my hand. With a quickening pulse, I gently sifted through the dark peat. I caught a quick impression of dark glints shining—the blackened silver of a pristine Roman denarius. I freed it from the soil: the proud aquiline features of the emperor, Augustus Caesar, could clearly be seen on one side. I gently turned the coin over and saw Caius and Lucius Caesar standing behind battle shields and crossed spears, signifying that Augustus Caesar had pushed out the frontiers of Roman dominion in almost every direction. The frontier between the subject province of Gaul and barbarian Germany was to prove especially troublesome, and the whole might of Rome was eventually to be challenged by one barbarian leader, Arminius, of the Cherusci tribe. But Arminius, whom Tacitus called the liberator of Germany, was not the first German to threaten Rome. Earlier, after pushing the Roman armies as far south as Orange, in the Gallo-Roman province of Narbonensis, the Germans had moved toward Italy itself. They were stopped, however, by Marius, one of Rome's outstanding generals. Marius defeated them at Aix-en-Provence in 102 BC and obliterated them at Vercelli the following year.

Germanic pugnacity engraved itself upon the Roman mind and tongue. A man of ferocious character was called "Cimber," and the *furor Teutonicus* was spoken of long after the tribe had disappeared. Although there was nothing yet approaching a German nation, Rome was painfully aware of the mass of Germanic peoples inhabiting northern Europe. The line of demarcation between the Celts in Gaul and the Germanic tribes to the east was vague, and though the Celts tended to concentrate west of the Rhine, there was still a lot of German blood and influence in that region.

In 58 BC, Julius Caesar strode across Gaul like a colossus. The territory he governed included not only the Adriatic coast and what is now northern Italy, but also the province of Gallia Narbonensis. After picking a quarrel with Ariovistus, a German leader influential in Gaul, Caesar proceeded to annex all of Gaul. The Rhine was established as the frontier between Roman and non-Roman land. And so Caesar crystallized the idea of a subject Gaul west of the Rhine and a free Germany to the east.

Half a century later, Augustus gradually pushed Rome's eastern European frontier to the Danube. But a frontier consisting of the Rhine and the Danube offered a long and devious line that included a right angle along their upper courses. An Elbe–Danube line, however, offered a much shorter front and better and easier communications, while potentially hostile tribesmen would be safely enclosed within the Empire. As a result,

Augustus' younger stepson Drusus crossed the Rhine to fight four successive campaigns in Germany. He reached the Weser and finally, in 9 BC, the Elbe. Roman-built fortresses studded the landscape, and the entire area from the Rhine to the Elbe was regarded as a new Roman province

The Germans were for the most part semi-civilized pastoral nomads. Tacitus, in his *Germania*, vividly described these people with their wild blue eyes, reddish hair, and hulking bodies—politically unstable tribesmen who loved a fight but disdained work. The Romans hated thee new province "bristling with woods or festering with swamps," but Roman influence gradually seeped in and modern excavations show that substantial trade was conducted between the Romans and the German tribes. One Roman governor after another fought difficult and bloody campaigns to consolidate the new conquests and frontiers. Unfortunately for the Romans, the shorter Elbe–Danube frontier could not be completed until Bohemia (now the Czech Republic) was also conquered. This became obvious when an astute German chief, Marobodus, led his entire Marcomannic tribe on a migration from occupied southwestern Germany into free Bohemia, and there established authority over the German tribes of Saxony and Silesia. The Roman government decided it was imperative to put a stop to Marobodus' expansion. In 6 AD, therefore, twelve legions were launched in a massive three-pronged invasion under the supreme command of Augustus' elder stepson and heir apparent, Tiberius. A huge revolt broke out in northern Yugoslavia, however, putting an end to the campaign against Marobodus. Still, the wily tribal chieftain sensibly came to terms with Rome and was recognized as a king and as a friend of the Roman people. Meanwhile, the Yugoslavian revolt, described by some as Rome's gravest foreign threat since Hannibal, took three long years to suppress.

People in the new province of Germany watched these events with rising excitement. The Romans were not, after all, infallible. They had been compelled to spare Marobodus. Prolonged resistance to their power was not beyond the bounds of possibility. Such were the circumstances when a new Roman governor, Publius Quinctilius Varus, reached Germany. Husband of Augustus' grand-niece, Varus was among the Emperor's closest friends and had a hard-won reputation for firmness and order. When he arrived in Germany, however, he quickly miscalculated the true situation that existed there. Varus considered the country subjugated, and believed he could impose civilian methods of control such as were possible in the rich, well organized provinces he had hitherto governed

*   *   *

Cassius Dio, a third-century Greek historian, described the situation:

> *The Romans held portions of the country, not entire regions but such districts as happened to have been subdued. . . . The soldiers wintered there, and cities were being founded. Gradually the barbarians adapted themselves to Roman ways, getting accustomed to holding markets, and assembling peacefully.*
>
> *But they had not forgotten their ancestral ways, their inborn nature, their old proud way of life, their freedom based on arms. As long as they were unlearning their ancient customs gradually and as it were by degrees, they did not protest against these changes in their mode of life, so gradual, they were hardly aware of them. But when Quinctilius Varus was appointed Governor of the area and in the course of his official duties attempted to take these people in hand, striving to change them, issuing orders as though they had already been subdued and exacting money as from a subject nation, their patience was exhausted.*

*   *   *

A few years earlier in 4 AD, Tiberius (who was at that time governor of Germany) had given the Cherusci, an important West Germanic tribe, the privileged position of a federated state within the Empire. Members of their ruling class, among them a young prince named Arminius, were made Roman citizens. Arminius entered the imperial service as an officer in its auxiliary military forces, gaining the status of a Roman knight.

By 9 BC, it looked as though Augustus' ambition to extend Roman territory to the Elbe had almost been achieved. But the Romans overestimated the extent to which they had successfully assimilated their new province. Encouraged by revolts in other parts of the Empire, German aspirations for freedom and their prowess in arms both found a champion in Arminius. His knowledge of the terrain and brilliant use of it helped make the German victory possible. His annihilation of the legions sent to maintain order shook the Empire to its very core. Rome was forced to abandon its dream of a province beyond the Rhine. The implications of that decision on the future of Europe were incalculable.

The Cherusci, whose territory reached almost to the Elbe, played a leading role in the arrangements of Varus. Like his predecessors, Varus proposed to winter on the Rhine and spend the summer at advanced posts deep inside the recently conquered province. And thus, in 9 AD, he established a summer camp for his three legions (about 6,000 men each) in Cheruscian territory. Two other legions were left behind on the Rhine. His own advance headquarters were on the west bank of the Weser. Varus befriended the Cherusci chiefs, Segestes, and his brother, Segimerus, little realizing that Arminius and Segimerus were even then plotting against him.

Some of the chiefs, in particular Segestes, tried to warn the governor of this impending treachery, as Cassius Dio later wrote:

> But Varus was persuaded to lend the conspirators legionary detachments, which they said they needed to guard certain posts and escort supplies for the Roman army. Moreover, when the time came for Varus to withdraw to the Rhine for the winter, the plotters persuaded him to change his route. He had intended to march back to his winter camp at Vetera by the military road, but the fictitious report of a local rising induced him to make a north-westerly detour through difficult wooded country. The conspirators saw the main army off from their summer camp on the Weser. As Varus took his leave, they asked for and received permission to rejoin their tribes—ostensibly to recruit men to help put down the revolt that they had invented.

The Roman column moved slowly. It was encumbered by a heavy baggage train and large numbers of women, children and servants. As it proceeded through the rough country, felling trees and making paths and causeways, a shower of missiles suddenly descended. The Germans were attacking. The legionaries were hampered by the wind, rain, and mud that had always made them dislike Germany. They were also woefully short of auxiliary troops—cavalrys, archers, and slingers—to strike back effectively. All they could do was press on and hope to reach the nearest fortress.

Discipline asserted itself sufficiently for a camp to be pitched for the night on high ground. Wagons and baggage were burned or jettisoned and next morning the march was resumed. The legions started off in better order over open country, but this left them vulnerable to German attacks, and they were again compelled to take refuge in the woods, where they spent a most disagreeable day struggling through natural obstacles.

They suffered heavy losses, some of them self-inflicted because of the difficulty of distinguishing enemy from friend. In the night they managed to huddle together in another makeshift camp, with a totally inadequate rampart.

When morning came, it was still raining. There was a biting wind and they could see that the Germans had received reinforcements. It was reported that one of the commanders of the legions, Numonius Vala, lost his nerve and rode off with the remains of his regiment and auxiliary riders, in the vain hope of reaching the Rhine.

Varus was suffering from wounds. He fully realized what the Germans would do to him if they caught him alive. To avoid this fate, he killed himself. Some members of his staff followed his example, and the two generals who were left in charge did not long survive. One mistakenly offered capitulation, which turned into a massacre; the other fell fighting as the Germans broke into the last encampment. Just as first light made its first attempts on the day, the remnant of the three-legion force, possibly only a few thousand legionaries, perhaps under command of one of the few remaining legion commanders, escaped under cover of darkness to flee towards the west and the safety of the River Ems. They only partly succeeded in their bid to escape, running straight into a well planned backstop ambush established by Arminius at the point where the northern edge of the nearby Berglands fell steeply down into a narrow gap between the hilly ground and the boggy moorlands beyond. It was a perfect pincer movement, and with the exception of a few handfuls of fleeing legionaries, all were slain. The entire Roman force, possibly up to some twenty thousand men in all, was slaughtered. Even those who were captured met their terrifying end at the hands of the German tribesmen, who took great pleasure in slowly torturing their prisoners to a grisly death.

*   *   *

The Varus disaster upset Augustus more than anything in his long life, and he adopted every countermeasure he could think of. He dismissed all the Germans and Gauls in his personal bodyguard. Determined efforts were made to replace the lost legions, but few recruits of military age were available. A force consisting mainly of retired soldiers and former slaves (who were not normally admitted to the legions) was entrusted to Tiberius, who had rushed back from Dalmatia. Tiberius led them to the Rhine to join the remaining two legions there and defend the entire line of the border.

As had been feared, the triumphant Germans were sweeping east toward the Rhine. Every advance fort east of the river except Aliso fell without resistance. Aliso's commander and a force of archers succeeded in holding out until their stores were exhausted. On a dark night the garrison slipped out—including women and children—and managed to make it to the winter camp at Vetera on the Rhine. There ,they found the province's two remaining legions, which Varus' nephew and legate, Lucius Asprenas, had hastily brought north from Mainz.

In the end, the Germans did not make it to the Rhine. Deterred by Asprenas and delayed before the ramparts of Aliso, they lost any chance of mounting a surprise attack. Moreover, an attempt by Arminius to convert his rebellion into a national German revolt came to nothing. Such a revolt was contingent upon the support of Marobodus, whom Arminius tried to intimidate in a gruesome manner. When his men found some of the Roman soldiers cremating Varus' body in the Teutoburger forest, the Germans seized what was left of the corpse and mutilated it. They cut off the head and sent it to Marobodus, appealing to him to join the insurrection. Marobodus, however, could not see an advantage in harnessing himself to the ambitions of Arminius. It seemed wiser to stand by his treaty with Rome. And so the head of Varus eventually reached Augustus in Rome.

Five years later Augustus died. Shortly before his death, he sent his brilliant young great-nephew, later called Germanicus, to take command on the Rhine. When Tiberius came to the throne in 14 AD, Germanicus fought three massive and expensive campaigns against the Cherusci. A long-standing quarrel between Arminius and his pro-Roman father-in-law, Segestes, flared anew, with Germanicus siding with Segestes. Arminius' wife fell into Roman hands, and although Arminius was urged by his brother to collaborate with Rome, he refused to do so.

The following summer in 15 AD, some six years after the defeat of Varus' legions, Germanicus formed the idea—which according to his uncle Tiberius was a very demoralizing one—of taking his troops to visit the site of the defeat. The occasion provided Tacitus with one of his highlights:

> *Now they were near the Teutoburgian Woods, in which the remains of Varus and his three legions were said to be lying unburied. Germanicus conceived a desire to pay his last respects to these men and their general. Every soldier with him was overcome with pity when he thought of his relations and friends—and reflected on the hazards of war and of human life. Caecina was sent ahead to reconnoitre the dark woods and build bridges and causeways on the treacherous surface of the sodden marshland. Then the army made its way over the tragic sites.*
>
> *The scene lived up to its horrible associations. Varus' extensive first camp, with its broad extent and headquarters marked out, testified to the whole army's labours. Then a half-ruined breastwork and shallow ditch showed where the last pathetic remnant had gathered. On the open ground were whitening bones, scattered where men had fled, heaped up where they had stood and fought back*
>
> *Fragments of spears and of horses' limbs lay there: also human heads, fastened to tree trunks. In groves nearby were the outlandish altars at which the Germans had massacred the Roman colonels and senior company commanders.*
>
> *Survivors of the catastrophe, who had escaped from the battle or from captivity, pointed out where the generals had fallen, and where the Eagles were captured. They showed where Varus received his first wound, and where he died by his own unhappy hand. And they told of the platform from which Arminius had spoken, and of his arrogant insults to the Eagles and standards: and of all the gibbets and pits for the prisoners.*
>
> *Germanicus gathered his commanders together and gave his orders: "Gather all the remains of our fallen brothers, from the beginning to the end here, clean the whole area, take down the gibbets and platforms, take all up into a place near here, and dig a grave with a funeral pyre. Light the fires and let us lay the ghosts of our brothers to rest. There is no merit in this place; it is not a place to honour. Let us be soon gone from here, and let the mists of time cloud its very existence . . .*

Soon thereafter, a large battle was fought between Arminius and Germanicus at Idistaviso, south of the main pass at Minden where Varus had established his summer camp. Germanicus claimed victory, despite the fact his legions and auxiliaries had been forced to retreat and regroup, as had Arminius' now much-diminished force. But the Germans were far from subjugated.

A few years later in 19 AD, Arminius picked a quarrel with Marobodus, the German king of the Marcomanni who had snubbed him. Although the outcome of a battle they fought proved indecisive, Marobodus lost much of his power and soon thereafter his Bohemian kingdom lost its independence. But Arminius' end was also at hand, as Tacitus describes:

> *I find from the writings of contemporary senators, that a letter was read in the Roman senate from a chieftain of the Chatti tribe, Adgandestrius by name, offering to kill Arminius if poison were sent to him for the job. The reported answer was that Romans take vengeance on their enemies, not by underhand tricks, but by open force of arms.*
>
> *However, the Roman evacuation of Germany and the fall of Marobodus had induced Arminius to aim at kingship. But his freedom-loving compatriots forcibly resisted. The fortunes of the fight fluctuated. Arminius finally fell victim to treachery from his relations; he was killed, probably poisoned, by members of his own family.*
>
> *He was unmistakably the liberator of Germany. As challenger of Rome—not in its infancy, like kings and commanders before him, but at the height of its power—he had fought undecided battles, but never lost a war. He had ruled for twelve of his thirty-seven years. To this day the tribes sing of him. Yet Greek historians ignore him, reserving their admiration for Greece. We Romans, too, underestimate him, since in our devotion to antiquity we neglect modern history.*

Tacitus was justified in calling Arminius the man who had freed Germany. He was not, however, a national chief. "He was only the leader of a faction even among his tribesmen," wrote another historian, "not a champion of the German nation, for no such thing existed. The very name was of recent date, an alien appellation; there was among the Germans little consciousness of a common origin, of a common interest none at all." Still, it was thanks to his extraordinary skill and courage that the Romans were excluded from Germany east of the Rhine. With the exception of a coastal strip of land and a tract on the upper Rhine and Danube, the province was abandoned. The Romans were forced to recognize annexation was impossible or inadvisable. Thereafter they treated trans-Rhine Germany as a client state, dependent economically—but nothing more.

Had Arminius not frustrated Augustus in his aim to establish an Elbe–Bohemia–Danube frontier, almost the whole of the present Federal Republic of Germany and the Czech area of Czechoslovakia would have been part of the Roman Empire. "Might-have-beens" are notoriously unprofitable, but it is likely that, in the end, these territories under Roman rule would have become as docile and Latinized as Gaul (modern-day France). Any idea of the Rhine as a frontier would have been irrelevant and forgotten. The whole concept of Germany would have been unimaginably different. And so, therefore, would every subsequent century of European (and much of world) history.

PART I

Chapter One

1987: The First Find

For more than six hundred years, people have searched for the site where the Roman army had been annihilated. Early in the sixteenth century, when the story was becoming widely celebrated, the Lippischer Wald was renamed the Teutoburger Wald. In 1875, a monument to Arminius was erected on the supposed site of the battle near Detmold. Nearly everyone with a strong interest in the battle had a theory as to where Varus and his legions met their end. In 1998, however, German archaeologists made a shocking pronouncement: after ten years of research and excavations, the location of one of the most important events in Germany history—in many respects, the birthplace of the German nation—was no longer in doubt.

In 1987, using the most sophisticated metal detectors available, I launched my investigation of what ultimately turned out to be the Varus battlefield. For three years I studied old maps and documents of antiquity, walked fields and woods, surveyed the land, dug into the soil, and pondered over the artifacts I was turning up. Thankfully, all of this was carried out with the blessing, assistance, and guidance of the German museum and local archaeological authorities.

This was not the first time the Detmold position of the battlefield had been seriously challenged. Archaeologists and historians had previously offered up some seven hundred and fifty alternative sites, but never before had the evidence so strongly favored a new location. Extensive desk research led me to the Kalkriese area, but the actual site was pinpointed almost by accident. One month after arriving in Germany in 1987 to begin a tour of duty with the Armored Field Ambulance unit in Osnabrück, I set off on a journey that would consume years of survey, research, and laborious days when it seemed as if the artifacts and the answers would never come. In the beginning, all I really expected to find was the odd Roman coin or artifact. It had been well established by the resident county archaeologist, Dr Wolfgang Schlüter, that not one Roman coin had been recovered from the Osnabrück area during his thirteen years in office.

My story began to unfold shortly after visiting the local museum, where I first met Dr Schlüter. He was naturally very cautious, but decided to take me at face value. After learning my main interest was Roman history and coins, he suggested I start my search in an area about twelve miles north of the city, saying simply it was worth further study. Among the documents and old papers consulted as part of the research on the area was a series of nineteenth century maps and a thesis by Theodore Mommsen, the nineteenth century German historian.

Like many other German historians before him, Mommsen believed he had correctly identified the probable site of the "Teutoburger Wald" Varus battlefield. He based his thesis on the fact that resident landowners of the area, the (Baron) von Bar family, had accumulated a large collection of Roman silver and gold coins, a good majority of which were from the reign of Augustus Caesar. Mommsen had originally been informed that the coins had been found by farm workers in the local fields over the previous centuries and accumulated by the von Bar family (whose family tree can be traced back to the early tenth century). However, Mommsen was also informed, perhaps as an adopted defensive stance, that many of the coins had been collected from finds made all over northern Germany, and not exclusively from the local parish area.

Nevertheless, he maintained his theory but was never able to advance it in the absence of further evidence.

After closely studying Mommsen's theory, I noted that a very old road known as the "Old Military Road" (*Heerstrasse*) ran through this area. I decided to center my main point of reference on a small crossroads in the middle of the parish area, and it was there my investigation began in earnest.

I read the small number of archaeological publications that described the coin and artifact finds made in the area over the preceding one hundred years. Obviously, the finds made more recently over the last thirty years would perhaps be easier to relocate than those made in the previous century. Because the majority of the publications had been written by Dr Schlüter, I was able to discuss with the author firsthand the basis for his writings. One of his early publications, *Osnabrücker Mitteilungen*, Band 88–1982, contained a complete listing of many of Mommsen's records. After careful study, I decided a "recent" find of a Roman denarius, recovered in 1963 by a young lad in a field near the military road crossing, might bear further investigation. I drove out to the area with Dr Schlüter to talk to the local farmers.

Having been introduced to residents living in the immediate area of the crossroads, I met the farmer who vividly remembered the find, for it was his own young son who had brought the coin home some twenty-five years earlier. Ironically, the coin was still lying around the farmer's house (regrettably they have never been able to find it again). The field where the coin had been recovered was a short distance from their house, and we walked over to look at the general area. I was given an idea of the area where he thought the coin had been found—some fifty meters square—but since time was pressing I decided to return the following day.

Early next morning I got up with the birds and was soon standing in the field, ready to proceed with my detector survey. I have always believed every field has a distinctive part that stands out from the rest. In my experience, it is always best to move to the central point of a field to "get the feel" of the land, so to speak: nothing magical, nothing strange, just a straightforward good spot to pick up the potential activity areas. I walked a few paces and noticed the early morning dew highlighted a very slight elevation running across the field, possibly part of an old track or trail. I moved onto it and tried to orientate its course with the other roads some short distance away, but initially there appeared to be no logical link. (Much later, in the winter months, the connection would become abundantly clear, but at this particular point in time I was a little foxed!) Very often I found the edge of tracks more productive than the center, and I began searching along the side of the grassy elevation.

Over the next few hours I carefully moved up the northern edge of the line of track and outward, meter by meter, toward the edge of the field. Other than the odd piece of silver paper and bottle top, I found nothing. I took a late lunch break and decided to change tack and cover the southern edge of the track. Five minutes later, as I neared the center point of the track, I heard a familiar double-ringed tone in my headset. Some years before I decided to use Fisher metal detectors from America. In 1987, I was using the 1265X model, which was always an infallible source of good finds for me. This occasion would prove no different. In fact, it was the beginning of an incredible series of amazing and wonderful finds which, to the present day (now seventeen years later) continue to amaze as they are unearthed from the soil.

I cut away a square of turf, checked that first and, when I did not get a signal, continued carefully to clear out the black peat from within the hole. I rechecked the signal tone then picked up a handful of soil. No signal in the hole. Painstakingly, I sifted through the contents in my hand, but I could see nothing resembling a solid object as indicated by the signal. I sifted through again and then I saw it: black, small . . . and round! A tiny glint of silver caught my eye. It was a perfect silver coin, blackened with age, with the same black hue as the peaty soil: a Roman denarius. I saw the proud aquiline features of Augustus Caesar on one side, and on the other, two figures standing behind battle shields and crossed spears. I could hardly believe it. I stood transfixed, savoring a combination of disbelief, excitement, and the pure exhilaration of finding such a wonderful 2,000 year old artifact from ancient Rome.

According to Dr Schlüter, no Roman coins had been found in the Osnabrück area during his tenure, and here I was, three months after my arrival in the district, holding a beautiful Roman coin in the palm of my hand. Rather than put it into a plastic bag in my collecting pouch, I carefully placed it on top of the inverted cut-away turf, and then checked the immediate area of the hole and surrounding area for other signals. At first there was nothing. Then, within a few paces farther along the side of the track, I picked up another clear signal. I repeated the process, but this time the coin proved to be much deeper than the first.

Nevertheless, the Fisher detector gave good signals and the second coin, an early period denarius, was recovered and placed on top of the second turf. Having checked the immediate area of this find without any further signal, I again proceeded up the line of the side of the track. Four yards had separated the first and the second coin, and seven yards further on, another clear signal produced the third find, another early period denarius!

For the next few hours my spirits knew no bounds. I paced up and down the track line, fired with great enthusiasm about the whole area. The military road nearby, the tales from local farmers, the finds made from centuries before—something was about! As I looked across the fields toward the rising hillside some 2,000 yards away, I asked myself over and over again, "Who lost these?" "Who was he?" "What was he doing: running, riding, walking?" "Who came this way?"

Looking up from my reverie, I noticed weekend walkers about, particularly around the small crossroads area about 100 yards away. Some seemed to be taking an interest in my activities, and I decided to withdraw quietly from the field. Holes were filled, turfs were carefully replaced, and after noting the exact locations of those three finds, I packed my kit carefully into the car.

Dr Schlüter was away on a short holiday during the following two weeks, and so I was unable to speak to him and tell him of the find. I was a little worried about revealing the location and finds to the German police at this early stage, not being fully conversant with either their expertise or the recognized procedures to be adopted in these matters. I therefore decided to await Dr Schlüter's return.

I was fairly busy at work during the following week. It was not until some days later that I had positively identified the three coins. Two were from the era of Augustus and a third was pre-Republican from 100 BC. As the doctor was not back at work until the following Monday, I decided to revisit the site on the weekend and see if I could locate any similar scattered finds.

Based on the position of the previous three coins, I decided to concentrate on a 50 x 20 meter rectangle with the coin-find sites as the center of the survey. The earth had been very peaty and very dark, and locating blackened silver denarii was exceedingly difficult. Even sifting the compressed peat in my hand had failed to reveal them straight away, so I decided to take a common garden sieve with me. For a change, I also took my son and daughter to give them a few hours out in the countryside while I searched for more coins. They both proved to be of invaluable assistance as the day wore on.

When we arrived at the area of the field early on Saturday morning, I carefully checked the find positions of the three coins and marked them with three small colored stakes. It was interesting to see, just one week later, that there appeared to be no visible evidence of the old track; it was as if the path had disappeared altogether.

Using the field fence posts as reference points from my logbook, I had my son and daughter lay out a rectangle of white tape straddling the coin find sites, aligning it with the general line of the "missing" path. Once this had been done, I carried out a search of the marked area. I have always believed in working outward from a find site and maintaining a straight-line search pattern. Across the marked rectangle in the grassy field I laid out two white tape lines running through the line of the left- and right-hand find sites. This internal rectangle I began to search first, my theory being that the line of the track may have been very relevant to the loss of the coins some 2,000 years ago.

My son and daughter had gone off to play at the very end of the field. It was a beautiful summer morning. Only the birds' gentle chatter could be heard, and though the main crossroads was not far away at the end of the field, nothing moved or disturbed the wonderful tranquility of the setting. I scarcely noticed anything going on around me after that, so intense was my concentration at this point. Adjusting my headset to a more comfortable position, I turned up the gain control a little more and carefully walked across the grass. After a few minutes, halfway up the first leg of my search pattern, I came upon the first coin of the day. I knew it was a coin even before I cut away the turf. The Fisher 1265X "loved" coins, and particularly relished Roman silver! It gave a great sounding signal. When I heard that double ringing tone yet again, I knew it was another good find. Cutting away the turf, I carried out the normal checks of turf first, then the hole. The ringing tones remained. I was amazed. From a good 30 centimeters down, I brought the black earth containing the coin to the surface. Again I found it very difficult to locate the coin. In the end, gently sifting away the excess, I uncovered another beautiful blackened denarius.

It was in marvelous condition, again showing the proud aquiline features of Augustus. On the reverse this time was a large bull, head lowered, as if ready to charge. I took out a small plastic bag and dropped it in, noting the site and depth of find in my small logbook. Considerably excited at this fourth find, I continued with my sweep of the inner marked rectangle.

During the next hour another five denarii came to light. Each one was carefully noted in my log. When the search of the inner rectangle was complete, I called my children over to sit down for a quick coffee and to discuss the remainder of the day. It was my son's birthday, and I wanted to ensure any plans of his for the rest of the day were not spoiled by my staying at Kalkriese. However, their enthusiasm was as great as mine, and they both decided to remain with me as long as was necessary.

I looked over my log and the map, trying to work out any obvious pattern in the scattered coin finds. I spent some five minutes attempting to orientate the location. First, I took the line of the old track, and then other obvious lines of activity across the field. Having now completed my first good sweep of that area, I decided to move outside the inner marked rectangle and search down the side of the path where I imagined it ran through the field. This was now a good twenty yards from the other find sites, and I had little hope that I would be as successful as before. I could not have been more wrong

I had only moved some five yards in this new sweep area when I heard the familiar Fisher double tone. I cut the turf away and laid it to one side, then swept the detector over the exposed area. Again the double tone, not once, but now three distinct separate "marks." I nearly forgot the golden rule, but swept over the cut-away turf as well. Another double tone! I gently pulled at the black earth on the underside and a small black coin dropped out. Only then did I start to imagine that perhaps I had found the center point of the scattered coin finds. I rechecked the turf again, both sides, and with a slight quickening of pulse moved the Fisher over the hole. The first coin I recovered was only some four or five centimeters down, but again the black soil was making recovery slow. I called my children over, gave them a quick explanation of what was happening and suggested we work as a small team. It was necessary to ensure each coin was logged as we went deeper into the hole, and I also wanted to avoid intrusive shovel work to ensure no damage was caused to the precious coins.

A large piece of black plastic sheeting was unfolded and placed over the complete work area. I had used it before for similar recoveries. I cut a large hole out of the middle to fit around the excavation area, leaving a large area of plastic around the sides to lay the soil on. In this way, when it was time to fill in the hole at the end of the hoard recovery there would be no trace of where we had been working: no tell-tale marks to reveal the site to inquisitive eyes.

I opened up a box of small freezer plastic bags I carried with me and placed inside the extra-special finds. With my son wielding the Fisher and my daughter holding the garden sieve on the other side of the hole, I began to pull out handfuls of the loose soil, placing each, one by one, into the garden sieve. My son swept the detector over the sieve after each handful, and after two or three handfuls came the first clear double tone. We could not see any coin, and my daughter carefully shook the sieve to remove as much surplus earth as possible. We got down to the bare minimum of small clods of peat but there was no obvious "find" to be seen. I carefully squeezed each clod and we were delighted finally to see yet another blackened denarius.

"That's the first of three," I said, and proceeded to repeat the exercise over again. Once we had recovered the three "signals" and logged the three coins, I indicated that my son should sweep the hole again. We had disconnected the headphones so all three of us heard the distinct but puzzling sound of a good metal tone, but no clear double tone indicating a coin. I eased a small trowel into the sides of the hole to loosen the earth some 10 centimeters from the epicenter of the signal, and proceeded to pull out more soil, depositing each handful into the sieve. Only two or three handfuls had gone in when a detector sweep again gave a clear double tone: not once, but twice! From that small accumulation of earth emerged two more denarii, one looking a little worn, but the other in very good condition. Another sweep, and again we heard that solid but non-specific tone. By now it was evident that there was more to this find than we originally thought.

I decided to widen the extremities of the hole to allow the detector room to sweep the bottom fully, now some 30 centimeters below. I cut away more of the center of the plastic sheet, then we cut more turf away from the circumference of the hole, and each time checked the grass clods. The detector was swept over the new exposed area. Two more specific double-tone signals! The same procedure was repeated; each handful of earth went into the sieve, and we recovered two more beautiful denarii. The hole was now some 50 centimeters in diameter. I placed the detector carefully into the bottom, making two short sweeps from one angle, and repeated at right angles. The central core signal was still there, as strong as ever, but was now surrounded by many other strong double-tone signals. I looked up and said, "I think we're going to need a lot of find bags for this. Before we go down into the center point, let's recover the outer signals, and get them out of the way."

Just as we were about to start, I realized that with all the excitement of the finds, I had not been aware how quickly the morning had passed. I took a cursory look over to the crossroads area 100 yards away, out of no more than idle curiosity, to see if there were any country walkers in the vicinity who might be taking more than an a passing interest in a man and two youngsters digging a hole in the middle of a grassy field.

I could not believe my eyes! A complete coach load of pensioner day trippers was slowly getting out of their coach. Four or five walkers were moving up the road toward the gate leading into the field and, on top of that, the farmer who had shown us the site in the first place was making his way toward us across the field from the other direction! What had been a quiet peaceful crossroads in the country now had all the makings of a city pedestrian throughway.

The approaching farmer was neither the owner nor the tenant of the field we were in (I had obtained permission from the primary landowner in the area to prospect and detect on the fields), and I felt a great need to preserve the secrecy of my finds. This was particularly important as neither Dr Schlüter nor the owner were yet aware of the treasure site. I carefully covered the find bags and the main hole with my large waterproof "poncho" groundsheet before standing up and telling my children to go to the car and get out the coffee and sandwiches we had brought for lunch. As they moved away, I walked slowly to meet the farmer. We exchanged a few pleasantries about the layout of my search pattern and the general methods involved, and I explained we were looking at one or two more interesting signals by sieving through the loose earth. Although this gentleman was later made aware of what had been recovered in those early days in the summer of 1987, I believed that at that time, I could not trust any person with the details of what we had found save Dr Schlüter, who was still away on holiday.

It was a long frustrating hour of waiting until all the trippers had faded away, by which time the day had slipped into one of those heady, tranquil summer afternoons. Thankfully, the farmer had left to take up his afternoon siesta. Once again alone with our work, I removed the waterproof sheet and began the recovery of the other singular signals lying around the central core. More denarii followed until finally, all that remained was the primary hard signal. By then, about twenty denarii had been found, logged, and bagged. In case of further interruptions, I took another short break to log the exact location of the hole, pacing out the distances from three distinctive markers around the sides of the field: a gatepost, a fence post and a lone tree.

Once completed, the hole beckoned me like a magnet. I returned to pulling away further handfuls of soil from the center of the large signal. For the first time I actually saw a single coin lying in the bottom of the hole, and as I went to recover it, the next sweep of the detector by my son produced a cacophony of double and half-toned signals. As my daughter gently shook the sieve, three or four denarii were revealed.

From a small amount of soil, seven denarii were eventually put to one side and bagged. Another handful yielded another quantity of small blackened silver Roman coins: more logging and bagging. The coins recovered from the sand table, which lay at a depth of about 40 centimeters under the top bed of black peaty soil, were not in good condition. Three small pearl-colored stones were also recovered from the center of the mass, but at no time did I see any form of purse or container for the coins, which at the time I found a little surprising. As the afternoon began to draw on, we finally reached the point where no more signals could be found in the bed of the hole.

It had been a most remarkable day. Within a few hours I had recovered 89 coins, six from the main rectangle, and the others from the hole itself, plus the three pearl-colored stones. Counting the three denarii from the previous weekend, there was now a total of 92 coins bagged, ready for Dr Schlüter's return the following Monday. It had been a long day and I decided that we should refill the hole and conceal all traces of our work. Before we commenced refilling, I laid two black dustbin liners in and around the sides of the excavation to ensure I could ascertain exactly the outer edges of the hole when I returned.

We refilled with the soil straight off the plastic sheeting, and then just before we replaced the grass clumps, I staked four metal tent pegs into the ground. Once the turfs had been carefully replaced and the area generally tidied, with the exception of the flattened grass there was no sign of our earlier excavations. Satisfied, and with the exciting prospect of browsing through Seaby's books on Roman coins that evening, I called it a day. We made our way back to the car, and home.

The following week I spent my evenings carefully washing the coins to free them of the black peat. I also began perusing the Seaby catalog in an effort to identify them. By week's end I was able to identify the great majority of the coins. Some 50 percent were pre-Republican, and the rest were Augustan, all in very good condition. One curious aspect of my initial dating of the coins was that none appeared to be minted later than Seaby 43, or Augustus 2 BC–AD 14, the coin that showed the head of Augustus Caesar on one side, and on the reverse his grandsons, Caius and Lucius Caesar, standing behind battle shields and crossed spears. Almost all of these were in pristine, newly minted condition. A spark in my mind began to turn into a glimmer of light. I was extremely impatient to get down to the museum and give Dr Schlüter a big surprise on his return from holiday!

That weekend, I returned to the field with a larger detector head on the Fisher. In the unswept rectangle lying on the other side of the central find site, I located a further seven denarii. Then, from a sweep of the complete site again I found a further six coins—all fairly deep in the peaty soil, and all in good condition. From a grand total of 105 coins recovered thus far, there were only three in an advanced state of deterioration. No more signals were found.

Monday finally arrived. I had already phoned Dr. Schlüter to say that I had a big surprise for him, whetting his appetite by saying I had found "one or two Roman coins." When I came into his office that memorable day, I carried a large see-through plastic bag with countless smaller plastic bags inside. I had segregated all the coins to protect them and to assist in the dating process for the photographic procedures to follow.

I placed the bag slowly on the table in front of him and stood back to await his reaction. I don't recall his exact words, but I do remember his incredulity and amazement, and my remark, "I think this is just the tip of the iceberg."

During those early days there was always a degree of formality between us; after all, he had no knowledge of my aspirations or intentions with regards to the recovery of archaeological finds. However, from that time forward, our relationship developed and became more friendly and easygoing. We both agreed that for the immediate future, the best course of action would be to keep the whole affair quiet for as long as possible to allow him to set up the correct line of registration operations. After all, such a major treasure trove had never been found in his area of responsibility during his thirteen-year tenure as Chief Archaeologist in Osnabrück.

As Dr. Schlüter removed each coin packet out of the larger bag, I took one particularly fine and attractive coin and looked at it closely. It was the coin we were to see so many more times in my future searches: the face of Augustus Caesar, looking to the right, and on the reverse, Caius and Lucius Caesar standing behind battle shields and crossed spears.

Chapter Two

July 1987: Alt Barenau

After the discovery of the first coin hoard, we preserved secrecy about the find and the site until the museum managed to contact other German authorities involved in the preservation of antiquities. By far, the biggest problem was that a find of this nature had not been made for many years in this area of northern Germany, and the resulting instant publicity that might follow could have far-reaching effects on the museum's plans for the immediate future. There were also other landowners in the district who would not be so enthusiastic at the thought of hundreds of curious sightseers traipsing across their fields. The local farmer who owned the site field, and much of the surrounding area, came from a family that had historical links with the region dating back more than 1,000 years. Although he approved of my surveys of the area, he made it clear he preferred they not be accompanied by other interested individuals and freelance hobbyists armed with detectors from other districts in Germany. Naturally, he strongly supported our request for strict secrecy.

Once the coins had been repackaged by the museum assistants, Dr.
Schlüter opened up the first line of communication with the
Münzkabinett (Coin Room), a department of the Kestner Museum in
Hannover. This department was managed by Frank Berger, one of the
world's leading experts on Roman and early coinage. He was a relatively
young but vastly experienced scholar, and the resident official at the coin
museum. Dr. Berger had always had an avid interest in recovered coins,
particularly those discovered from the Osnabrück area during the 1700s
and 1800s. His thesis was dedicated to those early finds. During those
earlier centuries, many of those coins had been collected by the von Bar
family, the oldest landowning family in the Kalkriese area. The von Bars
could trace their lineage as far back as 900 AD, and they still maintained
large tracks of land in the district. Strangely enough, my first large find
was from lands they owned.

It had always been assumed that the greater part of the coins
recovered during the eighteenth and nineteenth centuries had been
accumulated over a long period, either by the family buying up
individual small lots of coins from all over Germany, or the acquisition of
odd coins from their own farms that farm workers found during the
harvesting and ploughing seasons. By 1939, the von Bar Roman coin
collection was rather impressive—certainly for the northern regions of
Germany—and comprised many silver and copper coins, as well as some
gold aureii. Up until 1945, the collection was maintained in the newer of
the two family Schlösser (castles) in Kalkriese known as Gut Barenau,
(the older original family Schloss at Alt (old) Barenau, a little over one
kilometer away, dated back to 1305). Regrettably, however, the entire
collection was stolen during the final months of World War II, apparently
by occupying Allied forces. Not a trace of the collection was found until
forty-five years later in 1990, when Dr. Berger uncovered some startling
revelations concerning some of the missing coins (see Chapter Ten).
Thankfully, before its theft, the entire collection had been carefully listed
and cross-referenced, which enabled experts like Theodore Mommsen to
debate the real source of the coins and the reason for their deposition in
Kalkriese.

As a result of these lists, there emerged the first remarkable clue that
something far greater was afoot than just the discovery of a singular coin
cache. In Hannover, Dr. Berger examined his reference books to recheck
the original lists of the von Bar collection. He found an uncanny

similarity between that accumulation and the cache I had just recovered. It was not so much the comparison between similar coins, but the clear proximity in the spread of the age of the minting eras, particularly evidenced by the mass of silver denarii. The more he looked at the graphs of the age-spread of this coinage, the more convinced he became that the von Bar collection could never have been an accumulation made over many years from many districts in Germany. Indeed, it was now obvious the collection had been put together from coins found in the immediate area of the von Bar estates in Kalkriese.

Now, two very similar caches had been registered in the same area, and both from the same era. In neither collection were there coins minted later than 14 AD. Furthermore, the great majority of those minted 1–14 AD were in pristine condition—as if they had been issued and lost a very short time after they were minted. According to the mint marks, these coins were made between 2 BC and 1 AD in Lyons (Lugdunum) and issued immediately after 2 BC.

Dr. Berger quickly diverted his attention to another interesting source of information on the movement of Roman troops during their invasion and occupation of Germany. He studied anew the other coin finds that had been made over the preceding centuries. One of the main Roman Lager (forts) that had been positively identified and excavated during the late nineteenth century was the key fort of Haltern. It was one of many main Lager forts established by the Romans on the east–west axis through the German heartland, centered on the River Lippe. A few thousand coins had been recovered during archaeological excavations of Haltern. Although there was a marked ratio increase in the number of copper coins found there in comparison with the original von Bar collection and my own find, it would be natural for a Lager camp to use and retain more base copper coinage. Still, the denarius coin graphs showed a remarkable similarity in the era, age-spread, and condition of all three accumulations: in the Lager in Haltern, in the original von Bar collection, and now in the new cache I had uncovered.

Once Dr. Berger completed the initial and absorbing studies into the remarkable coincidence of age and condition between all three accumulations, he found himself confronted with an unassailable fact: some of the Roman troops occupying Haltern during that period had somehow—and possibly for some good reason—moved through the area of Kalkriese during the same year. Based upon the comparable condition of the Augustan coins, they did so during the same season as well.

The very clear and concise Roman historical archives as written by Tacitus, the Roman historian, and Cassius Dio, noted that Varus spent the early part of 9 AD in Haltern. Indeed, Varus' own personal mint-marked coins had been found there during excavations in the 1800s. These same records also discuss how Varus deployed to summer quarters—possibly out along the Lager camps on the Lippe toward the German highlands—and ultimately to his summer camp, most likely at Minden, where he remained until the end of the season. Thereafter, little is known with certainty because Varus and his legions (the Seventeenth, Eighteenth, and Nineteenth Eagles of Rome) never returned.

After this investigation, Dr. Berger decided it was time to visit Osnabrück and meet with Dr. Schlüter and me, and made arrangements to visit us at Kalkriese.

August, 1987

In Osnabrück, meanwhile, Dr. Schlüter and I recovered from our initial feeling of euphoria and began discussing our next course of action. He wished to ensure that before any future moves were made in Kalkriese, key landowners in the area were brought fully up to date, and the authorities in Hannover were provided a good opportunity to study the find. The legal aspects concerning the find itself, he advised, could be a long and drawn-out procedure, but the landowner should nevertheless be officially apprised of any future decisions when these were made known. In all cases, however, the state, and not the individual, assumes possession of all archaeological finds or artifacts, whatever they turned out to be, and I was therefore allowed to continue additional unrestricted surveys in the Kalkriese area.

Both Dr. Schlüter and I agreed the next important step was to formulate plans for the immediate future. He requested I continue my research and surveys in Kalkriese, unhindered by either bureaucratic agencies or landowners, and issued me with a certificate of authority identifying me as an honorary member of the museum's archaeological research team. This permit allowed me access to any area of interest I might wish to investigate in the future. He also decided to initiate a proper dig on the find site in the autumn months, and asked me if I would like to be provided with any further archive material that might prove worthy of further research. I readily agreed, but stressed that the most important thing I would do during the following weeks was to recheck the find site itself, and make further surveys of the fields and tracks surrounding the adjacent old military road.

With regard to the archives, I asked Dr. Schlüter not only to seek out as much material as possible on the whole area of Osnabrück, but also older local maps, particularly those that showed both field and road names. In addition, I asked for copies of any local folklore archives from the surrounding villages.

Dr. Schlüter's own staff was still heavily involved in excavations in the town center of Osnabrück in the area of the cathedral and, regrettably, he was unable to immediately provide me with any staff assistance. He was, however, extremely enthusiastic about going out to the site and looking over the area with me, and we agreed to do so the following week.

During the week I left work in the late afternoon and, after hurried meals of "sandwiches on the hoof," made my way back to the find area to continue my search during the early and sometimes late summer evenings. The immediate area of the cache site produced a few more scattered coins, but I spent most of the time reconnoitering the surrounding fields, meeting the various landowners, and generally orientating myself with the way the land may have looked some two thousand years before.

By midweek I had moved across to the northern extremities of the initial area of interest. There, for the first time, I met the older of the von Bar brothers who ran the local estates. As the senior brother, his full formal title was Baron von Bar. Being a farmer first and foremost, he was more than happy enough to dispense with any real formalities. After a few moments we were happily engrossed in conversation about the coin find. He spent considerable time regaling me about the collection of Roman coins the family had owned and subsequently lost at the end of the war and invited me to join him in a guided tour of the estates at the end of the week. He made it clear he was only too happy to show me the full extent of the family lands and property—including his two Schlösser. He was particularly enthusiastic about one or two historical points he thought might be of significance to me, and promised to dig out family documents for our forthcoming meeting on the weekend.

By now I was already getting a distinct feeling about Kalkriese, and began putting together ideas on routes and track lines running through the district. Maps of central Germany have always shown the main area of Roman interest to be the camps running north and south along the River Rhine, the camps running west and east on the River Lippe, and the movement of Roman troops through the north German plain between the River Ems and the more central River Weser, both of which were main links to the north German coast. It has long been believed that legions moving back west to the Rivers Ems and Rhine from the central northern plains, which were bounded by the River Weser, had done so on a military road or march line along the northern edge of the hill feature running from Minden to the north of Osnabrück and on to the west. Further research into this theory tended to support such an idea, mainly because of the recovery of scattered coin finds and artifacts along the line of hills itself. Other German historians from the nineteenth century (Hartman and von Altenasche, for example) strongly advocated the existence of two main routes between the Rivers Ems and Weser. Nevertheless, the fact remained that coin finds had been made in fairly large quantities in the Osnabrück area and, in particular, immediately north of the city. The recovery of yet another cache only strengthened the supposition that there had been a strong Roman military movement into and through the area—but from which direction into Kalkriese if not due east from the Weser?

I met up with Dr. Schlüter on the site that weekend, where we discussed our next move. I mentioned the enthusiasm shown by Baron von Bar and that I was to meet him again shortly, and suggested it was an ideal opportunity for the three of us to get together and finalize the immediate plans for the continuation of surveys in the area, including the planned dig for the autumn. Our meeting was successful. Afterward, Dr. Schlüter returned to Osnabrück for other business and, as promised, the Baron escorted me around the estates including the new schloss, Gut Barenau, which had been built during the 1800s, and no more than one mile away the old Schloss, Alt Barenau. The road leading up to it from the main moorland crossroads was lined with an eerie stretch of gnarled and twisted trees, each of which leaned away from the elevated tarmac road at bizarre angles. Initially, it appeared the weight of the traffic had slowly depressed the road substructure into the marshlands beneath, causing the trees to lean outward from the center. Subsequent investigation, however, revealed a lack of proper support for the tree roots in the deep roadside ditches as the cause of this curious phenomenon. One of the oldest lime trees in Germany also lined this causeway. It was pinioned by metal stays and uprights to keep it from falling over, its branches also gnarled and twisted with age. The tree was barely alive, and looked as though it had just been plucked from some nightmarish Gothic horror scene. The area had an ominous, brooding atmosphere, and reeked of age and times long gone.

The old Schloss was not nearly as awe-inspiring as its newer replacement, but it was surrounded with a quiet dignified aura. It had firm bricks but crumbling plaster, and its porchways had been bricked up, never to be opened again. The doors of the old carriageway entrance across the moat were now shut tight. In modern times, access had been created by a new small drive laid into the courtyard complex, and it was from there the Baron pointed out the main areas of interest. Most of the residence had been converted into small flats, where many of the farm workers in the Baron's employment lived. The courtyards and grounds were fairly run down. In some areas, however, large tracks of undergrowth had been cleared, and at one end of the grounds a JCB was parked along a large partially excavated hole. The Baron explained they were in the process of installing a new pond and linking it to the moat system in an effort to bring the grounds up to a better standard of layout and appearance.

As we moved around to the far end of the Schloss, the Baron pointed out where the original building had been cut short due to insurmountable structural problems. He explained that the original structure had been some thirty meters longer, and at the end there had once existed a small building that stood on its own just a short way from the end wall. Only a paved area of floor was still visible on the original site, and it was here the two of us stood for a while to take in the surroundings. The Baron asked whether I was interested in looking at some old documents concerning the building and its origins. During the early 1800s, he explained, Napoleon's army moved through the area of Kalkriese on its way to Russia, and many troops had camped in and around the grounds of the Schloss. Like most armies during most wars, they foraged and pillaged the land through which they moved to provide food for all their troops. Many buildings along the way were invariably taken over for the period by the command hierarchy of the advancing army. It was during this brief occupation, continued the Baron, that the French troops had fully explored the Schloss buildings, and had probably used the castle as a headquarters.

Our meeting reminded me of a story I had picked up in Kalkriese. During those times, French soldiers exploring the surrounding farming community stumbled upon a small but heavy cloth-wrapped bundle of short swords with heavy flat blades and large, ornamental bone handles—a description that matches well the short stabbing swords used by the Romans. These swords, so the story goes, were handed over to a local commander, who in turn presented them to Napoleon. The Corsican dictator, as history has recorded, was fascinated by the Romans and their Empire.

As is so often the case with old wives' tales and local folklore, these stories are based upon real events that had become "foggy" with the passing of time. Although no reliable documentation has surfaced to support this particular story, I found the association between the swords and the Roman troop movement through this area both interesting and plausible. It also promoted a desire to carry out a survey of the area surrounding the Schloss as soon as I could, and I indicated as much to the Baron.

We walked back slowly to the main building and he suggested we go back to his residence, a small farmhouse just off the main grounds of the new Schloss about one mile away. Here, the Baron produced a small set of documents that were part of an old magazine article printed in Gothic-type German print. Although not fully fluent in German, I had no great difficulty understanding much of what was written, and avidly studied the section indicating the family history and Alt Barenau. However, it soon became clear much of the real detail of what had actually taken place during Napoleonic times was lost forever, and the final tantalizing truth behind the story of the weapons would never be known. Nevertheless, it was an intriguing story from what had already become a most fascinating area. Before we parted, the Baron mentioned that there were other interesting documents in the family archives, and he would make efforts to produce them for our next meeting planned for a few weeks hence.

The following week passed quickly enough and on Saturday I arrived back at the old Schloss to begin my survey of the grounds. I quickly ascertained that the broader area surrounding the building was originally the wet bog area of the moor, much of it having originally been under water. It appeared my best chance of success for finds would lie in the grounds on the southern and eastern edges of the moat, where it was considerably drier, and where there would have been greater activity in previous years. The grass was fairly long but did not prevent a good close sweep of my detector head as I moved up and down the field next to the moat.

After but a few moments the sharp Fisher ringing tones rang out. Although not the double-barreled tone of a clear coin signal, it was a good firm sound. I quickly cut away the turf, laid it back and gently loosened the black soil. A patch of reddish-grey metal was easily seen and I gently pulled away the loose earth to reveal what looked like a small pyramid with a small eyelet at the apex. It was made of lead and was obviously some type of plumb or weight, but its curious aspect was the small eyelet at the apex of the pyramid. As the day progressed I found a few other lead objects, some not so readily identifiable, and a cross section of coinage from the 1700s and 1800s. Nothing else was uncovered as curious as the small lead pyramid. At the end of the day I packaged all the finds, and as part of the original agreement I had made with Dr. Schlüter, took them down to the museum during the course of the following week for his staff to examine.

During the next few weeks I was heavily involved with my military duties, but as the end of the summer drew near, my work and ongoing surveys in Kalkriese continued with unmitigated enthusiasm. Many evenings and weekends were spent crisscrossing the fields surrounding the site of the coin cache. Local farmers were quickly becoming used to the lone figure walking up and down the fields with maps and "electronic mine detectors," and were themselves an ever-increasing source of old wives' tales and area folklore from times gone by.

Each evening after a day's work, I packaged the finds and dropped them off at regular intervals at the museum staff offices. Nothing startling had been said about the curious lead pyramid plumb, and I thought no more about it at the time. That was about to change, however. I purchased several new reference books on Roman activity in Europe and was browsing through one when I noticed a simulated photo of a pair of

Roman soldiers measuring lines in preparation to laying down a road. Suspended from each part of the four-square plumb-line instrument were small inverted lead pyramids hanging upside down, their apex points being used as line of sight indicators! After a bit more study it became evident I had unearthed a Roman groma, a road-surveying device used extensively by the Romans when building military roads.

The following day I dropped into the museum and showed Dr. Schlüter my book and the relevant photo. He immediately went out to the restorer's office, where many of the artifacts were laid out for examination, and picked up the small lead pyramid. It matched the reference photo exactly, but Dr. Schlüter pointed out that the hole at the apex of the pyramid indicated a scales weight. Therefore, it was not an inverted groma. Although not necessarily of a "military" nature, the find was of great interest to both of us, and Dr. Schlüter asked to borrow the new reference book, as some of the other contents and photos were new to his experience.

Having now processed the legal aspects enabling archaeological work to proceed in Kalkriese, Dr. Schlüter informed me that excavations would begin on the coin site in the near future, and asked whether I would be available to help out on the dig itself. Regrettably, my work schedule did not allow for time during the day, but I would be able to drop in to the dig during lunch breaks, and possibly look over the spill soil from the dig in the evenings after work. He was anxious that I do this, and informed the dig team of my intentions.

I arrived at the site during the Monday lunch hour, where work was already well under way and a cross-hatch method of excavation had uncovered much of the turfed area. I was initially amused to see the huge clumsy metal detector that was being used by the dig team—a remnant of the Second World War and at first sight, more suited for mines than small coins and artifacts. Unfortunately, the old-style mine detector was missing many of the small silver denarii embedded in the soil. I suggested that I re-sweep the excavated dirt at the end of each day to ensure no artifacts and coins were being missed. I also requested that my specialist Fisher 1265X detector be put to use during the digging of the main areas of the excavations. At the end of the week, the dig team had recovered some 25 coins from the excavations. Much to the astonishment of the dig team and to the delight of Dr. Schlüter, I recovered a further 30 coins from the grass turfs and the dig spill soil at the end of each day.

During the week, Frank Berger once again came down from Hannover to visit with us and discuss the finds. All the coins were now being cleaned and photographed in the museum, and Dr. Berger asked that they be sent to Hannover for further examination. He also requested that future finds be made directly available to him for research. Dr. Schlüter readily agreed and confirmed that I was going to continue to survey Kalkriese during the coming autumn and winter months, and asked that I keep them apprised of developments. To date, more than 160 coins had now been recovered from my first find site and the surrounding area. I photographed the complete collection before it went off to Hannover.

It was an impressive accumulation and nearly a twin of the original von Bar collection—a fact well recognized by Frank Berger.

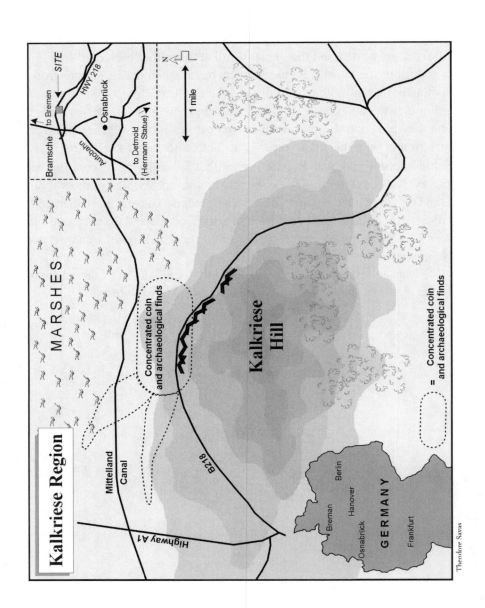

Kalkriese Region

MARSHES

Mittelland
Canal

Highway A1

B218

Kalkriese
Hill

Concentrated coin
and archaeological finds

= Concentrated coin
and archaeological finds

GERMANY

Bremen
Osnabrück
Hanover
Berlin
Frankfurt

N

1 mile

Bramsche
to Bremen
SITE
HWY 218
Autobahn
Osnabrück
to Detmold
(Hermann Statue)

Theodore Savas

Chapter Three

1987-1988: The Search Continues

During the autumn of 1987, I spent many hours in the museum with Dr. Schlüter and his staff. We poured over old records and maps of the areas surrounding the find site, and I spent as much time as possible in the field. Even at this early stage it was obvious the first main task was to ascertain where people and troops might have moved through the area in former times, and to identify the routes they took. Although the old military road cutting across the moorlands initially seemed the obvious answer, I was already getting a different picture. I marked coin sites from times gone by on modern maps. The result was interesting, and displayed a scattered effect between the Kalkriese Berg and the old military road.

I studied old maps carefully to locate field names of common interest: the Roman Wall, the Gold Field, Silver Corner, Bikks Camp, and many more with a high degree of interest value from Mommsen's notes. Those from the central area I joined by a process of trace lines, and those that linked into the military road were transposed to run back through a natural line of march to the east. This exercise produced an interesting discovery: finds from areas to the south and southeast, some 30 to 40 miles from the main site of interest at Kalkriese, indicated a possible line of march during Roman times well up from the accepted areas of concentration of main Roman activity lying to the south and the River Lippe. Over the next six months, well into the start of spring 1988, I filled countless bags with unusual finds of various artifacts, including more scattered silver denarii from the areas immediately surrounding the original coin-find site. Each time I delivered them, the museum's staff enthusiastically looked through the bag's contents.

These forays into the Kalkriese area produced many varied and interesting discoveries, including some bronze pieces (possibly from Roman uniforms and fittings), and many lead pieces. However, something I had recovered earlier and handed in unrecognized with other metallic material turned out to be a find of great significance. Three separate lead ovals generated a tremendous level of excitement with Dr. Schlüter and the museum staff. He quickly recognized them for what they were: lead slingshot—the first real evidence of a military presence or engagement (or even a battle) in the Kalkriese area. Further Roman coinage was also found scattered around the main crossroads area.

By now I had identified three main areas of interest, and each was significantly linked to areas of high or rising ground. When surveying an area for any possible lines of march, I had always surmised that any high or rising ground in such a flat area at the edge of the moor would have had a distinct military advantage. To troops moving through the area, such points would be used for both places of observation and control, and I made a careful recheck over each of these elevations. Two points of rising ground were situated on either side of the military road just to the west of my first main coin find. The third and main tactical point of rising ground was identified as the small knoll on the northern edge of the Kalkriese Berg, about 1,000 yards away from the main *Heerstrasse*. My further study was greatly assisted by Dr. Schlüter, who provided ground-content and soil-feature maps that clearly showed the varying soil structures. This made it easy to distinguish the dry areas of sand cutting through the wet moorlands. Overlaid on a normal map of the roads and trails running through the district, it was apparent that there had once existed other trails and paths in the locale that had long since fallen into disuse. It was already clear some form of link route existed with the Kalkriese Berg and the military road running east–west across the top of the moorlands. Luck would again play an important part in my ongoing search for clues.

A farmer who owned an adjacent field near the rising ground of the small knoll on the edge of the Berg shared with me an interesting story. His elderly aunt, long since passed away, had often spoken of a small cache of Roman coins recovered from the area of the edge of the field near the knoll, some 200 yards from his farmhouse. At the turn of the century, a large oak tree fell over during a storm. The coins were found under its roots when farm workers worked to clear away the fallen debris. The fate of the coins is unknown, but the farmer believed they may have ended up in the original von Bar collection. The farmer was happy to point where the oak tree had fallen. He went on to casually remark that on two or three other occasions at the turn of the century, single Roman gold coins had been recovered from his fields near the canal that ran east–west through the district directly toward my coin cache find site about 1,500 yards to the northwest. Although I had already gleaned this information from both Mommsen's notes, as reproduced by Dr. Schlüter, and archive maps showing the actual find sites, it was good to have firsthand confirmation from a knowledgeable landowner. From our vantage point on the edge of the knoll, I gazed out across the fields falling away to the great moorland, and looked out across the broad sweep of ploughed fields spilling out in front of us.

The main field to our front rolled away for 800 yards before coming up against the wall of the canal, and was perhaps 600 yards across at its widest point. I had no reservations about the time it would take to cover such an enormous area of ploughed field, but had to think carefully about how best to go about conducting such a survey. From my work folder I extracted a copy of one of the soil-content maps of the district and studied the plan of the ground. We stood at the edge of the knoll facing northwest toward the canal and the military road crossroads, which was about 1,500 yards away and out of our line of sight. The ground before us had been primarily wet moorland, with perhaps one or two strips of dry land running through it. The crossroads themselves lay across a narrow strip of sandy soil that split in two at the junction. Obviously this had been the crossing point on the boggy moorland for many centuries, with the military road running outward along a strip of sandy soil either side of the crossing. Running my finger over the map back to the point where we now stood, I could make out a broad patch of dry soil linking up with the two points, before converging again with the dry belt of land running around the Kalkriese Berg area to the east and west.

I decided to conduct the first field survey down the dry belt of land running away to the northwest, but even this was at least 200 yards square and would require considerable time and effort to be carried out properly. However, my first priority was to check the apex of the field and the knoll where the farmer and I now stood, and I arranged to commence a run over the general area during the following week. Unfortunately, many of the fields were still frozen from the harsh German winter, although most of the snow was long gone. Thankfully, a thaw was soon expected. I bade the farmer farewell and I hoped that, with any luck, the following week might see an overall improvement in the weather. I was not to be disappointed.

A few days later, the sun's rays burst through the clouds and the thaw quickly set in. That weekend I began searching the oak tree site, cordoning off about 30 square yards of the area. Strangely enough, there was not one single coin or artifact to be found. After moving 20 yards up the line of the knoll and again finding nothing of note, I suffered what most have experienced in similar circumstances: acute frustration and disappointment. It was exasperating that a solid firsthand lead by the landowner was not panning out. I have always maintained that perseverance and maintenance of a good search pattern produce good results, but on this particular occasion I decided to leave the position and move 200 yards across to the beginning of the raised ground leading away to the northwest, and the canal.

I would come to regret this decision. Even though the next series of surveys proved fruitful, if I had persevered with my searches at the apex point, the whole concept of my quest may have been dramatically affected much earlier. On the other hand, many other important discoveries would not have been made. Still, after a short time I began to recover more scatter finds of Roman denarii along the raised area of field. Nearly every find fell in a fairly straight line across the field in a northwesterly direction toward the heart of Kalkriese.

I called Dr. Schlüter out to the new find site, and he was again enthusiastic about the new discoveries. He was becoming increasingly convinced that with the recovery of the bronze artifacts, lead slingshots, and now these other coin finds, there was good reason to believe there had been some form of armed conflict in the area. It was becoming

increasingly obvious that more had occurred in Kalkriese than just
military troop traffic passing through the area on the military road or
round the Berg to the west. I suggested that I continue my sweep of the
large field during the coming months, and Dr. Schlüter asked to be kept
abreast of developments as they occurred.

During the spring and summer I maintained my efforts on the large
fields, even moving over the canal into the area some 500 yards short of
the crossroads. Slowly but surely, a cohesive pattern began to emerge
relating to the coins and artifacts. Lines began to appear linking the road
running east-west around the Berg through the knoll to the military road
also running east-west through the moor about 1,500 yards away to the
northwest. The picture was somewhat reminiscent of that of a large
starburst, with the stars shooting out in one direction. There was every
indication that a large contingent of people had spread out from the area
at the apex to the field and the knoll, fanning out in a 90-degree arc north
and northwest down to the crossroads, the military road, and the lands
beyond.

Perhaps they were fleeing from some unknown horror.

No Escape: Death of a Centurion

*He was running for his life. His lungs were dragging in great rasping
gulps of air. Sweat, salty and hot, filled and blinded his eyes. The deep
lush grassland, boggy and soft, clung to his every footfall as he pounded
down across the great moorland. It was as if he were in the middle of the
worst of nightmares, running but never making headway, never
escaping; the presence of death behind urged him on though drawing
nearer with each faltering stride.*

*Torn and bloodied from a great open wound stretching from
shoulder to hip, the Centurion continued on, his legs like leaden weights
dragging him down into the mire of the black peat bogs. All around him
were running legionaries, single figures or small groups of two or three
men streaming down from the hill to their rear, racing away from the
slaughter and screams echoing over the wooded knoll on the edge of the
nearby Bergland. Some were racing to the safety of the lands to the west,
though it was too far to the west for some. He threw an anxious glance
over his shoulder, half hoping, half expecting, and saw his worst fears*

and nightmares realized. A line of enemy warriors were racing down toward them, chasing them into the boggy moorlands morass. To his horror, a huge Cheruscian warrior was fast approaching from behind him, his giant strides less than 100 meters away. The bearded enemy face wore a determined aggressive snarl. The warrior's yellowed teeth were bared as would be a hound's just before sinking its fangs into the flesh of its prey. In one hand was a bloodied sword, and in the other a long stabbing javelin.

A fresh surge of adrenaline pumped through his veins, and with an audible moan of agony he forced his legs to even greater efforts. But the battle had been too long, the four days and nights of running, skirmishing, and harassment too exhausting. And then the demoralizing onslaught of the Cherusci warriors . . . it was too much to bear. His nightmares were real enough now as he stumbled his way through water and mud, a sucking morass of black horror that threatened to trip and engulf him with each difficult step. His legs were losing power, and his sodden sandals losing traction at every pace. For what seemed long periods, but in reality were but seconds in the short time that remained of his life, his mind drifted back to the horror of those days and nights since the three legions under Varus had left the summer camp at Minden. And he remembered . . .

Incredibly violent storms and foul weather had followed every step of the legions' march toward the Lippe. And then they changed direction, altering their course to march to the assistance of Arminius in the highlands to the northwest in search of a German tribal uprising. Hell arrived as the first day lengthened into late afternoon. Harrying ambushes, flights of spears and javelins whistling down at them from the wooded slopes, thrown by invisible hands. . . .

They had slipped and fallen while screaming in frustration at this godforsaken country, fighting back, yes, but unable to fight and effectively combat a largely unseen enemy. The godforsaken storms tearing through the woods only made matters worse, throwing trees and branches into their path, splitting their forces in the middle ground, and providing continuous ambush positions for the Cherusci hordes at every turn. But this was only the beginning. The attacks from the flanks were joined by deadly thrusts from the rear.

The three days and nights that followed were a hazy memory of mud and yet more mud, winds lashing bodies, horses screaming in fear and pain, their screams joined with the shrieks of their masters as iron-tipped javelins pierced flesh and smashed through bone and sinew. When the second day ended, the survivors had camped in a hastily made redoubt, a battle lager, earthworks and ramparts thrown together. Here they burned a large number of their baggage and stores wagons, a sad task made all the more difficult by the soaking wet conditions. They had been unable to move them through the entanglement of the forests and ravines, and their commanders had ordered them destroyed. When the fires died down, they huddled against the muddy earthen walls, shivering in the clammy mists of the forest.

The early light of dawn shone through the umbrella of trees around their embattled position. The storms had subsided, and the silence that had fallen over their position and the surrounding forests was ominous. Fear and despair coursed through the camp, for their situation was a desperate one. They had regrouped, and the march proceeded a bit easier, though their movement, always toward the northwest, was still hemmed in by close country and ravines. Just as small glimmers of hope were born, the harrying attacks began yet again, and went on throughout that day. Morale sank lower in all ranks of the remaining legion forces. That evening they broke free of the horror and the claustrophobic conditions of the Berglands into open country once more, again regrouping what was left of Varus' force. Another series of earthen ramparts were erected into yet another hasty battle lager. Some 13,000 soldiers of the original three legions who had stepped off on the march from summer camp had already been slaughtered, their bodies littering the hills and ravines of the Teutoburger ridge some 25 kilometers southeast of their last position. The remaining 7,000-8,000 disorganized legionaries and their sorely mauled cavalrymen spent the night huddled in the lager, each knowing full well the end was near. The cavalry broke out during the night in an attempt to thrust ahead through the hills due west, possibly through an area known as Borgwedde, and on to the friendly lands of the Ems—and beyond. They had progressed no farther than Borgwedde before a huge mass of Cherusci tribesmen, who had gathered in the hills in anticipation of just such a deployment, surrounded them; the mounted Romans were wiped out to a man.

Most of the Roman commanders, including Varus himself, decided suicide was preferable to the fate that would befall them if they fell into the hands of the Cherusci. At first light on the fourth day, the remaining commanders led the largest remaining contingent of legionaries in a breakout from the lager. The soldiers pushed northwest toward a narrow defile between the hills of the Kalkriese Berg and the Great Moor to the north. The wounded Centurion, who was marching as part of this contingent, would never know that those left behind in the comparative safety of the lager were quickly overrun by a screaming mass of predominantly Chatti and Cherusci tribesmen. The trapped Romans tried to surrender, but were slaughtered one by one until no one was left. The commander and a few legionaries tasked with the grisly job of burning and burying Varus' corpse were discovered and swiftly killed.

The breakout contingent managed to traipse but eight kilometers from the lager when they were attacked by German hordes lying in wait for them. The elaborate ambush was delivered from a prepared position of earthen ramparts disguised as grass banks. Hiding behind them, the tribesmen picked off the Romans as they attempted to squeeze through a narrow gap between the ambush wall and marshy bog across from it. Harried once again from the rear and left flank, and with no room to deploy and fight in an organized formation as they had been taught, the column disintegrated into chaos. The cries and screams of wounded men echoed across the surrounding hills and fields. Very few Romans escaped through the ambush pipe into the great moorlands beyond.

By now, the Centurion had lost all sense of direction. His only thought was to escape away from the slicing swords and flying javelins. And so he continued to run. What remained of his senses brought him slowly back to reality. Was there someone running beside him, screaming words he could not understand? The fear welling up from within his living nightmare prevented him from turning his head to confirm what he knew to be true. He was sobbing and gasping with fatigue and despair. He could no longer feel his legs. When he began to stumble, he knew he could escape from his destiny no longer. He turned his head and looked to his right.

The Cheruscian running alongside was not more than a meter from him. The bright red hair of his beard was laced with droplets of spittle, morning mist, and blood. His lips were spread in a wide grin of triumph that revealed a set of yellowed and blackened teeth, clicking together as would a hound in anticipation of sinking its fangs into the flesh of its prey. For a few moments the Centurion found it impossible to look away from his glowing bright blue eyes.

The German's stride easily matched that of the slowing Centurion. With a laugh of scorn he pulled back his bloodied sword and chopped hard and low at the back of the Roman's knee. The razor sharp edge severed the tendons in one slicing blow. The officer felt little except a dull punch. There was no pain; his mind had long since rejected his torn and bleeding body. Without even a whimper he crumpled forward to the ground. As he fell, his small purse of silver coins split open. The proud Centurion rolled over on his back to face his final enemy, his weight pressing the coins into the muddy black soil. Each had been minted before the end of 9 AD. All were denarii—the silver coinage of the marching legions.

He gazed blankly up at the Cheruscian warrior, huge wracking sobs coming from his throat as he drew air deeply into his lungs. Instinctively, he raised his hand before him in a useless gesture of self protection, his palm facing his executioner in a final plea for mercy. The warrior swatted the hand away with a flick of his sword, and without hesitation or emotion plunged the point of the weapon into the officer's throat. Several inches of the blade protruded out the back of the neck. The realization of how he would die gripped the Centurion for a few seconds and his eyes opened wide in shock. His hand, still half-raised in supplication, fell to the ground with a slight slap as it hit the muddy water. The Centurion's nightmare was at an end.

The warrior yanked free his sword and looked back in the direction of the site of the ambush 1,000 meters distant. Other Romans were attempting to escape from the ambush pipe. His bloodlust still unquenched, he turned to head them off.

The field where the Roman came to rest was well removed from the main battle area, although the noise of death and annihilation still echoed across the surrounding hills and fields. Under his outstretched hand was a lone coin embedded in the mud, a silver denarius of Augustus Caesar. The proud aquiline features of the Emperor were now encased by the wet peaty soil. It would remain so for many, many years.

Chapter Four

Early April, 9 AD: Regrouping at Haltern

Marcus Aius, Senior Tribune and the second in command under Quinctilius Varus, Legate of Rome, and Governor of the Northern Command in Gaul, stood at the front of the main first aid post of the lager at Haltern. He looked out across the steep slope and down to the southern edge of the fortress to the main quay and jetties on the river bank below. The River Lippe was swollen with spring waters running down from the highlands to the east, and the currents were making hard work for the boats moving up the river from the west. Their loads included reinforcements from the Rhine. A large number of vessels were stacked along the river bank downstream, impatiently waiting to disgorge their troops and stores at the main port area.

Essential supplies for the reinforcements were usually carried piecemeal from the forts along the Rhine. Because of the increasing number of reports of unrest in the northern command areas, the lagers on the Lippe were ordered to be reinforced with a complete change of guard.

This, in turn, would allow the resident legions under Varus to move farther east up the Lippe in preparation for their annual foray into the highlands and beyond to the summer camp at Minden, where they would collect taxes and payments in kind from German tribes.

Regrettably, many of Varus' troops were immunes, *a collective term used to describe the more common support elements of the legions. Simply put, they were not high quality legionaries. Many had become a bit soft during their comparatively easy tenure in the German province, where they carried out Varus' policing routines. Their duties made for a better soldier's life, but did little in the way of keeping skills razor sharp. Indeed, the majority of Varus' legionaries were soldiers who were, by their very conditions of service, granted exemptions from heavier chores and fatigues. These men worked at a wide variety of tasks and included surveyors, orderlies and dressers, ditchers, furriers, architects, shipwrights, artillerymen, glass fitters, smiths of all varieties, wagon makers, and many more skilled and unskilled workers. Included in the same category were butchers, huntsmen, animal keepers, workshop personnel, clerks, orderly room staff, pay clerks responsible for money left on deposit, clerks responsible for payments to the troops, grooms, horse trainers, armory Sergeants, trumpeters and heralds, and many more.*

The reason for this state of affairs was simple. Varus' role as Governor of the region required him to do little more than gather tithes and taxes from the local tribes, and oversee an area that had not experienced significant unrest or rebellion during his tenure in office. His command was no longer the high-caliber fighting force it once was. By 9 AD, it had become a stale, apathetic collection of men, whose primary responsibilities consisted of little more than standing guard in the forts along the Lippe and escorting the tax consul on his periodic visits to the local tribes.

Of better caliber were the German auxiliaries attached to Varus' legions. Their commander was Arminius, a fearless warrior with a sharp mind and a good grasp of tactics. Marcus Aius watched as Arminius moved up through the camp toward Varus' headquarters, laughing and joking with one of his unit commanders. Both were in high spirits at the thought of the forthcoming move upriver.

As was his habit, Arminius was gesticulating wildly while describing to his companion some tactical maneuver of a bygone action. The pair of

Germans passed within a few meters of where Marcus was standing. Arminius noticed him there, watching.

"Hail, Marcus Aius, Senior Tribune of the Legion."

Marcus nodded in reply.

"The troops are here in great numbers. We begin the move up the river soon," continued Arminius. "Will the gods look kindly upon us and serve us with good weather for the summer this year? My men are eager to get out from this stinking camp and breathe some good clean air in the highlands. What say you?"

"Do not jest where the gods are concerned, Arminius," Marcus shot back. "You may call up a mighty storm by your lack of respect, and storms we do not want when we move into the highlands on our march. Best you make an offering this evening and make penance for your flippancy, or the gods may make you pay for such remarks."

An amused Arminius laughed aloud. "Me, pay? I think not! The paymaster has arrived with his bags of silver and gold, and the face of mighty Augustus shines as brightly as ever on each and every new coin we have. Look, see here." The German shook out a handful of coins from his large money pouch. "You see how brightly these new coins sparkle in the sun! Tonight, I shall see how many more I can win when I challenge my man here to a game of chance. Perhaps you would join us, Marcus Aius?"

"No!" came the Tribune's curt reply. "I have no time for such matters. I must make preparations for the move and speak with Varus. We have not yet received our promised cavalry units. It would not be wise to move into the highlands before they have joined us." Marcus paused a moment before adding, "Again I say to you, do not mock the gods, Arminius. You may rue the day you took them lightly." With a quick nod of dismissal, Marcus Aius moved away toward the gate and the docks.

Arminius watched him for several moments before turning to his friend and fellow commander, Wodenicus. "It is not I that will rue the day but Marcus Aius. He and his fellow Romans will soon enough regret the day they set foot on German soil to rape and pillage our land. We have paid too many taxes and tithes to these accursed people, old friend. Soon we will put things to right and remove them from our land once and for all. Mark my words," he added bitterly, holding up a silver denarius clearly stamped with the Emperor's aquiline features. "This face will no longer haunt me in my dreams." With that, he threw the coin to the ground and followed it with his foot, angrily stamping it into the soil before moving off up the hill with Wodenicus to Varus' headquarters.

On the other side of the aid post, the chief doctor of the legion had been cleaning his instruments after performing several minor operations during the morning sick parade. A Greek by birth, he had overheard the exchange between Marcus Aius and Arminius. When the Roman commander had moved off, however, the wind changed direction slightly, and Arminius' acidic commentary to Wodenicus had been lost on the breeze. When he saw the expression of pure hate and rage on Arminius' face, however, a shiver shot up the Greek's spine. He watched in quiet shock as the German leader threw down a silver coin and stamped it with his boot. Once the warriors left, the doctor could not resist the temptation to walk over to where the men had stood. He continued cleaning his bronze gauge while scanning the ground with his eyes. A small glint of silver in the muddy earth caught his eye. The Greek looked furtively about before bending over quickly to pick up the coin. He turned it over in his hand. On the reverse side was stamped the picture of the brothers Caius and Lucius Caesar, standing behind battle shields and crossed spears.

The doctor clasped the coin tightly in his hand as he walked back to his instruments. The episode was highly unsettling. What could it possibly mean?

Chapter Five

A Lump of Gold

During the spring and summer of 1989, my search carried me closer to the wooded slopes at the edge of the Kalkriese Berg. Around the other side of the prominent hill lay the field where, during the previous winter, I had detected larger deep metallic signals still awaiting proper excavation by Dr. Schlüter's team. A time for their investigation had yet to be decided. For the present, most of my searches were centered on the large fields falling away from the edge of the Berg to the north and west.

Mid-April, 9 AD: Ready to Deploy

Varus' legionaries marched into the assembly points of the lager in good heart, having just received their annual wages in newly struck coins from the mint in Lyons. Silver and gold coins offered a small but reassuring weight in the officers' money pouches. The coinage passed to the men in the ranks was predominantly copper. Though not as plentiful either in quantity, weight, or value, the coins made good gambling chips on the long summer evenings. Except for those lucky enough to win the small pots of silver denarii during their gambling sessions, the legionaries were all paid in the Quartermaster's copper coinage, in asses and other base coins.

From some distance across the river, anyone paying attention could see into the sloping ground of the lager where the troops assembled, their thousands of burnished cooking pots and helmets reflecting the early morning rays of the warm summer sun. The view was not unlike a disturbed ant nest, with a continuous flow of movement spreading out and down toward the south gate of the fortress and the river below.

The legions had to fully deploy soon. The reinforcements were flocking in and they had to create room for the incoming troops. They also had to make the best use possible of the dry early summer months for their expedition through the German hinterlands to the summer camp at Minden. It was Varus' intention to get under way as soon as possible, carry out his tasks along the Lippe, and take up the summer occupation of the fort on the Weser. He also wanted to return in good time to avoid the end-of-season weather patterns that prevailed at the summer equinox in Germany. The late summer and early autumn storms were notorious for their ferocity and high winds that made movement and control virtually impossible.

The leading auxiliary reconnaissance elements of the three-legion command were led by Arminius. Although they were already well under way, Arminius had yet to join them. Varus intended to make a swift series of marches to gain the upper reaches of the Lippe as soon as he could, visiting each of the river lagers along the way.

Tribune Marcus Aius sat astride his striking black horse, gazing out across the forming lines of legionaries. He was ill at ease. Although the sun's early rays were already warming the air, the superstitious officer felt a chill of foreboding course through his body, as if someone was walking over his grave. His horse nervously scratched the ground with a front hoof, throwing its head up and down with a series of snorts and whinnies. The beast was restless and unsettled by something it felt rather than saw.

"You feel it too, my beauty," whispered Marcus as he gently stroked the horse's thick neck in an effort to pacify the excited animal. "I fear you

and I feel the same thing. There is something wicked in the air today—something not right. I pray the gods will bless this venture, but if there are problems ahead, at least I will have you to guide and carry me along the way, old friend. Come, let's see if we can find the Quartermaster and see how things are progressing with the move."

And with that the Tribune coaxed the animal forward down the main street towards the lager gates, and his destiny beyond. It was the spring of the year 9 AD.

* * *

Having completed as much survey work as was possible before the growing season took a firm hold, I decided to take a series of trips to visit the site of the Roman lager at Haltern. The old fort was about 100 miles away to the south of Osnabrück on the banks of the River Lippe. The lager that had once housed Varus' legions had been the subject of fairly comprehensive digs during the late nineteenth century and in more recent times as well. Dr. Schlüter had supplied one (and perhaps two) detailed booklets covering the site and its surrounding area, including material concerning the artifacts that had been recovered. I decided a firsthand look over the area, to acquaint myself with the actual site from which Varus' legions had deployed, would give me a greater insight into the ground and the distances the legions had sought to cover.

Before I ventured near the site, in 1988, I had traveled to the area museum in Münster to introduce myself to the resident archaeologist, Dr. Kühlborn, and obtain his permission to visit the lager area. Dr. Schlüter in Osnabrück had already made the necessary telephone calls to arrange a meeting. I soon found myself in a warm and friendly discussion with Dr. Kühlborn, who had closely followed my involvement in the Kalkriese area. He invited me to visit Haltern for a general look at the area of the lager, and possibly also to carry out one or two detecting surveys on his behalf. However, before that could take place, it was necessary that I secure a letter of authority from the County Offices to allow me unlimited access to the Haltern area. This required another visit to the museum the following week to collect the certificate.

In an effort to wisely utilize my present trip to Münster, which lay approximately halfway between Osnabrück and Haltern, I decided to go on to the site of the lager and carry out a basic reconnaissance of the extremities of the position. Today, the area is covered by a mixture of farmland, new building estates, and an intricate web of farm tracks and tarmac roads.

I arrived at Haltern around 10.30 a.m. and drove about to obtain a clear impression of the area of the town, which bounded the lines of the lager's original position. These were highlighted on the maps I carried, reproduced from the museum magazine articles supplied by Dr. Schlüter. Unfortunately, some two-thirds of the original lager had been covered with a sprawling housing estate, but the western edge of the complex lay under two or three large crop fields centered on an extensive farm complex.

I decided making introductions should be at the top of my priority list. I drove to the nearest farmhouse adjacent to the site of the lager to find the owner and, with a bit of luck, discuss plans for the future. Although the certificate from Münster was not yet in my possession, I had no problem establishing an immediate rapport with the farmer, who had already heard of my work and finds in the Osnabrück area. He also had an avid interest in the local history of the lager and the Roman occupation of Haltern. The farmer clarified exactly which fields he owned, and assisted in identifying for me the ownership of other outlying fields. He and I spent the next hour or so over a coffee and schnapps discussing the reasons behind my visit and what I hoped to achieve. One of the more interesting aspects of this visit came about when he mentioned that he also owned a small field south of the lager that covered the area of the original Roman port and river bed of the Lippe. This was before the river's course changed to its present long loop around and south of the town. Some of the port areas had been excavated a hundred years earlier, when the lager site was being archaeologically investigated. Several key points in the port area, however, had not had any meaningful surveys carried out on them since that time, and they might well reveal some interesting relics and artifacts that may have been lost in the water during the loading and unloading of the Roman boats and galleys.

Farther around the original river line east of the port, archaeologists had found the remains of a boathouse that had probably housed Roman boats. In 1973, a program of small archaeological excavations was initiated, both in the housing estates and the fields covering the southern extremities of the complex. Dr. Kühlborn told me that once the certificate was made available, he would like me to survey the land lying in the outer boundaries of the "Field" or Feldlager (as opposed to the inner main Lager, known as the Haupt Lager), which had produced large quantities of pottery shards as well as a few coins. Equally of interest were the crop fields that bounded the western side of the main lager and the original lager's western gate, which had also been excavated a hundred years ago.

After finalizing my initial discussions with the farmer, who was perfectly happy to allow me unrestricted access to his property, I tied up my first visit to the area by carrying out a complete reconnaissance of the inner and outer areas of the original lager, including the fields highlighted by Dr. Kühlborn, the Roman port, and the site of the original river bed.

One of the more fascinating aspects of my first trip to Haltern was being able to stand in the bed of the original river, which was now a long and sprawling field running away to the west. It was between 50 and 75 yards in width, bounded by a rising bank on either side. Its course was now split by a modern road bridging the field from north to south. This field was the bed of the original river line where the Romans had shipped their long boats up from the Rhine. Standing in the middle of this long banked causeway, it was easy to imagine what had once been water, four or five yards deep, and the large imposing Roman craft sweeping up the river from the west. What manner of relics and artifacts had been lost or tossed overboard? How many boats had sunk? Had anything of value been lost while the boats were loaded or unloaded at the port a little farther up the river? With workers carrying heavy loads of goods and supplies over small narrow gangplanks, perhaps they dropped the odd load as they slipped on the greasy planks leading to shore. Perhaps a purse of coins was lost when someone fell into the water from the quayside. It was almost certain that many wonderful relics and artifacts were resting immediately underfoot in what was once a deep and muddy riverbed. Perhaps they were too deep to recover by normal means of detection.

I felt the familiar surge of adrenaline that always comes when I discover a new potential site for detecting. I had other priorities to observe at Haltern, however. I marked the riverbed as a place worthy of further investigation should I ever find the time to do so. By the end of that long and tiring day, Haltern was no longer the great unknown. I had firmly established in my mind the scope and magnitude of one of the main Roman forts on the Lippe, the fort at which Varus had camped before launching his disastrous expedition into the German highlands. I now felt more rapport with the allied historical aspects of my searches in Kalkriese.

During 1988, and again in 1989, my visits to Haltern were not as productive or successful as my searches elsewhere in Germany. However, the discussions with Dr. Kühlborn at Münster, and with other interested parties from the local populace, accomplished more than just filling in details of the scale of logistical and political importance that was Haltern in Roman times. The visits provided me with a large portfolio of the many fascinating and priceless artifacts that had been recovered there, some of which, particularly the coin finds, would subsequently throw a revealing light on the movement of Varus' legions during 9 AD.

One particularly spectacular and unusual find was made there in the winter months of 1989. The discovery was during one of my short weekend visits. Dr. Kühlborn had earlier earmarked an area northwest of the lager just outside the Feldlager boundaries. The site included two cropped fields situated within the dense pine forests that surround much of Haltern, where pottery shards and other artifacts had been recovered some time before.

After driving down the long autobahn stretch south past Münster, I reached the outskirts of Haltern. Snow flurries dusted the air as I climbed from the car. The weather report had promised a cold sunny day, and although the sky was not very overcast, the snow came as a surprise. However, I had often gone out when the snow was thick on the ground, particularly when there was no frozen ground to contend with. When I arrived at the new site, I found that both fields were still soft enough to excavate with a small digging shovel. Within a short time, however, the snow began to come down a bit heavier and settle on the ground. I would have to work fast.

Both fields were surrounded by thick pinewoods. The smaller of the two fields was a mere strip of ground 50 by 30 yards running alongside the wood path about 300 yards from the Feldlager boundaries to the east. The larger field was farther into the woods on the point of the rising ground, perhaps 200 by 60 yards. This was where the majority of pottery shards had been found by field "walkers" working for the museum. It was this field I first reconnoitered, working the lines and sections of the ground for some two to three hours. On my second break for a warming cup of steaming black coffee, I considered whether or not to pursue my search in this area. So far I had not discovered a single metal artifact of note. There was a small bonus, however, because I had found a number of pottery shards in the loose soil when digging up the odd spent brass cartridge case. By now the snow had stopped falling and the whole area was deathly quiet. The snow and trees muffled any noises that may have been heard from the autobahn running through the woods about 400 yards away. These moments of tranquility were often the most satisfying result of working the fields. I usually used these breaks to formulate new ideas and revise search plans. "Taking stock" was always an invaluable exercise, and on this occasion particularly so.

Leaning back against the car, I stared out across the field. A hot cup of coffee warmed my hands while I thought the orientation of the field in comparison with the layout of the Feldlager as shown on my map. For some strange reason, the Feldlager boundaries were irregular in comparison to the walls of the main lager fortress. This anomaly raised questions in my mind concerning the location of the various main lager gates and entrances. Earlier digs carried out on the main lager had pinpointed the location of the main gates. One in particular sat astride the northwest corner of the complex. With my finger, I traced a line on my map outward from that gate through the northwest corner of the outer boundary of the Feldlager, and then into the wooded countryside beyond. The line stretched neatly onto the corner of the track some 200 yards away, which proceeded on a straight line running alongside the small field, the next on my job list for the day. I was now firmly convinced the track running through the woods was the path the original occupants of the Haltern fort would have used if they had moved northwest and then north from the main lager complex. The small field to the side would perhaps have been an ideal location for some form of sentry or lookout post during Roman occupation of the lager.

Finishing my coffee, I left the car and walked back down to the smaller field. The snow formed a thin layer on the top of the furrows and stood two to three inches deep between them.

The obvious area to check first was the edge running along the line of the track, so I stepped onto the bottom corner and began my search. Instead of moving along the furrowed lines, which always presented difficulties when attempting to make clean sweeps of the detector head, I proceeded to cover five-yard lines into the field and then back again to the edge, about one yard from my previous line. I had only progressed about fifteen yards up the edge of the field when I picked up the staccato noise of many separate hard signals spread across an area one yard square. The Fisher had always been a sound and reliable discriminator, and I now turned up the right-hand disc on the face of the machine to a higher reading to check for fadeout of the signal. The signal tones remained hard and positive, but I was puzzled by the number of different place signals. To save my ears and establish an easy dig pattern, I moved to the outer edges of the signal area, picked one positive separate trace to work on, and bent down to unearth whatever was waiting for me.

A few inches down I unearthed a large unusual piece of flat metal, its surface covered in bubbles that looked like blisters. It was blackened over much of its surface, with patches of red and gray showing through. I had no idea what it was, so I proceeded to the next signal and unearthed a similar piece of metal, this one a little smaller than the first. An idea was now nagging at the back of my mind that I had seen something like this before. Try as I might, I could not recall the occasion or the subject. I continued searching and unearthed many more similar pieces. After perhaps thirty minutes, I sat back and studied my finds. Next to me were fourteen or fifteen pieces of similar metal, all blackened with the curious blistering effect on both sides.

The one-yard square was now devoid of any further signals. I decided another coffee would not go to waste. The cold biting wind was gathering strength, sending snow flurries through the woods and across the field toward me. For some minutes I sipped the warm liquid and mulled over the strange pieces. And then it came to me. I remembered where I had seen similar metals disks before—larger than these and many years earlier when I visited a foundry works in the UK.

The metal was pig iron, a byproduct of the smelting process. The obvious question was how it came to rest in this particular field. No farmer worth his salt would have deposited it there as rubbish. It was equally unlikely anyone hauled such a small load deep in the heart of the woods just to dump it there. There was no readily obvious reason for its presence. I decided to proceed with my search up the line of the edge of the field and picked up where I had left off.

I had only moved a few feet when I came upon harder but less scattered signals than those thrown by the original pig iron find. Within a few minutes I recovered several smaller pieces of the pig iron. One piece proved particularly difficult. It gave out a strong signal, but I found it difficult to pick out in the sandy brown soil. I had to dig down a good 18 inches to recover it. At first it looked like a clump of blue-gray lead covered in a sticky coating of sand. It looked similar to a piece of fish coated with bread crumbs. When I picked it up out of the soil and gently rubbed some of the earth away, a flash of yellow gleamed brightly from beneath the coating of sand.

At first I thought it was a lump of brass, but I quickly threw out that idea when I found there was no visible discoloration in the bright yellow surface. I gently rubbed away at a few more loose particles of sand and yet more yellow metal revealed itself. My curiosity—and a certain disbelief!—was now very much aroused within me, and I quickly placed the piece in my finds pouch and quickly moved the detector over the rest of the area. From a total area of five square yards I recovered additional pieces of pig-iron, some small globules or balls of what appeared to be bronze, and two fairly thick strips of lead, but no more yellow sand-covered pieces were found.

The snow was falling heavily now and accumulating on the ground. It was already the middle of the afternoon. I spent another half-hour trying to pick up any other points of interest, but to no avail, so I packed up and made my way back to the car. I took out the reserve water container I carried, placed the strange metal object in its lid, and then filled it with water. The residual earth that stuck to the surface of the lump floated easily away, leaving behind the sand-covered blue-gray lump. The wash exposed more traces of yellow metal beneath.

I was not yet convinced the lump was gold, but I must admit I was quite excited by the possibility. Regardless of its true composition, it was evident the original metal had been dropped in a molten state into a bed of sand that must have produced the curious breadcrumbs coating effect. But was it gold? I told myself the first thing I would do on my return to Osnabrück was get out the set of chemical reactors I had purchased in the UK the year before and test the lump of metal for a gold reaction.

Once I arrived back home about two hours later, I unpacked my gear and took out the strange lump of metal. I set up the testing kit and took out the simple liquid tester for low-carat gold. I applied a small amount to the exposed yellow surface and half expected it to turn green straight away, which would signify a brass or bronze content. Instead, the liquid frothed on the surface without changing color.

Gold

I quickly drew a spot from the second container and gently applied it over the area of the first test. It changed slightly golden, but again, no trace of green. I sat back and exhaled loudly. The mass was pure gold. I knew the testers could not harm gold, so I dabbed one or two other areas of the sandy coating with the acids. As each small area came away clean, more yellow metal appeared, and after satisfying myself that the greater part of the mass was indeed pure gold, I stopped cleaning the lump in this manner. After washing it with warm water, I dropped it into a small plastic recovery bag.

I had in my possession a gold nugget, but it remained to be seen whether it was completely solid and I still had to determine its carat rating. This information would provide at least some indication of its possible age and manner of its creation. Nine-carat gold, for example, is something of a trend in modern times. Fourteen-carat gold was often associated with early European use, and eighteen-carat was highly favored by the French during Napoleonic times. Purer gold in excess of twenty-one carats was almost always a product of the early periods of history from the peoples of Europe and the Mediterranean, including the Romans. It seemed logical to me that if it had dropped to the ground or into a bed of sand in a molten state, it was a fairly safe bet it was solid gold—if the surface rating was verified as pure. An expert on precious metals would have to be consulted, so I made arrangements the following week to visit Herr Manfred Rutkies, a local jeweler and goldsmith.

As I suspected, Rutkies was utterly fascinated by the nugget, and even more fascinated by my visit to his shop. Apparently he had already read a little about my activities in Kalkriese in the local press. After an informal discussion concerning many of the Roman finds recovered in Kalkriese, he promised to give me an answer on the artifact within a few days. He also asked if he might drill a fine hole into the centre of the mass to test metal content all the way through it. I reluctantly agreed. I had already contacted Dr. Kühlborn in Münster and apprised him of the strange find, promising to drive down there as soon as the results were known.

A couple of days later, I returned to Rutkies' shop and, much to my delight, was informed the gold content was 90%, with a 21-carat rating. The lump weighed in at just over a fraction of an ounce! The sandy coating still clinging weighed a gram or two, but the fact remained that I had unearthed a one-ounce nugget of gold. Interestingly enough, the 10% of the lump that was not pure gold was a mix of silver and gold, the combination of which was otherwise known as palladium. Rutkies told me this was a relatively unusual mix, and the type of metallurgy often associated with ancient times. I thanked him for his report, which I was pleased to find had been given free of charge, and left his shop. With the entire afternoon free that day, I decided to drive down to Münster to show Dr. Kühlborn this remarkable find.

Kühlborn, naturally enough, was delighted with the unusual piece, although he expressed a little disappointment that the other field where the pottery shards had been recovered had not been productive. We discussed at length the various possibilities that may have been behind the location of the site of the nugget's recovery. After some debate, we agreed there were two realistic possibilities to account for the presence of pig iron, lead strips, and the gold: (1) There had been some form of Roman foundry situated on the site during the Roman occupation of Haltern, or (2) The remains from a foundry situated in the lager had been disposed of in the field or woods alongside the original track way. As the distance from the main lager to the find site was at least 1,000 yards, the second hypothesis was not given serious consideration.

Dr. Kühlborn thanked me for my ongoing work at Haltern and for sharing the find with him, which he assured me would be further investigated, possibly by mounting a proper dig at some time in the not-too-distant future. He asked if he could keep the gold nugget and show it to his colleagues at the museum and discuss its merits, promising to brief me as to the results. I assured him I was quite happy for the museum to retain the nugget permanently, and was not concerned with any awards equivalent to treasure trove, but would be very interested in ascertaining its true origins. Haltern still had many secrets left to uncover, and the pure exhilaration of making finds like this was satisfaction enough for me.

The following week, Dr. Kühlborn contacted me to ask if I could again visit the museum to discuss the find. When I arrived, he explained that, although the museum and staff were extremely excited about the artifact, the whole concept of archaeology was based on realizing historical fact based on time and place and people: in essence, dating. Although the hypothesis of a Roman foundry was the most logical reasoning for the nugget's existence in Haltern, it could not be exactly dated or placed in archaeological terms. The nugget, though of great interest, was not an object that could be placed in historical terms.

I thanked him for his efforts, and asked to borrow the nugget to show Dr. Schlüter in Osnabrück. Dr. Kühlborn was perfectly happy to allow this, and I drove back to Osnabrück with the nugget once again in my possession. I stopped off in the town to visit Wolfgang at the museum and show him the golden find. Our mutual interests had created a good friendship during the previous years, and we had already been on friendly first-name terms for some time.

"Who knows," he mused while studying the nugget. "Perhaps your next find will be the ring or bracelet the smith was working on when he dropped this globule of gold into the sand. Haltern is a key part of the Varus puzzle. It is where it started, and possibly Kalkriese is part of that. Only time will tell. There is much still to be recovered in Haltern."

He turned the nugget over in his hand and continued. "The finds and coins recovered from there have told us much about Varus' occupation and his movements during those times, but sadly we still have not recovered any coins of Varus' mint mark anywhere else in northern Germany, save those that were recovered in Haltern itself when it was partly excavated.[1] Even in the area of Detmold where the statue of Arminius now stands, we have never found coins from Varus. The three legions under him were certainly attacked by Arminius and massacred, supposedly in the Teutoburger Wald some time after they left Haltern or the summer camp at Minden, but exactly where is still the big question." He paused for a moment before continuing.

"With all your searching for the truth about Kalkriese, perhaps we are nearer than we think."

*   *   *

---

[1] New finds were made in 1997 northwest of Kalkriese on the banks of the Ems.

9 AD – Late April. The Band of Gold—Haltern

The blacksmith was standing over a large anvil. A short pair of tongs gripped in his left hand held a horseshoe, one of the heavy varieties worn by the draught horses. The shoe was glowing white and red as he beat away at its edges with his heavy short-handled hammer. The metallic clangs echoed within the confines of the lager. He had been both a blacksmith and a farrier for the legions for many years, the last two in this fort at Haltern (Castra Secunda). He enjoyed his work and the satisfaction he felt creating all manner of metal implements, tools, weapons, and horseshoes for the troops established here in the Roman province of Germany.

He was a respected member of the fort's community, and his expertise and standard of work were second to none. Many of the Roman legionaries came to him for advice on weapons and the intricacies of working with bronze and iron and, on some other occasions, silver and gold. At the end of a long day's work sweating over his furnace and anvils, he would often turn his attentions to the small and intricate pieces of jewelry and ornaments he so enjoyed creating. The fine work was a pleasant break from his heavier duties as blacksmith and farrier—and far more enjoyable. It was an excellent way to relax after a long and hot day's work.

One of the advantages of working as the camp smithy was that he could keep warm in the winter by laboring around his furnace, and cool in the summer by working outside to catch the delights of the sunshine and breezes. When it rained, he would simply move inside under the protection of the smithy roof and sit near the furnace, keeping the damp, cooling rains at bay while gently stoking his fires to maintain the furnace at an effective operating temperature.

He was German by birth, but like many of the ancillary workers and cavalrymen (including Arminius), he had been content to change his allegiance and work for the Roman occupation forces. After all, the terms of service were good. The pay was fair, and for much of the time he was his own man, his own master. He was a sociable man, and thus enjoyed the opportunity to come into contact with the rich and varied personalities that comprised the Roman lager community. He had views on nearly everything that happened from one day to the next, and was looked upon by others as a mine of information on myriad of inconsequential matters. He was also privy to the gossip and innuendo that pervaded life within the fort. He knew everybody else's business, but was well trusted to keep his knowledge to himself. There were few who were not on at least a nodding acquaintance with the lager blacksmith, and his smithy was a regular social gathering point for off-duty personnel.

This evening however, he was involved in a special and very private piece of work. A few days earlier, Arminius had taken him aside and personally asked for his assistance. The legions and their auxiliary forces were already well into their preparations to move out on their march up the Lippe. The main force of the three legions was deployed on its move toward the first lager on its route to Detteln (Castra Trentia), but the rear elements had yet to deploy, awaiting the new reinforcements shipping up the Lippe from the Rhine via Xanten (Vetera Castra). The composition of the guard force at Holsterhausen (Castra Prima), the second of the river line of forts, would remain the same, as would the force guarding the smaller lager of Aliso, situated a short distance up the mouth of the Lippe from the Rhine.

Normally, Arminius moved out with his lead reconnaissance elements, but on this day he decided to delay his departure until that evening for reasons best known to himself. Command of his men he left to his second in command. He would join them the following day.

The German warrior approached the blacksmith to inquire how the personal work on his piece of jewelry was progressing. Arminius had asked the smith to craft a special thick and heavy solid gold arm bracelet, adorned with crossed snake heads at the apex of each open end. It resembled a gold Celtic torque, examples of which he had seen in Rome when legionaries brought them home after participating in Caesar's invasion of Britain. The stunning arm bracelet was a present for Wodenicus, his lifelong friend and German cavalry commander—a gesture of comradeship to celebrate the innumerable battles and campaigns in which they had fought side-by-side. Each had spilled blood to protect the other; each would do so again.

Wodenicus had surprised him the previous week when he presented Arminius with a superbly engraved bronze and iron dagger embellished with gold and silver filigree at the hilt and handle. It was a beautifully balanced weapon, and Arminius proudly mounted it on his body cross belt, sheathed in a hardened and polished leather scabbard. How could he repay such a thoughtful gesture?

As Arminius drew near, the startled blacksmith looked up quickly. He was so engrossed in his labors that he had failed to note the approach of the German leader. As he did so, a spoonful of molten gold, sitting astride the small kiln he used for fine molding work, rattled on the lugs of the supporting frame in the jaws of the heated kiln before falling onto the main casing of the kiln itself. Small amounts of the precious metal splashed out of the spoon. With an audible gasp, the smith jumped back quickly in an effort to avoid burning one of his open-sandaled feet. The small mass hit the floor of the building, where it merged with the sand and rubbish a few inches from his toes. A sharp hiss and small plume of smoke erupted from the now unrecognizable globule. Two other splashes, both well away from the kiln, hissed and sputtered as they, too, burned into the sand. The blacksmith quickly grabbed the wooden handle of the large spoon before any more gold spilled, and carefully replaced it on the lugs of the kiln.

"You seem to be having a little trouble," laughed Arminius as he stopped a short distance away. "Are you almost finished? I am leaving tomorrow to join the legions, and I wish to take the bracelet with me."

"There will be no problem," replied the smith as he cast his eye across the floor in an effort to identify where the gold had landed. "I have made the mold castings for the bracelet, and that is the more time-consuming part of this job. I am about to pour the cast, just as soon as I recover what just spilled on the floor." The blacksmith swept his sandaled right foot through the top layer of sand in an effort to locate the globules of gold, which by now had hardened and were merging into the flooring. He kicked over one small lump that had landed near his foot, which he left to cool a bit more while he looked for others.

Arminius edged closer and, with his own foot, probed a lumpy mass near the base of the kiln. Traces of the precious yellow metal were clearly visible through the sand and bits of detritus clinging to it. When further searching failed to turn up additional gold, the smith bent down and recovered the two warm, hardened lumps. He dropped both into the molten mass in the pouring spoon and, a few seconds later, gently removed the slag from the top with a small drawing spoon. The large spoonful of molten gold was once again pure and unsullied.

"So," continued the smith, "we are ready. I can promise you a fine and beautiful gold bracelet in a short while. I must now concentrate on the pouring, for that is the secret of an unblemished ornament."

Arminius bent over and looked carefully at the mold. "What is that?" he asked, pointing to a thin white film inside.

"I have lined the casting mold with a fine layer of special fats so the gold will burn itself cleanly into the design without the bubbling, which often occurs during the pouring process—to amateurs, of course," the smithy added quickly.

Arminius smiled briefly before a shadow of seriousness covered his face. "Do what you must. I know you are the best, Smithy, and I eagerly await your finished article." The warrior lifted his eyes and looked into the distance. "I am going to get a cool pitcher of wine. Perhaps you would like some while we wait for your masterpiece! I'll see if I can find some roasted chicken to bring back as well." His words sounded more like an order than an offer.

"That sounds like an excellent idea," replied the smith as he bent forward to grasp the handle of the kiln spoon. "I need to concentrate now while I make the pouring, but will gladly join you when I have finished."

Once again thoroughly engrossed in his work, the smithy immediately forgot Arminius, who turned around and walked out of the small shop. With his tongue protruding from between his gently clenched teeth, the smith carefully poured the gold into the moldings before dashing water on the external casings. The sudden cooling effect produced an instant internal reaction that set the external surfaces of the gold, which absorbed and burned out the sheen of fats, to produce a lovely, unblemished glazed skin to the gold facings of the bracelet. He then meticulously cooled the whole cast until it maintained its casting warmth but was manageable to the human hand. He smiled to himself. He was indeed a master craftsman.

Once it cooled, the blacksmith picked up the small flat-bladed chisel he used to open moldings, gently inserted it into the prepared notch, and exerted just enough pressure to ease the molding open. The top half of the mold moved easily away and the smith set it aside. Inside was a beautifully formed torque in the Celtic style. A pair of beautifully carved snake heads rested at the end of each point of the open bracelet. The whole glowed with the magical sheen of pure gold. Its incredible beauty shocked even the experienced blacksmith, who felt both pride and awe swell within his breast. The smithy smiled broadly and nodded his head in approval.

"It is beautiful," whispered Arminius, who stood but a foot away looking over the smith's shoulder. He had again been so engrossed in his work he failed to hear the warrior's approach. "Here," said Arminius, holding out a pitcher and two chalices, "a good goblet of fine wine for the master. A freshly roasted chicken is on the way to us from the kitchens." The German warrior's scarred hand held an empty goblet, which he proffered to the smithy.

Nodding quickly, the smithy blurted out, "Just two moments, sire. The proof is still in the making." He gingerly picked up the base of the casting holding the gold band and turned it over into his left hand. The gold had contracted slightly during the cooling process, and without any additional effort, fell neatly out of its casting into its maker's palm. It was indeed perfect, a masterpiece. Arminius was ecstatic. He now had a fine present for his comrade-in-arms, Wodenicus. He would present him with it when he caught up with the legions the following evening. For now he would relax with the smith, sup their wine, and savor not one, but two roasted chickens, both of which had just been delivered. Arminius lifted the bracelet in front of him and turned it slightly this way and that, watching it sparkle as the last rays of the evening sun danced across its golden surface.

Neither man noticed the third splash of gold that was now hidden amongst the pieces of pig-iron and droppings from the kiln.

July, 1989

On July, 12, 1989, my son's birthday, exactly two years after I had made the first major coin find in Kalkriese, I returned to the apex of the woods that fell away from the large knoll on the edge of the Kalkriese Berg, the northern extremity of the Teutoburger Wald. There, I unearthed the first copper coin bearing the rare mint mark of Varus found outside the earlier discoveries registered from the lager at Haltern.

The half-As coin was inspected and cataloged by Frank Berger in the Münzkabinett in Hannover. He described it as one of the most important coin finds ever made in northern Germany. The mint mark stamped into the coin was one of the rarest imperial varieties. Some 1,100 copper coins were recovered from Haltern during the archaeological excavations of the 1800s and 1900s, but only eleven had been found with Varus' personal mint mark stamped on them—even though it was known he and his legions had lodged there for a considerable time during the years leading up to 9 AD. Except for this exceptional coin find in Kalkriese, not a single coin with Varus' mint mark had been found along the camps on the Lippe, in the Detmold area where the statue of Arminius stands today, or anywhere else in the North German plains and Teutoburger Wald.

Standing alone, the coin presented something of an enigma. When they began to be found in great numbers, the shadow that had been draped across the centuries began to lift. . .

*   *   *

According to Tacitus, "when the Emperor, Augustus Caesar, heard of the great loss of his three legions in Germany, he cried aloud, 'Varus, Varus, give me back my legions!'"

Chapter Six

The Mask

The find of the half-As copper coin was one of the most important and crucial discoveries in the quest to find Varus' lost legions. In fact, this single coin was the key that unlocked the outer door leading to the resolution of this ancient mystery.

After Frank Berger inspected and catalogued the coin, he confirmed it was indeed a rare copy with the imperial stamp mark of Augustus Caesar. Encouraged by this information, the archaeological team in Osnabrück went into overdrive to assist in my searches in Kalkriese.

Beginning in 1988, Dr. Schlüter permanently employed two of his staff with Fisher detectors in a day-in, day-out survey of the outlying fields and areas I had previously researched and inspected. These researchers always kept clear of my immediate work areas around the knoll of the Kalkriese Berg. The recovery of a find as important as the copper half-As bearing the imperial stamp mark of Augustus Caesar, however, convinced Dr. Schlüter that more intensive searches should be carried out in the immediate area of the single coin site itself.

Archaeological Surveys in Kalkriese, 1989

Armed with the knowledge that I had already pinpointed many deep metal source readings on the far side of the wooded knoll in the open ploughed field, Dr. Schlüter decided to initiate a new program for his archaeological team linked with my own work and surveys, and convened a new meeting at the museum to discuss plans. We had maintained a continuous series of discussions and meetings over the preceding two years regarding the discoveries, maps, archival material, and other related issues of interest to our search. But now there was a heightened sense of excitement in the air, as Dr. Schlüter came to realize that major archaeological surveys in the Kalkriese area were justified. Our conferences combined expert archaeological appraisal with the enthusiasm of the amateur hobbyist and the military mind's view of the way the legions might have marched through, and possibly fought in, the area under consideration.

During the previous two years, I had spent considerable time drafting maps of the region, drawing out ideas of possible lines of march and carefully linking up old and new coin sites. Tellingly, the same starburst effect of discoveries presented itself, with the burst of finds spreading out west and northwest from the bottom of the Kalkriese Berg knoll. The unearthing of an imperial coin of Augustus only strengthened the conclusions that were becoming obvious from my cartographic representations.

Together with members of the museum team and myself, Dr. Schlüter formulated a comprehensive plan. He decided to use exploratory archaeological slit trenches, beginning in the woods on the bottom reaches of the western side of the knoll and moving through the timber, up and over the rise, and ultimately to the open ploughed field on the other side. Additional detector surveys would be conducted on sites in the woods surrounding the knoll, which had been reconnoitered by me the year before. This time I would return and search them again with a highly expert and very active museum search team.

To ensure there was no doubling up of efforts, I told the team that I would remain clear of the trench works that would be crawling up and over the hill itself, and maintain my area of search in the woods and fields to the south and east. This would leave the survey team free to detect over the main feature, including its northern and westerly aspects. Although Dr. Schlüter was quite happy for me to work alongside the trench teams, both in and out of the digs, I explained it would be preferable for me to continue "proving the ground" on the far side of the knoll and looking over other spots that had now taken on a far greater degree of importance because of the unearthing of the copper half-As coin. This would also allow me to concentrate on my proposed "lines of march" theories. I also voiced another concern. As news of the digs and possible finds became more public, other "interested parties with detectors" were bound to arrive at the site and begin unauthorized searching. If the main exploratory trenches proved productive, the museum might be forced to fence them off and even introduce guard dogs to keep trespassers away.

During this meeting I again stressed that the main area of interest was likely the uppermost point of the knoll and the plowed field, known as the Oberesch, lying on the eastern side of it. This was the field that had already produced deep metal trace signals when I had used a specialized deep-seeker detector the winter before. I intended to concentrate my efforts on the far side of that field during the coming weeks. Some of my early forays into the Kalkriese area, which were based on the books and documents provided by Dr. Schlüter, led me to believe that a bronze scales hook, recovered in this area at the turn of the century, may well have been found when a nearby stream had been re-channeled as it ran through the farm complex lying just off the bottom northeast corner of the field. Regrettably, the local farming family who had lived in the area for many generations was unable to verify this theory. The story of the find was based upon a tale that implied the bronze hook had been discovered "while farm workers were digging a deep hole." Although Dr. Schlüter agreed with my thoughts on the plowed field (the Oberesch) in general, and the rising ground on the western edge in particular, he nevertheless believed the proposed series of exploratory slit trenches on the wooded part of the knoll must be carried out first as part of a systematic and comprehensive archaeological survey of the area. This would demonstrate whether the single mint-marked copper coin was a singularly important find, or one related to other important artifacts waiting to be recovered.

With the plan well established in his mind, Dr. Schlüter assembled his team and briefed each member on the work to be carried out over the coming months. He appointed Wolfgang Remme, a fairly young but very competent technician and surveyor, as the official in charge of the Kalkriese exploratory digs, with Klaus Fehrs as the chief prospector. Klaus had already been employed as one of the two people tasked to carry out full-time detecting in the area, and was an avid supporter of my efforts on the project. He greatly shared my enthusiasm and we exchanged ideas at every opportunity. The other—equally important—members of the archaeological team were Dr. Georgia Franzius and Günther Becker, the chief restorer who worked in close liaison with Wolfgang at the institute in Osnabrück.

The search was now on in earnest. A full ground investigation of the wooded knoll area would be carried out before the onset of winter, beginning with a series of small slit trenches in the apex area of the knoll. A full dig team was employed. The difficult nature of the terrain (with trees and heavy undergrowth in abundance) made it virtually impossible to use heavy machinery in the epicenter of the excavations. The trenches would have to be dug with shovels and other digging implements. Once the initial instructions for the outline work were issued, Dr. Schlüter turned to securing additional authority for the incursions required into the Kalkriese fields and woodlands.

*   *   *

During the next few weeks, as his team began its ground survey of the knoll, Dr. Schlüter (now promoted to Professor) obtained the necessary clearance for the ground digs to proceed. More importantly, he also secured extra funds to support the necessary labor force that would be used on the main excavations in the woods.

I received new movement instructions from my superiors about this time that sent me to my next posting in Hannover, 100 miles east of the Osnabrück area we were searching. Once I was settled into my new post, I began a series of regular visits to Kalkriese. Most were made on weekends, but I tried to get away whenever I could manage to do so. The 200-mile round trip was sometimes carried out daily. I would leave

Hannover as early as 5:00 a.m. and arrive about 7:00 a.m., which put me in the fields a short time later. Sometime I would stay for the weekend at one of the local farms. The locals now trusted and accepted me as a regular feature of the landscape in and around Kalkriese, trudging my way up and down the fields, stopping, stooping down, digging, inspecting, and then religiously refilling each hole before launching the process anew.

Once Professor Schlüter's team began its work on the wooded knoll, I moved my area of investigation away from the hill and back into the field on the eastern edge of the site. Harvesting was well under way. I managed to get a clear weekend to start work on the area nearest the farm pond, and the outlying field adjacent to it. I drove down from Hannover on a Saturday and arrived around 8:00 a.m. The early morning mists of late summer were still awaiting the sun's rays to burn through and chase away the last wisps of cool air from the surrounding woods. For a moment I stood at the edge of the field and looked across at the stubble left over from the farmers' crops, studying the rising ground to the knoll in the trees 200 yards away. Just a bit farther over the hill was the area that produced those deep, nagging and irregular metallic signals that now awaited the museum digging teams.

My eyes followed the track running along the northern edge of the field and into the woods, not far from where the teams were carrying out their initial digs. I sensed more than knew that the field in which I was standing and the track alongside it was the natural way for people to have moved through the area in times past. In fact, it must always have been the logical way to move from the eastern side of the Kalkriese hills through to the lowlands on the western and northwestern reaches. This was also where the large majority of my previous finds along the "starburst" lines had been found. As I sipped my first warm coffee of the morning, I perused the local relief map. On the northern edge of the track, much of the land was boggy and nearly always wet. Even during the hot summer months, the woodland soil retained a dank, moist texture. The majority of the trees here were young and sparsely sited saplings. The undergrowth was a confusion of bramble and fallen trees interspersed with areas of soft spongy ground, where fungus and leaf humus mingled with oddly-shaped toadstools clinging precariously to the sides of twisted and gnarled old tree roots.

What had been eluding me during years of map and ground studies suddenly became so very obvious. The only "dry" way through from one side of the Berg to the other, without going over the knoll, was along the path of the track. This encompassed a maximum of 50 to 100 yards of dry land, which quickly narrowed to a mere 10 to 20 yards running through into the northern wooded edge of the knoll centered along the track.

I performed a slow 180-degree pirouette, taking in every feature I could see. The farm complex was 50 yards away, quiet and unassuming. I looked south and southeast toward the adjacent field, which was hidden behind a thin screen of fir trees, before turning a bit farther and looking due southeast. Here was the "Gold Field," lying immediately south, and a waterlogged morass of bog and swampy ground running along the southern edge of the field into the nook lying on the corner edge of the Berg knoll. I turned back and examined the line of the track disappearing into the woods. Now I fully understood what I was looking at: the area effectively formed a bottleneck.

Metal detector enthusiasts spend much of their research time looking for such bottlenecks, not always of the same layout, but based on the same principle: old way stations, toll gates, fords, bridge sites, rivers coursing around the edge of hills, and features where the flat grassy river banks are no more than a few yards wide between hill and water. The naturally narrow pass like the one spilling out before me now fit the bill perfectly—an old track running between hill and water and boggy moorland.

I walked across to where the track disappeared up the wooded knoll. Once there, I turned around and gazed back across the expanse of the field before me. I felt like kicking myself when I realized it was the one view of the field I failed to examine when I had made my winter survey the year before. At the time, I had been consumed in the field area to my right, examining the many confusing and deep "ghost" signals reverberating in my detector's headphones. I studied my map for a few more moments and then drew three main trace lines from my current position: one running alongside the track to the east and through the farm complex; the second at 30 degrees to the first line running through the field across the fir tree line and into the next adjacent field; and the last, at 45 degrees, running through the opposite corner of the field across to the Gold Field.

"To the left, to the right, or through the center?" I muttered to myself.

In 1987 and 1988, I had made three forays onto the so-called Gold Field. My efforts had been rewarded with the recovery of a remarkably small quantity of recent coinage and not a single Roman coin or artifact of any kind—and certainly no gold. Yet, Mommsen had quite clearly written that Roman coins had been recovered there. I had bet Frank Berger a bottle of good gin that I would be the first to find a gold aureus (a particularly desirable Roman coin) in Kalkriese. The field beyond the fir tree line had yet to be surveyed, and it was always difficult to get onto because it was planted with sweet corn (as was the Gold Field), which was a late harvest in this shaded area of the local farming district. It was time to find that gold coin and claim my gin.

I elected to go down the edge of the field alongside the track and then carry out a series of sweeps across the bottom end. Thereafter, I would move back into the central area where the rise to the knoll began. By lunchtime I had recovered only a few relatively modern coins and the normal plethora of spent brass shell cases and empty toothpaste tubes. Just as I was considering taking a well earned break, the Fisher elicited that heart-warming double tone. It was so clear and specific I knew immediately I had found another solid silver coin.

I only had to go down four or five inches and gently push the black soil to one side to locate a perfectly formed denarius. I recognized it immediately because I had already recovered similar coins from earlier surveys on the far side of the hill. It boasted a blackened yet unblemished face of Augustus Caesar—the natural old gunmetal effect silver produces that so often enhances, rather than spoils, the natural beauty of old silver coins. I deposited the coin safely in a small plastic recovery bag and logged the spot.

The next hour was spent opening up the search area into a box survey of about twenty yards square. Oddly enough, the first find was a solitary one, as no further Roman coins were located. After surveying perhaps 1/3 of the lower reaches of the field by early afternoon, I finally took my break for lunch. I again perused the local relief map, carefully noting the location of the denarius in relation to the overall lay of the land. Taking a line from the point where the track disappeared into the wooded knoll behind me, I redrew the 30-degree line I had made previously. It now passed through the find site of the denarius. The line continued through the wooded pine belt and across the next field, now full with a crop of high sweet corn stalks. Should I concentrate additional energy on this field, or walk around to the farm complex, which abutted the corn field, and get a general review of the land there?

Instinctively, perhaps, I told myself I should concentrate on working back along my 30-degree line from the coin site to the wooded knoll, and do a thorough check of the central areas of the field to see if any other Roman finds came to light. As is so often the case on such occasions, a distraction broke the logical train of thought. (I would in the months to come curse this oversight, one of a number of errors of judgment I made during that time.) Just at that moment I heard the sound of a tractor laboring away on the other side of the fir tree line, and I decided to walk around to the farm and see what was about. I wanted to speak with the farm manager, and this seemed as good a time as any to do so. I had already had discussions with both the landowner, Frau Fisse Niewedde, and her farm workers, and I had been itching for some time to move on to the next field. As I walked into the farm complex, I took in the familiar surroundings of the small fish pond and the enclosed sweet corn field. The farm manager was sitting up on a large tractor, driving up the western edge of the field and harvesting the corn crop. I waited until he had completed the next leg of his sweep down the field before moving over to greet him. He told me all the corn would be cut down that day, and thus the field would be ready for me to search that evening or the following day. I looked at my watch. The afternoon was quickly slipping away. I decided to return the following day and bade the manager farewell.

I decided to spend the last hour of my day in Kalkriese with a short visit up into the woods on the knoll, where in the previous week the museum workers had started their exploratory trench excavations. As I walked back on to the track way and to the area of the field where I had previously recovered the copper half-As, a great sense of personal satisfaction and achievement with the way things were progressing coursed through me. This incredible sense of well-being stayed with me as I continued my way along the dirt track, dog-tired but pleasantly warmed by the afternoon sun. Only the low solitary call of a thrush disturbed the lovely serenity of the place.

The moment I entered the wooded area of the knoll and began walking up to the apex through the undergrowth, my whole demeanor changed. It was as if I had walked from the embracing cocoon of a summer afternoon's warmth into a chilly and foreboding atmosphere. Light barely managed to filter through the trees, and the silence was infinite, heavy, and palpable. An overwhelming deathly stillness pervaded the place, as if a black cloak had been thrown over the wooded landscape. I slowed my pace. My legs brushed though the ferns and undergrowth as I moved toward the top of the knoll. With each stride I felt more and more disturbed by the loneliness of the place, disturbed also because I had the strange feeling of having been through here before, but a long, long time ago. To this day, it is difficult to fully put into words the feeling that crawled up and down my spine that late afternoon.

Before long I came upon a large hole five yards square and perhaps one yard deep. Like ancient arthritic fingers, the gnarled and twisted tree roots exposed by the diggers stretched into the freshly opened ground. I lingered for a few moments before moving on. After another minute of walking, I found yet another freshly-dug hole. This time it was a slit trench, 20 yards long, two yards wide, and half again as deep. I came across three more similar excavations before I halted near the top of the western side of the knoll. I gazed down through the timber (which was not nearly as thick on this side of the knoll) to the sunlight and fields beyond, where I had made so many discoveries. The copper half-As had been recovered at the bottom apex of the woods. For a few minutes I remained, absorbing the atmosphere of the place. The open excavations reminded me of large mass graves waiting to be filled, and of long lost treasures still to be found.

*　　*　　*

It took a full month of exploratory digs on the wooded knoll before Professor Schlüter's team made its first significant find: a full perfect As of the Emperor Augustus Caesar with the stamp mark of Publius Quinctilius Varus. This coin, together with my earlier discovery of the imperial copper half-As, convinced the team members they were on the right track. Over the next few months, their slit trench excavations across the wooded knoll turned up many Roman bronze fibulas and additional copper coinage—including two more with Varus' personal stamp mark.

Meanwhile, I continued my efforts on the periphery of the dig area, where I was fortunate enough to stumble across another important find: a lone denarius and a bronze fibula. The coins were turned up on the steeply-banked edge of the stream running down the western edge of the knoll, which prompted more exploratory digs in that location.

The series of excavations continued to the very eastern edge of the woods, where a final slit trench was dug and the team uncovered what looked like the profile of a sunken earth wall. The discovery was perplexing. After studying the ground and pondering everything known to date about the surrounding area, Professor Schlüter decided it was time to move out into the field where I had made my first deep trace tests the year before. A large excavation about 150 yards long and five yards wide was made. Although Professor Schlüter did not know what to expect, it was his hope that the trench would uncover and link up with the beginning of the earthen wall uncovered at the edge of the woods.

And so the dig continued through the late winter and into the early spring of 1990. As the team dug deeper and deeper toward the sand bed below, metallic signals became stronger and stronger . . .

The Mask

It had rested in the bed of sandy soil for nearly 2,000 years, slowly submerging into the ground with the passing of each season. As the slow process of decomposition took place all around and then above it, it became as one with its surroundings, merging into a mass of unrecognizable contours and blemishes. The oxidizing effect of the soil and then the sand turned it a reddish-orange of honeycombs, a blackened hole on one side the only guide to what it once might have been.

The mask had fallen to the ground in times long gone by, when a nameless Cheruscian warrior slew an equally anonymous Roman legionary amid the screams of the dying as they echoed through the dank and wet woods. Its master's head had been cleaved from his body and fell to the bloody forest floor. The leather harness securing the mask to the helmet had come apart, separating them. The mask was made of iron and bronze, with silver and gold work embellished around its contours. Its sheen gave off a deathly pallor of grey and gold. It was an eerily beautiful thing.

The mask was trodden on before being picked up. It felt the heat of the hand that held it, and experienced the hot foul breath of the victor—just before the blade of his knife pried from their settings the gold and silver edgings along its outer rim. It was then thrown down, and many more feet trampled it into the stinking bloody mud, obscuring its proud aquiline features.

The mask had traveled with its master across much of the known world, from the sandy wastes of North Africa to Egypt and the Nile, throughout the Mediterranean to Greece and Athens, to Carthage, to the Pillars of Hercules, on the marches across the Alps, and across the great open plains of Gaul. It had witnessed the glory of great battles fought over many fields, its master carrying forward the proud aquiline features of his glorious Emperor, Augustus Caesar. As lovely as it was, the mask's appearance was coldly expressionless and cast fear wherever its master and his fellow Romans fought, unnerving their opponents in battle and presenting the face of their Emperor for all to see.

And then, from the lagers of the Rhine and the Lippe, the mask fell into a quagmire of storm and tempest, of fallen trees and dark stygian forests, valleys of mud and bog, where javelins and spears were hurled into the legions' ranks, and Cherusci warriors harried the columns at every twist and turn on the trail toward their oblivion—the final destruction of the legions of Varus.

The seasons came and went, and only twice in the early years had it felt any movement around it. The first time there were whispers and slow careful footsteps quietly treading around the site of the massacre. People unnamed stooped to part the leaves and ferns and pick up a sword here, a lance there. The second time there were many voices and many people, countless legionaries, comrades of its dead master. They spoke quietly to each other as they collected the butchered remains of their fallen comrades to take them away to another place. And then it became dark. The branches and leaves fell from the trees and formed thick layers above it as the mask began its long and agonizingly slow journey down deep into the heart of the wooded knoll to became as one with the dark damp soil surrounding it.

Many centuries passed before it sensed any further movement above it. Trees were being cleared from the forest, and small bands of workers were tilling and digging the soil above, sowing new life into the earth that had witnessed so much bloodshed and death. But it was so deep now that it was not disturbed. More seasons passed, and the centuries continued slipping by. Larger wars with greater armies tramped past the place of its sojourn deep underground.

By now, the mask's metallic content had fused into the soil and had oxidized all around its outer edges. Yet one of its two eyes remained open, as if it was waiting to see the light again.

And then, something happened. An electrical force gently caressed it, lost it, and then probed it again, seeking its core and shape, touching its top, its sides, before passing over again and again, until there was . . . nothing. Two more seasons passed, and again it felt strange powerful vibrations coursing down through the substructure of the soil, becoming more and more intense, fading and returning but always there, the pitch of noise from above becoming more sharply focused. For a short while it was quiet again. Finally, after nearly 2,000 years, a beam of light broke through the earth when the sandy soil was softly brushed away from its face. Its red and orange surfaces were indistinct, but its lone black eye gazed coldly up at those who had disturbed its resting place. The mask was highlighted from above by a fading winter sun.

It had been found. If it could, it would have smiled. But alas it could not, for it was the ceremonial face mask of the Roman legions, the profile of the Emperor, Augustus Caesar, made to be worn during battle and cast cold fear into the hearts of the enemy.

1990—Gisela in the Gold Field

She was a short stocky lady, with longish curly hair done up in the manner of dreadlocks. She always dressed very sensibly for the arduous outdoor work she and Klaus were undertaking, walking up and down the same fields I had first surveyed during 1987 and 1988, expanding the area of the search out into the other fields and pastures of Kalkriese. She was nearly always cheerful, regardless of the weather, and she loved her work with a passion that matched my own obsession. She and Klaus made a good team and they made many, many exciting finds over the years she worked on the Kalkriese project. But none was to match the excitement of her first major discovery.

It was in the dead of winter, and the team was more than pleased with the discoveries of the previous months. Like me, they did not take too much notice of the cold winter weather. Some of the most enjoyable times I spent in the fields were during the blustery winter months, with a light fall of snow on the ground, wrapped up snug and warm against bitter winds, searching across lonely empty fields very much at peace with the world.

Gisela liked those times as well, although in January 1990 the weather was more mild than usual. Just after New Year, on the second day of the month, she left Klaus in the area of the central excavations to forage out on to the Gold Field for a few hours. She knew I had been over the field many times without any marked success, but recalled that only a few months before, I had said to them both that when the finds start drying up, and you don't know what to do or where to go next, go back over the same ground again. And don't forget to reread Mommsen— again, and again, and again.

Each new plowing only turns the topsoil over some 90 degrees, or 25 percent by the farmer's plow. In theory, if a field is deep plowed only once a year, a searcher would need to visit it every year for four years before the topsoil had been comprehensively surveyed. So it was with the Gold Field. As noted earlier, I had surveyed this field without success at least three times during the previous years, and by 1990, was beginning to lose the incentive to return—particularly in view of all the other fields and meadows that were now revealing their buried secrets. The Gold Field had produced nothing noteworthy. We all know of the lesson that one should practice what one preaches. While I was busy rereading Mommsen, Gisela was chasing his shadows and revisiting these old sites.

According to Klaus, he and other team members were working in the main dig areas when they saw Gisela walking toward them from the direction of the Gold Field. She looked excited and was waving her arms in the air. Klaus turned to Wolfgang Remme, "Gisela must have made a good find. She seems very excited about something." When she finally joined them, she opened her hand and revealed a shining gold aureus of Augustus Caesar, the distinct aquiline features of the Emperor clearly visible even after two millennia. This particular coin had the same clear embossed head as its counterpart in the issues of the silver denarius, which were being found in prolific quantities in the Kalkriese battle area: Augustus Caesar on one side, and on the reverse, Caius and Lucius Caesar standing behind battle shields and crossed spears. I was happy for Gisela, but her discovery meant that I had lost my bet with Frank and now owed him a bottle of gin!

"It was nearly completely exposed, lying on the topsoil, clearly to be seen," Gisela later recalled. "No digging was necessary, and I thought it was a modern coin, as it was so clean and bright golden lying there on the surface. I actually thought Klaus and the others had played a trick on me and had planted a forged coin there for me to find. Now we know it is a real aureus. It is so wonderful to have made such a beautiful and exciting find. I think now I will never tire of walking the fields in the future—I will always be looking for that next exciting find!"

Gisela continued walking many fields, but nothing would surpass that wonderful discovery. Sadly, she passed away in early 1996 after a short illness. I know and feel she still walks those fields, a reassuring presence among the thousands of other spirits who, so very long ago, departed this life during the Varusschlacht, their whispers caught up in the will-o'-the-wisp mists of time that drift through the woods and glades of Kalkriese. She is greatly missed. Good hunting, Gisela.

Chapter Seven

1990: The Summer Months

The recovery of the oxidized clump of iron that turned out to be a ceremonial parade mask bearing the face of Emperor Augustus woke the imagination of every learned archaeologist and school of historical interest in the whole of Germany. Headlines proudly proclaimed that we had discovered the battle site where Varus had lost his legions, labeling it the most important historical find in German history.

To my amusement, one journalist compared my achievements with those of Heinrich Schliemann, the discoverer of Troy. (I lamented the comparison, for Schliemann had dug through seven or eight layers of important historical strata to get to the treasures he was seeking.) Many archaeologists and historians had scoffed at Professor Schlüter's expert supposition that this was indeed the true battle site, offering instead their own theories as to the location of the "actual" battle. The mask find, however, coupled with everything else we had unearthed, threw cold water on their own ideas, professional aspirations, and peer-reviewed articles.

Regardless of all the publicity for and against the establishment of Kalkriese as the lost battle site, Professor Schlüter's team went into overdrive in their work in the field on the edge of the knoll. By this time we were recovering a prolific mass of artifacts from the main dig area, so extra staff was brought aboard including, in June of that year, Dr. Susanne Wilbers-Rost.

Among the recent discoveries were a huge pioneer's axe and many bronze pieces, both small and large. Some were from Roman uniform fittings. They were carefully picked out of the soil bed using a combination of heavy tractor shovel scrapes to take the soil layers down inch by inch, with Fisher detectors being deployed at each scrape stage to ensure that even the smallest metal piece was recovered. I had convinced Professor Schlüter that the Fisher detectors we used, both the 1265 and the Gemini models, were an invaluable asset to both the excavations and the field work. In view of my own success with these instruments, he asked me if he could buy some for the team. I quickly placed the order with Joan Allen Ltd, the leading dealer in the UK for Fisher detectors, and two 1265s arrived the following week by express delivery. We were now in business in earnest.

Of course, shovel and brush were used once the dig reached the lower level of the excavation, but the detectors quickly came into their own as the excavations progressed. The Deep Seeker detector I had used both before the onslaught of the main digs on the knoll, and later when more large finds were made, proved to be of infinite value in assessing the overall picture of the ground, and in the recovery of many valuable finds. The primary artifacts, including those discovered on the knoll during the preceding months, were brilliantly restored by Günther Becker, the museum's chief restorer. It was tedious work. For example, it took many weeks for Günther to restore the battle mask and the axe to something resembling their original condition. Two fairly crisp winter months, January and February of 1990, prevented further serious work on the dig, and the excavations were closed down until the spring thaw.

By March, Professor Schlüter had decided to combine a "Grand Opening" of the Osnabrück Museum, with all of its previous archaeological discoveries, with the Kalkriese battle site discoveries. A new series of displays showing a selection of the artifacts that had been restored were introduced, including a special display of the mask and the axe. The opening was attended by various dignitaries from the county and the city, including the Minister of State for Archaeology and the Arts, and the Oberbürgermeister of Osnabrück, Herr Fip. I was invited as a special guest and, naturally, Professor Schlüter took center stage. The possibility that, at long last, the site of essentially the first important event in German recorded history had been found created tremendous excitement and debate within the German community. Nevertheless, there were still many who could not bring themselves to agree that Kalkriese was the place where Varus met his end, concerned as they were that future finds might disprove the dating of the events of two thousand years before. The March Grand Opening was a wonderful success. Large crowds of curious onlookers flocked in, particularly to see the Roman finds from Kalkriese. Only about 10 percent of what had been unearthed had been restored for viewing, but even this small amount was more than sufficient to support a major exhibition of "The Romans in Kalkriese."

With the onset of an early spring, the excavations progressed swiftly into the main field. They now covered an expanse of ground 200 yards long by 150 yards wide. During the careful scooping of the top layers of soil, I often dropped by to discuss the excavations and finds with Wolfgang Remme, Klaus Fehrs, and the rest of the dig team. There were few things I enjoyed more than to discuss the project with them and listen to their thoughts on the merits of further exploratory digs at the top of the hill. But with so much work being carried out on the main field, the team was forced to concentrate its labors on the area of the earthen wall in an attempt to follow that structure's line through the hill.

On the western side of the knoll, a small stream ran down from the hills above into a deep gully, or beck, where I had previously recovered a bronze fibula and a silver denarius. It was my belief that this gully would have been a natural "backstop" to the ambush position, and would have been a good defensive position for the German warriors if the Romans had broken through the ambush and regrouped to counter-attack from the western side. Professor Schlüter believed he would eventually need to explore the possibility that the earthen wall extended well beyond this gully, to fall into the natural contour lines that curved around the northern extremities of the wooded knoll and the Kalkriese Berg. He believed it was necessary to cut additional exploratory trenches into the sloping field on the far western side, but for the present, continue working with the major excavations in the field running along the eastern edge of the field: the Oberesch.

Fairly confident the battle site had indeed been located, I returned to my archival and other research materials to refresh my thoughts on the general description of the battle and the events that had followed that disastrous defeat for the Roman legions and the greater Roman Empire.

9 AD: May: Move Out to Summer Camp

The Seventeenth, Eighteenth, and Nineteenth Legions under Quinctilius Varus were on the move northwest of the upper reaches of the Lippe and tramping into the highlands beyond. The legions were spread in long formations of troops, six abreast, straddling a swathe of countryside 200 yards wide. From above, they looked like a formation of multi-colored ants swarming forward from the drop-off ports on the river. The boats that had transported their effects and support stores up the Lippe had disgorged them onto the quaysides, where they were loaded onto wagons that followed the principal legion forces along the primary axis of advance.

The main force of the mercenary auxiliary troops under Arminius was deployed forward and on the flanks of Varus' command, where they acted as scouts and flank guards for the three marching legions. Their reports were an invaluable source of information for the legion commanders, and reported not only on activity ahead of the marching troops, but on the general state of the ground and any obstacles that might lie in their path. The auxiliaries were also responsible for deploying a rearguard to protect the soft underbelly of the formation, where the quartermasters' wagons and carts laden with stores and food followed the phalanx of marching legionaries. Varus had ridden up the slope, away from the river, to watch his legions form and tramp away on their journey. With him was Marcus Aius, his second in command, and the three legion commanders.

Marcus Aius sat quietly astride his large black horse, brooding. In his ears rang the voice of Emperor Augustus, who had reviewed Varus' legions the preceding year before sending them to this wild and untamed land. An accomplished general in his own right, Augustus warned Varus of the dangers that lurked in the murky recesses of the German forests. "Varus, move forward carefully, behind an advance guard of scouts. Protect your flanks and rear at all costs. Always remember, and do not forget for one moment, that the most invaluable troops in your army are your scouts. It is the quality of your intelligence and advance reconnaissance information that will ultimately protect the safety of your soldiers." The Emperor had forcefully reiterated those warnings—again and again—until Varus' face took on a blank expression. He was no longer hearing the warnings. Perhaps he was embarrassed by the repetitive advice.

Marcus Aius' thoughts turned to the complex logistics required to sustain three legions in the field, together with a contingent of mercenaries, cavalry, and support elements bringing up the rear of the column.

The responsibilities of his command were substantial and unending, and he never ceased being fascinated and impressed with the intricate but effective organization of the mighty Roman legions. Each legion was commanded by a legate, usually a senator appointed by the Emperor. Under his charge were six Tribunes, the senior of whom acted as the legion's second in command, while the remaining five held administrative or operational positions on the legate's staff. The legion was comprised of ten cohorts, each of six centuries. With the exception of the first cohort in every legion, each century had a fighting strength of 80 men and was led by a Centurion, promoted to that position as a reward for distinguished service or gallantry in the field. The first cohort was special. It was comprised of five double-strength centuries and usually commanded by the five most senior Centurions, the senior of whom held the title of Primus Pilus.

The Primus was nearly always an exceptionally experienced officer. He attended every command and staff briefing, where his advice and military experience were counted as invaluable. He normally held his appointment for one year before either retiring or receiving a promotion to higher rank, perhaps Praefectus Castrorum—or third in command to the legate. The praefectus castrorum was responsible for the administrative staff and support elements, which included the medics, armorers and blacksmiths, and technicians of every category, such as the clerks and other back-up services.

A century of eighty men was made up of ten sections of eight men each, known as a contubernia. When in the field, each of these sections was provided with a tent and a mule to transport it. Some of the other heavy equipment also had to be carried, such as saws, axes, sickles, chains and rope, spades, and baskets. Many of these items were required for construction projects and clearing trees during a march, tasks the men frequently carried out when on active operations.

On some occasions, heavier items were brought up at the rear of the force by the logistical support groups under the command of the Quartermaster. Under these circumstances, legionaries marched with a stake over their shoulder, carrying with them a string bag for forage, a metal cook pot and skillet for cooking and eating, a sack containing rations or clothing, and a satchel or carrying bag with some of the lighter trenching and clearance tools. Having the soldiers carry the load reduced the requirements placed on baggage animals when the legionaries were not moving into an active service area, as was the case in northern Germany.

The result of all this was that the advance guards were lightly equipped, the bulk of their support stores and logistical support situated closer to the rear of the column behind the supply train.[1] The legions were ready to fight, if necessary, without the encumbrance of heavy stores and equipment. But every experienced military commander knew that even the best and most skillful army cannot sustain its efforts for any length of time without an intact logistical line of supply. The most essential of these were plentiful food and water, which were critical for the well-being and state of mind of the common soldier. As Vegetius, a Roman writer of military affairs succinctly put it, "Famine makes greater havoc in an army than the enemy, and it is more terrible than the sword."

---

[1] It is worth noting that the effectiveness and strength of the Roman legion command structure proved so efficient that much of it still exists in modern armies of today: We still find the soldier who works his way up through the ranks, changes and extends his service from a warrant officer to take up the Queen's Commission as an Officer. He is nearly always appointed as an Administration Officer, or a Quartermaster in charge of support elements and logistics.

Because he was not expecting any unrest among the German tribes or serious problems along the line of march, Marcus Aius had ordered the soldiers in the van of the column, and those ahead of the supply train, to carry only the basic ration of bacon, hard tack, and sour wine. The hard tack was a biscuit baked from a corn ration known as bucellatum. Three pounds per day were issued to each man.

Feeding the men was a formidable logistical problem. Between 50 and 70 tons of grain had to find its way into the hands of the men each day. Much of it would come from the scouts who foraged ahead of the army, taking what they could in tithes from the tribes and villages along the route as part of their tax-collecting duties. On an operational march, the column usually carried food and supplies to feed each man for 17 days. The majority of the food was hauled by transport animals moving with the supply train. These animals, as well as the cavalry horses, also had to be fed and cared for, and required about seven pounds of feed each day. More than 1,000 pack mules were thus required to carry all this food, tents, and general support supplies, with ox carts and horse-drawn wagons transporting the heavier loads.

The legionaries themselves were also capable, to some degree, of feeding themselves. As it was with all soldiers in every age, the men followed the general motto "If it moves, eat it." Badgers, moles, fox, voles, and mice were frequently seen roasting away over the camp fires at night. In addition to the occasional fresh meat, basic bacon, corn, and sour wine, their diet was often supplemented by beer whenever available, and venison, fish, poultry, and vegetables. Oxen, mutton, and pork were also eaten in large quantities.

The logistical marching order of Roman columns concerned Marcus Aius. Indeed, the legion's officers routinely debated the matter. Some argued that soldiers sensibly unencumbered by the paraphernalia of pioneer tools, other equipment, and excessive food rations, could form up and fight at a moment's notice, and could sustain themselves for up to 36 hours by what they carried on their own back. Before those hours expired, a battle lager would have been established and the rear echelon train would have arrived to supply the troops during any lull in the fighting. Or so it was argued. Others, however, believed the supply echelons should be positioned closer to the front of the column and immediately behind the forward legion, so the soldiers could be readily re-supplied and directly supported during the early stages of any battle.

As far as Marcus Aius was concerned, there was merit in both positions. However, the legions were about to move into the highlands and German forest areas, where the terrain would make it difficult or impossible for the legions to deploy into the open battle formations they preferred. It would also make it very tough for the quartermasters to effectively control the baggage train, and for the commanders to effectively control their legions.

Varus' senior Tribune had listened carefully when his superior voiced his thoughts on the matter of deployment. The information Marcus Aius possessed reassured him that there were no serious problems of unrest among the German tribes. Arminius and his mercenary scouts had supplied much of this intelligence. Marcus Aius digested this intelligence and Varus' suggestions, and reluctantly convinced himself that the support echelons could follow the rear of the advancing force in the normal manner, protected by a reserve force of other contingents provided by Arminius. The upcoming journey, however, was wholly unsuited for artillery wagons (carroballistae). He issued an order to leave many of them behind in the main lager on the Lippe. The few that would accompany the legions would roll in the main rear echelons, and would be ordered forward from that point if and when they were required.

As the marching Romans tramped past his position, Marcus Aius swivelled on his horse to address Varus. The commander was reclining on his travel litter, his eyes half closed against the strong sunshine as he studied his passing legions.

"General, our preparations are nearly complete. Arminius informs us there are no reports of any threatening activities from the villages northeast on our march route. The quartermaster is making good progress with the unloading of the final provisions from the galley port, and his echelons will be following us late this evening. His men will take their position as the rearguard, and Arminius has left a large contingent in the form-up point ready to follow after." The senior Tribune stopped for a few seconds, but when Varus did not speak, he cleared his throat and continued. "The weather reports, according to the scribes, are good, and they have assured me there is every possibility that we shall have a warm late summer, and complete our foray into the highlands long before the autumn storms arrive."

Marcus Aius paused once more. Varus again offered nothing in reply. "If it pleases you, sire," continued the officer, "we can join the deployment now and take up our position behind the Seventeenth Legion."

Varus' eyes widened as he contemplated the solid mass of troops marching below his position. Dust stirred from the tramping of thousands of feet billowed knee-high into the warm summer air. A wide palette of red and brown composed of Roman armor, the shimmers of burnished helmets, and the waving of multi-colored standards and banners offered a symphony of noise and movement. "A pity our scribes have not taken the equinoxes into account," replied Varus. "We are deploying late this year, and the spring equinox is already well behind us." He paused for a few seconds before continuing. "Marcus Aius, do you not recall the old adage, 'It is the choice of the right moment that controls all human action, and above all the operations of war?' Yes?"

Marcus Aius nodded. "Yes, sire."

"A commander must have an exact knowledge of the dates of the summer and winter solstices and of the equinoxes. These damned lands here, especially in the autumn months, are bedeviled by ferocious winds and rain—the worst storms one can imagine tear through this forsaken countryside and play havoc with troop deployments. We must ensure that the gods favor our journey and we must make further sacrifices to them. Order the scribes to speak with the priests and let us be favored with good omens." Varus sighed audibly, coughed once, and sat up. "Let us join the march as you suggest, Marcus Aius, and pray we enjoy a trouble-free collection of the taxes during the next few weeks. At the end of the summer, I want to return to the lagers on the river with satchels full of German treasure, and enough panniers of corn and wine to make even the surliest of legionaries sing with joy."

"It shall be done as you suggest, sire." Marcus Aius smiled in response.

"Let us go with good fortune now, Marcus Aius. You have my baton and the command of the legions. Signal the standard bearers to let fly the banners and advance now. Let us at least enjoy the sun while it shines and join the column." And with these words, Varus and his command began their march into the German highlands.

The standards of the legions provided more than just a rallying point in battle, and were never intended solely for purposes of pageantry. Their primary purpose was as a means of passing orders on the battlefield to distant formations and units that would then execute their oft-practiced battle drills. The effectiveness of this means of command was made possible by the cornu, a large rounded horn with a distinctive note that alerted commanders and soldiers alike to look inward toward the standards and banners. When the horns sounded their distinctive notes, the legions' subordinate commanders read the commands and transmitted them either directly or by runner. This system of signaling and communicating could be adapted to most battle formations, and its success depended entirely upon the army's training and discipline.

The cacophony of noise and movement quickened every man's pulses, excited the already nervous cavalry horses, and filled pumping hearts with a combination of emotion and excitement, of surging adrenaline, and of a distant fear of the unknown. The pungent sweat from this mass of humanity and animals on the move filled the nostrils of the men of the Seventeenth, Eighteenth and Nineteenth Legions.

*   *   *

A few months after the mask and other important artifacts had been recovered in Kalkriese during the spring of 1990, the archaeological team's survey of the excavations of the earthen wall straddling the northern contours of the hill was nearly complete. The nature of the objects and their age, which was established by a variety of accepted dating techniques, supported the premise that a battle between Romans and Germans had taken place here during the period when Varus' legions disappeared in the German forests. In the estimation of Dr. Wilbers-Rost, there was no doubt that an earthen wall had been erected through the cut of the hill, and its eastern edge had been supported by a series of timber posts, which were now visible as post holes in the sand base of the excavations. Her conclusion confirmed my own theories of the general layout of the battle site, which possessed all the hallmarks of a very effective ambush position. But was this where Varus lost three legions and his support troops and echelons—some 20,000 men? I was not completely convinced. The area was far too small to squeeze that number of men through the gap between the hillside and bog. In all probability, this site was the final, devastating, denouement of a complex running battle that had taken place during the day or days leading up to this location at Kalkriese.

The more I thought about and studied the evidence discovered thus far, the more confident I was in my conclusions. The original starburst of artifact activity on the western edge of the feature, narrowing back through the bottleneck to the lands to the east, indicated a march (perhaps orderly, perhaps harried and pressured) to a pre-planned ambush position, from which only a handful of Romans managed to escape. My educated hunch was that before the Romans reached this place, the great majority of them had been attacked many times as they moved up from their original route leading to the lager forts on the Lippe. I therefore decided to concentrate my research on this theory as my raison d'être, and make it the focal point of my work in the coming years.

*   *   *

I had already made many forays into the highlands to the southeast during 1988 and 1989. In April 1990, I began a series of intensive surveys that took me to more than 60 different sites throughout the highlands between the River Lippe and the Weser, to the east and northeast of it. Nearly all of these sites had been written up by Dr. Frank Berger from older records, and his reference documents and books proved invaluable in my research work. I decided to concentrate my efforts on the two highland wooded features north of the Lippe. The first, and by far most important, was the Teutoburger Wald (a Wald is a series of forested highlands), which runs northwest up to Osnabrück and on to the Kalkriese Berg. The other was the Wiehengebirge (ridge), which runs eastward from Minden and the River Weser and also joins with the northern edge of the Kalkriese Berg.

About a century after the loss of Varus' legions, Tacitus wrote the following: ". . . *ductum inde [from the Ems] agmen ad ultimos Bructerorum quantumque Amisiam et Lupium amnes inter, vastatum, haud procul Teotoburgiensi saltu, inquo reliquiae Vari Legionumque insepultae dicebantur.*" The general interpretation of this passage indicates Tacitus believed the battle had taken place north of the River Lippe and east of the River Ems, in what is now known as the Teutoburger Wald. According to Professor Schlüter, the former Osning (mentioned in old literature) is the Teutoburger Wald as we know it today. The Teutoburgiensi saltus was probably the western part of the Weserbergland, lying between the Wiehengebirge and the Teutoburger Wald.

This Wald ("weald" or ridge), runs up from the lands directly north of the Lippe, due northwest, and then curves away to the underbelly of Osnabrück. In this area the ridge breaks up into a scattering of hills that fall away farther to the north, with Kalkriese as its northern extremity. Beyond were the large wet moorlands of the Dieven Wiesen (Moorland Basin). Historians have long believed the Roman route ran from the River Weser in the central plains, across to the River Ems in the west, and across this northernmost point of the juncture of the Wiehengebirge and the Teutoburger Wald. But did it? I had my doubts (for reasons that will be presented in subsequent chapters). I believed Kalkriese was the site of the Varusschlacht because I believed the legions had marched up from the Teutoburger Wald, from their original route leading to the Lippe, and, lured on by Arminius, had changed direction and moved northwest toward Kalkriese.

Just as the first edition of this book was going to press, I received a communication from historian Derek Williams, who was in the final stages of writing *Romans and Barbarians: Four Views from the Empire's Edge* (St. Martin's Press, 1998). His book includes a substantial chapter on the Varian disaster. Professor Williams believes the early German scholars misinterpreted the Roman use of the word "saltus," and mistakenly understood it to mean "forest" or Wald. Livius (Livy) Book 25:5, 8, uses these words to describe the Battle of Thermopylae: "*Thermopylarum Saltum ubi angustae fauces coartant iter*," or "The Pass of Thermopylae, where a narrow 'gap' constricts the road." Tacitus, continued Williams, never meant Teutoburger *Wald*, but the Teutoburger gap, corridor, passage, or pass. As I later discovered, this idea had also been published in a 1992 essay by Herr Wolfgang Prauss in Berlin. Nevertheless, it was intriguing and helpful, for it tended to confirm the Kalkriese Gap—or the passes to the east between the Wiehengebirge and Kalkriese Berg hills—as the sites of the final slaughter of Varus' decimated legions. It did not alter my belief that Varus' legions marched up through the highlands of the Teutoburger Wald and through the Wiehengebirge passes in the region of Ostercappeln, on to Felsenfeld, and then into the Kalkriese bottleneck.

If such a large force had indeed passed through the highlands toward Kalkriese, its members would have left many small but potentially significant artifacts in their wake. Was the battle fought over several days in the form of a running or harrying series of ambushes that culminated with the final slaughter at Kalkriese? If so, there should be concentrated artifact sites scattered along the 18 miles or more of the Teutoburger ridge leading northwest up to Kalkriese—perhaps in even greater profusion than existed in Kalkriese itself. The best way to confirm this theory was to locate every recorded Roman coin and artifact find that had been made over the previous two centuries in this region, and plot them on a graph overlay of a map of the same area. This was no small undertaking, as I intended to visit each recovery site and, if possible, locate the exact areas where the finds had been made.

From Detmold north of the upper reaches of the Lippe, through the highlands of the Teutoburger Wald leading up to the northern areas of Osnabrück and Kalkriese, I began pursuing this mammoth task. Because I did not have sufficient time to confirm and survey every find site area with a metal detector, I had to settle with establishing the lay of the land and plotting the point on the map overlay before moving on to the next known recovery site. Some of the artifacts recovered at these sites were not relevant to the Varian period, and this fact had to be taken into account when recording the data.

Endless visits to farms and locating the right farmers and landowners to properly understand the events surrounding the discoveries themselves (some of which had been made more than a century earlier) was a daunting task. My free time was often limited to weekends, a time when farmers are not at home. Nevertheless, by the end of the summer of 1990 I had gathered sufficient information to enable me to accurately plot the series of Roman finds into some semblance of order, both in terms of dating them and visualizing the general line of the recovery sites.

I combined all relevant facts, location sites, and dates, and asked a colleague at work to compute the data and provide a graphic display of this information. The result was simply remarkable—an exceptional concentration of artifacts had been unearthed between the Weser to the east and the lands south of the Wiehengebirge and north of the Lippe, and up the Teutoburger Wald, running southeast by northwest farther to the west. The artifact concentration points continued up through the Berglands northwest to the Kalkriese Berg. Also telling were the small number of artifacts found north of the line of the Wiehengebirge ridge, between the Schwagstorf area and Minden.

*   *   *

During these summer months of 1990 while I carried out this survey, work steadily progressed in Kalkriese across the open field on the eastern side of the wooded knoll. The total area excavated now measured about 200 yards long by 100 yards wide. The team members established to their satisfaction that the earthen wall was originally at least 100 yards long (and subsequent excavations would increase that figure considerably). Archaeological finds continued to be steadily unearthed. The dig had already moved into the middle of the field, edging closer to the far side that had produced the lone denarius months earlier.

A particularly noteworthy find was unearthed one morning when the workers were carrying out another series of three-centimeter scrapes in the lee side of the earthen wall. A clear series of signals from the Fisher detectors indicated the presence not only of a solid item in the ground, but one of circular shape.

The double ringing tone that signified coins or other circular objects was already well recognized by the workers, and with some excitement they began brushing away the sandy bed of the dig. Within a short time, the first dull green glint of a semicircular piece of bronze was revealed. The artifact was gently removed and placed in a small box, after which the position was carefully marked before the worker again swept the detector across the small hole where the bronze find had been removed. Once more the double tone rang in the headset, and gentle brushing and loosening of the soil revealed yet another, apparently identical, semicircular piece of bronze. This, too, was placed in a finds box, and the team swept the area with their detectors a third time. Nothing else was found.

The boxes were taken down to the site hut for shipment to Osnabrück and the offices of the Denkmalpflege Institute. All finds were inspected and logged before leaving the area, but no cleaning of the items took place on site because this was the responsibility of Günther Becker at the Denkmalpflege. During the restoration work in Osnabrück, it was determined the artifacts were bronze armor clasps. The pieces comprised two parts of a whole clasp of a "Kettenpanzer," each linked to a central piece of the uniform fitting the shoulder, or possibly a cloak clasp.

Professor Wiegels, a leading authority on Roman history and artifacts, gently brushed away the earth and remaining sand residue and made a remarkable discovery: carved into the bronze was a name. Almost certainly it identified the owner who had perished at the Kalkriese battle site in the late summer of 9 AD, when the legions of Varus were lost for all time—until now.

These words were clearly engraved on the bronze clasp:

Marcus Aius
1st Cohort Fabricus

German Tribes

NORTH SEA

Ems

Hunte

Hase

Ems

KALKRIESE

Weser

Brukterer

Cherusci

Marser

Lippe

Chatten

Marcomanni

Schelde

Maas

Rhine

Main

Theodore Savas

Chapter Eight

May, 9 AD: The Lost Reconnaissance Patrol

The extended patrol of the eight-man reconnaissance team carried it into the most northern stretches of the rolling hills. It was one of a half-dozen such groups, dispatched by Marcus Aius to move stealthily but swiftly through the highlands to reconnoiter villages and larger settlements. Their task was to glean as much information as possible about the lands and temperament of the highland tribes, estimate the number of warriors and villagers in each of the areas the legions were to visit, and calculate the cattle and food stocks available in each of the village communities. Successful foraging was critical, for the soldiers could not subsist on the food carried in their wagons and on their backs.

Although Varus' legions were supported by Arminius' German mercenaries, who provided advance scout groups and flank reconnaissance parties, the Romans also maintained an independent reconnaissance company within their own formations. This outfit, comprised of the fittest and bravest Legionares, was selected from all ranks of the legions and formed into small, efficient squads. It was separate from the other contubernia that formed the basic unit of the Roman legions, but part of the first cohort—the senior cohort of each legion. Although many of the soldiers currently marching in the three legions were stale and second-rate warriors (and some were untested in battle), the men of the reconnaissance units were the legions' finest. Their vast experience gathered from countless expeditions and engagements made them the envy of their peers. The accuracy of the information they gleaned from the surrounding countryside, and the speed with which this information was communicated back to the legion commanders, was of primary importance to the health and safety of the army.

As the patrol moved forward up a long wooded rise in the heartland of the Cherusci tribe, the area known locally as the "Teuton Hills," the lead legionary caught sight of small wisps of smoke drifting into the sky from the other side of the rise. Without a sound, his hand signals spread the seven other soldiers out to the left and right. Not a man spoke as the soldiers quietly eased their way up toward the crest of the small ridge. Just before they reached the top, the lead scout gestured for them to go to ground. Within a few seconds every man was prone except the leader, who cautiously edged closer to the top on his hands and knees.

Though the hill held a thick undergrowth of oak, there was little undergrowth here and his view in every direction was good. As he approached the final level of the rise, he edged forward and slowly lifted his head. Nestled in the valley on the far side was a large German tribal settlement. He exhaled slowly as his eyes carefully studied the outwardly peaceful village. But something was wrong. An air of menace hung heavy in the haze of the afternoon sunshine: the settlement was dead quiet. Although smoke was drifting from a number of cooking fires, not a man, woman, or child was in sight.

The scout edged forward to obtain a better view into the central portion of the hutted settlement. After crawling through a large clump of forest ferns, he gently parted the palm-like fronds to look beyond. The soldier stifled a shocked gasp. The open central area of the village was now within view, as was a gathering of hundreds upon hundreds, perhaps even thousands, of tribesmen. Some were sitting, others were standing, but together they formed a huge circle. In the rear were hundreds of women and children. Every person present was listening in rapt awe to a tall pacing figure addressing the gathering.

The Roman knew enough about the Germans to know a meeting this large had to consist of several tribes besides the Cherusci. Who was the lone figure pacing, gesturing, and speaking to the gathered warriors? A force of German tribesmen this size was unheard of during Varus' two-year reign as Consul of the German province. A chilled realization struck the scout. There could be only one reason for pulling together such large collection of armed men.

His curiosity to learn more was tempered by a surge of fear and adrenaline. He had to get this information back quickly to the legions so the commanders could take whatever actions were necessary to quell what looked to him to be an uprising within the Teuton hill tribes. Although he had not been able to clearly see the chieftain at the center of the massed tribesmen, he could make out his strangely familiar winged helmet.

The scout was slowly easing his way through the ferns when he heard a blood-curdling scream from one of the legionaries to his rear. The terrified shriek ended abruptly, drowned out by the battle yells and howls of at least twenty Teuton warriors who burst from the woods on their flanks and from their rear, swiftly hacking and cutting into the prostrated Romans spread out and defenseless across the slope. A wounded Legionaire moaned and twisted on the bloody ground until a helmeted Cheruscian standing next to him lifted his sword and, with one swift stroke, cleanly decapitated the prostrate soldier. Another Roman a few yards away was on his knees, his sword arm nearly severed above the elbow and hanging limply down his side. Before he could pick up his gladius with his left hand, three large Germans hauled him to his feet and kicked and dragged him up to the crest and down the far side to the hutted settlement. A quick death on the slope would have been a blessing. Several Cherusci remained behind to strip the corpses of weapons and uniforms. Within a few minutes they, too, were on their way back to the village, laughing and refighting the ambush with hand gestures and fake sword and spear thrusts.

Stunned by the sudden lethal ambush, the lead scout forced himself to stay flat on the ground, surrounded by the thick bed of ferns. The afternoon sun beat down on him and his body dripped with sweat. It was not the sun that made him wet, but the screams of his wounded companion echoing up the rise from the village. The Germans were torturing him. His body was stretched upside down on a rack of wooden slats while his captors performed unspeakable acts of cruelty on his torn and bloodied form. They asked not a single question, for it was not answers they were seeking. They only wanted screams and suffering. The torture went on for several hours, and by the time the afternoon sun was nestled on the horizon, the soldier's tortured screams had fallen away into anguished whimpers of despair.

All the while the scout had remained still, listened, enduring, unable to render assistance. The sun dropped off the edge of the world, and as the evening shadows lengthened, he gently worked his way back through the undergrowth. Within a few minutes he was on the rear slope where his companions, stripped of their clothing and uniforms, lay naked, bloodied, and dead.

He rose to one knee and listened. After looking carefully in every direction, he began running down the slope, hunched over as close to the ground as possible. A final piercing scream, now far in the distance, chased him down the slope as a hot iron was laid on torn flesh. As he alternately ran and stumbled down the long hillside, he suddenly remembered where he had seen the winged helmet of the chieftain who had been addressing the massed tribes.

* * *

While the scouting team was being slaughtered, the three legions were resting in their temporary camp, three days' march from the river Lippe and the last permanent lager of Anreppen. Marcus Aius relaxed in the canopied porch of Varus' large sprawling headquarters tent. A warm gentle breeze wafted through the heat of the early summer afternoon and across the open porch, disappearing into the inner recesses of the marquee. He thought back over the three-day march to the highland. It had been a long, hot, and dusty journey. The heat of the early German summer permeated every pore of the body. Though not an easy march, the troops suffered it reasonably well. Sweating and cursing under their breath, as troops always have, they toiled step by step across the plains away from the upper reaches of the river and the security of the main forts. The unusually hot conditions slowed down the rear echelons of the column. Their oxen and carts, donkeys and horse-drawn panniers, with a snail's ponderous but determined rolling movement, made their lethargic way forward. Large clouds of dust rose above them and hovered lazily overhead. The usual five-mile spread between the main column and the supporting echelons lengthened as the hours passed.

Though outwardly calm, Marcus Aius' mind was not at rest. One of the reconnaissance patrols was missing. It was to have returned the previous evening with the others. The complete section—all eight men and the reconnaissance commander—had disappeared. It was a capable team, he assured himself. The men would arrive soon. The Tribune took a long drink of cool water and watched the early evening activity unfold around him.

The unending need for fresh water was one of the critical aspects in the movement of an army. Once on the march, Roman troops set a normal day's pace which, if necessary, could be doubled to a march-and-run pace no army in the world could equal. The first march of the day, normally an eight or ten mile stretch, carried them to a forward logistical point established ahead of time by reconnaissance parties. Once rested and replenished with food and water, the legions set out again on the afternoon march. By the time they reached the overnight camp (a position selected well in advance of arrival), the forward pioneers, guarded by elements of the leading legion, were already well on their way to completing the night's lager, establishing the security perimeter, and setting up the guard rosters. Only when these grueling preparations were complete did the men relax and prepare their evening meals.

The commanders' tents and accommodations were always speedily erected. This was done so when the center guard that maintained a protective shield around the litters and carriages of Varus' cortège moved inside the fort, the Consul could transfer from his litter to the cool recesses of the shaded porches of his tent. Chests of personal chattels were opened. Tables were set with gold and silver chalices brimming with water and wine. Bowls of fresh fruits were spread across the tables. Marcus Aius reached for some now, grabbing a handful of green sour grapes. A slight commotion at one end of the lager caught his attention. The head of the support echelon was arriving.

The rear echelons always had a much longer day, trekking behind their counterparts in the main force as fast as the slowest ox-drawn cart. The combination of fitful movement and overpowering heat and dust left them more exhausted than their comrades in the faster-moving forward legions. As Marcus Aius knew only too well, the rear elements would dribble into the overnight fort throughout the early evening, with the light from campfires flickering and blazing brightly to guide them. Legionaries at the head of the rearguard were cursing their plight as they arrived in the lager, spitting out the dust of the long day's march through dried and parched lips. Marcus Aius smiled to himself as he thought back to the days when he marched at the rear of so many long-forgotten columns.

The day's labors were not yet at an end. The animals had to be fed and watered, stores replenished and distributed, and the command reports submitted to the legion commanders. All these duties had to be performed before the troops could relax for the night. Only then would the scattered cursing and hot tempers be replaced with odd shouts of raucous laughter echoing across the compound as some lucky soldier won a profitable play of dice. A guard reported his station manned and secure. Another reported the same thing. And another. The rear echelons finally settled for the night, their marching comrades-in-arms already well into their slumbers or deeply immersed in a game of chance. Within a few hours the dice would be still and the legions soundly sleeping.

In Varus' marquee, the Consul was surrounded by his close entourage of legion commanders and his second in command. They were seated in an informal group, sipping wine and eating from the heavily laden tables of food laid out before them.

Varus approached and sat next to Marcus Aius at the tented porch entrance to watch the buzz of activity surrounding them.

Varus turned to Marcus Aius with a cup of wine in one hand and a leg of grilled chicken in the other. "Tomorrow, I want to change the tactical formation of our order of march, Marcus Aius. I have had to wait a long time for our rear echelons to catch up with us today, and my supplies and Quartermaster's special provisions for our own pleasure and sustenance have been sadly missed—until now. Even my wines were not brought forward quickly enough!" He gave half a laugh before turning to face the echelon commander. "What say you, Commander Flavius?"

"Your lordship's wishes are but my command, sire," answered Flavius. "With your permission, sir, on the morrow the full echelon will move forward centrally in the horn of the legions' advance, and when we halt again tomorrow eve, you will have all your comforts and sustenance

immediately to hand. I personally guarantee it." Flavius shot the Quartermaster a meaningful glance.

"Sire," interjected Marcus Aius, "I have no wish to appear to disagree with your order, but to have the main echelons traveling in the horn of the advance will sorely hamper any tactical deployment we may have to make. The wagons, hod carriers, and store packets will make control of all elements near the front difficult to maintain—particularly if we have to make a radical short-notice change in our order of battle."

"Marcus Aius," answered Varus, "you are without doubt one of the finest commanders Rome has ever seen. Your command and control in many campaigns and battles will be forever etched in the annals of our mighty Empire, and you are my true and valued adviser and friend. But I must disagree with your reservations. Why should we make our life unbearable? Here in this Teuton wasteland of Germanic tribes we are omnipotent, we are unbeatable, and we are here merely to continue our occupation and gather taxes and tithes from these uneducated, long-haired, so-called tribes. They are no threat to us." Varus finished his leg of chicken before continuing, wiping away the grease with the back of his hand. "The only thing that concerns me is that we should finish this foray through the highlands to our summer camp well before the next summer heat wave strikes us. By then, I wish us all to be tucked up safely in our quarters at Minden, alongside the pleasant waters of the Weser, where we can bathe and relax, and consider the next partition of the German hinterlands to the east."

"I understand well, sire," Marcus Aius carefully answered, "but it is my duty to warn you of my tactical concerns, and I still have reservations about the reorganization as you propose." Marcus Aius fixed his gaze squarely on the Quartermaster. "We will make the integration of the echelons into the horn of the legion an orderly and controlled event. I task the Quartermaster to ensure that order is maintained throughout our advance, particularly when we move deeper into the Teuton Hills, where it will be difficult to deploy into our normal battle formations under the best of circumstances."

And so the decision came to be made, a fateful one that would doom Varus' legions when they moved back to winter quarters at the end of the long hot summer.

*   *   *

The surviving commander of the reconnaissance patrol ran through the woods for the better part of an hour without stopping to rest. His only thought was reaching the main column and warning the men that enemy tribes were gathering and treachery was afoot. Out of breath, he finally allowed himself to stop for a few moments when he reached the bank of a fast-running stream. As he stood, hands on his hips and his breath coming in deep gulps that burned his lungs, a javelin from a nearby line of trees hissed through the air and embedded itself in his back. He looked down with shock at the bloody metal tip protruding from his chest. With a strangled cry, he threw his arms into the air, waded a few staggered steps into the quick-flowing water, and pitched forward into the current.

*   *   *

Spring 1990

By the late spring of 1990, the full extent of the enormous archaeological digs in Kalkriese was visible for all to see. The digs had moved well out of the line of woods from the knoll and were spreading inexorably across the open field. There were now excavations more than 200 yards square and two yards deep. More cuts were being made as the archaeologists pursued what they now believed was the site of the battle of the Teutoburger Wald.

Was it really here that the Seventeenth, Eighteenth and Nineteenth Legions under Varus, Governor of the Germanic tribes in northern Europe, met their end? Nobody could yet say for certain how many legionaries had died here at the hands of the Germans. The cries of thousands of men caught in the middle of an ambush, dying in the hundreds, could not actually be heard 2,000 years later in the hazy spring of 1990, but they could certainly be felt, as the enormity of the massacre became more and more apparent as the digs progressed and the Roman artifacts came to light.

I sat quietly on top of one of the high banks of excavated earth and sand, watching the archaeological teams at work in a huge hole in the ground. Sketching, drawing, measuring the lines, checking the finds and artifacts, plotting the length of the ambush wall as it curved away toward the far eastern side of the field where the year before, among my many other finds, I had recovered the lone denarius. I stayed a while atop the mound, taking in the atmosphere of the place, my thoughts tugging away at the various questions the ground investigations raised nearly every day. There were so many questions waiting for answers.

By this time, there was really no longer much doubt that this was the site of the final battle, where Varus' legions had met their end. Still, nagging uncertainties about the full extent of the action at this point of ambush were a source of considerable debate and argument. I had re-examined much of the original archival material, including the early historians—particularly Tacitus—and was slowly but surely becoming convinced that his interpretation of the Varus battle was the correct one.

According to Tacitus, once Varus realized he was about to be defeated, he had taken his own life on "the second" night or "the final" night of the engagement. If true, it was logical to assume the action was some form of a running battle spread across two or more days—or even longer. If so, it was also likely the fighting had covered many miles through the wooded highlands. If so, from what direction had the legions come? What route did they take to arrive at this final place of annihilation?

According to the few survivors who lived to tell about the horrors they witnessed, the weather had been exceedingly bad. A late summer storm had caught them in wooded highlands, its force striking them in the flank. And it was from the flanks that German tribesmen had picked and pulled the disciplined ranks of the legions to pieces. Hemmed in by the storm and the wooded hills, the Romans had not been able to deploy into their normal tactical formations for battle. Their problems were further exacerbated by the presence of the rear echelon train in the core of the advancing three-legion force.

The scenario painted by the survivors, if accurate, does not support the other favored theory: that the legions had made a normal westerly advance from Minden, along the northern flank of the Wiehengebirge, which ran east-west to the Kalkriese feature, with the wet moorlands lying immediately to the north. The summer storms in Germany always blow out of the west, triggered by a mixture of warm and humid fronts rushing into the gaps created as other warm fronts rise and draw in additional currents, creating enormous deep depressions. They are notorious for their ferocity, and if the legions had advanced from Minden, they would have met the storm head-on—not from the flank. If so, forward progress would have been nigh-on impossible. Furthermore, there are no highlands between Minden and Kalkriese, as such, but just the foot of the Wiehengebirge ridge line with the wetlands to the north. The Romans would never have unnecessarily put themselves into a compressed formation by moving along the top of a ridge line. In my estimation, the Minden theory was heavily flawed.

But if Varus had not approached from Minden, he must have come up from the highlands between the River Lippe and the lands to the north, the long range of rolling hills known as the Teutoburger Wald, which swings northwest to the underbelly of Osnabrück before petering out to the north, where it converges with the Kalkriese Berg. The legions must have moved through one of the passes east of Kalkriese. If so, they almost certainly would have been attacked there as well, in an early bottleneck.

Another thought crossed my mind. If Varus committed suicide (as Tacitus claimed) in his final overnight camp position, perhaps inside a hastily erected lager, the remnants of his command must have broken out from the lager and moved westward toward the friendly occupied areas of the Ems and Rhine rivers, perhaps during the early morning, perhaps at first light, when the enormity of their commander's disgrace and their looming defeat became a horrifying reality.

Kalkriese was slightly more than six miles from the first main pass that led down and through to the south and east and the rolling hills of the Teutoburger Wald. Six miles was not far for the Legionaries to traverse. Even if they were sorely tired and had wounded with them, they would have been able to cover that distance in a relatively short time and reached the narrow gap lying between the morass of the Dieven wetlands and the Kalkriese Berg, capped off by a small wooded knoll. What I needed were extensive aerial photographs of the land to the east, where the main passes cut through to the Teutoburger Wald and beyond.

My reverie was cut short when an excited cry rose out of the excavations 100 yards away from where I was sitting. I quickly rose and trotted to the dig site. The excavating team had been ordered to preserve some modicum of reserve as they carried out their work, so as not to bring particular notice of any find to interested onlookers passing along the main highway south of the digs. On this occasion, however, the excitement of the two workers was readily apparent when they called out to attract the attention of the archaeologists busy in the work huts off to the side of the excavation site.

A whole area lying along the northern edge (the Roman side) of the ambush wall was currently being excavated, the two Fisher 1265Xs busily ringing out their "good find" tones as the searchers cleared each section to enable the diggers to take the level down a few inches more. Tucked against the base of the wall, a prolific number of artifacts were now coming to light. These included uniform fittings, shield bosses, spear and javelin heads, bronze buckles, and many smaller uniform link plates.

When I arrived at the trench I discovered the reason for the excited shouts. There, in the archaeologist's palm, were two small embossed bronze seals. They were found a short distance from the site that gave up the cloak clasps of Marcus Aius. The seal matrix looked to be a relief of Varus' head, as portrayed on his own minted coins of Achalla in North Africa.

AD 9—Mid-May on the Route to Summer Camp

Centurion Gaius Claudius Suebus strode into the Consul's tent, saluted Varus and, in turn, Marcus Aius, and then issued a startling report: "Sire, we have found one of the missing cohort scouts. He is badly wounded from a spear in the back, and will likely not live much longer. He is delirious and trying to speak, but it is difficult to understand him."

Marcus Aius jumped up from his chair. "Where was he found?" snapped the Tribune.

"He was clinging to a log floating down the river north of our location," answered the Centurion. "He was in the water for some time. The surgeon is attending to him now, but he says there is little hope. Do you wish us to bring him here?"

"'No," said Varus, who was also standing by this time. "Marcus Aius and I will accompany you to the sickbay. Lead the way, Gaius Suebus, and bring my quarter guard with us."

The men made their way through the central concourse of the temporary lager to the surgeon's post and sickbay. The Romans had perfected the art of medical care in the field, from basic first aid to the most advanced medical treatment possible. Each legion, each auxiliary unit, infantry battalion (cohort), and cavalry regiment was equipped with its own medical team, headed by a doctor. This team included trained nursing orderlies who could be seconded to the Legion Centuries for operational reasons, or when a subunit was on detachment.

The Praefectus Castrorum, or second in command of a legion, was responsible for the sick soldiers and the medici (medics) who looked after them. Hospital buildings were normally provided within permanent legionary fortresses; until these were built or when a unit was on a campaign, a field hospital was set up in tented accommodation.

With Varus in the lead, the men converged on the third cohort's sickbay and entered the complex. In the dim light of a flickering torch they could make out the Greek doctor bending over his newest patient. The wounded soldier had sailed with the legions in the central sea and marched and fought all across the Empire. Twenty years in the army, and now his life was about to end on top of a trestle table east of the Rhine in the wilds of Germania. He was still alive but delirious, muttering and babbling like some demented soul. Life was fast ebbing from him, his focus fading. Suddenly, he fell silent and calm as a strange but peaceful serenity enveloped his body. His senses began to float as the light from the torches flickered lower and lower. A shadow crossed his dulled vision. For a few seconds he thought he could see leaning over him the winged helmet he had seen on the head of the German warrior chieftain in the center of the massed German tribesmen. His eyes widened for a few seconds and his mouth muttered a few words—a low but succinct oath. And then his eyes glazed over. He was dead.

"How strange," whispered Varus as he looked over at his auxiliary commander. Arminius had entered the tent and gazed down at the soldier just before he died. "For all his delirium, the only one thing he seemed to recognize was you, Arminius. Do you know this man?"

"No, my lord," answered Arminius. "Although my scouts trained the cohort reconnaissance teams, I have no knowledge of this soldier."

"Well, we have learned nothing about this scout and how he came to meet his end. Where is the rest of his patrol? From what direction flows the river down to us, Marcus Aius?" The Tribune paused for a moment in response, which Varus used when he turned and faced the surgeon. "How long would you say he was in the water?"

"A few hours perhaps, sire," answered the Greek doctor. "Probably no more than that, but it is difficult to know for certain."

"Arminius," said Varus, "Take a large patrol forward in the morning. Ride up the river and see if you can determine what happened

to this man and the rest of his patrol." Varus let out a long sigh. "For now, I am going to retire. Walk with me a short way, Arminius, and tell me all you have been doing today. I need to take a little air."

As the men left the tent, the Greek doctor turned to Marcus Aius, who was standing next to the Centurion. "Did you hear what the scout said when he saw Arminius?"

"No, I could not really hear much of it save the name. Something like, 'It is you, Arminius?' or words to that effect. A greeting of some sort."

"No," said the doctor. "He said, 'It was you, Arminius.' Those were his dying words."

Marcus Aius let the accusation sink in for several seconds as his eyes met those of the Centurion's. Then he fixed his stare at the Greek. "What are we about here? Do you mean what I think you mean?"

Unsettled by Marcus Aius' sharp look, the doctor backpedaled. "I hope not, I hope not, sire," he answered quickly, tripping over his words. "I have enough to do with the ills of the legion as it is without worrying about politics, intrigue . . . and other matters."

Marcus Aius cooled his gaze and shrugged. With a short laugh he remarked, "You Greeks are always involved in intrigue and politics. You see a demon around every corner! We will find out tomorrow whether Arminius can produce an answer to explain this man's fate. I have orders to attend to." The Tribune turned and, accompanied by the Centurion, left the hospital.

The doctor merely raised his hand in farewell and turned to the attending medics. He nodded toward the dead man and ordered, "Take him out and bury him deep. Otherwise, the pigs here in this abominable land will be using his carcass for fresh meat. They can sniff blood and flesh from miles away."

Twenty miles distant, on the slope of a wooded hill, a family of wild boar were squealing and snorting as they feasted on the remains of the lost patrol.

*   *   *

April 1990

In April 1990, three years after my arrival in Osnabrück and the start of my involvement with Kalkriese, I established a link with a Professor

Schoppe from the Institute of Hamburg. He, too, was a keen amateur Roman historian interested in the Varus project. Dr. Schoppe had links with the German Luftwaffe and offered his assistance in securing the aerial photographs I required. The idea was to photograph the complete region, including the first main pass area some six miles due east of Kalkriese. The over-flights began during the early summer as I undertook other extensive investigations of the highlands of the Teutoburger Wald. Once the large photographs were taken, they were given to Professor Schlüter to be examined during the coming months.

Professor Schoppe and I continued pursuing our photographic interests through the end of that year, as more and more artifacts and information was being unearthed from the dig site and surrounding area.

*   *   *

Roman historian Cassius Dio wrote:

> The shape of the hills and mountains in this region were irregular, their slopes being deeply cleft by ravines, while the trees grew closely together to a great height. While the Romans were struggling against the elements, including a violent downpour and storm, the barbarians suddenly surrounded them on all sides at once, stealing through the densest thickets, as they were familiar with the paths. At first they hurled their spears from a distance, and then they closed in to closer range as the storm raged.

A storm of another sort was rising in 1990: Desert Storm in the Middle East. As a member of the British military, I knew sooner or later I would have to concentrate totally on my military duties elsewhere and leave the enigma of Kalkriese until a later date. A great sadness washed over me at the thought of having to delay my quest to seek the lost legions of Varus and the men of the Seventeenth, Eighteenth and Nineteenth Imperial Legions of Rome.

Chapter Nine

The Summer Camp at Minden

I have long believed Varus left Haltern at the beginning of the year in 9 AD, after the first rushes of spring, and moved along the forts and camps on the River Lippe. It is almost certain he did so in the spring, marching northeast away from the Lippe to the main summer camp at Minden, where he remained for much of the season. At the end of the summer, probably in September, Varus gathered up his three legions to move back to the forts along the Lippe, to the main camp at Haltern, for the winter. It was during this journey, southwest through the Teutoburger Wald toward the River Lippe, that Varus was drawn northwest by reports supplied by Arminius of an uprising in the highlands.

I am convinced the movement and the general course of events surrounding Varus' legions, as described in the preceding chapters, took place on the spring march to summer camp, at the banks of the Weser at Minden.

*   *   *

9 AD—Late May Daydreams and Arrival at Summer Camp

A rain shower late in the day produced a breeze that swept gently from the west across the plains leading up to the banks of the mighty River Weser. The cool air was welcomed by the men marching in the drawn-out mass of three legions as they wound their way out from the highlands, happy to be on ground better suited for marching. The army's baggage trains and heavily laden mule and ox carts were tightly packed in and around the Legionaries and cavalrymen as they trekked their way forward.

The extended column, now five or six miles long, bore little resemblance to the disciplined troop movements the men had executed when they had first arrived in the German hinterlands two years before. Varus' complacent attitude toward the Germanic tribes had filtered down into the ranks. He had ordered the legions to advance with all the comforts of the baggage train close at hand for his personal use. Even the camp followers and slaves were intermingled with the troops and echelon support elements.

Despite Marcus Aius' reservations, Varus was convinced the German tribes did not pose a threat to his large army. As the governing Consul of Germany, Varus had thus far maintained complete and unchallenged control over the tribes in the lands east of the Rhine. There was no need to make unnecessary demands on his men and himself during these long forays to gather taxes and to reinforce his subjugation of the Germans.

Quinctilius Varus, Consul of Rome, Legatus Augusti pro Praetore for Gaul, and Supreme Commander on the Rhine. It is all such a heady title, Varus thought to himself as he lounged on his gently rocking litter. He cast a lazy eye over the eight muscular slaves toiling to keep his litter steady as they moved across the moorland, tucked inside the central horn of the advancing throng of the legions. Surrounding Varus were twenty of his loyal consular guard—handpicked soldiers who had been with him during his long campaigns and former governorships in other lands. His mind wandered back to his life in mighty Rome and his strong friendship and links with the house of the great Augustus Caesar.

Varus had been on this earth for nearly fifty-six years. His family was descended from old Alban nobility who, in earlier times, were neighbors of Rome and eventually settled into the Roman community. According to legend, they may have been companions of Romulus, the founder of Rome. The clan of the Quinctilians was patrician and belonged to the cream of the Roman aristocracy. His name—Varus—was typical of the momentous Republican era and was, he believed, most likely a hereditary personal name. His father committed suicide when Varus was very young, and during his childhood he had lived near the town of Tivoli, where relatives raised him as their own.

Political intrigues during the despotic governorship of Tiberius damaged his family's name in the eyes of the Emperor. The politically astute Varus began weaving connections with the family of the general Germanicus, the son of Drusus, who in turn was the brother of Tiberius. Germanicus was also disliked by the Caesar. With the crowning of Augustus Caesar, Varus' life took a considerable turn for the better. In 21 BC, as a Quaestor under the new ruler, Varus accompanied Augustus on his forays into the eastern provinces. In 13 BC, Varus was appointed a Royal Consul of Rome, an honor bestowed upon him not by his patrician contemporaries, but by Caesar himself. His chest filled with pride as he remembered those heady days. Augustus Caesar had just returned from Gaul, where he had reintroduced Roman rule and subjugated the tribes after the defeats suffered by Lollius on the Rhine in 16 BC. As the new pontifex, or priest, it was Varus' responsibility to oversee the games held in honor of Augustus' success.

It was during this time the most significant altar was conceived and erected in Rome: the Altar of Peace, the Ara Pacis, *created to mark the pacification of the whole known world under Augustus Caesar. Varus' participation led to even closer links between his family and the house of Augustus, connections he further cemented by marriage to his third wife, Claudia Pulchra, daughter of a niece of Augustus Caesar.*

From that time forward, Varus never looked back. After an interval of five years, Augustus appointed him Legate of the province of Africa. It was there Varus ordered the first of his own coinage to be struck—an honor from the Emperor that was bestowed on few at that time. The years drifted by, and even more wondrous gifts and treasures were laid at his feet, many of which were directly passed on to his Caesar as an offering of servitude, gratitude, and unswerving loyalty. It was a time of much happiness in his life. His service in Syria, an important imperial province on the frontier with the Parthians, changed all that. Varus despised every hour of his service in that desolate and abominable land. The threatening

Parthians were an old and warlike people who had always provoked unrest in the lands surrounding their borders, never more so than during 7-5 BC.

It was during that period he proudly bore the title Legatus Augusti pro Praetore *for the first time; a Governor of the Empire with the rank of Consul—one of the highest positions a Roman could attain.*

Distracted for a moment from his daydreaming, Varus settled his gaze on a large white horse that had pulled up a short distance away. It was Arminius, sitting easily astride his mount, his face as expressionless as it always was. The bouncing litter bobbed past the weathered face of the German warrior, whose men were patrolling the advance and flanks as the legions drew near the summer camp of Minden, now just a few miles distant.

Varus did not think deeply of Arminius' sudden appearance, but it did remind him of the unusual incident on the previous week's march. With the exception of one lead scout, an entire reconnaissance cohort had disappeared. The single man who returned to the legions died within a few minutes of his recovery from a river, unable to give a report on what had transpired. A thrusting wound had torn into his back and ripped through his organs. No reports of rebellion or insurrection within the Germanic tribes had reached his ears, which led Varus to believe the scouting patrols had come across a collection of German raiders who had cut down their small patrol in the wooded highlands. Arminius' extended search the following day returned empty-handed. Not a trace of the patrol or any band of German raiders who might have perpetrated such an attack was found.

Arminius' German mercenaries were fierce and warlike—even more so than their brothers in the tribes from the German heartland. They had battled long and well for Varus over the years, a competent and disciplined force that added speed to the legions and made his force stronger and even more irresistible. Varus reflected on the ease with which the mighty Roman Empire had encompassed and defeated so many varied peoples and nations, many of whom now fought alongside the Roman legions. Some, like Arminius, were now honored as knights and noblemen in Rome.

His thoughts drew him back to his occupation of Syria, part of which later became Palestine, and to the annexation of Judaea under its king Herod, to whom Varus had acted as counselor. After Herod's death in 4

BC, revolts broke out among the oppressed Jewish population. Varus crushed the uprising with an unforgiving hand. He launched a military campaign of occupation that ended with the public execution of the ringleaders. One of his three legions was left to oversee Jerusalem. Unrest, however, plagued that accursed land. Financial procurator Sabinus, whom Varus had left behind to command in Jerusalem, was besieged in the city when another Jewish rebellion broke out. "I soon dampened their enthusiasm for revolt!" thought Varus. "I hit them hard where it hurt them most. I overran their temples and smashed them into small pieces. I took their sordid little books and chattels, their so-called church treasures, and brought their praying houses down about their ears. So they spread their revolt across Judaea! It mattered not. I crushed them in Antioch, crushed them in Jerusalem, and again in Judaea, and then burned their lands until their petty revolt was finished once and for all." A smile formed on his lips as he savored the memory of his victories there.

Even the memory of the horrific sight of the 2,000 Jews he had ordered crucified along Appian Way did not wipe the small grin from his face. The men were transported to Italy solely so they could be executed along the historic road south of Rome. He had slowly moved up the long road, standing erect in his double-handed chariot as he gazed dispassionately at the torn and bloody bodies hanging from the high rough wooden crosses. Their moans and cries of pain and pity fell on deaf ears as his four black Arab stallions pulled his chariot slowly along the cobbled street. Varus had no conscience on such matters. It was the accepted punishment of the day: arms and legs were lashed to heavy wooden crosspieces, and heavy iron nails were driven through the wrists. A longer iron shaft was hammered through the crossed feet, which inflicted even more agony, for the legs remained half drawn. It was an excruciatingly terrible way to die. The whole body was racked by throbbing masses of cramps and torn limbs.

One of the most surprising things about those who were crucified, remembered the guards who watched over the condemned, was that a great many died with a prayer on their lips. Few so much as cursed their Roman tormentors. "Religious zealots," mumbled Varus under his breath, "too concerned with their outlandish gods and temples rather than the good of the Empire." As far as he was concerned, crucifixion was well deserved for their rebellious activities in Rome's distant province. They could pray as long as they liked, but they still died the death they so richly deserved.

Varus' iron fist did not end with the mass execution. The town of Emmaeus was reduced to ashes, though other population centers were spared. He considered his diplomatic maneuvers masterful, for the Jews believed they had won concessions from him. He allowed the Jewish community to make representations against the Jewish monarchy, and he supported the establishment of a Jewish province under Roman rule. His success in the distant troubled province established Varus as a permanent member of the ruling elite in Rome and in the Senate.

He sighed while thinking back to those golden days of his rise to greatness and the splendor and mightiness of the Roman Empire shining like a beacon in the middle sea, the Medi-terra, *with Rome as its core, its very essence. By 6 AD, however, he grew bored of his opulent lifestyle in the Middle East. His frequent visits to Rome to report to Caesar did little to assuage the monotony of his life. He was growing older. Were his accomplishments all behind him? He needed, yearned for, a change.*

Augustus noticed it immediately during his next visit to Rome. Varus was unhappy, restless. The Emperor had taken him aside after a particularly pleasant evening at the Forum.

Augustus took Varus gently by the arm and led him away from the other senators. "We have need for a firm hand to hold down the Consulship of Germania, which is now under the command of Sentius Saturnius," whispered the Emperor. Varus knew of Saturnius, for he had replaced him in Syria many years earlier. "Quinctilius Varus, my friend," Caesar continued, "I have the greatest of positions for you. I can only send the best of my many administrators to the Rhine. I fear we need your firm hand there to maintain our incursions east of the river into the German interior. We still have but a toehold on the province. I wish to push out the frontiers of our eastern borders, occupy and subjugate the German tribes, take our tithes and taxes, and turn the German province into another stepping stone in the glorious expansion of our great Empire." He paused and shot a glance at the distant senators.

Varus was nearly speechless. "Whatever you desire, highness."

"I want you to take over from Saturnius." It was not an offer, but an order. "Your great successes in Syria are what I need to consolidate the forays we have already made into the new province of Germania. You may well be a peaceful, calm and restrained man on the outside, my great

friend, but I know well your unyielding hand and expertise in such matters. There are others not so discreet with their opinions of your military skills and tactical appreciations." Augustus paused and looked into Varus' eyes. "Yes, I have heard the wild talk and know these criticisms to be unfounded, spoken by ignorant and vain fools who have themselves become soft-bellied, wallowing in the drinking and whoring houses of Rome. You are my sword, Varus. You carry my baton with the royal seal." He patted Varus' right arm, adding, "My right-hand man and my trusted friend."

For a moment the daydreaming got the better of Varus, whose eyes pricked with tears of emotion, his chest swelled with pride, as he remembered those words spoken to him by the great Augustus Caesar. He was proud of his achievements, and even more proud that it had been the very Emperor he worshipped who had confirmed his status in Rome.

A clatter of hooves broke his reverie and he looked up see Marcus Aius riding toward his litter on his fine black stallion. The Tribune reined in his mount and proudly announced, "The Commander of your summer camp extends a warm welcome to you, sire, and wishes you to know that all is well. The wine is cool and the bathing waters are ready for your Excellency. A great feast is being prepared, and we have made a sacrifice to the gods in your honor. Hail, Quinctilius Varus!" The Tribune's salute was echoed by the immediate concourse of consular guards surrounding Varus' entourage, "Hail, Consul of Rome and the mighty Augustus Caesar! Hail, Quinctilius Varus!"

The verbal salute was picked up by the surrounding legionaries, who also echoed the cries. Within a few seconds, thousands of throats raised forth in a tumultuous roar of sound, the shouts accompanied by the strident tones of horns and trumpets from the advance and flank guards of the sprawling mass of advancing legions.

"Hail, Consul of Rome and the mighty Augustus Caesar! Hail, Quinctilius Varus!"

The scene was an incredible, awe-inspiring experience that sent horses skittering nervously across the scattered formations with frightened snorts and whinnies. To a man, the cacophony of sound and surge of excitement raised the spirits and morale of all who marched in the Varus legions.

They were at summer camp. Here, finally, they could relax, bathe in the waters, launch casual forays into the German heartland, and return

*to enjoy the comforts of the lager—and the women camp followers! It was
a time to rest and enjoy the summer sun. Soon enough the season would
end and they would set off again for the Lippe forts and Haltern, now
many miles away to the southwest.*

*   *   *

*Arminius sat astride his horse on the last small rise just beyond the
outer reaches of the summer camp. Varus established the occupation
lager two years earlier, when he had assumed his Consulship of the
German province. The German's gaze swept over the thousands of
marching Romans. Their clattering accoutrements and constant carping
ground away at his nerves. He cleared his throat deeply, turned his head
to the side, and spat into the dirt. These troops were lazy, undisciplined.
He wheeled his horse around and cantered to join the marching throng.*

    Soon, he thought, very soon.

1990—Hannover

The excavations at Kalkriese continued as the months of 1990 slid
by. Professor Schlüter was well pleased with the archaeological
investigations and the artifacts the digs continued to unearth. The buried
earthen wall was being carefully analyzed by the field archaeologists,
and additional slit trenches were being made to ascertain the wall's total
length and historical significance.

Many conferences were held to update the various finds and their
significance in relation to the battle. Based upon these meetings,
Professor Schlüter devised a forward-thinking plan of action for further
excavations. Although there was still pessimism in some professional
circles concerning the validity of the Kalkriese site, it was not held by
those participating in the digs. Given the pace of the excavations and the
productivity of the site, we all realized the project would extend over
many more years. According to my theory, the running battle was
probably fought across many miles of ground to the east. If that was true
and excavations confirmed my hypothesis, the archeological effort could
continue indefinitely.

By this time, museum field surveyors were now armed with their own full complement of Fisher metal detectors. Klaus Fehrs and Gisela carried out their own vastly more comprehensive examinations of the fields surrounding the site than I could ever have hoped to achieve using only my free time and a single detector. The large plowed fields in this area were extensively scanned, yard by yard, and soon acre by acre, as they painstakingly combed each field I had already searched.

Even in those early days, a historical tapestry was beginning to emerge from the recovered Roman coins and artifacts lost all those centuries ago.

Unfortunately, matters playing out on the world's stage set in motion a series of events that rippled through the Kalkriese excavations for several years. The surge of events in the Middle East, including the final throes of the horrendous war between Iraq and Iran, the cruel slaughter and genocide of the Kurdish tribes, and the subsequent invasion and occupation of the small principality of Kuwait by Saddam Hussein, pushed Kalkriese back into the shadows of history. Work was still being carried out week by week, but the results of all this remarkable work continued without the publicity it had once garnered from the world's press. In hindsight, this withdrawal from the media limelight could not have come at a better time. Professor Schlüter finally had time to take stock of what he had thus far accomplished and consolidate his plans for the future, without being unnecessarily influenced by the politics of media supply and demand. He no longer had to meet the expectations of the optimists who believed the site would soon produce the final answers, or concern himself with the many pessimists who scoffed at the idea that this was the actual site where Varus and his legions were wiped out.

By now I had been warned I would be moving from my post in the hospital at Hannover to the Ministry of Defence in London at the end of the year. Once I moved back to England, events unfolding in Kalkriese would, at least for me, have to take a back seat, so I decided to concentrate my remaining time in the region on the quest for the lost legions.

When I arrived in Hannover the year before, I introduced myself to Dr. Cosack, the archaeologist in charge of the northern area of Germany surrounding the large city. Initially, I believed this area of Germany was outside my immediate interest concerning the Varus legends, but Dr. Cosack proved to be an infinite source of information concerning Roman movement in general, both during the Augustan and later periods.

In 13 BC, Augustus Caesar ordered his two stepsons, Drusus and Tiberius, to launch a series of campaigns against the Vindelici and Rhaeti tribes straddling the borders and lands of what now are parts of Switzerland and Bavaria. Drusus' aim was to conquer the lands east of the Rhine bordered by the Elbe River farther to the east, or some 180 miles into the heartland of the German provinces. Tiberius took up command of the legions occupying the lands east of the Adriatic which, until a short time ago, was collectively labeled Yugoslavia.

Drusus established key camps on the Rhine at Xanten and Mainz, with the fort at Xanten (Vetera) acting as the linchpin to the other forts he established running east along the course of the River Lippe, on the eastern side of the Rhine. Some were marching forts only; others were major centers of Roman occupation. One such camp was the fort at Haltern (Castra Secunda) . . . where Varus assumed his command of the German province in 7 AD.

By all accounts, Drusus met his untimely end in 9 BC, though the location of his death has not been identified. Some historians believe he died on the very eastern edge of his incursions to the River Elbe, shortly after his successful attacks on the Chatti and Marcomanni tribes. Tacitus, however, described Drusus as having taken ill on his way back to Rome and dying en route. The site of Drusus' demise has always intrigued me, and I decided to pursue the matter during my remaining time in Hannover before I would leave for England in early 1991. Dr. Cosack was keen on the idea, and supplied me with valuable information surrounding the possible routes Drusus may have taken on his deployment from the Rhine to the Elbe.

My interest was also sparked by other information concerning Drusus and his establishment of Roman lines of supply into the German interior. He had constructed a large waterway at Ijssel linking the Rhine to Holland and the North Sea. This provided Drusus with access to the northern reaches of the coast of Germany, where he could ship supplies and reinforcements down into the German interior on the Rivers Weser and Elbe. At the mouths of both of these waterways, the young general established key fortifications to act as control points to water-borne traffic moving up and down the main course of the rivers. Almost certainly he established other staging ports down to the southern reaches of the Weser. Indeed, when Varus established his summer camp at Minden some years later, it was possibly built on the site of one of

Drusus' original Weser ports. As mentioned previously, many Roman historians fail to understand or accept the fact that the Romans were not free to march everywhere, that they had to have adequate supply lines established both on water and land, and that they used the waterways as much as possible in support of their armies.

I had about six months remaining in Germany, which was precious little time to conduct the investigations I had in mind. I needed a coordinated plan of action. Kalkriese was progressing well and would continue to do so with or without my immediate assistance, though I admit to some frustration that it was such a long haul down to Osnabrück and back from Hannover every weekend. Thus, being able to pursue associated points of Roman historical interest in the local area proved both tempting and therapeutic.

During my stay in Hannover, I was a regular visitor to the *Münzkabinett* at the Kestner Museum, where coin specialist Dr. Frank Berger worked. I visited him there many times to drop off coins unearthed during my searches in Kalkriese. This, in turn, allowed him to log and photograph each one for his reference book before they were handed over to Professor Schlüter in the museum in Osnabrück.

Frank wrote a fascinating article concerning the recovery of Roman silver bullion bars from the Weser, north of Minden. The three large bars were uncovered by peat diggers from the previously flooded lands along the edge of the Weser. Each bar was engraved with Roman inscriptions. According to the article, the excavations carried out around the find area were only some five by three yards square! When no other bars came to light, no further digs were pursued. What if this had been a Roman port area, and the bars had been lost overboard during the unloading process, or dropped from a broken case? The possibilities were endless, and the excavations wholly inadequate.

All of this left me in a quandary, for I did not know which line of inquiry to investigate first. Ultimately, I decided to pick up the short-term quest for answers to Drusus' occupation and death, for Dr. Cosack was positive he had one or two avenues of inquiry worthy of immediate investigation south of Hannover on the approaches to the Elbe. The Weser, with its ports and camps (including Minden), would have to wait a while longer, as would Varus, the men of the Seventeenth, Eighteenth, and Nineteenth Legions, and the storm clouds gathering in the heartlands of the Cherusci.

*   *   *

The last staging post or fort on the River Lippe was Anreppen, the key jumping-off point for further incursions to the east across the mighty Weser, and on to the Elbe, and northeast to the area of the summer camp at Minden.

On October 17, 1868, a large cache of Roman gold and silver chattel and household effects was found by a musketeer digging a local defense trench in the side of one of the surrounding hills. The discovery was one of the most extensive and priceless finds of Roman artifacts and tableware ever made in northern Europe. Although the massive find was considered to be from the period 70-100 AD, it nevertheless raised questions about how, and by whom, such a large set of rich household silver had come to be deposited in that place.

Several theories were advanced. One was that the goods may have been found in another area of Germany, transported to that point, and hidden away. Another suggested that the treasures were stolen centuries later during the troubled final years of the Roman Empire, and then buried to protect them from periods of unrest or war. I do not subscribe to either theory. To my way of thinking, given the content of the treasure and its discovery in the heart of what was once Cherusci territory, it was more likely part of the loot taken after the destruction of the Varus legions in 9 AD. Perhaps they comprised personal effects and belongings taken by Arminius as his share of the spoils of the battle, still housed in the large treasure chests Varus had ordered hastily buried at the time of his final hour. After carrying the chests of silver and gold back to his homeland, Arminius may have secretly buried them for safekeeping.

The safest place for such a treasure would have been in the ground, but the implications of such a find, recovered in its original condition and in its original burial site, were self-evident. Whoever had carried out the burial of the treasure had taken the secret with him into the afterlife. And that theory fits in with what we know of Arminius' final years. About twelve years after his victory at the *Varusschlacht*, Arminius was killed—not by the many wounds he had suffered in the countless battles fought against the Romans, but by poison administered by members of his own family, who sought to prevent his kingship of the Germans. Did Arminius carry the secret of the Varus treasure chests with him to his grave?

*   *   *

As one emerges out of the highlands from the west, Hildesheim sits astride a natural stretch of open land near the River Leine south of Hannover. From the upper reaches of the River Lippe at Anreppen, about 60 miles away, the natural route through the hilly country to the east was northeast to Blomberg, and on to Hameln, which sits astride the Weser itself.

From this point it was only one good day's march of 18 miles to the River Leine and the present-day area of Hildesheim, a couple of miles beyond. Other historians believe the more direct route (due east through the towns of Benhausen, Neueheerse, Brakel, then Hoxter, and onward toward the Elbe) was a more logical line of forts and *lager* through the highlands surrounding the lower reaches of the Weser. This would also support the theory that Hoxter was a main Roman port. But from there, the natural way toward the east leads one again northeast through the valleys and Holzminden, and then on to Alfeld on the Leine, also located in the Hildesheim sphere of influence.

Movement directly due east from Hoxter, however, penetrates through the highlands, across the Leine at Einbeck, and then again through the massive Harz Mountains before reaching the Elbe—an arduous and doubtful route to the east.

It would still be more realistic to assume that the one day march from the Weser at Hameln, to the Leine in the Hildesheim area, would be an ideal link to progress farther east into the German interior. This line of march bypassed the northern tip of the Harz Mountains. It would also be both tactically and strategically advantageous for any force of men and stores to move through open country after disgorging themselves at Hameln from the Roman boats that would have carried them down the Weser from the North German coast. The route from Hildesheim east to the River Elbe at Magdeburg was a straight line across the flat broad expanse of the North German plain. From Anreppen (Castra Octal), the last known fort on the Lippe, it was a logical route to take to reach the eastern borders of the German provinces.

It was during the middle months of 1990 when I was provided with more historical background surrounding Drusus and his untimely death in 9 BC. The source of my information originated from Roman historical records, and one of the more intriguing highlights concerned the lost location where Drusus may well have met his death.

". . . [A]nd where the river Saale ran into the greater concourse of the other river . . . this is where Drusus died . . . "

Many students of the period believe this passage means Drusus reached the edges of the German provinces along the River Elbe near Magdeburg, where the wide concourse of the River Saale ran into the wider stretches of its sister river. There were no recognized areas of Roman influence in that region, either historically or as revealed by modern archaeological research. (Magdeburg had slept in the time warp that was East Germany until the fall of the Berlin Wall.) There appeared to be no way to viably pursue the matter and carry out investigative research and map work in an area so far removed from my more immediate interests.

On the following weekend, and for the first time in many months when I did not travel to Osnabrück, I set out to look over the ground south of Hannover, where Dr. Cosack had briefed me on a number of Roman find sites. Some were not far from the rolling hills in the rural area surrounding Hildesheim, where the legendary Hildesheim Silver Treasure had been uncovered.

Dr. Cosack provided me with numerous large-scale maps. I eagerly ran my eyes over them, taking in one or two curious field names in the process. Field names have always provided a source of information in my research into the Kalkriese project—but never more so than on this particular occasion. Through many years of antiquity, and in the absence of any positive identification to the contrary, field names and "walls" were often called *Römerwall* (Roman wall) or *Römerfeld* (Roman field). However, I subscribed to the premise that there was no smoke without fire, and avidly sought out unusual names with Roman connotations that routinely appeared on German maps.

My curiosity did not disappoint. Almost immediately I spotted a field with the familiar *Römerfeld* emblazoned across it, not more than 3,000 yards northwest of one of the find sites pointed out by Dr. Cosack. This was potentially important, another small discovery that quickened my pulse: a nearby field was called *Silberflecken*, which in English means "silver pieces." At this particular juncture, however, I missed the one key clue to the whole area, an oversight for which I still kick myself. Still, the "silver pieces" field almost certainly indicated that Roman silver coinage had been found there. It warranted investigation.

During a lunch hour the following week, Dr. Cosack and I discussed the terrain in general and the two highlighted fields in particular. He was extremely interested in my overall impression of the area, particularly in my thoughts concerning the more logical lines of march that may have been the route taken by the Romans between the upper reaches of the River Lippe and the River Leine. He was not as enthusiastic about the various field names. As was often the case, Dr. Cosack believed these names were not necessarily synonymous with real Roman activity, as they were often named by farming communities and over-imaginative farmers based on local folklore and old wives' tales.

As we studied the large-scale maps provided to me by Dr. Cosack, and debated the merits and arguments surrounding Roman activity in the area, a name jumped up off the map and branded itself on my consciousness. The small tributary running down from the west over the northern edge of the two field areas and into the main concourse of the River Leine was called "the Saale."

"Where the River Saale ran into the greater concourse of the other river . . . this is where Drusus died."

A sense of disbelief and skepticism washed over me and our lively conversation stopped in mid-sentence.

Within a few seconds we were at it again, debating the obvious potential of this entire area of Roman activity. If there was ever a site that matched the rumored advances Drusus made into the German interior, culminating with his untimely death in 9 AD, it was surely here and not at the site of the other River Saale flowing into the Elbe. What might now be discovered there? Were we about to unlock yet another part of the puzzle surrounding the Roman legions and their activities in the German provinces?[1]

---

[1] What might now be discovered there? During the succeeding months, Dr. Cosack and I carried out additional surveys in the lager and adjacent fields. This work prompted Dr. Cosack to launch a series of archaeological projects that are still ongoing. As with all important historical investigations, it is always prudent to confirm the facts before speculative statements are made public. Hopefully, one day in the not-so-distant future, we hope another missing link of Roman history will be revealed.

9 AD—Early June Summer Camp at Minden

Varus lounged at the long low dining table laden with meats, fruits, breads, and flagons of wine. His silver and gold platters, goblets, and tableware offered a portrait of magnificence and wealth rarely seen outside the opulent halls and houses of privileged of Rome. He drank deeply from a gold chalice. The visit to the summer camp was progressing well.

Marcus Aius, accompanied by the generals and senior legion commanders, lounged about the banquet table. Some of the officers had slave girls draped about them, feeding the Romans grapes and meats and plying them with watered wines and mead. A general air of cheerfulness permeated the atmosphere, and laughter and old war stories abounded. While Varus and his officers feasted, hundreds of soldiers took their evening baths in the cut-away quadrangles lining the side of the Weser on the edge of the lager.

"What news of the supply vessels from the northern sea port, Marcus Aius?" inquired Varus while holding aloft his empty glass. "You promised me more of this excellent wine from Gaul on our next shipment, and my thirst on these beautiful summer evenings remains unquenched! Have we news from the runners?"

The Tribune leaned forward to answer. "Sire, the latest report indicates the ships entered the mouth of the Weser late yesterday evening, but will require a brief stopover at the next staging port north of our camp to drop off supplies to the garrison there." He turned and wiped away the wine running down his chin before continuing. "With this fair weather we should see the ships on the morrow, highness, although as you know, the current on this stretch of the river is very strong and requires heavy oarsmanship in order to proceed at speed. You may rest assured your wine from Gaul, as I promised, will be on your table tomorrow evening, and we will toast the Emperor, the mighty Augustus, yet again!"

When Varus smiled and nodded in response, Marcus Aius stood and raised his goblet. "We need no excuse to wait until the arrival of new wine when we have plenty of this wine to drink now. Sire, if you please," he added, nodding his head toward his commander, "I propose a toast!" The officers, Arminius among them, collectively stood and raised their cups in the air. Varus joined them. "To our Emperor, to the Caesar,

Augustus!" proclaimed Marcus Aius. With one voice the officers shouted, "Hail, Caesar! Hail to the Emperor! Hail, Augustus Caesar!" The wine, which had already flowed freely, now flowed faster as the tent filled with laughter and merriment.

Arminius stretched out at the table opposite Marcus Aius, his manner somewhat restrained and contemplative. Although he had raised and toasted from his goblet along with the other commanders, there was no obvious celebration in his outward expression for Caesar.

"What ails you, Arminius," called Varus. "Your thoughts seem elsewhere this evening. Do you have some attractive wench waiting for you to bed her tonight, or are there other matters more serious that make you so somber and withdrawn?"

"Sire," replied the German, "I am concerned by repeated reports from my scouts that there is some form of trouble brewing in the local tribes. I cannot yet explain what the unrest is about, or pinpoint its exact location. I am frustrated that I am unable to locate the cause, and I intend to go out tomorrow with a small contingent of my riders to reconnoiter the highlands to the west."

"I think you concern yourself unnecessarily, Arminius," laughed Varus in reply. "You should stay here and drink the new wine from Gaul when it arrives tomorrow. We have much to thank our dear departed Drusus for establishing the canal through to the north coast and his port at the top of the Weser. After all, had it not been for him, we would not be so well served." Varus' tone assumed a more serious note. "I understand your frustration. I suffer from my own. We do not know the exact location where Drusus lies buried in these German lands. That frustrates me. His untimely death and loss to Rome was incalculable. When I think that a commander of his standing should be left to rot in an unmarked grave—that grieves me." Varus sat up and looked directly at Arminius. "Take your men and go with my blessing, and with that of the Emperor. And another toast, gentlemen," he shouted, raising his goblet yet again.

"Hail, Augustus! Hail, Caesar! Hail to the Emperor!"

The cries echoed across the lager and the men of the Seventeenth, Eighteenth and Nineteenth Legions in the vicinity of the headquarters laughed at the revelry pouring forth from Varus' tent. The ranks proffered their own boisterous toasts in return, though with wording less respectful in both tone and substance.

Arminius smiled in his cup and lifted it slowly to his lips while his thumb and forefinger on his left hand rubbed a silver coin. It was another newly minted denarius from Lyons, boasting the proud aquiline features of Augustus Caesar on one side and, on the reverse, Caius and Lucius Caesar, standing behind battle shields and crossed spears . . .

Chapter Ten

1990: Hannover and the Weser Silver Bullion

I walked into the *Münzkabinett* in the Kestner Museum, near Tramm Platz in Hannover, and asked to see Dr. Frank Berger. As my coin finds at Kalkriese increased, the number of meetings we held together naturally increased as well. I enjoyed dropping in to spend an hour discussing the latest developments unfolding, both around Osnabrück and in the area of Hannover. Frank's knowledge of Roman coinage is extensive, and every time I saw him there was always something different on the agenda to discuss.

During this period, he was extremely busy writing up his records of every Roman coin discovery made in northern Germany. His intention was to create a series of historical reference books for others involved in his profession. During his research, he often came by interesting snippets of information concerning Roman finds, although not all involved Roman coinage. Frank's office was crammed full of reference books stacked from floor to ceiling like some prodigious library, the shelves sagging under the massive weight of the countless tomes and journals. His desk was strewn with photo plates, slides, old manuscripts and much more, a fascinating accumulation of facts, figures, and knowledge.

He greeted me warmly on my arrival; our meetings were always very convivial, and comprised a welcome part of the rare social activities surrounding my own intensive research and associated free-time work. I sat down and noticed some old reference works he had on his desk. Before I had a chance to inquire what they contained, he opened up the conversation with one of his "throwaway" questions that often provoked much debate between us. Frank is a master of understatement, and I greatly enjoyed the lead he took in our meetings. This occasion was about to unfold into a very special meeting, and provided an intriguing insight into some of the remarkable work Frank performed.

"I've now spent many months poring over the German archives from the last war, about what our museums held and where the various accumulations may have disappeared to," Frank began. "Obviously, in the East, everything went back to Russia, and indeed much remains there today, locked away without the likelihood of ever seeing the light of day again. It is doubtful anyone will ever see much of what went back to Moscow; they consider it war repayments of a kind, I suppose; but who knows, one day that might change."

Frank was interrupted by the sound of a car backfiring as it coughed its way past his window. The vehicle was a Trabant, or "Trabbie" as they are affectionately known, one of the plastic sewing machines that were mass-produced by the East German auto industry. The Berlin Wall was no more, and now the autobahn and streets in the vicinity of Hannover were strewn with broken-down Trabbies. Those still running poured out plumes of exhaust smoke. Dying engines were strewn across the countryside as the East Germans streamed out of their former prison to experience the freedom of the West, with the mass exodus of other East Europeans yet to come.

"Perhaps that time might come sooner than we think," I answered. "Doors are opening in Eastern Europe, some faster than others. Anyway, let's get on with your story, I'm fascinated. But where is it taking us?"

"Well," he began again, pausing for effect, "the curious part about all this is that a large amount of the treasures that were originally gathered by museums and family households, well before the Third Reich and still lying in their original places of storage, were also stolen by members of the Allied Forces as they swept through Germany at the end of the war."

"To many it must seem a little like poetic justice, really—stolen in one hand, and removed from the other. But, obviously, many would today say differently. There was so much theft and embezzlement on all sides during those times that it must be difficult to judge one way or the other. However"—I smiled—"are you going to tell me different?"

"Yes," Frank replied. "It is part of my job not only to recover, through the various national and international auctions, all the known interesting coins that were part of our original legacy from the last few centuries of exploration, but also to trace, if possible, all the other hoards and singular rare coins that went missing at the end of the War."

"As you may recall,' he continued, "the coin collection the von Bar family in Kalkriese accumulated during the 1700s and 1800s was stolen at the end of the War. We believe, based on both our own and Allied Forces' archives kept by the Americans here in West Germany and in Berlin, that it was either a Canadian or British contingent that stayed at the main von Bar *Schloss* of Gut Barenau, which was set up as a temporary headquarters when they passed through the area in the final throes of the War. It is also believed the person responsible was an officer, but we have never been able to confirm this and, regrettably, could not throw any more light on the matter, until of late. Thankfully, the complete collection was recorded by museum authorities and local historians, including, most notably, Theodore Mommsen himself. As you know, he was the man who originally surmised that Kalkriese was the site of the Varus battle—based just on the make-up of that coin collection. Mommsen knew none of the coins in that collection were minted later than the Augustus denarius showing Augustus Caesar on one side, and on the reverse, Caius and Lucius Caesar, standing behind battle shields and crossed spears."

Frank paused for a few seconds before continuing. "Anyway, here's what's happened. As a result of my inquiries on these misappropriations, and keeping an eye on the markets for any of the Kalkriese von Bar collection itself, I came across some interesting snippets of information."

I could barely contain myself. "And . . .?"

"I have now applied the same close observations on the European and Swiss auctions and believe I have found three of the original silver denarii that formed part of the von Bar collection. I am flying to

Switzerland this week because I received exciting news from the main auction house in Basel. An employee of the firm Münzen und Medaillen AG, with whom I studied history and numismatics in Münster, Dr. Lutz Ilsch, acquired these three coins. They were reported to have belonged to the von Bar collection. In fact, Mommsen mentioned them in his writings. The auction house gave the three denarii to the Kestner Museum as a donation."

I was thrilled at this information. "That's marvelous news, Frank! Perhaps more will turn up in due course. What's next on the agenda?"

He paused for a moment, and then asked, "Can you come back next week? I have something else I want to show you, but have to research it further. It directly relates to the Roman occupation of North Germany, and in particular the area of the Weser. I think you will enjoy my next find from the archives, something for you to search for, another set of clues to put together. I know you enjoy that sort of thing, so perhaps if you can spare an hour next week? I promise to have it ready for you then." I assured him I would be back without fail, and we agreed to meet again the following Wednesday at lunch time.

That night I dreamed of all the marvelous treasures and artifacts lying in fields and hills waiting to be found—and the stories they could tell. And then the dreams turned into a nightmare when my visions beheld barren fields, plowed and plowed again, the air and chemicals slowly corroding and destroying the precious treasures. The artifacts, at least in my dream, were lost forever.

9 AD—June: The Watchtowers at Minden

Arminius sat straight as iron on his horse on the upper reaches of the hills surrounding the gap at Minden. His eyes were fixed on Varus' summer camp stretched out far below. Through the summer haze he could see it, lying alongside the western banks of the River Weser. He lifted his eyes and took in the German plains sweeping away north and south of the Minden gap, with the Weser winding up from the southern highlands. Both sides of the Wiehengebirge ridge gap, about one mile across at its widest point, had been cleared of its timber and undergrowth by Roman pioneers. Heavily fortressed lookout points now crowned each height. The woods had been cut three hundred yards from the leading edge of the ridge lines where the forts had been erected, and another fifty yards down the precipitous slopes below.

Each fort was manned by a reinforced guard, which was regularly changed with soldiers supplied from the legions stationed in the lager far below. Communications between the two observation forts and the main fortress were maintained by a heliograph system during daytime; at night, signal pyres were readied in case the urgent need for reinforcements arose. Deep and narrow trenches linked the forts to each pyre site. An attack on these positions, however, was deemed highly unlikely. The hours of darkness also witnessed a series of small fires along the outer edge of the closest defensive trenches encircling each position. Their glow cast a light across the cleared ground without creating a glare in the eyes of the guards or restricting their line of sight.

Arminius rode up to the hill fort with his large contingent of cavalry. He was to check the guard on behalf of the summer camp commander before setting out on his reconnaissance into the Bergland of the Teuton Hills. The previous evening, Arminius told Varus that rumors of "trouble" in the lands to the west required investigation. Under this guise the German warrior was free to pursue affairs of his own. From this high point, he intended to ride the ridge line along the Wiehengebirge to the western reaches, fifty miles away to the borderlands of the Bructeri and Cherusci. The open parade ground opposite the western hill fort's front gate was crowded with hundreds of heavily-armed cavalrymen jostling about on their mounts. They had pledged their oath of fealty to Varus and the Emperor, but the Germans were loyal to Arminius alone.

They were essentially a mixed force drawn from the various tribes of the north German plains, including the Chatti, Marcomanni, Cimbri, Bructeri, Marsi, and a handful of the famed Teutons. The remnants of this tribe were now little more than a depleted and scattered force. They had been sorely defeated and decimated a century earlier by Roman legions led by Marius at Aix-en-Provence, and then slaughtered again, nearly to a man, at Vercelli the following year. They never regained their former status and strength.

Arminius had even more men to depend upon from his own tribe, the renowned Cherusci, than just those who rode with him. Five years earlier, in 4 AD, Tiberius, at that time Governor of Greater Germany, granted the tribe the privileged position of a federated state within the

Roman Empire. Members of the Cherusci's ruling class, among them Arminius, were made Roman citizens. As a new citizen of Rome, Arminius entered the Imperial service as an officer in its mercenary auxiliary forces. His status was further enhanced when he was given the prestigious award of Roman knighthood. Cherusci territory extended from the upper reaches of the Lippe to the Weser and on to the lands bordering the mighty Elbe. Its "pacification" enhanced Roman power and prestige. But the Cherusci people were unhappy with Rome. Arminius and the tribal chieftains were angry at the manner in which the Romans under Varus occupied and administered their lands and peoples, issuing orders to the Germans as if they were slaves and not free men of a Roman federated state. Heavy tithes and taxes were extracted from the populace, further exacerbating the simmering pool of Cherusci discontent.

Arminius knew the time for action was approaching. The Romans were relentless and overbearing, but they were also vulnerable. If he could take the battle to the Romans—not on ground of their choosing, but some place in the highlands of the Teuton Hills, at the end of the summer on their return to winter quarters at Haltern—they could be beaten. Exasperated and discontented, the tribal chieftains were angry much of the time and vociferous in their debates and tribal gatherings. Arminius planned to meet with the senior chieftains again.

His last meeting a month earlier was a rousing success. With the support of their gods, they would at last push the Romans from the German plains forever. The conference was interrupted by a small Roman scouting force that was quickly eliminated. A lone Roman survivor had escaped, but the badly wounded man had died before he could reveal what he had seen. Still it had been close thing, and Arminius believed Marcus Aius had grown suspicious of him. Certainly he was cooler lately, distant, more reserved. It was time to finalize plans for the end of summer. In a few months the legions would pack up and move southwest again. It had to be then.

Before Arminius turned his horse a movement on the Weser caught his eye. Approaching Varus' summer camp were a number of galleys rowing slowly up the river from the north, pulling hard against the current sweeping out toward the northern sea coast. Arminius sought out his chief auxiliary. Wodenicus was a short distance away, speaking quietly with several riders, waiting for his commander to finish his reverie and order the move. Feeling the hard gaze of his commander, Wodenicus looked up to see Arminius nod in his direction, urge his horse forward, and move across the open ground toward the wooded ridges beyond. Wodenicus passed the order to the subordinate commanders. As he rode by the northern edge of the fort, Arminius offered a lazy wave of his hand to the fort's commander, who was leaning over the battlements watching the impressive German mounted troops form up and ride off. Arminius gave a short tap of his heels and urged his horse to a canter. The rest of the auxiliary cavalry force followed slowly in his wake. The soft breeze carried the sounds of the moving column back to the fort: the soft clatter of hoofs on the soil, an occasional whinny of a horse, and the odd muted call of a nameless rider encouraging his mount forward.

Before five minutes had passed, the three hundred riders had completely disappeared into the timber. A haze of dust lingered in the air behind them over scattered piles of droppings, the only evidence of their presence at the hill fort.

Centurion and post commander Gaius Claudius Suebus slowly raised his arm and returned the wave as he watched Arminius's men disappear from view. He lowered his hand just as slowly as he had raised it. Something was amiss. Although the sun was warm he shivered, an icy cold feeling coursing down his back. "By the gods," he cried, "who is walking over my grave today?"

A guard pacing nearby, one of the standard-bearers and a friend and companion from many campaigns over the years, laughed in reply. "With respect, sire, if the steps were heavy then it may well be my wife's mother. She is still cursing you for taking me away from my wife's side all these years, and you know well that her tongue is long and inventive!"

"Indeed, Brutus Maximus, you may well be right. I remember your mother-in-law well. Her vocabulary is awe-inspiring, far more advanced in color than many of the ladies of the bathhouse! When the runner leaves again for Rome, you must send a special missive to her. Explain how much we think of her and your dear wife, for I can do without these cold footsteps up and down my spine!"

The Centurion looked out toward the black expanse of the dark woods into which the auxiliaries had disappeared. "Perhaps your wife's mother may not be responsible for my chills, Brutus." His voice was softer now, just above a whisper. "Did you notice how withdrawn the Germans were? Far too quiet for my liking. Indeed, unnaturally silent.

Except for Arminius, not a one spoke or waved farewell. Strange, very strange." Suebus leaned over the rear wall of the upper walkway of the fort and called across to the heliographer, "Signal the fort that Arminius has left, and that all is well. Ask for more wine and fruits. I see the boats with the new stores arriving with the excellent wines from Gaul!"

Down at the quay, the first boat was drawing in, the cry of "Ship . . . oars!" echoing across the water as the craft bumped along the sides of the jetty. "Rest . . . oars!" rang out, and the oarsmen fell forward over the transoms and the well worn handles of their oars.

*   *   *

The horse cantered smoothly beneath him as Arminius' mind worked over the stunning course of events spread out before him. He had joined the Roman forces as a young man, and was grateful for his new status and the lifestyle his position afforded him in Varus' command. But now wrath and hatred consumed him. He could no longer stand by and watch his people grow more oppressed with the passing of each season. It was all he could do not to draw his sword and cut down Varus each time he stood near him.

Arminius' speeches to the various German chieftains had become more strident with the passing of time. At the last several gatherings he had openly called for them to take up arms and follow him to victory against the Roman jackals. United they could defeat the enemy and keep them west of the Rhine. Divided, he admonished, we would all become slaves. There was only one tribal leader who was against such an uprising. Each time Arminius urged action, he called for diplomacy and patience. It was against this rhetoric—cowardice in his eyes—that he now moved with his contingent of cavalry. He would resolve the matter once and for all. Before the sun rose again he would have the full mandate of all the tribes to conduct his plan, to remove the loathsome legions under Varus once and for all. Arminius urged his horse on faster along the woodland trail, the drumming echo of the hooves of three hundred pounding stallions echoing through the darkened timber.

*   *   *

1990—The Weser Silver Bullion

By the autumn of 1990, my time in Germany was fast coming to an end. I had spent the past two months working with Dr. Cosack surveying the areas south of Hannover. Each day, the frustration of returning to England now, of all times, welled inside me. Leaving Kalkriese behind me would be painful indeed.

I would remain with the Ministry of Defence in early 1991, but the rest of my colleagues at the Military Hospital in Hannover were notified to prepare for deployment to the Gulf in support of Operation Desert Storm. They were also in a mixed state of emotions, for the idea of facing biological and chemical warfare was a much more unpleasant thought than leaving an archaeological site.

That September I decided to visit Kalkriese again to see how work was progressing and perhaps improve my state of mind. I had heard from Wolfgang that the dig had gone slightly "dry" for a time, but had picked up again as new trenches were opened up toward the center of the battlefield. I spent the weekend there. After meeting old friends and looking up some of the local farmers who had been so helpful during the early stages of my work, my spirits lifted a little more.

Eating away at me was the the information Frank Berger in Hannover had waiting up his sleeve. Before leaving Kalkriese for Hannover, I decided to look over some of the large rolling fields surrounding the battle site. They had always been a great source of pleasure over the years, and were still coughing up the odd find here and there, although they had been scoured by both me and the museum survey team over many seasons. The local farmer, by now a devout enthusiast of Famous Grouse whisky, had cut his yellow fields of corn and deeply plowed the soil. When I arrived, the field offered the best detecting surface I could remember, a gray porridge-like sponge of finely tilled soil, every lump long since removed. I just hoped there were some sweeteners in the mix! The field was huge. It was split into three separate segments, with another field at the back leading on to the battle-camp knoll itself. Over the years, this ground had given up many secrets and treasures, and I had a great affinity for one or two special areas of my own, sites where denarii and other coins and bronze uniform pieces had revealed themselves in all their glory during my early days in Kalkriese.

I decided to concentrate on two small areas that had, until the previous year, maintained a steady flow of artifacts and coins. The areas had appeared to "dry up" at the end of the last summer season, and no fresh finds were made after the spring plowing a few months earlier. But the ground looked so very inviting (a wonderfully flat tilled field and a Roman battlefield to boot!) I could not resist the opportunity to make the best use of a warm sunny day. My spirits were already raised, and I set to with added vigor to mark out the two quadrangles I intended to prospect.

Three hours were expended working the first grid—to no avail. Disappointed, I retired for lunch with my favorite flask of coffee and an apple. Feeling a bit tired, I dozed for a few short minutes in the hope that I would awake refreshed. Recharged, I climbed out of the car and moved off to the second quadrangle. The entire area was totally quiet and still, one of those sunny days in the country when hardly anything happens to spoil the scenery: no people, no traffic, an occasional bird call, and not much else.

I was making my way along the left-hand edge of the second field, sweeping the ground before me, when I heard the familiar sharp double ringing tone from my Fisher detector headset. I had only been at it again for a few minutes. The short nap also changed my luck! I knew the sound meant I had found a coin, but was it Roman? I was not to be disappointed. I carefully moved the soft soil to one side. The coin was only a few inches deep. The black peat core to the topsoil not only preserved the older silver pieces, but made it very difficult to locate the find or determine quickly what it was. This time however, it was different. The proud aquiline features of the goddess Venus were quickly revealed. I gently cleared away the crumbling earth from the reverse side and made out a walking figure carrying what was later identified as his father on his shoulder, with "Caesar" clearly embellished alongside. Julius Caesar had himself minted the coin in North Africa in 47 BC. It was a brilliant pristine denarius! That single find would have been enough to maintain the adrenaline and interest in the laborious process of sweeping detectors over sometimes barren lands for an entire month. My spirits soared and my exhaustion fell away. I logged and marked the spot of the find and continued my search.

Another thirty minutes passed before I heard the familiar double ringing again. I was by now absorbed by the success of my survey. I cleared away the soil with my hands, for no trowel was necessary in this soft ground. This time the coin was a little deeper and more difficult to locate. It turned out to be yet another fine silver denarius, but with a picture I could not instantly identify. It looked somewhat Egyptian, with a *sympulum*, axe and hat. Memories of similar finds only slowly came to me. The reverse, however, revealed an old friend, a wonderful bull elephant, the same that had cropped up on some of my original finds three years earlier. It was a perfectly defined elephant, huge in bulk, with its head lowered and trunk raised. The fine coin was another from Julius Caesar. I carried out the necessary logging procedures, left the coin at the site, and moved on.

The afternoon was drawing on, and I knew that in the absence of any further finds, within the next quarter hour I would have to pack it up and call it a day. I stopped for a short rest, using a "locked in" technique I had perfected over many years of fieldwork and military life that allowed me to stand still and yet rest. I looked out over the large field and noticed, for the first time that day, people walking slowly along the northern footpath about five hundred yards away. I doubt they even noticed my presence. I daydreamed a short while, thinking of Romans and Germans, warriors all, of running battles and bloody swords, of cries of anguish and horror, of pain and fear and death. These fields had witnessed many individual bloody fights—apart from the main debacle that had unfolded on the other side of the knoll to the east. I found it easy to imagine the mass of Romans spilling out from the ambush gap a short distance away, fleeing for their lives as they ran into the bogs and swamps. There, they would have quickly discovered they had but two options: turn and fight the vicious hordes of German warriors, or beg for mercy. In either case, the unforgiving enemy would have hacked them down where they stood—or fell. *Arminius' plan had been brilliant, effective, and devastating . . .*

The day was ending and I decided to pace out the last two legs of the search area, and then pack up. I walked no more than three paces when the wonderful sound once again echoed in my headset. It was hard to believe such a cleanly researched field could continue producing rare Roman coinage—particularly when it had failed to produce anything during the previous year. At about a foot under the surface, this coin was much deeper than most I had turned up, but my powerful Fisher still gave off a clear resounding signal. I gently cleared away the soil. I suppose I should have guessed what it would be. I had found so many examples of this particular coin during the previous three years that I could read it like an old book one takes down from the library shelf, dusts off, and opens to the familiar passage . . . of Augustus Caesar, facing right, and on the coin reverse, Caius and Lucius Caesar, standing behind battle shields and crossed spears.

The unearthing of the silver denarii from the killing fields surrounding the main battlefield did much to alleviate my downed spirits. My faith was now restored in my link with the project in Kalkriese and capabilities as a searcher. Thus encouraged, I returned with my finds to Hannover. During a lunch hour the following week I went down again to the Kestner Museum *Münzkabinett* to see Frank Berger and to discover just what he had been withholding from me.

August 1990

I was ushered into Frank's office by the museum front attendant. Curiously, Frank was not there, but when the attendant assured me he would return shortly, I leaned over the desk and browsed through some of the books in his large library. Before too long Frank came bounding into the office, full of vigor and enthusiasm. His hands clutched a small set of pamphlets.

"Hi, Tony," he greeted me. "I am sorry to keep you waiting. We have been hastily looking for some particular documents I think you will find extremely interesting. Last time you called, I remembered seeing them during the writing of my last coin reference book, but I had a little difficulty remembering where I had put them. No matter, I have them now. Have you had any more success?"

"My turn this time, Frank," I replied. "Three very nice denarii for you to see." With that I pushed a small plastic container across his desk towards him.

The three denarii inside, recently removed from the black peat, were in near-perfect condition and Frank was naturally very impressed with them. He picked up his magnifying glass and carefully studied each one in turn. He leaned forward and opened up one of his reference books.

"No need." I smiled when Frank looked up at me. "The left-hand one is Julius Caesar, 47– 46 BC." This is the coin I did not initially recognize. "The next coin is Julius Caesar, 49– 48 BC, and the right-hand one is

Augustus, our old friend, from 9 AD, Caius and Lucius Caesar on the reverse." By now, I was becoming a bit of an expert myself.

"One hundred per cent correct," replied a rather surprised Frank. "But the condition is incredible—even Julius Caesar's coins are in a very fine state. I will have them photographed and catalogued, and then get them down to Professor Schlüter. Does he know you have found them?"

"No. Wolfgang is away this week and I won't see him until next Monday, so these will be another nice little surprise for him."

"Well then, here is a fair exchange, as you say in English—my next offering to your Roman research." With that, he passed over the sheaf of documents he had brought with him into the office. "There are some photo prints on the last two pages of these papers. Have a look. One shows some men standing in a field, with long farming shovels in their hands, all posing for the photographer. Behind them"—Frank leaned over and deftly turned the pages to the appropriate print—"you can see a large windmill on the field rise. I know the area is near one of the small villages lining the Weser north of Minden, but the exact location of where these men were standing is not known to me, and I cannot find a reference to it, either. The important thing about this scene is what follows . . . ."

And with that, he settled back into his favorite position and began a most fascinating discourse.

Chapter Eleven

Tilting at Windmills

"In March, 1888, three field workers gathered to cut peat from the old bed of the River Weser." So began Dr. Frank Berger's remarkable account. This is the story he told me.

"The site, close to the original shoreline, was north of the pass at Minden. The only documentary evidence of their effort is two photographs, one depicting the three workers standing in the grassy field, and the other a record of what they uncovered. The photos were taken by the resident local archaeologist. The field workers had been cutting peat from ground that originally had been the river bed of the Weser." Frank pointed to one of the photos. "The banks behind the men and this side of the windmill look to be no more than two meters high. One would imagine therefore, that the water had perhaps been two to three meters deep, and over the centuries the bed had silted up a little before the Weser changed its course, as rivers are prone to do over the centuries, leaving this particular area dry.

"During their digging, the workers came across a small group of three dark black and brown colored bars of metal. They picked them out, examined them, and then realized that they were most likely silver. The markings on either side of the bars were also indicative of their importance. However, these men took the bars into the local town that evening, and for a groschen (a silver coin worth little more than one-thousandth of the value of the bars), sold them to another gentleman in the bar. He, in turn, sold the bars to the local provincial museum for a little more than his outlay of one silver groschen, but still nowhere near the true value of the silver bullion.

"Strangely enough," continued Frank, "it was not until February 1889, during the reasonably mild winter, that a small archaeological excavation was made on the find site. Even then, for some inexplicable reason, the dig was only carried out over an area of three meters in width by five meters in length, and only to a depth of half a meter. The archaeologists believed that, from this dig, the three bars had been a one-off find, possibly lost over the side of a ship in former times, to disappear into the muddy bed of the river.

"The inscriptions on the bars included the stamp VRBS ROMA, a well known marking indicating the bars were stamped in Rome. Some of the other markings led one to believe the bars were stamped during the period of Valentian III, and with the other markings of Theodosius and Placida, the bars could not have been stamped later than 450 AD. However"—Frank hesitated as he reached across the desk for another sheaf of papers—"it is not necessarily the right interpretation to put on finds such as these. There were many occasions where existing bars of bullion, unmarked, and cast as a result of the gathering of other valuables—some taken, some stolen, and some the result of taxation—were moved around for many years as trade items, and then re-smelted and stamped many years after their original casting. These same bars may have been stamped around 450 AD, but as I said, they may have been cast many, many years earlier."

Frank flicked over some of the documents in front of him, found what he was looking for, and smiled. "To my knowledge, no one has since investigated the site or done anything to locate the exact site of the digging that was carried out. It remains one of those dead-end stories, but very interesting nonetheless."

"Frank, this is wonderful, a marvelous story," I replied. "If you are correct in your estimate of the location of the site, I think it falls in Dr. Cosack's area of responsibility. I think it would be a great job to look around on the Weser and see if I can find the original field. It shouldn't be too difficult—after all, how many windmills are there on the upper reaches of the Weser? I'll talk it over with Dr. Cosack and see if he minds me looking for the site, and then check back with you if I can locate the area we're looking for. In fact, I think this coming weekend would be ideal. Can I use your phone? I want to check to see if I can meet Dr. Cosack this week and talk it over with him."

I was flying again, eager to act on this latest gem of information. I knew I had to leave my friends and interests in Germany soon, but I still had a few months left to pursue these fascinating and totally absorbing searches for hidden treasures and times long lost.

It was indeed a fair exchange—Frank was very happy with the three pristine denarii, and I was charged up with the opportunity to locate a treasure of a different sort, not necessarily more silver bars, but something perhaps of even greater importance. With a little luck I might find one of the Roman stopover ports on the northern reaches of the Weser, which must have existed during the period of Varus and before that, during Drusus' early forays into the hinterlands of Germany.

During the following week I dropped in to see Dr. Cosack, who greeted me with his usual warmth and hospitality. We discussed other matters still extant in his area, including our mutual interests to the south of Hannover where the lines in a field still remained to be excavated. We also discussed the other find areas farther down the line of the Weser as it coursed its way through the pass at Minden, and south beyond Rinteln toward Hameln and Hoxter. However, I was keen to take up the issue of the silver bullion, and having secured his approval to investigate the matter further (he had wished me luck into the bargain!), left his office in high spirits.

*   *   *

The mighty Weser is some 300 miles long, with its source being the junction of the Fulda and Werra rivers near Hannover in central Germany. After passing north through the Minden gap, the waterway maintains a fairly disciplined line for some twelve miles before it splits into larger tributary areas of lakes and minor waterways that stretch the greater width of the river, in places more than a mile wide. Farther north, the river comes together again as a main concourse, passing through the North German plain on its way to the North Sea, where Drusus built his sea forts at the mouth of the German rivers. The stretch of land I had to cover was about thirty miles long, but with the older maps supplied by Dr. Cosack, I was able to reduce the area to be covered. After all, how many windmills could there be bordering the Weser? I was in for a surprise.

Through a gradual process of elimination, I figured out a stretch of land about six miles long was worthy of investigation and, like Don Quixote, I was soon looking at windmills as my focal point. To my dismay, this stretch of the river boasted a large number of windmills with a wide variety of shapes and sizes. I had no idea such a number of windmills existed in this part of Germany. There were all manner of windmills. Some were perched in the right place with the right expanse of land to the front, but never like the picture in the mind's eye, with the windmills incorrectly situated relative to the backdrop of the original photo from 1888. Two weekends passed, and I had nothing to show for my efforts.

*   *   *

I remember well the drive to my last choice. It was not easily accessible from any main road, and as I drew near the river line in the vicinity of the site, I stopped at a minor crossroads that looked over the land and waters to the east. My mouth dropped open. I parked and got out of the car, not quite believing my eyes. Behind me was the original site of the windmill, though there was no sign of the structure's previous existence. Before I went down to the silver bullion site, I knew I needed to have the former existence of the windmill confirmed, so I made inquiries at the farm on the crossroads. The farmer was very helpful and related how there had been a fire many years ago that required the windmill be pulled down.

I thanked him for the information and walked across the road junction to look over the field leading down the slope to the river line. I gazed over the area to the east and, once again, could not believe my eyes.

I was looking at a perfect quadrangle of blue water, enclosed by river banks on three sides, open to the east and the main concourse of the river seven to eight hundred yards away in the distance. If there was ever a safe-water port or intermediate loading/unloading quay on the banks of the Weser in Roman times, this was it. The field where the three peat diggers had posed for photographs one hundred years earlier was once again underwater. But even then I could imagine . . .

9 AD, June: Storm on the Weser

The heavily-laden supply boats were lined up thickly along the sides of the quay. On the docks and banks were long lines of legionaries, most of whom watched as German workers and slaves bustled up and down the short gangplanks carrying heavy sacks of grain, flagons of wine, the odd chest of precious stores and belongings, and all the other items of great value being hauled away to Rome from the German hinterlands. Tithes of furs and skins, honey, amber, and other forms of wealth used to pay taxes, including a special consignment of silver, were all being loaded into the shallow galley holds for the long journey back to the Medi-terra Sea, back to the heart of the Roman Empire.

A dozen large oak chests full of silver bullion were lined up under guard awaiting shipment. Each box was packed with twelve silver bars, and each bar was carefully wrapped in sackcloth for the long voyage ahead. The chests were heavy, as one slave quickly discovered when he hoisted one up on his shoulder and began walking up the gangplank toward a low-riding galley. He had yet to recover from the long and rough trip upriver from the northern sea; pangs of nausea had left him weak and unsteady. Without warning, he slipped on the wet wood as he staggered up the gangplank and fell sharply to his knees. The combination of his weight and that of the bullion chest snapped the weathered wood beneath his body like so much kindling. Both slave and chest crashed into the muddy waters below and quickly disappeared from sight.

The commander of the galley had been carefully overseeing the loading process to insure that the flagons of wine shipped down to Minden were kept separate from the stores being loaded aboard. Varus himself was looking forward to new Gaul wines, and the master was determined to assure the loading procedure did not damage the liquid or make it difficult to easily unload. The process was moving too slowly for his liking, especially with a storm approaching. The hot air of the summer's day was becoming heavier and more oppressive by the minute. The change was so marked one could nearly smell it in the air. A faint whistling approached from the southwest, growing louder as the seconds ticked away. As he pondered the weather, a sharp crack of breaking wood and splash of water seized his attention. Whatever its cause, it could not be good news.

The slave felt his feet drive deeply into the soggy quagmire of the riverbed. The chest, lighter now, he let fall away, and some of its contents spilled out into the river bottom. The heavy Hessian-wrapped silver bars buried themselves deeply in the black gripping morass. Only five of the original dozen silver bars remained inside the oak box. Waving his hands and squirming his legs, the slave finally struggled free of the clinging mud and a few seconds later broke the surface, gasping for air as he thrashed the water to stay afloat. Few slaves knew how to swim, but it made little difference when the shallow draft boats sank beneath them in the heavy seas to the north. Manacled to the holds of the galleys, they drowned where they sat, chained to their sinking ships. But this slave grew up along the North African coast, and so learned how to swim as a young boy. He was comfortable on and below the water. With his lungs clear, he began lazily paddling his way toward the dock a few yards distant.

"You!" shouted the galley master as he leaned over the gunnels of his vessel, a crooked finger pointing accusingly at the slave. "You have two choices! Swim back down with a rope and recover that chest and its contents and live, or go back under and don't come up again!" In the commander's other hand was a coil of thick rope.

Nodding vigorously, the slave spat forth a garbled response in a tongue the master did not understand. It was clear, however, that the African understood what was expected of him and was more than willing to try and recover the lost bullion to save his life.

"Here," shouted the commander, throwing the rope into the water. "Take this damned rope and get me that chest back up here!"

The rope had barely hit the water near the slave when the weather noticeably changed for the worse. The galley master had seen and heard it all before; he knew what was coming. "Hell's teeth," he cried. "Secure all lines and hatches, lift all gangplanks! There is a storm coming fast! Quickly, you dogs! Secure the ship or we will founder where we sit!" Hoisting his whip from the rail, he cracked it mercilessly about him as he continued to berate his crew and the toiling slaves.

Menacing clouds, thick and black, lined the horizon to the west, scudding across the sky toward them at an incredible speed. "By all the gods," he whispered to himself as he stared into the maw of the approaching storm. "Look at the speed of the beast!" he cried aloud. "Hurry, hurry, we have no more time left!" His commanding cry was still echoing around the small port as the other galley captains quickly followed the master's lead and prepared their craft to weather the approaching storm. A sense of panic spread across the quay as the legionaries rushed about, trotting up and down the gangplanks to release their loads and hurry into the holds of their galleys to take up their positions at the oars. The legionary oarsmen had easier access to the cargo area than the slaves, who were shackled anew into the wooden slide running along the leading edge of the hold.

The slave in the water, meanwhile, had slipped beneath the surface to recover the chest, and had missed the shouted commands and pandemonium swirling around him. With the crisis nearly upon him, the galley commander had utterly forgotten about the lost box and swimming slave.

Within a few minutes of his first shouts of warning, the massive summer storm, pushed by a sledgehammer of hot driving winds, rolled into the port area. The cooling fronts from the north had sucked in the overpowering heat of the high pressure formation above the German highlands to the southwest. The result was a massive vacuum that sucked in the black storm clouds of the rain fronts behind them. High waves splashed up and across the quays and the moored vessels, sending those slaves who had not reached the comparative safety of the holds sliding off gangways and decks into the roiling cauldron of water below. Unable to swim, they flailed away as they sank beneath the surface.

After nearly a full minute underwater, meanwhile, the African slave surfaced to discover a different world than the one he had but recently left. The wind and rain lashed his face, and visibility was little more than a few yards. Without sound or warning, behind the last wave that splashed over him loomed his galley. Unable to hold under the pressure, one of the boat's lines snapped and the water pushed the craft rapidly *away from its mooring. The slave was instantly pinned against the galley's port side and ground to a bloody pulp between the sides of the ship and the stone stanchions of the quay.*

The maelstrom was only just beginning. By the time it passed thirty minutes later, more than a dozen galleys had been smashed into matchwood against the harbor walls, and two dozen slaves and several legionnaires were missing. The other boats, their hulls cracked and leaking, were torn from their moorings and thrown out into the greater reaches of the river, where they foundered. Not a single galley was left on the water.

As the winds blew, the ships splintered and sank, taking screaming men down with them. The same whipped sediment on the riverbed that cushioned the sunken ships engulfed the last exposed edge of the lost silver bars.

1990–1991: The Search Continues

The following week, I visited again with Dr. Cosack to inquire whether he intended to undertake an investigation of the site to verify what I believed was a Roman port. He was, naturally, very interested in our discussions about the Weser site, but he was still swamped with work south of Hannover. Mounting an underwater investigation in the near future was out of the question. However, he made it clear that he would be pleased to give his blessing to any efforts I wished to launch.

It was now the end of the summer. Even with professional backing, there would not be enough time to launch a serious project before I had to leave the country. As anxious as I was to prove my theory, I would have to delay any additional exploration until I returned to Germany. I bade Dr. Cosack farewell and dropped in at the *Münzkabinett* to see Frank Berger. He was sympathetic with my frustration at not being able to pursue the silver bullion matter further. We promised to keep in touch after I returned from England, and I left him at his desk, engrossed in some other historical gem from his archives.

The time had nearly come to leave Germany. It is difficult to express the frustration I felt at leaving. We were rapidly approaching archaeological proof as to what happened to the Varus legions—one of the great mysteries of the ancient world. I knew the answer was there, in

Kalkriese. I wanted so much to uncover everything as fast as the dig teams could work. Wolfgang brought me gently down to earth with his quiet and reassuring manner. The Professor rarely raised his voice or lost his temper, and he was always considerate to everyone involved with the project. Indeed, he was now fondly referred to by team members as "Papa Schlüter."

"Tony, these digs could go on for ten years or more, just centered here on the main site at Kalkriese," he said to me during my final visit to Osnabrück. "There is so much more to follow up both to the east and west of the site. When you can, you will come back and see us. The fields will still be here, and there is so much ground to be searched that not even the full-time efforts of Klaus and Gisela will unearth all the secrets lying here in the fields; they will not be able to search it all." His words were a great comfort, and I know he could see that by the expression on my face. "I will keep you up to date and will write to you periodically to tell you of the latest finds and how the digs progress," he assured me. "Keep in touch, Tony. You have found the site, and you can rest assured I will not allow that fact, or the work you have carried out since then, to be forgotten." He was a man of his word.

I left Germany in January 1991. In February, Operation Desert Storm swept into Kuwait and Iraq, and the world focused its attention on matters more important than a small hill in Germany.

Chapter Twelve

1991-1992: Impasse and Breakthrough

During much of 1991 and the final death throes of the Gulf War, I remained at the Ministry of Defence in London. Finally, in 1992, I made a series of return trips to Kalkriese to continue my liaison work with the project and conduct a search of the large areas surrounding the battlefield. For some inexplicable reason, the project had dramatically slowed down. Work had not progressed beyond the excavations central to Kalkriese and the point of ambush. In a way I was inwardly pleased; the complete scope and potential of the lands was still to be discovered.

The enormity of the battle site was staggering. In all likelihood, it extended anywhere from six to twelve miles east (and perhaps farther) in the direction where the running battle probably began. Given what we knew about the battle and its archaeology, the fields immediately to the west and beyond also held important artifacts waiting to be unearthed. Their excavation, sadly, would have to wait. Although archaeological excavations are sometimes laborious and frustratingly slow (at least to my way of thinking), I was keenly interested in everything these efforts uncovered. My preference, however, was to revisit the surrounding fields, where I was always happy and at peace with the solitude of my fieldwork and metal detecting. I was also still very keen to examine new lines of investigation, particularly the march route traversed by the legions to arrive at Kalkriese.

The team surveyors had done an extraordinary amount of work, both in the digs themselves and in the outlying fields, where Klaus and Gisela spent day after day searching for clues to help increase our understanding of the Varus battle. They extended their search both east and west of the main battle area, where they went over the same fields numerous times to glean from each as much as possible.

Two long and very hot summers allowed the central digs to be enlarged to the size of a football field. Then, without warning, the finds dried up. About this time the digs also lost the line of the buried earthen ambush wall, which the archaeologists originally believed ran fairly straight across the line along the forefront of the ambush position. The searchers were thus forced to change tack halfway across the field, and initiate further exploratory trenches to seek the missing wall by following the contour lines running southeast by northwest.

Given all that had transpired, Professor Schlüter decided to implement a radical new measure: excavate a large quadrangle into the woods on the western side of the field, beginning just outside the timber line of the knoll. This was the same area that earlier produced an enormous number of finds, including the battle mask and pioneer axe along the front of the wall. Apart from the obvious sensitivity relating to chopping down mature forest, the inherent problems of excavating through varying levels of tree roots and undergrowth were not to be taken lightly. Special authority had to be sought to cut down the timber before any digging could begin. Earlier exploratory slit trenches were dug through the wooded knoll between the pine trees, which required minimum effort, spared most of the trees, and reduced the labor of having to hack through heavy root spread.

By this time about one-half of the main field around the knoll had been open to the elements for a considerable time, but all the measuring and plotting work had been completed. Professor Schlüter decided to fill in the massive archaeological excavation before any additional explorations were undertaken to relocate the temporary line of the ambush wall. Thereafter, the work would be concentrated on the western side of the knoll, into the forest up to a point only fifty yards from the top of the wooded rise—from where I believed it probable Arminius controlled the final day's battle of the Teutoburger Wald.

AD 9 – July: The Death of Wodenicus

Arminius rode his horse hard. The thrill of the exhilarating ride down through the forest trails sent his spirits soaring. The trees flashed by, the bulk of the magnificent stallion beneath him thundering and heaving, twisting and turning as one with the curves and rises of the ridgeline path. Ickerland was still some miles ahead down the western side of the Wiehengebirge hills, out of the series of small passes running through Ostercappeln and into the hills to the north of Osning. The tribal chiefs were gathering at Icker for a council of war called by Arminius. It was time to decide on the final plan for the defeat and removal of the Romans from Germany.

The German auxiliaries—fellow Cherusci warriors and other tribal companions of many campaigns who had fought alongside the Roman legions during their years as mercenaries—whooped, yelled, and screamed with excitement as they chased after their commander through the undulating wooded glades. They knew they were speeding toward a royal feast, for one accompanied every major tribal gathering. Beer, wine, and women in any order and in large quantities, dancing, and singing, would be followed by hazy days (and headaches), followed once again by evenings of feasting on wild pig stew, venison, and many other grilled meats.

The long column was thundering through the woods when Wodenicus' horse approached a blind left curve at a full gallop. Wodenicus realized he was in trouble but did not react in time for the steed to lean into the camber of the trail. Both rider and horse disappeared over the banked side of the track. The stunned beast tried to counteract the loss of hard traction beneath its hooves by tacking to the left to regain its balance, and the force of its sudden change in direction threw the rider over its thick neck. Wodenicus somehow kept his wits about him long enough to execute a perfect double sideways somersault through the air before landing in the thick undergrowth beyond. His mount, perplexed and confused by what had just occurred, fought its way to a stop forty yards later, where it stood nervously scratching at the ground with its fore hooves. Other riders passing by erupted into fits of mirth at the site of the flying Wodenicus. Each cackled with laughter as he galloped past in Arminius' wake. Not a single warrior stopped to go to the aid of the fallen comrade. The race down the Berg to the feast at Icker was far too important to risk being the last to arrive!

Within a few seconds the echoing peals of laughter faded away into the forest, the thundering mass of riders had passed, and Wodenicus' horse was left alone. The beast walked back to where his master lay on the ground, spread eagled upside down and buried deep in a holly tree thicket. Blood ran from his nose and face down his forehead and into his thick matted hair. Wodenicus moaned as he tried to ease himself from the thorny holly branches. His left arm was at an awkward angle, either broken or dislocated at the shoulder, and his hand throbbed with pain. It took a few minutes for his head to clear and for senses to return.

"Here, boy, come here, boy," he whispered to his horse, clucking his tongue to encourage the animal toward him. The horse whinnied softly and cautiously advanced to within a foot of his crippled master. The bridle hung loosely from its sweaty neck, and the warrior gently reached with his good hand to grasp it. He quickly twisted it twice around his wrist so it would not slip off. With a groan and cry of pain, Wodenicus slowly pulled himself down from his inverted spread-eagle into a sitting position. The pain coursing through his damaged arm and shoulder was excruciating.

After resting for a few more minutes to gather both strength and senses, he pulled himself slowly to his feet. When he flexed his injured hand to test his fingers, he winced as a stab of pain coursed up his arm to his shoulder. Clenching his teach he gently lifted the top of his tunic away from his shoulder. It was as he suspected: a large lump protruding on the peak of the joint—a dislocation. It could have been much worse. The warrior slowly walked back through the undergrowth leading his horse by his good arm, cradling the other tight to his body across his chest. He stopped and leaned against the nearest tree, the sweat streaming down from his brow. The waves of pain struck him with every movement he made. He knew what he had to do: either lean into the dislocation with a sharp movement to snap it back into its socket, or arrange a sudden jerk on the end of his arm, either way with a pad or roll pinned under his arm to produce the lever effect to help draw the dislodged ball into the socket. He had seen it done before, but now he had to personally endure it. His eyes watered at the thought.

He raised his head and looked around the small clearing until his gaze came to rest on a small log lying a short distance away. It looked the right size for the job he had in mind. With a slow faltering step, he led his horse forward. When he reached the log, Wodenicus carefully stooped, picked it up with his good arm, and walked slowly back to the large tree. He closed his eyes for a few moments to rest when he heard it—the snap of a twig or leaf underfoot.

The German's eyes shot open and darted left to right before comprehending a hazy image of a lone figure standing twenty yards from him. Was it one of his comrades, finally returned to help him? A smile spread on his lips and he was about to speak a greeting when he saw the glint of flashing light swiftly winking its way toward him. The identity of the glistening circle of spinning light and shadow came to him too late, just a split second before the massive German axe split his skull in two, pinning his head into the oak tree. The severed skull burst like a ripe pumpkin, spurting blood brain matter into the face of the warrior's horse. The stallion reared up in fright, and in so doing, freed the bridle from the dead warrior's hand. As other men ran toward the frightened steed, it turned away and made for the woodland trail, where it galloped off after Arminius and his riders. The warrior who had thrown the axe stepped forward, gripped the weapon's handle, and with one swift jerk freed the iron weapon from the oak. The dead Wodenicus slumped to the ground at the base of the tree.

The warrior turned to his comrades and loudly proclaimed, "And so die all traitors and renegades who wait at the feet of the Romans! A curse on all these jackals who call themselves Germans but fight for the Roman scabs!" He rounded on the slumped body and kicked it before spitting into the bloody mess that was the slain Wodenicus' face. "They should be hunted down like dogs and wiped from the face of the earth. They are worse than the lowest form of life, and deserve to die. Any more of these so-called auxiliaries who fight for Rome should be the first to die when Arminius and our tribes join to fight the Varus legions. Mount up for Icker! Arminius will have already reached the camp before us. He will be pleased when we tell him of the death of this lone scout of the Romans sneaking forth to spy on us. He will spy no more. Another meal for the pigs!" Laughing, he wiped the axe blade on the tunic of the dead auxiliary.

He was about to move off to his horse when he noticed the dead warrior was wearing an attractive gold amulet about his wrist, a simple but beautifully crafted torque of twisted gold with snakes heads' at each cross-over point. He bent down and pried it free, slipping it over his own wrist. "A fitting tribute from one German traitor to a German who will soon be of the nobility when I wed Segestes' beautiful daughter!" he cried. "Come on, mount up—the feasting starts at Icker!"

With a final round of laughter and coarse remarks about the maidens of Icker, the group mounted their horses and rode for the gathering of the tribes at the encampment in the Osning hills of Ickerland.

The War Conference at Icker

Icker was a sprawling village community spread over many acres of grassy pasture in a natural bowl of land in the highlands to the north of Osning. It was a conglomerate of small encampments, comprised mainly of members of the Bructeri and Cherusci tribes, with smaller representative contingents of other tribes: the Chauci, Marsi, and the Chatti, who at this time were temporarily living on the western flank of the surrounding area. The Cherusci tribe was ruled by a Council of Elders headed by its chief spokesman, Segestes. The tribe had been a thorn in the side of the Roman invaders for many years. Its warring parties harried the Romans at every opportunity before disappearing into the hills and moorlands to the north and west of the Teutoburger Wald.

The Germans had long understood the limitations of their methods of fighting, but meeting the highly disciplined Roman legions in the field in a pitched battle was unthinkable. The Germans had few helmets or breastplates, and most preferred to fight with shields and large crude broadswords. Their light but deadly spears called frameae *were fitted with short, narrow iron heads with sharpened edges, and could be thrown or used as a slashing and stabbing weapon in hand-to-hand combat. Although they enjoyed pitched battles, the Germans were more adept at surprise attacks, ambushes, and feigned withdrawals, attacking and then retreating to lure the enemy into ground of their choosing.*

Their forces were comprised of mini-regiments of about one hundred warriors each, their strength lying in their mutual alliance and high morale. As Tacitus wrote in his Germania, *"that to aid their chief, to protect him, and by their own gallant actions add to his glory were their most sacred aims and beliefs." The German battle creed was simple: each man on the field of battle had to be seen as brave and heroic as his chief, and had to equal his prowess in combat. A people proud of their warrior status, they did not take kindly to the Roman scourge invading their lands.*

The Roman armies were trained and equipped to deal with an enemy who had cities and arable lands to protect. For the most part, the Germans had no such fixed assets. Their strength was primarily rural and scattered. The loss of a village meant little to them, so it was difficult for the Romans to strike a resounding blow against the more rebellious tribes. Much of the Roman military hierarchy failed to realize the strength and training of the legions were substantially weakened when they were forced to move through forests and swamps to get at the German populace.

As he neared the outskirts of Icker, Arminius slowed the approach of his cavalrymen, the thrill of the gallop down through the Wiehengebirge ridge line now well behind them. The warriors took in the enormity of the rolling mass of hutted encampments stretched out before them. The cooking fires sent lazy plumes of drifting smoke into the early evening sky, and the smell of grilled meats wafting across their nostrils made their bellies ache. The feeling was one of coming home—even if Icker itself was not the land of their birth. The hordes of men, women, and children gathered in and moving around each of the many settlement areas waved and called their greetings to Arminius' troops as the mounted men walked their horses through the encampment.

Scouts and guards deployed around the hills surrounding the tribal gathering had reported Arminius' approach some time before, and word of his arrival had already reached the main council area. Segestes, Arminius' uncle, Inguiomerus, and other important chieftains and elders, including Arminius' own brother, were sitting in a large semicircle waiting for the warrior to reach them. On one side of the council was a huge roasting pit that crackled from the drippings of an entire wild pig. Segestes' brother Segimerus, one of Arminius' friends and supporters seated within the gathered circle, nodded in acknowledgement at his compatriot's presence.

As Arminius and his riders approached the gathering, a curtain of beautifully worked deerskins over the entrance to the central hut behind the council was drawn aside, and a tall young woman appeared at the entrance. She was beautiful. Willowy and graceful, her hair flowed in long blonde tresses far down her back, her features soft and tanned from the early summer's sun. She wore a clock of light linen that fell to her sandaled feet. A large gold clasp with a large semi-precious stone linked the cloth at her shoulders, accentuating the rise of her firm young breasts as they pushed forward against the fall of the gown. She gazed out across the gathering and took in the slow approach of the riders. Her gaze finally settled on Arminius—his proud masculine features, commanding presence, and piercing blue eyes. They were as blue as hers, though sharper and with a steely glint that studied deeply the council members spread out before him.

She had heard of Arminius; who had not? A Roman knight, but a man of the Cherusci peoples who had never forgotten his background and his loyalties. It was rumored he was now the authority in the land, a leader calling for his fellow countrymen to take up the challenge with him and rid the German lands of the Roman invaders.

The woman was Segestes' daughter Thusnelda. She was betrothed to a Chatti warrior named Dagan the Hunter, whose detachment of cavalry was on its way to join the huge gathering of tribesmen at Icker. They were to be married that year, perhaps in the fall. The wedding had originally been planned for the spring just passed, but the tribal gatherings and the war conferences of the last few months had preempted all social ceremonies. Thusnelda's father was a respected elder of the tribal communities, but he had always preached appeasement with the Roman invaders, defending his stance with stoic and labored pronouncements on how it was better to live well and at peace in occupied lands than to live in fear, at war, continuously harassed by the oppressive Roman legions.

Arminius' warriors dismounted and tied their horses to the tether posts with feed bags dotted around the encampment, moving off to join the smaller groups of men and women seated around the dozens of cooking fires. The collection of so many multi-tribal groups, though unusual, did not pose any danger to Arminius and his men, for the throng

Denarius of Augustus Caesar (above and below), minted between 2 BC and 1 AD in Lyon, southern France. The obverse of the coin above features the proud aquiline features of Augustus Caesar (left), with his nephews Caius and Lucius Caesar on the reverse, standing behind battle shields and crossed spears (right). The author discovered large numbers of these coins during his search for the site of the Varus battle. To date, nearly one-half of all the coins recovered from Kalkriese and other related sites, including the lager fort at Haltern, are of this denomination. Schlüter

The first major exploratory digs on the eastern side of the ambush/command hill, circa 1989-1990. Seen here are Klaus Fehrs (right) and an official from the archaeological authorities. Schlüter

Early days of the first exploratory digs in the "Oberesch" field, where the famous silver mask and other important finds were made. Here, Professor Schülter (right) and author Tony Clunn (center) discuss the progress being made with Klaus Fehrs. Clunn

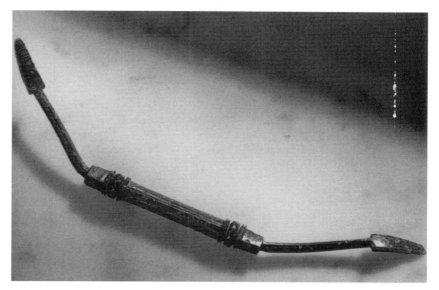

(Above) A surgeon's gauge. This wicked looking instrument was used to extract arrowheads, spear tips—and even teeth. Schlüter

(Below) The golden nugget. The author found this remarkable artifact in the area of the Main Lager at Haltern. This was the encampment from which Varus set out from winter quarters on the River Lippe to his Summer Camp on the River Weser. The nugget undoubtedly came from a metalsmith's kiln. (Pig iron was also recovered in the vicinity). Schlüter

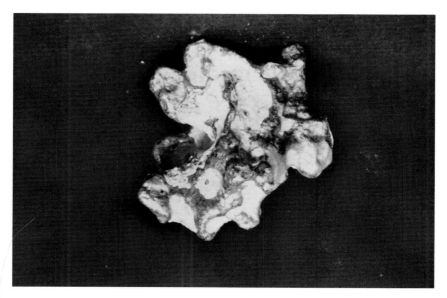

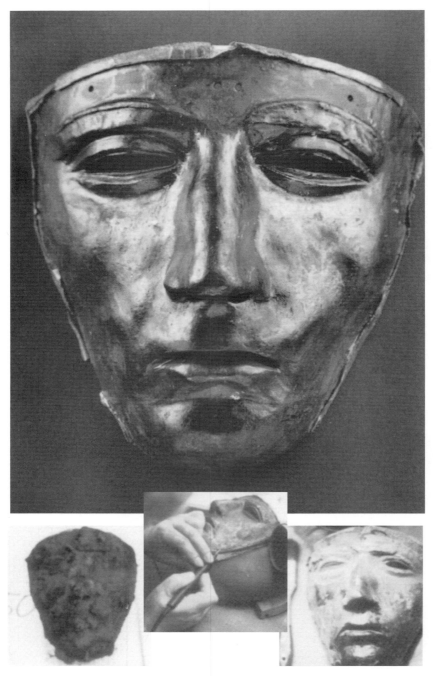

(Top): The iron mask. It was originally embellished with silver and served as a face mask on a helmet. (Below row of images, l to r): The mask as originally unearthed, and the evolution of the restoration process. Schlüter

This exploratory slit trench (above) was cut in the woods on the Kalkriese hill a short distance from the ambush wall. Schlüter

The discovery of three lead sling shot (right) helped confirm that Kalkriese had ties with military aspects of Roman life. Schlüter

(Right) A unique bronze phallic cloak clasp-harness piece excavated near Kalkriese. Schlüter

Bronze snakehead cloak clasps—one of the most interesting finds at Kalkriese. The front (above) shows the detail of the craftsmanship. The reverse (below) of each is inscribed. On one is the owner's name: "Marcus Aius." On the other is his affiliation: "1st Cohort Fabricus." Schlüter

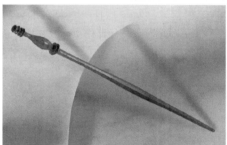

(Top) An "As" stamped with the mark "VAR" (Varus), found by the dig team. (Left) A beautiful bronze lady's hairpin. (Below) Four bronze seals with head relief used to emboss wax seals. Schlüter

(Above) The peat diggers at the site of the dry Weser riverbed, where three silver bars (below) were unearthed. Schlüter

Pieces from the Hildesheim Silver Treasure. (Above) An exquisite gold and silver plate. (Below) A large finely detailed silver urn. Did these treasures belong to Varus? Schlüter

Coins of Julius Caesar found on the Kalkriese field. (Top) 47/46BC, minted in Africa; (Middle) 46/45BC, minted in Spain; (Bottom) 49/48BC, minted in Rome.

(Right) A gold Aureus of Augustus Caesar. This is the same as the silver denarius of the same period, but a gold aureus. 2 BC–1 AD, minted in Lyon. Schlüter

(Above) The obverse of a Roman Scribona, 62 BC, minted in Rome. (Right) The reverse of the same coin. Schlüter

A roughly minted gold Aureus of Augustus Caesar, 2 BC–1 AD, minted in Lyon. It was discovered during a routine battlefield dig. Schlüter

A bronze wild boar's head and shoulders found with a denarius near the Venne Beck crossing. Schlüter

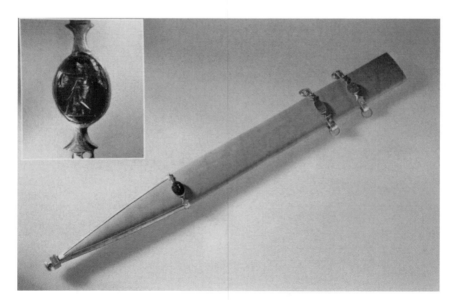

The silver retaining bands of a Roman sword scabbard, including a figure of a Roman/Grecian lady holding a mirror, set in resin (inset). Both were found in open fields west of the central battlefield area. Schlüter

One of Kalkriese's most intriguing discoveries including the unearthing of several large bronze keys designed to unlock Roman chests. All were found during the battlefield digs. Why were Roman soldiers carrying keys after several days of fighting? And what happened to the chests? Schlüter

A silver measuring spoon. This example may have been used by a doctor to measure out doses of medicine. Schlüter

Digging for a metallic signal at least four meters beneath the surface. The object seemed about 150 cm x 75 cm x 50 cm. For many reasons, we were unable to dig deeper than three meters. Author Tony Clunn (leaning on the ladder), with Willy Drager and others. Only one treasure chest was found in Hermann's tribal areas in the late 1800s. The number of chest keys found so far at Kalkriese indicate there were many more treasure chests, either buried near the battlefield by the Varus Legions, or recovered by Hermann's warriors and reburied by Hermann nearer his own tribal domain. The search goes on. Clunn

The search for buried treasure chests from the Varus Battle. Using a Fisher Deep Seeker Detector to relocate the signals, the author utilizes a cross section technique to establish exactly where the deep signals emanate from. The trench is already 2.5 meters deep. Clunn

The discovery of the Varus Battlefield generated enormous interest around the globe. The significance of the find is difficult to overstate. Three men—Jim Corless, with Model Production/Time Machine Miniatures, together with Doug Cohen and Chris Tubb—were so excited about Major Clunn's discovery they spent years crafting a diorama of the demise of the legions. This photo represents one small segment of their work. Corless

Professor Wolfgang Schülter (left) and author Tony Clunn (right) after looking over some of the interesting excavations at the battlefield's central site. Their partnership during the early years of discovery played a pivotal role in preserving the battlefield for posterity. They remain good friends, and continue to meet up whenever the opportunity arises. Although Prof. Schülter has retired, he closely monitors progress at the site. Clunn

Major Tony Clunn being presented to Her Majesty Queen Elizabeth II on the occasion of the presentation of the Member of the British Empire medal in January 1996. Clunn

was calm and largely unified in purpose. The majority of the assembled warriors and their families were excited and happy to be at this great gathering, and they opened their family circles to welcome the "Roman–German" mercenaries.

Arminius tied his stallion to the nearest post and stood in front of the horse for a moment, soaking in the atmosphere of the settlement. He turned to some youths standing nearby. "Feed him well, he is the greatest horse you will ever see, for he is the mount that will carry Arminius into battle against the Roman legions, and finally drive them from our lands. If you talk to him quietly enough, whisper in his ear, he will talk back to you. If you don't believe me, try it." He gave a short chuckle and made his way toward the central figure of Segestes, who rose to greet him, as did the other council elders.

This was not the first of the tribal meetings leading up to the battle with Varus, but it was the largest. Two full moons before, the main contingents and elders of the tribes had gathered in a meeting in the Teutoburger Hills fifty miles to the southeast, where they deliberated Arminius' fervent call to arms. A Roman patrol had been found and captured spying on the gathered Germans, but had been quickly dispatched.

"Welcome Arminius," said Segestes. "Your presence has been long awaited. We are pleased you have come to discuss once again your plans with us. All the elders and council members are full of praise for your determination to take up arms and fight Varus and his legions, but some still believe this might not be the best way to deal with the Romans. Perhaps further discussion and encouragement from you will convince those of us who doubt the sensibility of your proposals. But before you speak"— Segestes turned and looked across the short distance to the open doorway of the hut behind—"let my daughter bring you some chilled wine. You must be thirsty after your long ride. Come, daughter," he commanded, "bring the chieftain some good food and drink."

Thusnelda bent down and picked up a pitcher of wine and a platter of grilled meats recently removed from the spit roast over one of the many cooking fires. Arminius was struck by her gracefulness, for she appeared not to walk, but float across the ground toward him, her gait silky smooth with a gentle swing to her hips. Her cool blue eyes held his own as she moved forward. For the first time in his life he was totally and utterly mesmerized by a female. Segestes held out an empty chalice in front of

Arminius, which Thusnelda filled with her pitcher of wine. Segestes was not blind to the ways of youth and noticed immediately the effect his daughter was having on Arminius. He frowned when their eyes locked together. The dutiful daughter filled her father's cup as well, set the pitcher and tray of meat at their feet and, with a last lingering look at Arminius, turned and made her way swiftly back to the hut.

Arminius raised the cup to his lips, and said quietly, "You have a beautiful daughter, Segestes. She will make a good wife for some tribal prince. I salute her beauty, and you and your wife, to have produced such a daughter." He drank deeply of the cup's contents.

Segestes' face briefly clouded with concern before a smile eased across weathered features. "You are kind with your words, Arminius. Yes, she is beautiful, and she is betrothed to Dagan the Hunter of the Chatti tribe. They will wed in the fall during the Harvest Festival celebration. She will make him a fine wife, and he will undoubtedly become the chief of his tribe in due course. He is on his way to join us here, and should arrive before the sun sets. You will meet him then. Dagan the Hunter rides with his own mounted warriors, and they will be as hungry and thirsty as your own men! So let us attack the food and drink first, for there will not be much left after they arrive!"

Arminius said nothing as he followed Segestes toward the group of waiting elders. Segestes waved his arm, offering the stage to the younger German chief. Arminius cleared his throat and raised his voice. "When we wage war against the Romans, we will need every strong arm and steady horse we can get. The time is fast approaching, my brothers, when we will remove this Roman scourge from our lands! Who is with me?"

One of the chiefs stood and looked squarely at Arminius. "And how can we possibly defeat Varus and his thousands? They are better armed, better trained, and there are many more of them beyond the Rhine that will come even if we are able to defeat the scourge now occupying our lands." A faint ripple of applause rose from the seated elders.

Arminius nodded slowly. "You speak clearly and with knowledge of our enemy. We will not meet them in pitched battle, for that would be foolish. There is another way." And with that, Arminius began slowly unveiling his plan to defeat the mighty Roman army. He did not tell them everything he had in mind, but just enough to convince them his idea had merit and, with their support, a likelihood of success.

When he finished thirty minutes later he was greeted with a wall of utter silence. The seconds ticked past until one elder stood and shouted out his support. Another stood and did the same, and then two more. Within a few moments the groundswell of approval had become a tidal wave of support, as thousands of chiefs and warriors raised their swords, spears, and voices in a chorus of thunderous emotion. When banging drums and a throaty tone of horns joined in, the cacophony of noise grew into one indistinguishable, deafening roar. Ickerland trembled as the echoes of coming battle rolled through the surrounding hills.

Dagan the Hunter reeled in his mount to a sudden stop when the wall of noise washed over his mounted column some three miles from the encampment. "By the gods, they are celebrating without us!" he exclaimed. "What great events are we missing, my warriors?" Without another word he dug in his spurs and urged his horse forward into a speedy gallop. The golden wrist torque that now adorned his arm flashed in the early evening sunlight as he pounded toward Icker.

1992

In late 1992, Professor Schlüter initiated the drastic step of cutting back from the western side of the field into the eastern edge of the forested knoll. The authority for the excavation had finally arrived, and the shallow pitch of pine undergrowth was quickly cleared from the site. The digging had barely begun on the 30-yard square excavation when it became evident that the professor's decision had been wise indeed.

A number of key artifacts were uncovered, and as the hole deepened, some of the most important aspects of the layout of the ambush site were finally brought to light. This archaeological success was so compelling it induced the professor to make a definitive public statement: the site of the Varus battle was no longer in doubt. It was time to form a museum exhibition, he said, and present, in as many display cabinets as necessary, the remarkable artifacts unearthed during the first three years of the investigation.

Chapter Thirteen

Summer, 9AD: The Gathering of the Tribes

Professor Schlüter decided that it would not be appropriate to present the Varus artifacts to the public in static display cases at the local Osnabrück Stadt Museum. The best way to share the remarkable items dug from the north German soil, he believed, was to exhibit them on a grand tour in as many of the main cities of Germany as possible. The exhibition could be kicked off with a special opening ceremony at the Osnabrück museum before moving around the country in the late spring. The work involved preparing such an undertaking was staggering.

First, the professor had to appoint the right person to run with such a project, someone who could visualize and create the displays in a manner that would appeal to the viewing public—and not just to the learned and authoritative members of the archaeological fraternity. In other words, the exhibition had to strike a chord with the average German citizen, most of who look at archaeology as a stuffy and rather uninteresting subject.

Thankfully, there was a man born for exactly this task: Dr. Achim Rost, who was now married to Dr. Susanne Wilbers-Rost (one of the site archaeologists). The couple had worked together as students at the site of the initial dig, after my initial treasure finds from the autumn of 1987 had been recovered. Achim was the logical choice to breathe life into Professor Schlüter's vision. He was enthusiastic, very able, and knew the historical aspects of the project inside and out. The professor was confident he would make an excellent choice for the position of executive in charge of the exhibition. But time was short, and Professor Schlüter was anxious to open the exhibition to the general public in early March of 1993. All of us knew the importance of the finding of the actual battle site.

The great majority of the German population had been raised on the historical importance of Arminius' defeat of the Varus legions. Indeed, the site of the disaster was widely considered to be one of the greatest and most sought-after locations in the annals of German and European history. If presented correctly, a touring exhibition featuring the early finds from the site would capture the imagination of the masses. It would also lend weight to our public belief that the battle site had indeed been discovered. We all hoped there would be another benefit: the publicity from the media would help the professor generate the funds necessary to continue the many years of work that still needed to be carried out at Kalkriese.

We were a bit uneasy with the commercialization required to produce the various posters, books, and catalogs necessary to support such an ambitious venture, but if we wanted to spread the word and obtain the funding required to continue, there was little choice but to do whatever was necessary to achieve the desired end. The first ports of call were meetings with the money men—the bankers and the Stadt purse holders. Herr Fip, the Oberbürgermeister of Osnabrück and an avid supporter of the venture, lent Professor Schlüter the full weight of his office to help open a wide variety of doors to the various financial organizations and institutions.

As soon as Achim Rost was given the go-ahead, he initiated plans for the design of the various display cabinets that would house the traveling exhibition. They would have to be sound, yet lightweight, to enable them to be moved safely and with a minimum of effort into each of the city's museums. Professor Schlüter was kept more than busy pulling together all the strings necessary to make the tour a success. He contacted various city museums and authorities throughout Germany, ticking off one by one each success on his main plan of action.

Work at Kalkriese, meanwhile, continued under the watchful eye of Professor Schlüter, with Dr Wilbers-Rost as the on-site archaeologist in charge of the investigations surrounding the main digs. Unfortunately, I was back in England again and unaware that the new excavations cutting back into the wooded knoll had proven so fruitful. However, it was not long before Professor Schlüter contacted me again at the Ministry of Defence in London to tell me the wonderful news. I was delighted with the latest turn of events, and even more so when I received a personal invitation from the Osnabrück Stadt authorities, headed by the Oberbürgermeister, to attend the opening ceremonies in March 1993.

Other good news followed. Joan Allen Ltd, of Biggin Hill, the company that had supported the Kalkriese project with priority dispatches of Fisher detectors when the archaeological team required new and more advanced models, was equally excited about the continued success. Word soon reached Jim Lewellen, the manager at Fisher Laboratories in America, who suggested a sponsorship geared toward the opening ceremony in March. The idea was well received, so much so that Masten Wright Inc. of Connecticut, the major distributor for Fisher Laboratories Ltd, headed by distribution manager Erik Christensen, decided to personally attend the grand opening ceremony at Osnabrück. There, he would present the museum with a donation of various top-of-the-range Fisher detectors, including the Gemini III, the company's latest state-of-the-art deep-seeking detector. And so 1992 passed into 1993.

March arrived soon enough. A mass of media, Erik Christensen from America, and professors of archaeology and historians from across the continent gathered at the grand opening. The proof the German people had sought for so many hundreds of years of the Varus battle—the first historical landmark in the annals of early German and Roman history—was displayed in all its splendor for everyone to see. Yet, it was just a scratch of the surface. This incredible display of coins and artifacts had been unearthed from no more than a tiny fraction of the running battlefield that had been fought over during the late summer of 9 AD.

"... [T]hey dealt a succession of terrible blows to the Romans. A violent downpour and storm developed, so that the column was strung *out even further, and suffered many casualties and were quite unable to counter-attack,"* wrote Casius Dio. *"Accordingly they pitched camp after taking possession of a suitable place. The next day they marched on in somewhat better order and even broke out into open country, though they could not avoid suffering casualties. Moving on from there they reentered the woods, but suffered their heaviest losses in this action. The fourth day saw them still on the move, and again they experienced heavy rain and violent winds which prevented them from advancing or even finding a firm foothold . . . . every soldier and every horse was cut down without resistance . . ."*

*   *   *

I stood at the side of the large excavation cut into the forested knoll. Erik Christensen, a manger with Fisher Laboratories, walked with me on the battlefield, soaking in the somber atmosphere of the early spring day. A small gathering of people had assembled to gaze down into the open ground. I recall thinking how much it resembled a funeral, with all of us standing around the grave speaking in muted whispers. The place had always felt heavy to me; brooding, even sinister, but never more so than at this time. The darkness of the surrounding pine forest leading to the point where Arminius probably orchestrated the final stages of the battle felt like a black abyss, and I had no interest in walking deeper into the foreboding timber.

And then a strange phenomenon occurred. After the semi-vigil ended and most of the people turned around to walk away, a tall band of light danced around the center of the excavation. It was a trick of the sun's rays as they struck the various coverings draping the sides of the excavation pit. It was far more eerie than words can possibly convey. I did not need any further encouragement to hustle back to the car with Erik. Before I left, however, I snapped a photograph of the sun's weird reflections.

As one might expect, the trip to the field impressed Erik. It was a great pleasure to guide him around the area and point out the scope of the battle and the site where Arminius executed the final phase of his brilliant plan. As promised, before Erik left for the USA he presented Professor Schlüter with the invaluable Fisher detectors that would be put to so much good use over the years to follow.

9 AD, July: Dagan the Hunter and Thusnelda

The wild approval of Arminius' plan to defeat the Romans cut the palpable tension of the gathering of elders in the Icker encampment. The vast majority supported him and accepted his call to arms, but many were secretly fearful of his violent temper and astonishing expertise with the broadsword. Arminius tolerated neither fools nor enemies, and was quick to rise to answer either an insult or a foolish remark with swift and devastating action. He was one of the finest warriors the Cherusci had ever produced, and now with his vast experience of waging war with the Roman legions, he was a feared opponent of everyone who crossed his path.

Arminius was now entirely at ease. Vigorous discussions by warriors and chieftains alike swirled around him; many eventually sought out his point of view on a wide variety of matters. One or two of the more elderly members of the tribal council still expressed their doubts about the call to arms, seeking instead to convince their contemporaries that if they left the Romans alone, the Romans would leave the tribes alone—in peace.

But for every elder who preached appeasement, there were five others who supported Arminius and argued his case. Some were outspoken and vehement in their criticism of the weakness shown by the pacifists. Others were displaying open ridicule. In one particularly heated exchange, the elder of the two antagonists involved rose to his feet and stood over his opponent, shouting at and berating the reclining warrior, calling him a young upstart and a fool to boot, whose obvious lack of intelligence and maturity clouded his mind with foolish and impossible dreams of defeating the mighty Romans in battle.

The reclining warrior openly grinned at the old man, whose spittle and froth shot forth as the heat of his outburst intensified. Some near the exchange cast anxious glances at Arminius, trying to gauge how he would react to argument against his proposals. Arminius, however, was not even paying attention. Instead, he reclined against the resting mats and quietly gazed around the vibrant settlement. When his eyes fell upon Segestes a quick frown creased his brow, but Arminius had other things on his mind than the old man's platitudes and pacifist statements. His eyes fixed on the closed entrance through which Segestes' daughter had disappeared.

The continuous haranguing from the elder stopped suddenly in mid-sentence when the reclining warrior held his hand up, palm out toward the statesman. It was an unspoken order for the verbal onslaught to stop. In one fluid motion, the warrior leapt to his feet like a cat and threw himself in front of his old opponent. A hush fell on the gathering as the younger man's hand moved to the hilt of his sword while his eyes stared long and hard into the face of the old man. Perhaps he had gone too far, thought the elder, who drew back from the challenging figure looming before him. The warrior leaned forward until their faces were separated by no more than three inches. Beads of sweat formed on the wrinkled old brow. A muted tension of excitement filled the air as the possibility of sudden combat and bloodletting loomed.

The warrior bared his teeth and emitted a low growl. Just as suddenly he grinned and began chanting, "Eee-aaw . . . eee-aaw . . . eee-aaw." Then, louder and louder, "Eeeaaw, eee-aaw!" His imitation of a mule was not lost on the gathering as the majority, particularly the younger warrior chieftains, picked up the chant. It increased in volume and variety to include the sounds of chickens, dogs, and many other animals, each of which implied cowardice. The innuendo dug deeply into the council elder, who was now acutely embarrassed and angry. Without a word he stormed from the gathering, glaring at Segestes as he stomped away, shaking his head when he saw the chieftain look down to the ground, apparently to disown their association and friendship.

Although he had not joined in to humiliate the elder, Arminius was now openly laughing at this turn quick turn of events. As soon as he stood, the noisy catcalls began to fade. His right hand was held up high to ask for silence, and the command was observed almost instantaneously. In his left he held something tight against his thigh. "We are gathered under one moon, with one thought, as one people. We have come together to make a plan to rid ourselves of Roman rule, which holds our lands and lives in bondage. I do not like to be tied to a people who treat us like slaves, to be tried and imprisoned in our own homes and villages."

A murmur of agreement rippled through the throng. "I was captured by them, I grew stronger with them, I fought with them, but I never loved them," continued Arminius, his voice rising to overcome the effusive chatter. "They seek to dominate, to conquer, to extract fealty—and now, with this Varus, to enslave us, to turn us into dogs and mules!"

Arminius held his right hand up to silence the gathering. "I want no more of them! Join me, fight with me, let me lead you to victory!" He drew his sword and held the point high in the air. "These jackass Romans can be beaten! We must fight them on our ground, on our terms. Lead them into our traps and woods, fight them from the trees, hack them down from the darkness! Let us be their worst nightmares come true! If we do not do it soon, we will be conquered and occupied by these scum for all time. Live and fight now, with me, or live forever under the yoke of oppression! Hesitate, lose the warrior blood of your forefathers, and you will no longer be warriors—you will be mules, chickens, cats, and lowly dogs, and no more will you be a warrior of the Cherusci, of the Chatti, of the great Teuton tribes our fathers seeded in us." He stopped again and waited for the men around him to quiet down.

"My friends, my blood brothers. I will fight your fight whether you are with me or not. I will fight on my own, if necessary, but if our tribes come together as an effective force against the Romans, we can defeat them!" He paused, noticing for the first time that many of the villagers and warriors from the surrounding encampments had been drawn in by the sound of his voice echoing across the flickering campfires and the hills of Icker.

"I am yours. My life is yours, my dreams are yours. Join me, and let us bleed the hearts of the Romans until they lose stomach for this land. At the equinox, I will call you. I will call all the peoples, all the tribes, you, the warrior chiefs and your men, and we will lead Varus onto our swords, and our spears."

With that he extended his left hand. In it was a large chunk of raw meat. With a grunt, he tossed it high into the air and skewered it on the end of his sword. The raw flesh quivered on the end of the blade as its blood ran down the metal and tickled over the warrior's clenched hand. The crowd erupted with screams of approval.

"Fight with me and I promise you victory. And with victory, I promise you the plunder and booty the Romans have extracted from us and our peoples!" yelled Arminius. "I have my men who will follow me to the death." Arminius searched the sea of faces before him for his friend Wodenicus. Where was he? "With all of us together we will not be going to our deaths—it will be the Romans who will be going to their bloody deaths!" At this every warrior within earshot drew forth his long

broadsword and brandished it in the air, calling and shouting, voicing their support and enthusiasm for the call to arms.

Arminius was working the gathering when Dagan the Hunter entered Icker. The rest of his column remained behind at one of the outlying encampments. Dagan rode ahead to alert the elders of his arrival and spend the night with Thusnelda. Arminius was about to pull the meat off his sword that he had stabbed from the air when he spotted the lone rider slowly approaching the outer circle. For a moment he thought it was Wodenicus. It was not his missing friend. Nor was it anyone he recognized.

Dagan drew up to the outer circle and quickly dismounted. He passed the reins of his horse to the same young boy who had tethered Arminius' white stallion and then moved to join the assembly. As the cocky stranger strode forth Arminius' eye spotted a glint of gold on Dagan's forearm. The stranger's other hand rested on the haft of his broadsword. Dagan stopped in front of Arminius and extended his right hand to take up his forearm in the customary form of greeting. And then he saw it: the familiar snake heads, the golden torque, the gift of friendship he had the smith create for his lifelong friend Wodenicus after leaving Haltern just months before—on this stranger's wrist!

Arminius' blood froze. He lifted Dagan's wrist and asked quietly, "How come you by this bracelet?"

Dagan smiled, thinking Arminius was praising him for its beauty. "I took it from a Roman mercenary who was on his own on the eastern ridge line." A few onlookers cheered the response.

The German chieftain's eyes burned brightly in response. "I have seen one exactly like this worn by a great friend of mine, and not many hours ago. It was I who gave it to him this very year before we left our winter quarters. There cannot be two like it. I ask you again, how did you come by it?"

Slowly, Dagan began to understand the import of Arminius' words and the lurking menace behind them. It was an accusation, an inquest. Arminius continued holding Dagan's right forearm. Not one used to being questioned before others, Dagan ripped his wrist out of Arminius' steel hold and moved his hand swiftly across the center of his body, holding it a short distance from the haft of his broadsword. His left hand had dropped to his belt directly under the haft, ready to hold the scabbard should he need to draw his weapon. The move was not lost on

Arminius, who stood without moving, his bright blue eyes fixed on Dagan's own.

"Has your tongue lost itself, or are you about to tell me you found the torque on the trail?"

"I make no pretence of how I came about this bracelet," replied Dagan, holding his wrist up to show the article to the encircled mass of chieftains and warriors. "As I already said, I took this from a Roman, a mercenary, who was on his way here to spy on our gathering. He was one of the accursed traitors to our tribe who joined and served the Roman pigs, and even fought against out own people during the early wars. He was a lone scout." Dagan paused to let the next three words sink in. "I killed him."

Dagan waved his arm in the air. "This gold is a trophy of war, and I do not regret nor seek justification for my actions!" He looked again at Arminius and added, "Do not ever accuse me of a misdeed. I killed a traitor. I took a prize. I answer to no man for my actions." Dagan stepped back a few paces and again placed his hand near the haft of his sword. It was a challenge.

Word of the confrontation spread quickly and soon reached those in camps immediately surrounding the central gathering. Like a flood, the men in the outlying areas poured into the central Icker encampment, where they saw Arminius and Dagan facing each other in the center of the large gathering. Many of the newcomers were members of Arminius' cavalry force. They quickly took in what was taking place and quietly, but swiftly, blended into the inner ring of the circle of elders.

Arminius continued staring intently at Dagan, barely able to contain the rage boiling within him. Wodenicus had been slain by this impetuous puppy of a warrior from Segestes' camp? It could not be so—except that it was. Almost as bad was the accusation that Wodenicus was a traitor. Dagan's statement implied that everyone who rode with Arminius, including Arminius himself, were traitors for having fought with the Romans. His decision made, he drew in a long breath and exhaled. How would what he was about to do influence his plans with the other tribal elders and chieftains? He was unsure, but Dagan would have to pay for the death of Wodenicus and his insults. And then he heard Segestes' words in his mind: "Yes, she is beautiful . . . and she is betrothed to Dagan the Hunter, of the Chatti tribe; they are to be wed in the fall . . ."

"Wodenicus was my greatest friend." Arminius spoke quietly, clearly, almost without visible emotion as he stared hard into Dagan's eyes. "Any man who calls him a traitor, and has slain him for that very reason, must now be prepared to join him in death. For you, Dagan the Hunter, are now no more than Dagan the Dog, a low-life who deserves to live not a moment longer. Prepare yourself, for I fight with no mercy, and no call of mercy will stay my hand. This day, you die."

With a swift movement—some would say faster than the eye could see—Arminius' long and heavy broadsword suddenly appeared in his grip, its point but a few inches from Dagan's throat. The surprised German gasped and stumbled backward with an oath, drawing his own sword and hacking downwards to meet Arminius' blade. The movement was wasted. Arminius slipped to the blind side of the sword as it cut through the air where he had stood a brief second before. His own blade cut back quickly, slicing through Dagan's hamstring in a deft move that drew a deep groan as Dagan sank to his knees, his sword raised to protect himself from the overhead blow he knew would follow. Arminius' sword found nothing but raised blade, but the mighty blow sent painful shock waves racing up Dagan's wrist and arm and the sword slipped from his nerveless fingers.

Sensing victory, Arminius pulled his sword back and around for a final sweeping death blow. Dagan, however, rolled sideways and backward, freeing as he did so his large double-headed axe, which had been secured across the back of his shoulders. With blood running down his leg and a pained grimace etched in his face, he stumbled to his feet to face Arminius. His axe was held across his body, ready to block any cutting movement or strike if an opportunity presented. Arminius stepped to one side to attack from another angle when he saw fresh smears of blood on the blade of Dagan's axe. Unable to contain any longer the anger roiling within, he emitted a shout of fury, raised his sword high above his head, and brought it down on Dagan's axe. Once . . . twice . . . a third time. Faltering a bit more with every strike, Dagan slowly hobbled backward until the fourth powerful swing of Arminius' broadsword swept the axe away from Dagan's grasp.

The encircling crowd held its collective breath as they watched in rapt awe the death-duel being played out in front of their eyes. Dagan was now defenseless, his chest heaving in search of air, his body tilted to one side in a half-crouch to favor his good leg. In an act of supreme bravery, Dagan slowly drew himself up to stand a little more erect, refusing to look away from his opponent or ask for mercy.

Segestes stood at the edge of the circle, his hands framing his face in horror. "Have mercy, Arminius! He is soon to be my son-in-law!"

"No longer," shot back Arminius angrily, who swept his broadsword in an upward-curving underhanded sweep. The broadsword was originally designed to hack and chop, its weight sufficient to cleave its way through the most hardened of shields and protective clothing, but its edges were blunted. Arminius' sword was of a similar design, but its edges had been honed to a razor's sharpness. The sword whistled through the air and cut sharply through Dagan's body, beginning at his waist. Continuing on its bloody journey, the blade swept on, opening his breastbone from sternum to throat, narrowly missing his jaw as it ripped free from Dagan's flesh and slipped past his head. Dagan was dead even before his insides spilled out of the gaping cavity and slopped onto the ground. The corpse collapsed to its knees, remained upright for a few seconds, and then slumped forward in a sticky pool of blood and gore.

Arminius had avenged his friend's senseless death, but he felt little as he gazed dispassionately at the prostrate body before him. As the heat of mortal combat slowly ebbed from his body, he raised his eyes and stared at the subdued mass of tribesmen gathered around the circle of elders. No one said a word or even moved. As the seconds ticked past he realized there would not be an adverse reaction to the death of Wodenicus' executioner. In fact, his display of honor and valor in slaying Dagan may have eliminated any lingering opposition to his plan.

Without a word, Arminius knelt by the corpse and pried away the gold torque from Dagan's wrist.

He held it aloft for all to see. "This man killed my greatest friend, and took this as a trophy for his deed. I have now repaid the debt to my departed friend, with Dagan's life as payment."

Arminius, however, had more on his mind than the gold bracelet. "I am not satisfied with so small a payment! Under our laws I have taken Dagan's life in legitimate combat, and now I have the right to take his horse, his lands, and all his possessions. I want none of these! Instead, I claim the right to take his woman, his wife-to-be. Segestes!" called out Arminius as he turned to face the white-faced chieftain, pointing his broadsword straight at his chest. "I claim the right. Your daughter will be mine, and I will wed her when I have defeated Varus and his accursed legions. Say it—proclaim the right, Segestes. I call on your agreement now. Let all gathered here under this moon hear your acceptance of my rights."

Segestes looked befuddled, unsure what to say as he lowered his gaze to Dagan's corpse. He held the form with his eyes for a full minute before locking his eyes on the sword pointing directly in his direction. The crowd silently awaited the outcome of this latest turn of events. Segestes turned his head and looked at the hut that held his beloved Thusnelda. To his astonishment, and almost as if on cue, the skins across the entrance parted to reveal the girl. How much had she heard? Did she know Dagan was dead?

Before she could speak Segestes made his decision. "I agree. My daughter is now your betrothed, Arminius, in accordance with our laws. If you defeat the Romans"—he emphasized the word "if"—you may wed my daughter."

When the words reached her ears Thusnelda's mouth fell open and she gasped in response. A flush of both fear and embarrassment engulfed her body, for she still did not fully comprehend what had taken place, only appreciating that somehow she had become the center of attention. She shot a look at Arminius, but when his blue eyes bore again into her own, she quickly drew back into the hut without speaking a word.

"I will wed Segestes' daughter, because I will defeat the Varus legions. I will defeat them because I have your support, the bravest warriors from the greatest tribes Germania has ever produced. With you, I can defeat the very devil himself. Who is with me, who is with Arminius?" he cried.

The response was again electrifying. A mass of voices, all excited at the prospect of war and battle, rose in a tumultuous roar of approval. Shields were beaten and trumpets blown in a noisy accompaniment to the cheers and shouts of support for Arminius' call to arms.

He had won the day. Now he had to win the battle. He held both his sword and hand aloft, beckoning the crowd once again to silence. "I must now make plans with your chiefs and elders, plans for our victory. For now, enjoy the food and wines. I will meet you all again when the time arrives for us to face down the Romans. I salute you all."

Arminius moved across the circle, ignoring Dagan's corpse as he walked toward the other chieftains and elders. Segestes remained to one side, where he murmured under his breath, "Every dog has his day, Arminius, but I promise you will have your comeuppance."

*   *   *

And so Arminius brought the tribes together during the summer of 9 AD. He would fight his battle in September on his ground, at a time of his choosing, and on his terms of engagement. It was not a victory he was seeking, but the annihilation of the men of the Seventeenth, Eighteenth and Nineteenth Legions of Rome.

PART II

Chapter Fourteen

9 AD: Aspirations and Judgments at Minden

Varus' summer camp at Minden was a hive of activity. Drusus had established the camp during the early years, when the Romans forged their way into and through the German heartlands. Traveling up the waters of the Weser, which flowed about 1,000 yards from the eastern edge of the lager, the Roman galleys cut their way upstream from the coastal regions of the northern sea and through the link ports leading up to the summer camp. Thereafter, they passed through the broad gap of the Wiehengebirge ridge into the upper reaches of the river that coursed its way through flat and unimpressive flooded meadowlands before merging into the steep valleys and gorges of the range of hills sitting astride it, passing through the towns of Hess Oldendorf, Hameln, and on to Hoxter. Here was the junction of the upper reaches of the east–west land route from the last of the forts on the River Lippe into eastern Germany and on to the Elbe some 120 miles distant.

Minden was also a key junction between the north–south course of the Weser and the northerly east–west land route, stretching from the

River Ems across the north German plain to the Weser, and again, on to eastern Germany and the Elbe. Minden was one of the most important link fortresses in Germany—as important to the Romans as the link fortresses of Xanten and Aliso, sited on either side of the junction of the Lippe and the broad sweep of the Rhine river.

A short distance north of the Wiehengebirge ridge proper, the summer camp was overshadowed by the ridge's lofty heights on either side of the Minden gap. Here the legions established small but well fortified lookout forts, with commanding views of the surrounding countryside for many miles in nearly every direction, save the wooded areas of the ridge. Even here, the Romans cut back into those forested areas to establish lines of sight protected by a series of impenetrable ramparts and staked ditches.

The summer camp was a desirable posting for the Roman occupation forces. Sited against the side of the Weser, the pioneers had cut into the nearside river banks, establishing small backwater areas where bathing and swimming could take place, safely removed from the dangerous currents swirling along the main concourse of the river. In the heat of a summer's day, the pools were nearly always full with officers, soldiers, and their attendant slaves.

It was now August, the religious month during which all Romans commemorated the elevation of Augustus to the rank of Caesar. It was usually the hottest and most uncomfortable of the summer months, humid and utterly unlike the hot but clearer airs of Rome.

It was almost time for the legions to move back to winter quarters at Haltern and Xanten (Vetera), a march they would undertake during the coming month. Meanwhile, they worked hard maintaining their foothold in the German tribal areas of the northern plains. These tasks included building roads between their various bases along the east–west line between the Weser and the Ems, mapping the features of the surrounding countryside, and sending out detachments and foraging parties to the various German villages as a show of authority and to collect taxes.

Varus often held court inside the summer camp, lording it over his domain, challenging the laws and decrees under which the German tribesmen and elders lived, and imposing his own Roman courts of justice in matters concerning the fate of various offenders and minor transgressors. His reputation as judge and jury was well known, and not many of those involved in the day-to-day petty disputes were pleased when their cases ended up before the Roman commander. Most of the local disputes were resolved by the various councils of village elders. Varus, however, saw himself as not only a representative of the mighty Augustus, but almost as a Caesar in his own right. As was the manner of every dictator, Varus tried to enhance his own status by exaggerating the importance of otherwise modest judicial proceedings. A man accused of stealing a flagon of wine, for example, was given a punishment befitting a rapist or murderer: inverted crucifixion. A village that had not paid sufficient taxes was ordered razed to the ground, its animals and grain seized, the men put to the sword, and the women and children imprisoned and hauled back to the summer camp as slaves.

Varus saw to it that semi-permanent detachments were posted in the outlying districts to maintain discipline and continue the oppression of the German tribes. Several small march lagers and hill forts were established within a 30-mile radius of Varus' thriving central camp on the Weser. Almost one-quarter of his army was deployed in these outposts at any given time—a large number considering that almost that many were also at work mapping and building roads across the length and breadth of the north German plain. Varus, however, was not overly concerned about this dispersal of force. He was confident in his omnipotence and belief that the German tribes posed no threat to his three mighty legions: the Seventeenth, Eighteenth and Nineteenth Legions of Rome.

His complacency would be his undoing.

*   *   *

The pioneer detachments strewn across the length and breadth of the north German plain, including the passes in and through the massive Wiehengebirge ridge line, were tasked with opening the main axis of advance Drusus had established between the Ems and Weser rivers two decades before. It was their responsibility to construct reinforced highways and repair and re-lay roads (Holzmoorwege) *over the boggy moorlands to the west. They were also ordered to reconnoiter and pave new routes through the key passes running from the northern reaches of the Teutoburger Wald into the highlands of the Wiehengebirge and Kalkriese Bergs.*

The work was a high priority in Varus' development plans for the region, and would serve to alleviate the pressure on the movement of essential stores and supplies up and down the main concourse of the German rivers, freeing barges and shipping for use elsewhere. The major undertaking of the first stage should have been the construction of a series of assault roads to support immediate operations. Varus' lackadaisical and complacent attitude, however, although challenged by his second-in-command, prevented the establishment of better lines of communication between the various outposts.

Manning these detachments naturally diminished the number of men Varus had available at the main camp at Minden. Marcus Aius had challenged the plan, to no avail. Varus believed his primary mission was the continued oppression of the German tribes by keeping up a direct and continuing presence in the main German settlement areas—with Roman soldiers on public view at all times.

It was normal practice for Romans to upgrade tactical routes to strategic main roads and highways, running near, but not necessarily along, earlier lines of march. Although building these roads was a long-term project, in the end they reduced the need for ongoing maintenance on the provisional tactical routes, and thus saved precious resources. But Varus would have none of this. Instead, he insisted that Germania would continue to be a subverted land, its people part of the greater Roman Empire; in due course it would become another Roman province. As far as Varus was concerned, building roads along direct lines of approach was far more important than working along tactical routes and lesser avenues of advance and withdrawal. There was no further need for such roads, believed Varus. It was time to begin the more lengthy process of building permanently established highways in preparation for the new Roman province of Germany.

*   *   *

Some modern engineers claim the amazing feats of engineering achieved by the Romans during the establishment of their Empire provided a yardstick thereafter for every nation. Roman roads and highways were a prime example of their engineering expertise. In the boggy moorlands of the north German plains, their ability to construct and maintain sound and reliable crossings was both vital and effective.

For example, Romans usually utilized a workforce of one thousand men, each working ten-hour days, to construct a causeway or road across approximately fifty miles of moorlands. The length of time it took to construct the road varied (see below). These highways, many originally established by Drusus, or refurbished using existing *Holtzmoorwege*, were built to the following specifications:

A. A cleared width of 8 to 9 yards with all trees and scrub cut at ground level;
B. A leveled carriageway of 2.6 yards marked by timber curbs;
C. Minimal or non-existent drainage;
D. A "corduroy" (log) surface over swamps.

Achieving such unparalleled engineering feats took time, and the time it took varied depending upon the type of terrain over which the roads were laid:

Grassland: 40 man-hours per 100 yards
Forest: 600 man-hours per 100 yards
Heathland: 450 man-hours per 100 yards
Swamp/Moor: 625 man-hours per 100 yards

In order to help interpret and fully comprehend the above figures, let's consider what it would have taken to construct a road from Ems to Weser, a distance of about 75 miles. Such a project would have consumed 570,000 man-hours, a work party of 1,100 men, and taken 70 days. Thus, if the tasks given the pioneer detachments had been no more than to repair and maintain the key routes within a 30-mile radius of the summer camp, it would not have been necessary to commit such large forces to man the outlying guard detachments and pioneering contingents deployed as decreed by Varus. Occupation and oppression, according to Varus, had to be seen by the locals as effective. Few commanders questioned whether occupation and security of the ground was of paramount military importance.

Varus, however, simply did not believe the Germans could or would combine to become an effective threat against his legions. Indeed, the ability of the Germans to respond to a central authority and pool their strength seems never to have occurred to him. During his occupancy of the summer camp, Varus stretched his legions to the breaking point without ever realizing they were in danger.

*   *   *

As each day passed, Marcus Aius became more despondent with the realization that on each passing day in the summer camp, his position as second-in-command became less secure and less effective. Varus had aspirations for an eastward advance. He intended to erect a bridge directly adjacent to the eastern exit of the lager and establish a new crossing of the Weser. He read often about the great Julius Caesar and his early forays and battles with the German tribes who had invaded Gaul in 55 BC. The event that specifically sparked Varus' interest was Caesar's counterattack across the Rhine to repel the German invaders, a momentous event only a few months before Caesar initiated his first invasion of Britain. The bridging of the Rhine was thus an important tactical exercise that provided valuable experience to Caesar's engineers and pioneer detachments before they would be forced to perform similar logistical feats during their invasion of Britain and advances through Kent and across the Medway and Thames rivers.

Caesar left an extensive account of his activities during the Gallic Wars:

> *Such, then, were my reasons for crossing the Rhine; but to do so in boats appeared too risky and was certainly below the dignity of a Roman general. To build a bridge would be a difficult operation because of the river's width, depth and swift current. Nevertheless I came to the conclusion that the difficulty must be overcome or the whole idea of crossing abandoned. Construction was therefore begun on the following plan. Two piles, eighteen inches thick, slightly pointed at the lower ends, and varying in length according to the river's depth, were fastened together two feet apart to form a truss. They were then lowered into the water from rafts and driven firmly into the river bed with piledrivers.*
>
> *They were not set in the usual vertical position but inclining in the direction of the current. Opposite to them, and forty feet downstream, a similar truss was fixed but this time leaning against the stream. The trusses were joined by a transom two feet wide, the ends of which fitted exactly into the spaces between the heads of the*

four piles. The two trusses were kept apart by iron 'dogs', which secured each pile to the end of the transom; and added strength was given by diagonal ties running from one pile to its opposite number on the same side.

In this way the rigidity of the whole structure naturally increased in proportion to the current's force; additional piles were driven in obliquely on the downstream side to form a buttress supporting each truss and helping to take the weight of the water. A series of these trusses and transoms were connected by timbers laid at right angles so that if the natives attempted to destroy it by floating down tree trunks or boats, these fenders would lessen the shock and prevent damage to the bridge.[1]

Ten days after the collection of timber for the bridge began, the work was completed and Caesar's army crossed without significant incident. The Germans, awed by this seemingly unstoppable force as it poured into Germania across an amazing feat of engineering, withdrew. Caesar spent no more than eighteen days beyond the Rhine before recrossing into Gaul. He destroyed the bridge behind him. Despite the fact that this bridge had been constructed in a remarkably short period of time, the delay of ten days might have been unacceptable in the cut and thrust of a full-bloodied battle, when the establishment of a military bridgehead would have been essential.

The Romans reduced this waiting time, when necessary, by the building of pontoon bridges, which occured during Caesar's incursions into Britain and the crossing of the Medway and Thames. His engineer and pioneer detachments may have used similar bridging techniques to quickly seize land on the other side of the crossings, in order to establish safe and secure bridgeheads. According to Roman historian Vegetius, the crossings carried out by Caesar were swift and speedy tactical maneuvers that triggered both surprise and alarm in the withdrawing British enemy:

---

[1] Much of today's modern warfare and engineering works in pontoon bridging derived from Caesar's amazing feats of engineering and tactical military skills honed during this period.

Navigable rivers are passed . . . in an emergency by fastening
together a number of empty casks and covering them with boards.
The cavalry, throwing off their accoutrements, make small floats of
dry reeds or rushes on which they lay their arms and cuirasses to
preserve them from being wet. . . . But the most commodious
invention is that of the small boats hollowed out of one log and very
light, both by their make and the quality of the wood. The army
always had a number of these boats upon carriages, together with a
sufficient quantity of planks and iron nails. Thus, with the help of
cables to lash the boats together, a bridge is instantly constructed,
which for the time has the solidity and stability of stone. . .

Now, more than half a century later in 9 AD, Varus was laying his
own plans to create a greater Germanian province for the mighty Roman
Empire under his personal rule. He enjoyed his position of power, which
included his weekly "courts of justice," as he laughingly called them.
Disciplinary problems within the legions were at this time relatively
rare—especially when compared to the uprisings and mutinies of earlier
times, which had been put down with swift and merciless punishment. As
a result, the vast majority of judicial matters heard by Varus (who
enjoyed applying the full weight of his office) concerned only minor
matters of local interest. It was while one of these hearings was in session
that Arminius returned from the war conference of the German tribes at
Icker.

*   *   *

Charged with stealing chickens from his neighbor, the defendant
knelt before Varus' elevated couch as the Consul looked out across the
sea of faces gathered to witness the hearing. A member of the Roman
judiciary, a nobleman selected from one of the elite families of Rome to
accompany Varus in his occupation of Germany, recited the man's
offences and related the gathered testimony.
The plaintiff had returned to his homestead from a foraging
expedition in the forest to find four or five of his chickens missing.
Initially, he thought a fox was the culprit, but the absence of either
feathers or blood convinced him otherwise. As the man crossed the
meadow to the other side of the valley, he drew near his neighbor's hut
and small vegetable garden. He was about to change direction and

continue up the length of the woods alongside the meadow, when he noticed his neighbor carrying two dead chickens, their necks obviously broken. Both birds bore a striking resemblance to the black and red chickens that had gone missing from the plaintiff's coop, and he had purposefully moved forward to challenge the accused, and demand to know where he had come upon the two birds. Knives were drawn and voices heated by the time a small detachment of Romans came upon the scene. When his inquiry was not satisfactorily answered, the commander arrested both men so that the case could be heard and judged at the weekly judiciary hearings in the lager at Minden.

Varus sat easily on his lounging couch, his eyes hooded as he gazed lazily at the managed performance unfolding before him. The villager accused of stealing the chickens from his neighbor was kneeling before him, his arms spread out as if in supplication. The prosecutor continued reading the charges committed by the man, outlining the case for the benefit of the gathered throng of spectators who waited with barely-concealed excitement for the result of the trial.

The neighbor who had lost his chickens was standing to one side, his head bowed as he sought to maintain a low profile and avoid the piercing eyes of the Consul. Varus appeared nearly asleep as he half-listened to the droning tone of the prosecutor, the heat of the day lingering into the breathless late afternoon air inside the canopied area of the entrance to the Praetorium. Everyone assembled was fully aware of how quickly the Consul could change his manner, and they were just as aware of how cruel and vicious he could be when it pleased him.

The prosecutor was still droning on when Varus suddenly appeared to waken. "Enough! Enough! By the gods, I have had enough of this sorry tale! This man before me, what has he to say to his accusers? Let him speak to me." With that, Varus raised a finger to one of the nearby Centurions and pointed to the prostrate villager. The Centurion swiftly stepped across to the accused and roughly shoved him in the side with his sandaled foot, demanding his attention. The German raised his head and looked up at the Centurion. Following the officer's nod, the frightened man slowly turned his gaze up to meet Varus'.

"Ask him what he has to say in his defense," barked Varus to his interpreter. "Why was he supposedly stealing this man's property! That is," Varus paused for a moment and turned his gaze in a different direction before adding, "if what this other man says is true."

Although the German who owned the stolen chickens believed his case was sound, he cringed when Varus settled his cold gaze upon him. He had not fully understood what the Consul had said, but the menace in his tone of voice was obvious in any language, and it unnerved him. Why would the Consul direct such a tone at him and not at his neighbor? Sweat broke out on his brow as he suddenly realized his position was as unsafe as his neighbor's.

"Come on, hurry," said Varus to his interpreter. "I have spent long enough listening to this boring tale. What says the man? And tell him to be quick; I tire." He brought a goblet of cooled wine to his lips from a gold and silver tray at his side.

The interpreter hastily questioned the frightened villager. It soon became abundantly clear to all assembled, including Varus, there was more to this story than just stolen chickens. "My lord," said the interpreter, finally turning to face Varus, "the man admits to taking the chickens, but only as revenge for a crime against his family by his neighbor. He states his neighbor was responsible for his wife leaving him a few days ago, after she disclosed their neighbor had forced his way with her—ah, he raped her, sire. She was distressed and ashamed, and vanished the following morning, at which point the accused went to confront the other man but found him gone as well. In the heat of the moment, sire, he claims he chased the chickens from the coop, killing two or three later as they ran about in the woods. According to him, sire, his neighbor's actions constitute the crime to be answered, and his actions were no more than a minor form of retribution."

Varus thought for a moment before asking quietly, "Then why was he carrying the dead chickens back to the hut? Was he intending to convert the heat of the moment into the heat of his cooking pot?" Varus laughed aloud at his double entendre and waited for the assembly to do likewise. Regrettably for the two co-defendants, the joke produced only muted and stifled chuckles instead of the open and boisterous laughter he had expected.

Varus furrowed his brow and held his tongue, a sure sign of barely controlled anger. Gesturing to the Centurion, he beckoned the officer to bring the accuser before him. The soldier grabbed the villager by the elbow and shoved him roughly forward to face the Consul. By this time the man was quivering with fear, for the lies told by his neighbor had changed the entire tenor of the proceedings. He stood meekly, head bowed, trembling, stomach churning, as a flood of nausea rose from his gut and fear gripped his mind. Beads of sweat broke out on his brow. He waited for the opportunity to speak in his own defense. The opportunity never came.

Varus looked at the Centurion and pointed down to the ground in front of him to indicate the villager should join his fellow German face down in front of him. The Centurion grabbed the man by the shoulders and forced him to his knees before pushing him forward, banging his head on the floor.

Varus gently sipped from his goblet of wine, enjoying the hushed expectancy of the assembly as the onlookers awaited his next turn of mood. The silence was deafening, and Varus milked it for another full minute. His earlier attempt at humor had failed to endear him to the gathered throng, and so he decided the only other course of action was to give them something more than they bargained for—a swift and exacting punishment to fit the crimes presented him. Although neither case had been proved or disproved, the crowd was itching for swift Roman justice. The opportunity to show the omnipotence and authority of Rome was not to be missed.

"I have decided," he began, pausing for the desired effect. The crowd held its collective breath. "The man who stole the chickens is obviously a thief. The patrol reported the chickens were dead and found in the man's possession, and they were obviously not his property. He is found guilty, and will suffer the appropriate punishment for thieves. He is to be crucified. His post will be erected up by the western lookout position on the ridge, so all can see his demise." The interpreter repeated the ruling in a hushed tone to ensure all would understand the Consul's decision.

Varus continued, "As for this other low creature, the taking of another man's woman—rape within a parent community—is not to be tolerated. It causes unrest and confrontation. There appears to be no reason why his case is not also found guilty, but his crime is more despicable than that of the thief. He shall be tarred and fired in animal skins, as is our punishment for such crimes."

Even before the interpreter finished, the villagers had jumped to their feet to weep and protest the unexpected outcome of the trial. Varus rose, a sure sign the hearing had run its course, when one of the accused raised his head and began chattering loudly toward him. Varus paused.

Something about the look in the man's eye caught his attention even more than the sharp guttural tones of his language. Turning to the interpreter, he asked him to translate.

Before he could do so, the Centurion standing next to the ranting villager stifled the outburst with a swift blow to the head with the flat of his sword, felling the tribesman, who sat on the floor and rubbed his head, stunned by the sudden blow.

"Sire," began the interpreter, "he says that if you spare him he will tell you all he knows of an uprising by the tribes, planned to take place at the end of the summer. He says he has much information about the leaders of this rebellion, and what form the uprising will take. He says there are many thousands of tribesmen coming together to form an alliance to fight against us. He pleads for his life in exchange for this information."

Varus chuckled softly. "Any man who nears his own death will clutch at any straw to live. He will search his soul for any way to stay alive, to remain on this earth, even if it means inventing amazing and incredulous inventions." Varus yawned as if bored. "The German tribes are entirely subjugated. Our forts and patrols report all is quiet, and neither I nor my commanders have received even an inkling of an insurrection. What say you, Marcus Aius?" Varus turned to face his second in command, who had been standing off to one side observing the proceedings.

Marcus replied, "You are entirely correct, sire, although I am curious whether this man really believes what he is saying, Lord. I request a few minutes to conduct an interrogation of him concerning his statements."

"No, Marcus Aius! Absolutely not. I want no more of this. It has dragged on far too long for such a trivial matter. On the morrow, I want these two to go to the posts as an example to others. I do not believe one word of his plea—the rantings and ravings of a condemned man. If a few Germans attempt anything foolish, I am confident you can put it down easily and quickly, Marcus Aius, though I doubt the tribes have any further stomach for such enterprise. Let us close this sorry case. I want no more of it. The accused will meet their gods tomorrow. Take them away!."

With that, Varus exited the front chambers of the Praetorium. The sobbing and moans of the two villagers soared above the chattering conversations of the assembled throng as the Centurion and a small party of legionaries dragged the men away from the forum to the bloody fate awaiting them.

The outcome of this latest judicial proceeding quickly traveled throughout the confines of the lager at the summer camp. The cruel fate dealt by Varus generated debate deep into the night. The sun slowly settled in the west, and the evening shadows drew in as the lager and its occupants prepared to bed down for the night. Outside in the quiet darkness the trumpets sounded for the first watch of the night, and the orderly officers "stood to" to carry out their late rounds of inspection.

Footsteps sounded outside the western guardhouse, and a red light glimmered at the window. The two officers inside moved out together to meet the duty Centurion, who stood outside holding high a flaring torch. The clashing Roman salute of fists to breastplates was exchanged, and the three officers set out on a tour of the darkened fort, moving from sentry post to sentry post along the rampart walk, from guardroom to guardroom, exchanging quietly as they went the password of the day. Finally, the trio reached a small lighted room at the rear of the Praetorium, where the pay chests and gathered taxes were kept, as were the standards of the three legions. A separate contingent of the guard force was on duty here, and between rounds the duty Centurion sat with his sword drawn and laid on the table before him throughout the night.

Across from the main building, the two prisoners lay curled in their cells, cold and afraid, waiting for the night hours to pass into morning, when they would be taken out to meet an agonizing death at the hands of their Roman captors.

Chapter Fifteen

9 AD: Summer Camp

The summer sun rose over the eastern sky and the lager guard force was preparing to change the overnight picket duties. With a stretching of tired limbs and much yawning, soldiers hurried to the washrooms and toilets to prepare for the day ahead. As campfires and furnaces were stoked and reheated, the fortress slowly came to life as men and women went about their duties, heating water for the officers' tents and unit commanders' quarters, and preparing bread and hot gruel for breakfast over open fires. Cauldrons simmered and wisps of steam hovered on the chilly early morning air.

The day started with the trumpets sounding reveille from the ramparts and ended with the late rounds of the overnight guard force, which involved a succession of complicated parades and fatigues, while patrols deployed and others returned to the lager. After the start of the day, the cavalry stable stewards set to their early morning tasks, and the arms drills and reports made for a hive of activity, as if a bee's nest had been stirred.

Breakfast was under way in the officers' mess, with the quartermaster, the Greek chief surgeon, and a full complement of ranking Centurions gathered for their victuals. The senior officers always came to the mess a little later, gathering in a separate forum of the mess to partake of the morning meal and discuss the plans and affairs of the day. The assembly was normally a boisterous and good-natured meeting of the senior commanders, during which they debated the issues at hand in the day-to-day affairs of the legions before Marcus formally reported the results to Varus later in the morning.

Varus always slept late and was irritable and belligerent if aroused early. As a result, Marcus Aius usually delayed their morning meetings as long as he could. Let a sleeping dog lie, he thought wryly, as he held a discussion with one of his subordinates. However, on this morning the conversation was muted and restrained. The Legionaries were used to witnessing punishments within their own ranks when warranted, and against conquered opposition when their bloodlust was high. But they were fighting men, and thus had little or no interest in inflicting unnecessarily severe punishment upon villagers. The result of the judicial hearing of the previous day had spread like wildfire throughout the lager, and neither officers nor their men were impressed by the judgments Varus had meted out to the two men. An eye for an eye was accepted practice, but cruel oppression for minor offenses only made their job in the German hinterlands more difficult.

More unsettling were the rumors of a possible insurrection within the tribes of the north German plains, and that the legions might have to battle the combined tribes. But it was all rumor, and gossip of every type was common in a legion's camp. Nothing had occurred during the occupation of the summer camp to indicate any particular area of concern in the surrounding tribes. Yet the rumor lingered as strong as the pungent smoke from the fires of breakfast. The impending executions of the two villagers only served to exacerbate the tense atmosphere now hanging like a dark cloud over Minden.

When one of the legion commanders brought up the subject of an insurrection, Marcus waved away the issue with an outstretched hand and turned the discussion toward the topic of the morning: a proposal for a series of patrols planned to explore the possibility of extending Roman control over and beyond the eastern reaches of the Weser—and ultimately to the Elbe, where Drusus had overstretched himself twenty years earlier. Also discussed was the possibility of raising a bridge across the Weser. It would be a massive undertaking, and the engineers were hesitant to undertake it. The current in this area was particularly vicious, which would make the effort difficult, time-consuming, and dangerous. There were also early, though admittedly sketchy, reports that the large flotilla of galleys bringing food, wine, and other stores to the lager via the north German coast had been hit by the severe summer storm several days earlier. A large number of boats had sunk without trace, some carrying barter and tithes, including a special shipment of bullion collected from the legions operating in the north German coastal areas.

The conversation had drifted back to the pending executions when the curtains were thrown aside at the forum entrance and Varus swept into the room, wide awake, smiling, and looking as fresh as if he had come from the heated baths on the Weser side of the lager. His sudden entrance startled everyone, including Marcus, who had never seen Varus up and about so early. He quickly stood to greet his commander, as did the other officers.

"Let's get on with it, Marcus Aius. I want the executions to proceed as soon as the morning guard watches have been posted," began Varus. "I think the sooner the local peasants are reminded of our standards of behavior and justice in Germany, the better life will be for everyone. These two peasants have tested my patience; they shall test it no more." Varus had overheard some of their conversation. He continued. "After the loss of our galley fleet and my favorite fine wines and finest sweetmeats, I am feeling extremely annoyed with life as it is here. These irritating peasants and their low-life problems and crimes make me ill."

With that, he sat down on one of the unoccupied low couches, reached for a drink and some breakfast, and broke into a story. "I recall how one of the great leaders of Rome became irritated by a local in . . ."

August, 1993: Return to Germany

I returned to Germany in August of 1993. My return had me traveling to Berlin to take up my next appointment, working as the Berlin Medical Group Practice Administrative Officer and Headquarters Medical Staff Officer. I would be working out of the British Military Hospital at

Spandau, where Rudolf Hess had spent some time just a few years earlier. I was now a Major and remember well the sense of anticipation I had about my new responsibilities as I drove from Hamburg up the autobahn to Berlin. The August heat wave was well advanced, and the temperature during that long drive reached 105 degrees, something rarely seen this far north in Germany. Although I was anxious to get into my new post and start work, I had been given a week to settle down into my new surroundings, so I decided to spend the weekend renewing my interest in Kalkriese and Osnabrück.

Wolfgang had earlier sent me an invitation to attend the first "Open Day" at Kalkriese (*Tag der Offenen Tür*). Regrettably, my time had been taken up with my move to Berlin and unpacking in my new quarters. However, having heard from him there had been many thousands in attendance at the open weekend, my interests were so aroused I determined to make the long haul down to Osnabrück. I had waited years to take up the subject of the silver bullion from the Weser north of Minden, and decided it was time to visit that site during my weekend outing.

I left early on a Friday to avoid the unholy build-up of traffic that accumulates on the Berlin–Hannover autobahn at the end of each week. I arrived in Osnabrück that afternoon and spent some time making the rounds to visit old friends, both in town and later that day, in Kalkriese. Several longstanding farmer friends offered to put me up for a few days, and certainly it was pleasant to be back among people who accepted me as one of their own. By Saturday, I was experiencing a distinct sense of déjà vu, having visited every find site in the local area. These included the new sites revealed by Klaus and Gisela during the months since my last visit in March. However, something was still nagging at my mind, something I had put off for far too long: what, if anything, had happened to my proposed "port" area on the Weser, north of Minden?

I drove back early Sunday morning, but decided to take a route past the site where the silver bullion had been recovered so many years ago. I had not been in direct contact with Dr. Cosack for some time, and was not exactly sure what had transpired since I had left to go back to the UK in early 1991. On Sunday, I made my farewells, expressed my gratitude for the hospitality, and traveled along the road from Kalkriese to Minden, through Venne, and on to Schwagstorf, which was becoming such an important and key point in the quest for the lost legions. From there I drove due east, directly on to Minden, along the northern flank of the Wiehengebirge ridge. As I approached Minden, I turned north up the Weser and toward the area of the port. I turned into the track running down into the farmhouse alongside the still waters of the open-sided quadrangle.

Nothing had changed in the two and one-half years I had been away. I drove down into the farmyard and met the owner, who remembered me from my previous visits. We spent some time discussing my interest and the possibility this had been a small Roman port. To my relief, he did not voice any objection when I asked whether I could return and look over the surrounding fields. When I mentioned the possibility of recovering artifacts from the water-filled quadrangle, the farmer offered a most important snippet of information—without being aware of the ramifications of his statement. As I would later discover, his observation would lead me to a final and most amazing outcome in my search for the truth surrounding the recovery of the Roman silver bullion from the mighty Weser.

I stood at the edge of the river bank surrounding the quadrangle of blue-grey water, my mind full of thoughts and pictures: of galleys being unloaded of stores and cases of wines, others being loaded with boxes and chests of treasures, some of which had lain on the very bed of the river not thirty yards from where I stood, some a mere three yards down, lost so many hundreds of years before. I looked up across the broad expanse of water to the east of my position which ultimately joined up with the waters of the main course of the Weser. A large dredger was operating some way out, clearing up the riverbed. As I later learned, the area produced large commercial amounts of stone ballast for use in various road-building projects in northern Germany. I knew I had to return to this site to carry out a full investigation, and hoped I would be able to do so in the near future. What I did not know then, however, was that all of my attention would be again drawn to Kalkriese with a series of mind-blowing discoveries. More hidden secrets were about to be revealed, and the ghost of Varus was about to raise its head yet again.

As I drove back to Berlin, I pondered Varus' movements during 9AD, recalling the events of that momentous year as described by Tacitus and Cassius Dio. Were their accounts accurate? There are two schools of thought about these writers. Some historians claim Tacitus, who wrote about one century after the Varus battle, was something of a romantic.

His version of events of Roman affairs, they claimed, was written so as to be acceptable to Roman aspirations and self-esteem. Because Cassius Dio wrote some two hundred years after the events, he was more removed and his version more solidly grounded in actual historical truth. The other historical school believes the reverse is true: that Cassius Dio's personal interpretation of historical events embellished the record, and that Tacitus was the master of his art in factually recording the history of Roman affairs.

Of course, it is difficult to know at this late date whose accounts are the most accurate. However, based upon my understanding of the terrain, Roman army organization, and the archaeological record, I find Cassius Dio's descriptions of the battles Arminius fought against the Romans, both during Varus' Consulship and later against Germanicus, vividly realistic. Suffice it to say that both writers are invaluable sources for the events of 9 AD.

As I drew near Berlin, a particular passage from Tacitus regarding the fighting between Arminius and Germanicus in 16 AD scrolled through my mind:

> When Germanicus crossed the Weser, a deserter gave him information. Arminius had chosen his battleground. The Germans had been marched to a level area called Idistaviso, which curves irregularly between the Weser and the hills; at one point an outward bend of the river gives it breadth, at another it is narrowed by projecting high ground. Behind rose the forest, with lofty branches, but clear ground between the tree trunks. The Germans occupied the plain and the outskirts of the forest. The Cherusci alone occupied the heights, waiting to charge down and across when the battle started . . .

Something nagged at me as I drove eastward up the autobahn. It took some time to sort out the thoughts revolving in my mind and bring them into line. The pieces came together slowly rather than as a flash of inspiration, and at the center of the puzzle were Arminius and the battle he had fought at Idistaviso against Germanicus in 16 AD. I was already aware (and have heretofore discussed) Roman movement across the north German plain from the Ems to the Weser. A more southerly route ran directly to Minden through Kalkriese and Schwagstorf, while the more northerly road ran across to the Weser and finished at an unknown point on the river north of Minden and across the other side *to a level area called Idistaviso, which curves irregularly between the Weser and the hills; at one point an outward bend of the river gives it breadth.* Another battlefield I intended to seek out in the years to come.

Arminius' Return from Icker

Arminius drew up at the highest point of the ridge line, near the farthest point of the western end of the Wiehengebirge about one-half mile short of the Roman tower overlooking the Weser. As he looked at the tower, his mind drifted back to his painful ride from Icker. His journey had taken him back along the ridgeline to recover the body of Wodenicus, which he found at the base of the tree where he had met his death at the hand of Dagan.

Arminius and his riders had slowly gathered about the tree, taking in the scene of Wodenicus' bloody death. Arminius climbed down from his steed and knelt quietly by the corpse, gazing down at his dead friend for several minutes. Only the gentle snorting from the anxious horses and the creaking of saddles and girths, as the animals altered their stance to take the weight of their riders, broke the silence of the moment.

Arminius lifted his head. Anger burned in his eyes. "Build a pyre. We shall send him on his way. Do it quickly, make it good wood and make it plentiful. I want the smoke to be seen for miles around, so that all who see it shall ask who merits such a large plume of smoke to carry his spirit up and onto the winds. And when it is done, I swear Wodenicus' talisman"—Arminius held up his wrist to show the circle of riders the golden torque bracelet on his arm—"will stay with me until all the accursed Romans and their followers are driven from our lands forever." Arminius stood and exhaled loudly. "Only then will I take it up into a high place and let it rejoin Wodenicus on his travels on the wind."

Arminius' band watched for some time as the flames of Wodenicus' pyre licked the wood and sent him on his journey. They mounted and rode from the clearing as billowing clouds of thick smoke surged upward in huge roaring clouds of fire and fumes. They walked their horses slowly in the direction of the eastern edge of the ridge toward the near side of the Weser. The trail veered northward along the very edge of the escarpment, where the broad expanse of the flatlands leading east into the fields verging onto the Weser and Varus' summer camp revealed themselves.

Arminius' wandering thoughts were jarred into the present when the rider ahead of him reined in his horse with a curse and pointed across the plain to the summer camp. Arminius followed his gaze and after a few seconds swore under his breath. Two large wooden crosses were silhouetted against the landscape of the cleared area around the lager as the sun's rays tipped over the edge of the ridge behind them. Even at a distance, the figures mounted and spread-eagled upon them could be seen. One was clearly human, but the other was more a misshapen mass attached to the beams. The men spurred their horses closer to the execution site.

"By all that is holy!" spat Arminius through clenched teeth. "What manner of a beast plays with men's lives this morning? I doubt those poor bastards are Roman. The day of atonement is approaching, but it cannot come soon enough for me. Our brothers, our countrymen, our peoples, are strung up like pigs on a spit after the hunt. I am not sure I can wait for the right time when these Romans leave their summer camp and the safety of the lager, when we can cut out their hearts, cut out their entrails, cut out their livers, and cut out their very tongues."

He paused a moment, and then continued. "Perhaps we should not cut out their tongues, just sew up their mouths, so they can scream to their heart's delight, but not so loud as to disturb me. I want to rid us of this plague, and may the spirits give me the patience until the time is right! Varus is to pay for his godlessness, and all his men will pay for his sins against our peoples. I tell you now, my friends, they will pay most dearly for their cruelties; for ours, our cruelties, will be a source of constant fear to their legionaries when we take our payment by wiping out Varus' legions from the face of this earth."

The group of riders reined in their mounts. Arminius continued his meandering discourse. "They will suffer mightily, I promise you this! But if I should fail in my promise to rid our lands of the Roman once and forever, then let me also slip away from this world with an unmarked grave—perhaps near Wodenicus, for he and I spilled our blood for each other, shared our love for our lands and our country, and sang the same songs through many years of battle and bloody campaigns. You and I are friends and comrades, but he was my blood brother. I will take out payment in full for his death, but it will be Roman blood and flesh that will foot the bill, not misguided German foolhardiness."

As he brooded over the scene, a plume of smoke erupted from one of the crosses. A fire had been lit at the base of the cross. The mass attached to the wooden structure immediately began a macabre dance as the flames licked and curled their way up the wood toward the writhing figure.

* * *

Varus, together with Marcus Aius and many of his commanders, watched as the condemned were mounted on the rough wooden crosses. The chicken thief was cross-hatched and nailed firmly into place. Unrequited screams of agony left his gaping mouth as the iron spikes tore into his wrists and ankles. Repulsed, Marcus Aius slowly edged away until he was standing alone, several yards removed from his fellow officers.

The second villager suffered an even crueler fate. Bound and spread-eagled on a wide wooden bench, he screamed with all the energy he could muster as hot pitch was poured onto his naked body. As he was sobbing great gasps of pain, he was wrapped in the skin of an ass. The animal's head, recently severed and still dripping blood, was firmly set over his own. With a nod from Varus, the executioners impaled the man on the wooden cross in the same manner as his neighbor, and raised the cross toward the heavens.

The man accused of rape was being afforded the punishment befitting that of a murderer or serious criminal. His moans and cries were interspersed with those of his contemporary, who languished on the other cross just a few yards away. When his eyes flickered open and saw the rolls of bracken and kindling being piled against the base of his cross, he screamed anew and pleaded once again for his life. The flames soared forth and quickly ignited the cooling pitch that had adhered itself to the man's skin. Within a few seconds he burst into a fireball, the excruciating heat tearing into his senses. His flesh and bones continued to jig, crackle, and spasm long after life had left the man.

Marcus Aius narrowed his eyes as the pungent scent of burning flesh filled his nostrils. He turned away as the smoke rolled in thick black billows toward the heavens crowning the Wiehengebirge ridge. As he did so, he noticed another plume of smoke rising from the highest point of the ridgeline, perhaps a mile due west of the outpost. The smoke spread out about the high ground, twisting itself into a long spear- like shape above the distant tree line. What was its source? Was this a sign from the gods? Did it portend something ominous for the Seventeenth, Eighteenth and Nineteenth Legions?

A chill gripped him and ran up his spine. The Tribune shivered and clutched his red cloak more tightly about him.

*   *   *

A quarter hour after the twin crucifixions, Arminius and his men rode slowly into the outer reaches of the lager. Small clouds of dust puffed out from the hooves as their steeds walked up the trail leading to the fort. The riders topped a small rise and stopped a short distance from the death site. One of the crosses had collapsed in ash and twisted flesh. Other than the grinning teeth of the villager, there was little to identify the corpse as human. On the upright cross hung the other victim, cruelly fixed, dripping blood, and moaning in misery.

Arminius stared intently at the scene before him. One man was already dead; the other was alive but facing a long and lingering death. Only a handful of guards remained to secure the execution site. It was exactly as he thought: the men were German villagers. With his anger barely contained, Arminius gently coaxed his horse toward a series of open spear stands holding a number of frameae throwing spears and javelins. The weapons were there for throwing practice, which the men carried out as part of their daily routine training drills. The warrior reached down and extracted one of the long lances, turned his horse about, and rode in front of the lone upright cross. When they saw what was happening, the Centurion and several soldiers moved quickly to intervene, but the German cavalrymen quickly wheeled their mounts about and cut them off.

Arminius paid them no heed. Instead, he stared long and hard at the transfixed figure, who understood what was transpiring and nodded his fevered head several times. With a muttered oath that each of the legionary guards heard but none understood, Arminius drew his arm back and launched the javelin into the chest of the hanging body. The man's eyes opened in shock at the sudden pain, but no sound escaped his *lips. His eyes focused one last time, and in their final moment of clarity recognized the winged helmet and face of Arminius. With his last breath he muttered, "Thank you, brother."*

Turning his horse away from the crucified figure, Arminius walked toward the gate of the fort. His riders followed. The Centurion and his men stood behind them, their mouths open in shock at the quick turn of events.

Just before Arminius entered the gates of the lager, he turned into the distance toward the high ridge line. Just as Marcus Aius had a few minutes earlier, so too did Arminius notice the long thin cloud of smoke that was still rising from Wodenicus' funeral pyre.

"May the spirits take you far and high, my friend," he said quietly to himself. "We will send many more to join their gods, soon, so very soon. I promise you."

With that, Arminius heeled his horse and cantered into the fort.

August, 9 AD

Within three weeks, at the beginning of September, Varus would begin to close down the summer lager for his slow return journey west to winter quarters on the Rhine. His route would take him toward the upper reaches of the Lippe, and then down along the march lagers to Haltern, Holsterhausen, Aliso, and finally across the Rhine to Xanten. But first, preparations were under way for the end-of-summer feast to which Varus had invited all the friendly dignitaries, nobles, and tribal elders from the surrounding tribes—including Segestes.

The gathering was a bout of feasting, drinking, and entertainment few German tribesmen had ever witnessed: a bacchanalian of gorging and sexual depravity that left nothing to the imagination of men.

Chapter Sixteen

Early Autumn, 9 AD: Departure from Minden

Both Cassius Dio and Tacitus left detailed accounts of Varus' heavy-handed administration of the German province. These histories help us understand how the anger against the Romans increased, and how Varus came to be viewed by the local population.

According to Cassius Dio:

> *When Quinctilius Varus became Governor of the province of Germany, and in the exercise of his powers also came to handle the affairs of these peoples, he tried both to hasten and to widen the process of change. He not only gave orders to the Germans as if they were actual slaves of the Romans, but also levied money from them as if they were subject nations. These were demands they would not tolerate. The leaders yearned for their former ascendancy, and the masses preferred their accustomed condition to foreign domination. They did not rise in open rebellion, because they saw that there were many Roman troops near the Rhine, and*

many within their own territory. Instead, they received Varus, and by pretending that they would comply with all his orders, they lured him far away from the Rhine into the territory of the Cherusci and toward the river Visurgis [the Weser]. *There they behaved in a most peaceful and friendly manner, and made him feel confident that they could live in a state of subjection without the presence of soldiers.*

The result was that he did not keep his forces concentrated as was advisable in a hostile country, but dispersed many of his troops to those regions which lacked protection, supposedly to guard various vital positions, arrest outlaws, or escort supply columns. Among those who were the most deeply involved in the plot and took the lead in its planning and in the subsequent fighting were Arminius and Segimerus; these men were constantly in Varus' company and often present in his Mess. He thus became complacent to the point of rashness, and since he expected no harm, not only disbelieved all those who suspected what was happening and urged him to be on his guard, but actually reproved them for being needlessly alarmed and for slandering his friends

Tacitus echoed these sentiments:

Segestes (a local chieftain and brother of Segimerus) had often warned Publius Quinctilius Varus that rebellion was planned. At the feast which immediately preceded the rising, Segestes had advised Varus to arrest Arminius and the other chiefs, and also himself, on the grounds that their removal would immobilize their accomplices and Varus could then take his time in sorting out the guilty from the innocent. However, Varus was to fall to Arminius. Segestes had been forced into the war by the unanimous feeling of the Cherusci. But relations between the Germans were still bad. Domestic ill-feeling contributed because Segestes' daughter, engaged to another man, was stolen by Arminius.

September, AD 9: Varus' Last Supper and Summer Storms

Arminius carried with him to the summer lager a heavy heart and a rising sense of rage. The final war conference at Icker during the waning days of August had solidified the tribes. He knew how much was as stake, and so managed to keep his feelings under wrap. Only his nearest friends realized his troubled state of mind. Outwardly, Arminius portrayed himself as a man of patience and a friend of the Romans. Inside, however, he detested every minute, hour, and day of Roman occupation. Yet he knew he must wait until the Romans departed the Minden camp for their return to winter quarters. Only then, when the enemy marched for their western camp on the Lippe, beyond the border of the Rhine, would he and his kinsmen have an opportunity to punish Varus and his hated legions.

Arminius had maintained a quiet but courteous relationship with all the Roman commanders, and in particular Marcus Aius and Varus himself. Varus did not doubt his loyalty and support.

Indeed, as far as Varus was concerned, Arminius could do no wrong. He was a favored member of the Consul's Mess, and Varus' warmth of feeling toward the Cherusci chieftain, Roman knight, and companion in his German campaign was second to none. Marcus Aius, however, was a different matter. His eyes and cautious advice demonstrated openly that he was suspicious of Arminius and his warriors. Without any proof, however, Marcus was unable to substantiate his misgivings. And though Varus relied upon his second-in-command, he did not tolerate his words of warning against Arminius—even in the normal day-to-day "baiting" that was often part of mess life, where light-hearted discourse was a regular feature of the informal gatherings and feasting.

Now that September had arrived, the final preparations for the move back to the Rhine were underway, as was the feast to mark the end of the summer. Every local dignitary and chieftain was in attendance including Segestes, Arminius' main competitor and antagonist. It was his daughter who had so inflamed Arminius' desires and clouded his reason at Icker.

The feasting and drinking, punctuated with performances by actors, skilled artists, exotic dancers, and musicians, was little more than a lengthy round of licentious partying straddled across many nights and days. Varus enjoyed the festivities and believed such grand affairs promoted his standing and status in the community, both in the eyes of the German tribesmen and, more importantly, in the eyes of his commanders and soldiers. The more impressive his feasts, the more people would equate him with the grander concepts that existed in Rome itself, with the greater reputation of the Caesars themselves. Perhaps some of the same esteem and awe people held for the great Augustus Caesar would fall upon him. Like a peacock, Varus' inflated ego was matched only by the pageantry of his colorful displays and posturing.

Arminius watched and listened as the sounds of revelry and peals of raucous laughter thundered within the lager and erupted from the central gathering of the German guests of honor inside the Principia *(Headquarters). The music and singing were mixed with boisterous shouts that echoed across the fort and surrounding fields. He clenched his teeth in disgust.*

While he retained his studied pretense of servility with the Romans, Arminius worked hard to keep his friendship strong with the German tribal chieftains. He was only too well aware that his relations with Segestes were tenuous at best. Even after the war conference at Icker, he knew Segestes was not fully behind his plan and would likely continue his attempts to appease the Romans. Would he openly betray Arminius' intentions? He doubted Segestes would outwardly condemn him to Varus or reveal the intent of the Icker gathering, though rumors had reached him that Segestes was criticizing Arminius in front of the Roman Consul and questioning his loyalties. Varus, however, would have none of it. Throughout the celebrations he laughed at such propositions. Determined to show his support for Arminius, Varus sought him out, placed his arm warmly around his shoulders, and loudly extolled his virtues and comradeship to the delight of everyone gathered within earshot.

One of these men was Marcus Aius. The Tribune had been closely watching these events with more than passing interest. Something was amiss, though exactly what he could not say. A passionate though undefined undercurrent was prevalent in the gathering of German tribesmen. Somehow, this time around, their casual though meaningful looks and nudges were different—different in meaning, different in intent, different in suggestion. The whispered comments between men gathered in small pockets, removed from their Roman allies, troubled Marcus, who was beginning to believe even Varus subconsciously sensed (but would never admit) something, somehow, was different with their German friends. The Consul's own emotions ebbed and flowed as Varus laughed one minute and grew angry the next at Segestes' insinuations. Was Segestes' prodding reaching too close to the truth for Varus' comfort?

The troubling situation warranted investigation. Marcus resolved to organize a few trusted commanders, who were not so friendly with Arminius and his men, to keep a careful eye on the gathered German tribesmen, and particularly on their leaders—especially those who were not obviously endeared to the German elder Segestes. Regrettably for the men of the Seventeenth, Eighteenth and Nineteenth Legions of Rome, the plan Marcus intended to implement was smothered by events that swept over them with unimaginable speed.

Unbeknownst to Romans and Germans alike, the oppressive heat of the summer was drawing in hot damp pockets of high pressure from the west, while simultaneously pulling down low pressure fronts from the north and east. The confluence of these fronts created the conditions necessary to trigger one of the sudden late summer storms that often blitzed their way across the north German plains during September and October. The outbursts opened without warning and with frightening intensity, usually with a devastating wind followed closely by a massive deluge of driving rain and, on occasion, hail. A lull in the intensity of rain and wind followed when the eye of the storm circled above, during which beams of sunlight would pop through the layers of heavy clouds, deceiving those unaccustomed to the autumn weather of north Germany. Within a short time, however, the rear pressure waves arrived to repeat the exercise all over again. It was not uncommon for these frontal systems to circle overhead for days, throwing downpour after downpour against the earth below, swamping the slopes and valleys in the hills and immersing plains and lowlands. These storms of wind and water crippled normal human activity. Soon, very soon, the Romans now safely huddled inside the lager at Minden, would set out for the Rhine, marching across the upper reaches and highlands of northern Germany.

The approaching weather front was similar to the storm pattern that had reduced the galley fleet to a few beached wrecks littering the banks of the Weser north of Minden. And the advance warning signs of its approach were already visible. The tell-tale smell of highly charged ozone hung heavily in the still summer air. The whisper of breezes and swirling eddies of air picked up speed and intensity as the hot wind rushed across the plains from the west. On the cleared ground surrounding the lager, particularly on its western side, the dry scorched earth left by the long hot summer released large pockets of dust and debris. Spumes of sand and dry soil rose in small tornadoes and spun themselves in a wicked dance of nature. The winds struck so quickly that guards on lager point duty along the fortress walls did not have even a chance to seek shelter before clouds of dust made both observation and meaningful communication impossible. Coughing and choking, their eyes streaming with tears at the invasion of stinging sand and dust, the guards crouched behind the ramparts in an effort to shelter from the onslaught. Those inside did not fare much better. Even those safely ensconced within the Principia *Headquarters were unable to avoid the rush of dusty air that shot into every room and hall within the fort.*

Though the initial dust storm was of relatively short duration, another followed it just minutes later, whipping through the lager with enough intensity to disrupt Varus' feasting troops and guests. The dust and wind overturned plates of food, filled wine goblets with grit, and choked off words of protest in mid-sentence. Almost as soon as it began, the second wave of wind died out, leaving the festivities in its wake in turmoil. Well into his cups, Varus laughed in an attempt to make light of nature's intrusion. "What next will the Gods throw at us!" he exclaimed, calling out for new wines and foods to be brought forth from the kitchens. As the stewards scurried about to comply with his orders, the lull in the conversation was palpable. The atmosphere in the hall was restrained and defensive, its occupants poised for the next round of wind or some other revelation of nature. It was not long in coming. The next sound they all heard above the unsettled silence of the hall was the crowing of a cock. Varus' face blanched. The bird was often used by priests to predict the future affairs of men; why would it crow now, so late in the day? Many of those who heard it were suspicious-minded men, and many spines were chilled by the unexpected sound.

Arminius had taken advantage of the turmoil created by the wind and dust to confront Segestes. The dirt had barely begun its swirling dance through the Great Hall when he stepped quickly across the distance separating him from Segestes. Seconds later he stood squarely before the tall elderly tribal chieftain. With one hand resting lazily on the pommel hilt of his sheathed sword, he placed the other firmly on Segestes' shoulder. Arminius' cold blue eyes bored into the old man's and their menace was unmistakable. But an easy smile spread across Arminius' lips as he leaned forward and placed his mouth within an inch of Segestes' ear. To anyone watching, the men appeared in the middle of a

friendly conversation, the winds preventing anyone other than Segestes
from hearing his words of warning.

"Hear me, old man, and hear me well," spoke Arminius. "You may
well wish to play lackey to the Romans for the rest of your days, and feel
free to do so. But should you continue to ingratiate yourself with Varus
and accuse me of treason, let me tell you what will be the result of your
folly. First, old man, your daughter will be slain." At this, Segestes
gasped aloud, though only Arminius heard it. "Listen well, and smile
while you do so, old man, lest I order the deed done now." Segestes
nodded in reply. "I have already left instructions for my men to take your
daughter into custody in a secret place in the hills, far removed from your
protection and care. She thinks you have approved these precautions to
be taken before the planned campaign and is entirely happy with her
circumstances—at present. She is well cared for, waiting for me to take
her for my bride, as I foretold."

Arminius paused long enough to lift his head and look deeply into
Segestes' eyes before leaning closer to his ear and speaking anew. "If
you betray our people, she will die the most fiendish death imaginable.
Even the remains of the brothers on the cross outside the fort will pale in
significance compared with what I will have done to her. Their fate will
bear no comparison to her pain and sufferings, and her bloody head will
grace your next table of fare. Second, I will order your whole family
slaughtered, but not before they have all been tortured across many days.
My men are even now standing by to take them prisoner should I so wish
it. Finally, old man"—Arminius paused once more to support Segestes at
the elbow when he noticeably sagged as the words tore at his heart—"I
will come for you, cut out your tongue, and then tear out your heart from
your body while you still breathe."

By this time the wind was dying down and Arminius caught sight of
an approaching Marcus Aius. Arminius lowered his voice and continued
speaking to Segestes with a wide smile covering his face. "And so, old
man, smile. Smile, damn you or I will give the order now! Do not think for
one moment you can turn traitor so easily." With these words Arminius
half turned to encompass the presence of Marcus, and with a well acted
airy dismissal of his conversation that had left Segestes pale and ashen,
said, "So, good friend, never doubt my commitment and loyalty to our
comrades-in-arms"—implying   the   Romans   but   meaning   the
Germans—"They have my right arm and my mighty sword to serve them,

to sink into many more pale bellies, and sever many more painted heads before my time is due." The smiling German warrior briefly nodded a greeting to Marcus and walked off, leaving Segestes and the Tribune standing together.

Marcus watched him strut away for a few moments and then turned to Segestes. The old man was visibly shaken. *"What ails you, Segestes? Has Arminius been taking you to task for your remarks to Varus? You look as if you've seen a ghost."*

Segestes attempted to recover his composure, but failed with every effort. He looked nervously around the hall, searching desperately for a friendly face, a friendly German face in which to confide his troubles. Suddenly, he realized how very alone he was, a friend to the Romans and estranged from his own countrymen, many of whom were pointedly avoiding his gaze. Segestes turned to face Marcus, a look of pleading on his face, a countenance of deep desperation and fear. He was trying to decide whether to speak when he saw Arminius stop and turn back to stare at them both. Segestes blanched and a wave of nausea swept through him when he thought of his daughter being held at the mercy of Arminius. The old man put his trembling hand to his mouth to swallow the sickly bile rising in his throat.

Marcus tried again. *"Come, Segestes, tell me what ails you."*

Segestes shook his head violently to make sure Arminius saw his reply. Just then, the noise of the second front of the approaching storm reached the ears of those gathered in the hall. The waiters and entertainers jumped up to prepare for the coming turmoil, shutting doors and slamming shutters, pulling drapes, and generally battening down the Great Hall.

At this point, Varus cried out loudly across the hall, *"Marcus Aius! Enough is enough of this damned weather! In the morning we make preparation to close down our stay here. It is time to make an early move back to winter quarters."* Turning to the gathered German leaders and tribesmen, Varus raised his chalice of wine and cried out, *"Thank you for joining me here at our festivities, good friends, but it is time for us to prepare for my return to the Rhine until next summer, when I will join you once again. For now, good health, and I drink to your friendship with Rome, and your Caesar, the mighty Augustus!"* With that last remark, Varus drank deeply as the guards and legionaries echoed his toast. He *failed to notice that the great majority of the Germans had raised their goblets, but did not drink from them or echo his toast.*

1993–1994: Journey from Berlin

Having settled into my new role in Berlin, I was anxious to get back down the long road to Kalkriese as soon and as often as I could. However, the demands of my new job were more intensive than I imagined they would be, and Berlin also had its magical points of interest for me. After I completed the initial tourist visits to the highlights of the large sprawling city (which included some wonderful visits to the eastern side of Berlin and the fascinating areas of Potsdam—both of which had been in their own time warp since the end of the Second World War), my interests turned back westward toward the other time warp that existed: that of Varus and Arminius, the Teutoburger Wald, the Wiehengebirge ridge, the Weser and Lippe rivers, and the new revelations coming out of the earth from the fields of Kalkriese.

My drives down to Osnabrück from Berlin, although fairly long and often demanding, always deepened with interest the farther west I drove into the heartland of north Germany. Every time I approached Hannover I smiled, for that is where I had enjoyed the professionalism and friendship of Dr. Cosack, and where Frank Berger, even now, sits at his desk in the *Münzkabinett* of the Kestner Museum studying the Roman coinage still being recovered from Kalkriese by the Osnabrück archaeological team (and on occasion, by my own hand). Farther west, beyond Rinteln, is where the Bergland and country trails have produced Roman coin finds. And beyond there flows the mighty Weser, which winds its way southwest as it lazily curves toward its source in the south highlands.

Farther down to Porta Westfalica, as I approached the autobahn turn-off leading toward Osnabrück, I would look right toward the river bridges and the fields lying beneath, sprawling outward to the river. In the distance was the gap to the north through which Varus and his legions had marched so many years before. The road carried me along the southern side of the underbelly of the high Wiehengebirge ridge. Out the left side of the car looking southwest were the Teutoburger Wald and the hills rolling toward Detmold, where the statue of Arminius stood another fifty miles beyond. This was the land Varus never reached, having been so cleverly lured away from his march toward the Lippe, baited instead to tramp northwest up through the rolling Berglands toward Kalkriese. He and his legions were unwittingly drawn upon the horns of the raging bull that was Arminius and the German tribes in 9 AD . . . where Varus and his Legionaries disappeared into the mists of time.

I was driving back to Kalkriese to continue to feed my insatiable appetite for the truth and to help search for the marvelous artifacts and archaeological treasures still waiting to be recovered. But with each mile west I slipped deeper back in history. The splashes of color from the surrounding countryside flashed by, merging into shadows and patterns of shapes that carried with them my daydreams . . . into a close phalanx of marching legions . . . to scores of men and wagons . . . to troops marching and cavalry riding . . . to men, horses and carts and oxen . . . to whips and cries . . . to horns and banners . . . to a bedlam of military might that had lost much of its cohesion and discipline and was now lazy and lethargic, indolent and unworried, as it made its way away from the summer camp, through the Minden gap, and southwest toward the Lippe.

How would it all have begun? A message likely reached the legions at about this point. I could picture a runner approaching from the northwest. His pace would have been steady and controlled as he held his leather message pouch close to his body. He had no idea the communication carried with him would change the course of history.

September, 9 AD: Departure from Summer Camp

He was sweating profusely and breathing heavily when he ran into the command cell, dropping to one knee and bowing his head as he opened his pouch and took out his scroll for the quarter guard commander. He had reached the legions' central command area. The Centurion on duty took the message, moved across to Varus' entourage, and placed the scroll into the outstretched hand of Marcus Aius.

The Tribune studied it for a moment, turned his mount, and cantered a few yards to Varus, who was lounging in a shaded litter.

"Sire, I have a message from one of the outposts to the northwest of the ridge line," began Marcus. "Three of his road-building parties have been attacked, and he has lost a number of men. He has prudently ordered his remaining patrols to return to the safety of the march lagers.

He believes there is some form of insurgency brewing within the local tribes in his area and requests that we send a patrol to ascertain the strength and purpose of the attackers as soon as possible."

Varus was listening to his second-in-command when Arminius drew up alongside the litter. Before Varus could reply, the German interrupted his thoughts. "Sire, I know the area to the northwest well, and my men are ready now to ride with all speed. May I take my flank guards and scouts and report on this outrage? It would give me great enjoyment to draw my sword in such a skirmish, if indeed there is to be one."

Marcus gazed long and hard at Arminius. "Why do you need the flank guards and scouts, Arminius? You have a large force of mounted auxiliaries under your command. I do not think it a good idea for the scouts and flanking forces to be reduced under these circumstances— particularly while we are marching. We must first ascertain the size and intentions of the tribal forces arrayed against us." Arminius met the Tribune's hard gaze with his own steely look.

"I think Marcus Aius is correct, Arminius," said Varus, whose words interrupted the locked stares of the two soldiers. "The flank guards and scouts will remain at their positions around the legions, and we will continue on southwest toward Anreppen. We must get on before we have a repeat of the damned storm that hit us last week in Minden. Take your cavalry, my friend, and give me news as soon as you can of what transpires in the hills to the north. I have no wish to commit our cavalry to those damned hills and gullies. You are better versed in that, and enjoy the Bergland of the countryside more than the legionaries." Varus stopped and pursed his lips a moment. His furrowed brow revealed his own concerns. "Make good speed, and report as soon as you are able." Then, as if to make light of the report, Varus gave an airy wave of his hand and dismissed the German, leaned forward toward his porters, and ordered his retinue forward.

Marcus Aius sat on his mount watching Arminius collect his men and give his orders. Within a few minutes they rode off toward the northwest, where they disappeared up the wooded slopes. Long after they vanished Marcus remained where he was. As the legions tramped past him, he searched his mind for what it was that had sparked his suspicions about this train of events, to no avail. With a troubled look on his face, he turned his horse about and moved forward to rejoin Varus.

He left a few seconds too soon. A few yards behind was the legionary runner who had carried the message. The man was drinking thirstily from a chagal of water. When some of it spurted from the upraised pigskin, he cursed aloud but quickly stifled himself when he realized he had exclaimed in guttural German instead of Latin. Some of the surrounding legionaries laughed aloud when the water spilled down the front of the runner's tunic, but Marcus heard none of it.

*   *   *

I left Berlin in October 1994 to take up a new appointment at the British Joint Headquarters in Rheindahlen. The British, along with the French, Americans, and Russians, were withdrawing from Berlin and the long process of drawdown had finally come to its conclusion. I was sad to see our interests in Berlin drawing to a close, for the city was possessed of a magical aura, even more so now that there was free access to its eastern regions and to the time capsule of Potsdam in all its former glory.

Before I left I had the pleasure of meeting Wolfgang Prauss, a well informed and widely published historian on Roman affairs in Germany. He had contacted me to discuss his interests in the *Varusschlacht* and other facets of the Roman occupation of Germany during the days of Varus and of Arminius.

I was extremely impressed with his fervor and obvious passion concerning the Romans in Germany, and have maintained an extremely interesting and informative exchange of ideas with him. Along with Mommsen, Hartmann, and other more modern historians, Prauss has his own passionate views on the circumstances surrounding the *Varusschlacht*. Although we have sometimes agreed to differ in our concept of what actually transpired in Kalkriese, his interests (one might say obsession) very closely matched mine in seeking the answers to not just one, but all of the imponderables of the Roman occupations of Germany, including the "Lost Grail" of the site of Aliso.

However, I had other duties to perform, and with a sad farewell wave to the new friends I had made in Berlin, I left for that last long drive down the autobahn . . . from the Elbe, to the Weser, and on to the Rhine beyond.

Chapter Seventeen

September, 9 AD: The Sacking of the Outposts

The legions continued their long, slow, drawn-out way across the flat expanse of the plain areas on the western side of the Weser, moving southwest toward the Teutoburger Wald some twenty miles away. They made relatively good time considering the enormous baggage train, ox carts laden with camp followers, servants, women and children, and lines of pack mules, all of which combined to hinder the speedy rate at which the legions normally marched. Still, the pace was too slow for Marcus Aius, who urged the men and wagons along at every opportunity. The heat of the late summer day had weakened the men. Dry mouths, cracking lips, and sweat running freely inside helmets and uniforms limited the bantering conversation that normally flowed within the ranks.

Marcus watched the men march on as he walked his horse near the front of the moving legions. Alongside rode Gaius Numonius Vala, commander of one of the legions. Vala had recently assumed command of Varus' cavalry when its commander had died after a serious illness shortly before their departure from Minden. Vala appeared deep in thought, absorbed with matters far removed from their present circumstances. Marcus could not help but notice Vala's somber distracted mood.

"What ails you, Gaius?" inquired Marcus. "You seem miles away from us. Are you dreaming of returning to Xanten, or have you lustier thoughts of your return to Rome later this winter?"

Several seconds passed before Vala replied, and then only after exhaling a long, drawn-out sigh. "I have slept badly these last few weeks, Marcus, and for no apparent reason. Every night I have the same dream, over and over. I see the mask of Augustus coming toward me, but stripped of all its trimmings—just the bare mask, as if to haunt me. Behind the mask, a little distance away but always behind it, is a winged beast, like our legion's Eagle, but like a helmet with large wings. Then, when the mask comes off, the head that wears it comes off as well, and there is blood everywhere. Finally, the mask itself screams in agony and I awake—hot, sweating, anxious, and terribly afraid, because I have to go back to sleep and dream it all over again."

The hair on Marcus' neck stood on end and a chill crept down his spine. "Gaius, it is only a dream, though a terrible one."

"Yes, I know this, Marcus, but I swear I have never felt so much fear from my sleeping moments, and I am so very tired. My joints ache from such sleepless nights."

"My good friend," replied Marcus, "why do you not seek solace from the medicines and potions of the Greek physician? He is known to have many draughts to aid sleep and assist a man to relax during his rest periods. A potion of Valerian from him has been known to soothe even the most rowdy of our besotted legionaries, and helps grown men sleep like babies. Why do you not try him?"

"I may well do that. I had not thought of it, Marcus," confessed Gaius. "Sound sleep may well be the cure, but I think I need to take a little more drastic action as well, for I believe I also carry part of my nightmares with me." He reached down to his back saddle pannier. Attached was a cavalry mask for training and parades, and a helmet. The helmet's mask was embellished with silver and gold and linked to the helmet with studs and fasteners. The helmet was heavily decorated around its edges with attractive flutes and winged elements.

Gaius drew the helmet free from its fastenings and gazed at its glorious shapes and veneers. The mask was the face of Augustus. To carry the face of Caesar wherever the legionaries were deployed was an honor. Though crafted for use as a parade and training helmet, when worn by a charging cavalryman in the van of battle, the awe-inspiring and utterly expressionless caricature instilled fear in the enemy. Dismounted legionaries had also worn the mask in battle with the same chilling effect.

"I think we must honor others from time to time, Marcus. Perhaps this is my nightmare and I might release it from my mind if I passed it to someone else."

As he spoke, Gaius Vala looked on as the mass of legionaries marched past. His gaze finally rested on the figure of the Eagle and standard-bearer for the Seventeenth Legion, Brutus Maximus, who had recently finished his tour of duty at the watchtower overlooking the Weser. Maximus had been promoted from Standard-Bearer to Aquilifer shortly before the legions had departed from the summer camp.

"Bearer of the Seventeenth!" Gaius called out as he kicked his horse into a walk. "Are you of a mind to carry the Caesar's face on your marches across these accursed lands, as well as the mighty Eagle of Rome? I am in a generous mood today, and wish to divest myself of this helmet and mask. You have been promoted a worthy carrier of such an honorable duty that you should also have my parade helmet. What say you, soldier, do you wish to take this prize?" Gaius Valla held the helmet and mask aloft for the soldier to see.

Brutus Maximus continued marching, holding the pole to the Eagle tightly in his grasp. His gaze was keenly fixed upon the upraised helmet. "Sire," he said, "I would consider it a great honor to carry not only the Eagle of my legion, but also the face of my Caesar. Yes, I would consider it a great honor and would wear it with pride whenever we again confront our enemies."

"By all the gods, Marcus Aius!" said Gaius. "How alike you and he look! I have never seen two men not twins who look so similar in face and figure. Have you ever seen your face in such a mirror? He could well be your brother."

Marcus studied the face of the Aquilifer and admitted to himself there was indeed an uncanny resemblance between himself and the slightly older soldier. "No, he is not my brother, Gaius, but he carries one of our Eagles, and is therefore my blood brother. However," he joked, "he obviously carries a good face of his own if it resembles mine. Should one *pay him the misplaced honor of wearing Caesar's face as well, to cover such a handsome one of his own?"*

The officers burst into a laughter that left Gaius feeling relieved, finally free from his earlier stress. He urged his horse gently sideways, closer alongside the Aquilifer. "Here," he said, half-leaning over with the helmet and mask outstretched, "take your Caesar with you, Aquilifer, and remember always that it was Gaius Numonius Vala who gave you such a treasure. It is yours for as long as you wish to keep it, and one day it may sit above your grandchildren's place in Rome as a reminder of our travels here in Germany." Vala stretched across to place the helmet into the hand of the marching soldier.

Brutus Maximus deftly hooked the helmet on to his belt, and replied, "Thank you, sire, I will carry it with pride, and if we go to battle, will wear it with pride. I thank you for the opportunity to be afforded yet another great honor. These last few weeks will stay with me for the rest of my life as my proudest moments. Thank you, sire."

Marcus listened to the exchange and nodded, thinking of similar memories from his distinguished career. Gaius Vala pulled up his mount alongside Marcus' horse and said, "By all the gods, it seems as if I have passed a great weight from me, Marcus. Perhaps the responsibilities of my office have dogged me more than normal. My Caesar expects so much of me, and even my own marked coinage stares back at me with the face of our beloved Caesar that I fear he is always judging me. Perhaps it was the right decision by Varus that we leave the summer camp early this year. We all need to retire to less stressful duties on the other side of the Rhine." The officers urged their mounts forward and walked along the marching column.

"I suspect you are very right, Gaius. It has been a long, drawn-out affair this year, and I must admit I have been unable to relax much myself," answered a sighing Marcus. "I have long feared trouble is brewing, and yet it never appears. I admit to feeling anxious most days about our circumstances, particularly at this time. Segestes was a troubled man at the feast in summer camp, but he would not tell me why. I felt unease, even animosity toward us during the celebrations, but . . ." he fell into an uneasy silence. "Perhaps I also am imagining the worst things in life and should relax a little more. However, Arminius has taken his riders to unknown pastures and unknown insurrections, and I fear I will not be able to relax. I am keen to know what he finds out to the north

and west from here. The highlands are there, as are marshy valleys, and I like the thought of neither area. Still, it would appear I have found a long-lost brother!" laughed Marcus as he looked across at Brutus Maximus and his soaring Eagle. "I should be thankful for that. It is good to know the faults in my profile are shared by others!" His words aroused a few chuckles of laughter from the marching legionaries at the expense of Brutus Maximus. Marcus Aius lifted his gaze and looked in the distance. Ahead loomed the Teutoburger Wald.

*   *   *

The detachments at the watchtowers overlooking the Weser had witnessed the departure of the three-legion force with a mixture of satisfaction and relief. Their task was to man the key posts overlooking the river and pasturelands to the north and south of the great divide, to ensure no enemy followed in the footsteps of the departing troops through the Minden pass. Their orders were to wait two days, pack up the small forts, clear out their belongings, close down the basic facilities within, and depart the area. Their route back to the Rhine was, at least initially, slightly different from that taken by the legions. The detachments would form up on the western side of the Weser and after one crossed the ford a short distance to the north, both would march along the Wiehengebirge ridge due west.

The detachments were directed to pick up the road-building and mapping detachments based in numerous small forts some twenty-five miles to the west, stationed both north and south of the ridge. Once complete, the entire force would continue marching southwest toward the Lippe to join with the slower-moving legions.

Varus and his legions had barely disappeared when the Germans attacked those left behind. The sun was dipping near the horizon when masses of painted long-haired enemy warriors poured out of the woods at the edge of the clearings. Unlike past attacks, there was no noise, no screaming, no blood-curdling battle yells—just a fast-moving force of sweating, pounding bodies streaming across the open ground that surrounded the forts. By the time the duty guards realized what was happening, it was too late to change the course of events already underway, too late to call out the Captain of the Guard, too late to raise smoke signals to warn other outposts—too late to do anything but fight and die where they stood.

The Germans had planned well. The attacks were a complete surprise and took each fort and detachment with surprising ease. The tribesmen, tight-lipped and frighteningly quiet, flooded up to the gates and walls of the bastions and towers, threw up ladders and scaling poles, and poured forth a relentless flood of painted bodies armed with swords and axes, spears and knives, and spiked clubs, all ready to stab and cut, sever and strike, and pound human flesh into unrecognizable gore. Only then, when entry had been gained and the Roman guards were falling under the massive weight of enemy numbers, did German blood-curdling yells and screams fill the enclosures with a bedlam of noise and aggression. The Romans never stood a chance.

Men died with questions forming on their lips as they rushed out of their accommodations and administrative areas, only to be met with the sight of falling comrades and a corpse-strewn internal parade ground. Legionaries littered the ground in a mass of stricken and slaughtered bodies, severed limbs still twitching in the sand, bloody heads held triumphantly aloft by hysterical dancing tribesmen in the throes of acute ecstasy at so much bloodletting. Adrenaline ruled the day. Hysteria grew with each passing minute as the tribesmen realized total victory—and the spoils of war—was within reach. After the slaughter of the guard forces, the tribesmen searched every nook and cranny, not only to seek out the few legionaries desperately trying to hide in darker recesses, but also (and now more importantly), to gather the spoils of war—the Roman silver and copper coins, clothes and personal possessions, and the accoutrements and trappings of Roman civilized life.

When the day was done, the two main forts were little more than shells, their former occupants slaughtered to a man. Less than one hour after the attacks were launched the Germans were gone, swallowed by the forests they knew so well. A somber, deathly quiet descended with the darkness on the stricken watchtowers. The only sounds that could be heard were those of wild pigs feasting.

The Roman detachments at the forts and watchtowers were only the first to suffer a quick but terrible death. Every picket duty detachment working in the surrounding countryside, some conducting map-making surveys and others constructing roads, was overrun and put to the sword. Those posted to occupy and garrison outlying villages around the

Wiehengebirge ridge and surrounding hills were struck down without warning. Soldiers stationed on the northern edge of the ridge, in the flat surrounding lands verging on the moor and the larger Dieven Wiesen, never knew they were under attack. Roman legionaries engaged in idle conversation with German tribesmen suddenly discovered unsheathed swords sliding into their bellies, or sharpened knives slicing across their throats, cutting away any chance of a shouted warning to their fellow soldiers. The Germans did not overlook the small port stations lining the Weser north of Minden. Each was, in its turn, wiped out to a man.

By morning it was over. Every Roman within half a day's march of Varus' summer camp was dead. Not a single outpost or manned picket force north of Varus' line of march, which ran southwest toward the Lippe and Teutoburger Hills, remained. A few men from the smaller outposts, who had been spared during the initial onslaught, later wished they had died at their posts, such were the unspeakable horrors performed on them by their victorious opponents. Torture awaited any prisoner unlucky enough to fall into German hands, and the Germans were masters of their art.

The first phase of Arminius' operation had been well planned and flawlessly executed.

*   *   *

Cassius Dio left an engrossing account of how the early stages of the operation to defeat the Varus legions unfolded:

> Then an uprising broke out, the first to rebel being those people who lived at some distance from him. This had been deliberately contrived to entice Varus to march against them, so that he could be more overwhelmed while he was crossing what he imagined to be friendly territory, instead of putting himself on his guard, as he would do in the event of the whole country taking up arms against him simultaneously.
>
> And so the plan unfolded. The leaders escorted him as he set out, and then made excuses for absenting themselves. This was to enable them, as they made out, to prepare their combined forces, after which they would quickly reassemble to support him. They took command of their troops which were already waiting them in readiness somewhere. Next, after each community had slaughtered

the detachments of Roman soldiers quartered with them, for which they had previously asked, they fell upon Varus in the midst of the forests.

*   *   *

By this time, Varus' legions were drawing near the outlying higher reaches of the Teutoburger Range, which waited for them to the southeast. Arminius, as he had so carefully planned, plied Varus with messages every few hours: an increasing number of small bands of rebellious tribesmen were congregating in the surrounding hills, but Arminius was successfully rooting out these pockets of unrest and did not require assistance from Varus, who was advised by Arminius to continue marching toward the Lippe and the line-of-march lagers there; Arminius would rejoin him later when his task was finished.

Unbeknownst to Varus, the only pockets of resistance being wiped out were Roman.

The Krebsburg and Borgwedde

Arminius rode into the temporary hill camp established at the Krebsburg on the eastern edge of the Schnippenburg hills. His encampment straddled the slopes overlooking the valleys and passes that allowed a north–south passage through the Bergland of the Wiehengebirge ridge and northward to the flatlands and moors of the Dieven. The main camp established farther west on the Schnippenburg dated from the Iron Age, and had been reoccupied by the Chauci some years before. Now, however, Arminius needed a temporary control point at the more easterly Krebsburg to enable him to control the north–south passes, through which Varus' legions were to be drawn.[1] Icker was but a few miles away to the west, tucked away in the Icker Bowl.

---

[1] One thousand four hundred years later, a fully walled German permanent camp would be built at the Krebsburg, most likely in order to have the same controlling elements on the north– south passes that Arminius made use of.

The land immediately to the north of the Schnippenburg and Krebsburg escarpment was one of the earliest settlement areas in northern Germania, its east–west routes cutting through it interspersed with Stone-Age monuments and Hunengraber *(Stone-Age graves). Farther westward, situated within a narrow valley through which ran a small but busy watercourse, was one of the most important ceremonial and religious areas of the local German tribes. Numerous standing stones lay on either side of the trail before it rose up into the Bergland towards Icker. At the place known as Borgwedde, a large* Sonnenstein *had been erected thousands of years earlier. It had been adopted and used without interruption at this place to reflect the religious affairs and spiritual needs of the tribesmen. Tucked away in the darker recesses of the woods bordering the track and the stream, the stone cast a gloomy and foreboding aura. Whenever local tribesmen passed along the track by the monument, they made a form of obeisance as a sign of respect to the "God of the Woods." Unlike the Romans with their worship of lofty heights and heavens in the sky, the Germans had always believed their spirits' world was in the hills and valleys of the woodland glades, in the darker recesses of the forests, where the gods of hunter and warrior carefully guarded their quiet, dark somber areas of residence; Borgwedde was just such a special place.*

At first, Arminius made a short stopover in his temporary camp at Krebsburg, where the first phase of his battle plans against Varus was to be put into action. He also wished to see Thusnelda for a short visit to reassure her of the future and let her know of his plans for the forthcoming battle. After Thusnelda he would visit the holy place of his forefathers at Borgwedde, there to submit himself to the power of the spirits and pray for a successful and overwhelming defeat of Varus and his hated legions.

The meeting with Thusnelda was brief but laden with emotion. In the short period they had come to know each other since that fateful day of the gathering of the tribes at Icker, they had fallen in love and been stricken by their desire for one another. Arminius had explained to her the circumstances of Dagan's death, but she harbored no regrets, no animosity toward Arminius. On the contrary, she could not restrain herself from revealing her true feelings to this warrior and chieftain of the Cherusci.

Just before he left, Arminius carefully described the difficult situation he faced with respect to her father, and how he had forced Segestes to clarify his intention and position regarding the Roman occupation of his homeland. He made it clear to Thusnelda that he believed he had every right to take the sword to her father for his acts of appeasement and treachery. However, as a token of respect for her, he swore that whatever the outcome of his forthcoming battle with Varus, he would not take up arms or strike against her father—neither now nor at any time in the future. He told her this knowing that Segestes' treachery had only been stilled and silenced by his own lie that Thusnelda was being held as his prisoner. Segestes did not know that after the pending battle, Arminius intended to marry his daughter.

As all lovers do, Thusnelda gave Arminius her blessing and prayed for his success and safe return to her. In turn, he promised her that after the battle was won, he would mark the defeat of the Romans by taking her up to the loftiest heights around them and marry her in full view of the Roman gods, to let them bear witness to the might of his sword and of the Germanic tribes. Arminius left her with a deep feeling of contentment and soaring spirits as he made his way to Borgwedde and the "Sunstone" of his forefathers.

As the sun set in the evening sky, he rose from his kneeling position in front of the large gravestone and turned to face his adjutant, who had quietly dismounted a few moments earlier to join Arminius' entourage.

"Is it done?" inquired Arminius.

"Lord, there were none who escaped us. All but a few Romans have been put to the sword, and those few who we took prisoner are now dying a thousand deaths. We are ready."

Arminius smiled and slowly shook his head. "We need no prisoners now," he answered in a gentle rebuke to his captain's description of the treatment being meted out to the Roman captives. "It is not a time to punish and make the Romans pay by torture. It is a time to kill them, to kill off the plague, kill as many as we can. If we are ready as you say, then send the message to Varus. He must come to help me now, help me fight my fight against these rebellious German dogs."

With a loud laugh, Arminius threw his arm warmly around his adjutant's shoulder, and continued. "I have had a great vision here by the Sunstone today: the God of the Woods has promised me that if we use the woods, use the glades and the hills and valleys, we shall beat the

Romans. Not by a head-on attack, but from the flanks, from the rear, as we planned. Steer him up here to the ground of our choosing, perhaps to the very slopes of the Krebsburg itself, and when we have finally drawn them here, then, my captain, then we will finish them. Completely."

Back to Borgwedde

I first met Frau Beckmann, who owns the small *Schloss* at Borgwedde, during the summer of 1988. I was drawn to the area by the stories of Roman coin finds in the sand hills and dunes farther west, above the stream valley. As on previous occasions, before I set foot on new lands and fields, I established contact with the local landowners. They often have a wealth of knowledge to impart, which on many occasions had saved me hours, and even days, of traipsing across empty fields and miles of woodlands in my search for Roman artifacts. I remember driving into the small entrance leading to the *Schloss*, a track bordered on either side by large boulders and stones of the same type used by the Stone-Age dwellers who had established the many graves and special places erected in the surrounding areas thousands of years earlier.

Twenty yards into the grounds I saw the full facade of the long building. In front was a small and shallow pond holding a pair of swans within its restricted confines. I stopped the car, stepped out, and stood for a few moments to take in the ambience of the small *Schloss*. It was a long-fronted building without much depth. On one end was the burned-out shell of what looked like a circular wooden chapel. The massive oak beams of the skeletal remains were still very much in evidence, and the framework of the building added a strange and somewhat eerie presence to the setting and grounds. A little farther on were large farm-type buildings and a barn. Behind the main house was a small but imposing lake.

My reverie was interrupted by loud barking, followed by the sudden appearance of two very large black dogs bounding down the double-sided steps of the main entrance in my direction. A small lady stepped outside and stood in the open doorway. She called out a sharp order to the dogs. I recall very much hoping her directive was to behave and not bite the visitor, but I certainly wasn't sure at that time! I remained perfectly still as both dogs raced up to me. Though still barking, they sniffed at my legs and did not seem intent on doing me any damage. The lady ordered the animals to withdraw slightly, permitting me to walk slowly forward and make my way up the front steps to greet her.

After I introduced myself and explained my reason for visiting her property, Frau Beckmann warmed to my presence and showed a great deal of interest in my investigations. She offered me a complete history of the area in general and, in particular, the local history concerning the many Stone-Age graves and special stones very much in evidence throughout the hills and valleys surrounding her estate. I have long believed these ancient graves and areas of religious activity fascinated all those who remained in, or later moved into, these areas after their erection, and indeed, became places of worship or ritual during early tribal eras. For example, today in England, people still actively worship at the annual summer solstice at Stonehenge.

Frau Beckmann was a goldmine of information on such matters. On my frequent visits to Borgwedde over the ensuing years, I chased down the many shadows of the folklore and old gospels she told me about. Her words instilled within me an absolute fascination for the area. One must understand that every time I drove to or from Kalkriese over the years, literally thousands of times by now, my route nearly always took me through Borgwedde. However, I rarely stopped there, for my searches in Kalkriese consumed my interest and time. Whenever I did stop to talk with her again it was like making a small pilgrimage, for regardless how long it had been since my previous visit, she was always pleased to see me and regaled me with additional snippets of local information she had stored and retained for me.

During that early visit in 1988, Frau Beckmann had fired my imagination with a startling revelation that involved a story of an unpublicized and little-known large stone grave that did not appear on any survey maps as a gravestone, a special stone, or *Teil* in its own right. According to her, this stone was a huge and alluring edifice that in modern times had been used as a marker stone in a small family cemetery. Historians of old and the former inhabitants and worshippers of times long gone by had once known of it. However, as Frau Beckmann explained it, the stone was hidden away in the leafy glades and shadows of the Borgwedde stream and valley, and so today hardly anyone knew of its existence. At the time, I had no way of knowing that this marker from the past would help me better understand my quest for the lost Varus legions.

Throughout the years, this ancient stone remained at the forefront of my mind (driving regularly through Borgwedde as I did, and still do), but much as I was fascinated by this treasure of a previously unpublicized place of worship near Kalkriese, it was of secondary priority in my ongoing investigations at that time.

One day arrived, however, when I decided I would take the time to examine the stone. With Frau Beckmann's help I sought out and found the marker. I remember standing before the great stone, broad at its base but more elongated than the usual tall marker stones of old. It was nevertheless as foreboding as any I have seen and of great weight and shape, much of which was now buried under the accumulation of thousands of years of leaves and foliage. The dark shaded glade in which it rested offered a quiet yet somewhat menacing atmosphere to the setting.

Just over halfway up the leading edge of the stone was a concave recess large enough to accept a simple offering (should it have been used for such a purpose). The cut-away recess held a small posy of flowers (which supports my thesis), a strangely evocative and thought-provoking gesture on such a large edifice as the stone. Frau Beckmann told me the recess was called *Teufels Back Trog*, or "Devil's Baking Trough." Borgwedde itself was originally called *Borg am Heiligen Hain*, which roughly translated means "Hill at the Holy Grove."

Men had stood before this holy stone for thousands of years to visit, pay homage, or pray to their gods. Nestled quietly within this foreboding forest glade, the stone had witnessed the passing of the millennia. The great historian Theodor Mommsen had traveled here and visited the site of the Roman coin finds less than one mile from the stone, but had left without ever learning of its existence. Not a single latter-day German historian, save one, had spent any time researching this remarkable stone. The lone exception was Hermann Hartmann. I found many of his thoughts and writings astoundingly similar to some of my own theories. Some of his hypotheses are amazingly comprehensive and revealing, particularly in his studies of possible Roman activities in and around northern Germany.

Hartmann the Historian

In the 1800s, Hartmann described the Schnippenburg as follows:

The Schnippenburg near Ostercappeln

Considering the most important valleys of the Wiehengebirge, through which nowadays the main highways run which carry the main traffic from north to south, one finds all cross valleys guarded by ancient barring fortifications—all but the Ostercappeln Pass. One is struck by the fact that this pass, one of the most important, through which today the main traffic passes from the Weser via Osnabrück to the Rhine, and on whose northern side an old *Heerweg* and trade route led from the Ems near Lingen via Freren, Furstenau, Bramsche, Engter, Pr Oldendorf, Lubbecke, and on to Minden past the Weser, has been left without any fortification.

In the opinion of von Opperman, the guarding of the Western Pass at Ostercappeln had been left to the fortified camps on the southern side of the hills. If so, at least a watch post would have been stationed there, just as the Wittekindsburg in Frankensundern seems to have served as such for the main camp at the Wittekindsburg near Rulle. Now, however, a fortification near Ostercappeln has at last been found, and it is a fortification that does justice to the importance of the pass. Thus the line of defense along the Wiehengebirge has become complete.

The fortification lies to the west of the Paris–Hamburg railway line, where the line cuts through the Wiehengebirge touching the "Krebsburg." The name of the newly found fortification is Schnippenburg, up to now known to locals only, of course also under the name Wittekindsburg, and as far as I know it has hitherto not been described by anyone, anywhere.

It lies on the western side of the gorge formed by the Ostercappelner Berg, and Venner Egge, south behind Venner Egge, on a foothill which falls steeply to north, east and south, and towards the west the hill slopes into Vehrter Bruch and, significantly, it lies in the fork of two brooks which conjoin at the western slope. The brook then flows past Ostercappeln and into Leckerbach. The distance from the Schnippenburg to the Krebsburg is 1.5 kilometres in a straight westerly direction. (The name "Schnippenburg" probably stems from the triangular form of

the foothill on which it is situated. The word *Schnippe* is still used
for the triangular small cloth at the front of a woman's cap, part of
traditional clothing, or costume.) Shape and position make the
Schnippenburg appear very similar to the other wall fortifications in
our district. I have, however, so far not noticed in other
fortifications what I found here; the mixture of wall earth with
charcoal and with stones blackened by burning—was this from the
destruction by fire of fortifications on top of the walls? The hidden
position of the Schnippenburg, 100 meters high, behind the steeper
Venner Egge, some 250 meters, was on the western side of the
Ostercappeln Pass excellently suited as a pass barrier, and as such it
is undoubtedly to be thus regarded.

The Schnippenburg forms an egg-shaped walled camp. The
walls have a width of 3 to 5 meters. The most extended length of the
camp from east to west is 166 meters; the maximum width from
north to south measures 108 meters. The area of the camp amounts
to 15,000 square meters, amounting to 1.5 hectares approximately.
Along this track bronze buckles of horses' harnesses, and "an iron
fighting axe" have been found. . . .   The Schnippenburg is
surrounded by a ring of heathen monuments, which point to the
significance of this area also in relation to heathen cults. At the
southern slope of the Wiehengebirge, in Vehrter Bruch, there are
two stone monuments, locally named Devil's Baking Trough, and
Devil's Baking Oven . . . in the area of Borgwedde, by the "Hill of
the Holy Grove.". . . Above here, on Vehrter Egge, there lies an
obelisk-like stone, the famous *Sonnenstein* (Sunstone), probably
put up in memory of an important event. Perhaps it is a Germanic
victory monument signifying the defeat of the Romans here in AD
9? On the northern slope there lie three *Hunenbetten* (stone graves)
enclosed by large grave hills at Darpenne, another at Driehausen,
and three at Felsen in the community of Schwagstorf.

*   *   *

As I gazed at the stone, I felt—and more importantly, *believed*—this
stone had been a special feature in days long gone. This ancient marker,
on a par with its brother up in the hills, the *Teufels Stein*, the "Devil's
Stone," and its accompanying line of gravestones, was an adjunct to the
worship and spiritual needs of men in the woodland glades of Borgwedde

in days long gone, in the days of Arminius and Varus, and the demise of the Roman legions in 9 AD.

Chapter Eighteen

Into the Teutoburger Forest: The *Varusschlacht* Begins

Varus and his legions were now close to the eastern reaches of the Teutoburger Forest and the hills beyond. They had made fairly good time over the preceding few days across the flatlands, even though they were spread about in a fairly haphazard and ill-disciplined fashion. The huge baggage train and its support wagons and carts were spread out among the marching legionaries and various military elements of the three-legion force. Arminius had departed the previous day with his numerous auxiliary riders to investigate the rumors of an insurrection somewhere to the northwest of their line of march. Other than general situation reports, no messages of any import had reached Varus—until the end of the first day of Arminius' absence.

The German chieftain stood near the crest of one of the many hills northwest of the legions and looked down upon his marching enemy. He did not wish to be seen, and so stood back from the edge of the forested slope in front of him to conceal his presence. He need not have been so cautious, for the advance scouts and reconnaissance troops riding at the head of the advancing Roman column, as well as Varus' flank and rearguard elements, were Germans to a man and aware of what was about to befall the hated enemy. Still, Arminius knew the unexpected could appear suddenly and ruin his strategy, and he was not about to throw away months of careful planning when prudence was called for. Arminius stared down into the distance. The time had finally arrived to implement the most important part of his plan: lead Varus onto ground of his own choosing, where the Romans would be unable to wage effective battle, and where Arminius could strike the legions piece by piece until there was nothing left.

Arminius turned to his aide. "Send down the messenger to Varus, and make sure he knows exactly what to say. Tell him to be careful and wary of Marcus Aius, for he is suspicious by nature, and does not believe I am to be trusted!" With a chuckle he continued. "Make sure he gets word to our scouts. They must wait for our signal before they leave Varus and join us in the flanks of the vanguard. We must make sure once the Romans change direction to come our way, the rear quarter of their force is closely followed by our scouts, who are to join with the rear force of our cavalry."

With a large stick in his hand, Arminius etched his plan into the soil for the aide to better envision its various parts. "The Romans must never be allowed to turn about once we have started our attack. They are to be harried from the flanks and rear only. Varus must be prodded and led on to our final position near the Krebsburg. He must always believe he is coming to join up with me to fight you despicable German dogs!" Arminius gave a short laugh before adding, "Then, only then, will we have Varus right where we want him."

The aide quickly nodded his understanding before turning to pass the orders on to one of the local commanders, who in turn moved off to brief the messenger and ensure he was fully conversant with his orders. Once this was done, the runner was sent on his way down through the valley toward the haze and dust of the tramping legions, as they marched southwest across their front from left to right, completely unaware of what was planned for them.

A German auxiliary operating with the flanking guards saw the runner approaching from the northwest. The guard called out to his nearby commander while pointing in the direction of the rapidly approaching courier, who soon drew up and delivered his message.

Within a few minutes he was standing in the central command area of the legion force at Varus' mobile headquarters. The commander of Varus' quarter guard took the message and passed its contents on to Varus himself. When he realized the import of the words, Varus bolted upright in his litter.

"It would appear Arminius has taken on losses, my lord," the officer was saying. "He has met with a large force of enemy tribesmen and was ambushed as they moved into the hills some fifteen miles northwest of our current position."

When the young man paused, Varus snapped, "Continue! Is there not more to the message?"

"Yes sire," he replied calmly, fully used to his superior's biting demeanor. "The messenger reports Arminius himself has been wounded, and he requests urgent support to assist him in putting down the uprising. Although he has lost men through ambushes, sire, the enemy he faces still appears to be fragmented and not necessarily a cohesive force of tribesmen. He believes that if you come to his aid, sire, the sight of our legions will panic the enemy and help us easily put down the uprising."

The officer paused as Marcus Aius suddenly appeared. He had been informed that an important message from Arminius had arrived. "According to the runner, the great majority of the tribesmen are dismounted, and therefore do not pose a serious threat to our cohorts."

Varus slumped back down into a sitting position and leaned his chin on his palm, brooding over this latest turn of events. Several minutes passed in silence before he looked up at Marcus Aius. "What do you think, Marcus Aius? You have heard all the news?"

Marcus drew himself up straight. "Yes, sire. I was briefed by the flank commander while I was making my rounds. I came with all speed. Is it true that Arminius is reported to be wounded?"

"Yes, apparently so," replied Varus.

"I cannot imagine he would suffer the ignominy of taking a wound delivered by one of his fellow tribesmen, so he must assuredly have been surprised as he claims. Still . . ." Marcus hesitated as he sought out the right words.

"Now is not the time to hold back, Marcus. Say whatever is on your mind."

Marcus cleared his throat and continued. "I find it difficult to believe Arminius' situation is as bad as has been made out. He is an outstanding leader and knows this land. How could he have been ambushed? I must again advise you to proceed carefully where Arminius treads, sire. I do not rest easy with his intentions or allegiance, and think it would be prudent to send out a patrol to gain further intelligence before we commit a large body of men into an area of which we are unfamiliar."

"Marcus—you know my feelings on this matter!" snapped Varus in reply. "Arminius is true and loyal to me and to Rome and he has proved it on many occasions. I am honor-bound to assist him when he calls for aid." Varus stood up and faced his Tribune. "I have decided. Turn the legions about and march northwest. Maintain the flank guards and reconnaissance forces, and when we deploy in the morning maintain the present marching order. I am not going to order battle formations at this stage, based on some minor skirmishing ambushes that have caused some discomfort to Arminius. We march as normal and retain the echelon and support forces in the van of the march."

"Sire, I must protest against this move and advise all due caution," Marcus cautioned. "Should I not at the least order the leading legion to form into battle formation and probe forward with the reconnaissance cohorts?"

"Oh, very well, commander," sighed Varus with a slight souring of his voice as he conceded the advantage of the debate to Marcus. "Put the Seventeenth into battle formation, but leave the remainder of the column as it is. I want no more disturbances. The threat appears to be head-on from the northwest, so the Seventeenth will have the capacity to sort out any enemy and skirmishes its encounters. Make the changes now, and then make camp for the night."

As Marcus made to leave, Varus reached out and touched his forearm. "Marcus, in the morning let us march to Arminius and sort out his problems for him—yes? Frankly, I suspect nothing will come of all this, but I wish to join Arminius quickly, resolve whatever matter he has stumbled into, and continue our march to the lagers on the River Lupia, then onward to Castra Secunda, and the Rhine."

"Very well, sire," Marcus nodded once, firmly. "It shall be as you wish. I will give the necessary orders and present the briefings tonight at the Orders Group conference. The Seventeenth will lead on the morrow." With that, Marcus Aius saluted and left to rejoin his legion commanders.

That evening, the runner who had carried with him the latest message from Arminius moved around the German flank and rearguard soldiers and spoke quietly with individual commanders, confirming with them the events soon to follow. Before daybreak, the nameless runner had vanished from the legion's encampments to rejoin Arminius in the hills and valleys of the Teutoburger Wald. His withdrawal from the legion's overnight camp went completely unnoticed.

As the messenger slipped away to the northwest, Marcus Aius was roused from his fitful sleep by the duty Centurion. The first thing he noticed was the soft light from a lamp that always burned in his tent. As always, he awoke instantly. "What is it, Centurion?" he murmured, quickly collecting his wits about him.

"The sentries on the north rampart report signal fires to the north and northwest of our position, sir, and one signal fire—we think it is a signal fire—many miles in the distance south of our position."

Marcus furrowed his brow as he lifted himself out of bed and swung his heavy military cloak over his tunic. He had slept fully clothed.

"You have seen these fires yourself?" he asked.

The Centurion moved to one side to allow Marcus to pass out of the tent into the half-light of the early dawn. "I have, sire, and I have noticed there is a clear series of signals passing between the lights to our front and the light to our rear. They are not just fires to brighten the darkness," he added ominously.

The two soldiers moved quickly across the main concourse of the overnight lager and approached the northern rampart. The shape of the sentry's helmet stood out against the breastwork. A rustle and thud followed as the sentry grounded his pilum *in salute. Marcus stood before the breast-high parapet. The sky offered a brilliant array of stars, the Milky Way emblazoned across the blackness like a million sparkling fireflies. Not a breath of air stirred. Marcus, listening intently, stared into the distance and immediately spotted the small pinpoints of light. He sucked in a sharp breath and held it. They were indeed signal fires. A sense of overwhelming remorse, followed quickly by a deep foreboding, reached into his very soul. His throat tightened as a chill stepped up each vertebrae of his spine. For a fleeting instant he thought of his wife, and that he would never see or feel her love again.*

When he heard the Tribune catch his breath, Centurion Gaius Claudius Suebus cleared his throat and spoke. "Sire, I mean no disrespect, but did you feel as if someone had clutched your heart, and walked across your grave just now?" Marcus did not move; neither did he laugh away the Centurion's question. "I had such a feeling just before I departed the watchtower duties on the Minden heights," continued Gaius Suebus. "I thought then it was my mother-in-law telling my wife what she thought of me, but then I realized it was only these damned German hills and woods; they play will-o'-the-wisp with our imaginations, and the very damp of the early-morning mists play havoc with our bones and spirits." Marcus remained silent. "There is no magical genie out here that cannot be put to rights with a touch of a Roman blade, sire. Whatever is out there, it will be of no match for us."

"Listen," was all Marcus said. "Listen."

Gaius Suebus cocked his head, held his breath, and waited. Somewhere out in the darkness a hunting owl screeched. And then silence. Gaius Suebus was just about to turn and ask Marcus what he was supposed to listen for when he heard it—a faint and formless sound of movement, gone so quickly he might have imagined it.

Marcus saw the Centurion tense. Did he hear it too? Marcus asked himself. Both men watched as the signal fires disappeared one by one and the heavy looming silence became a physical presence, something tasted, sensed.

"I don't think I heard anything, sire," said the Centurion after a long pause. "For a moment I thought the woods were rustling about as if men were walking softly through them, but it stopped suddenly, so it could not have been such a thing. And now the fires are also out. Shall I stand down the guard? It will be dawn soon."

Marcus turned and looked in Gaius Suebus' dark eyes. He exhaled softly. "No. I may not be long remembered as the second in command to the Consul, and the Seventeenth, Eighteenth and Nineteenth Legions of Rome's finest, but I will be remembered for doubling the guard each time I imagine a potential enemy stalking around our camp. And those signal fires were not of allied origin. I am going back to my quarters to prepare for our march north. Double the guard and turn out the cohort to action stations. We may as well start this day as we mean to go on—ready for mischief, although I know not of what sort." Marcus pulled his cloak tightly about him. "I fear it does not pay to take chances, especially now. We have been too long in this province without the need to fight our corner. I fear that time draws near."

"You are of course right, sir. Better to be safe than sorry. I will give the order now," replied the Centurion. "There was a full moon last night, and the gods are up and about their business."

Marcus had no need to ask him what he meant. In their world the gods showed themselves in full moons, in seed-time and harvest and, in particular, at the summer and winter solstice. If there was to be an uprising or a local but concentrated attack by the Germans, the full moon would be the time for it. And the moon was full now.

"Yes, let us be safe rather than sorry, my friend," said Marcus, and with a touch of humor and irony that he neither felt nor enjoyed, added, "let us also hope it is only your mother-in-law who troubles you, although I fear there is more to this day than the animosity of our relations." With that parting remark he departed the camp perimeter and made his way back to his billet, and then to headquarters.

The cohorts were duly turned out to action stations. At daybreak, when the sun began to rise on the eastern horizon, the legions quickly made their preparations to take up the march again, making all speed with a hasty breakfast; washing and shaving were luxuries not to be indulged in before a march to possible battle.

Within a short time the three legions were forming up, the lead elements of the Seventeenth Legion already snaking their way out of the overnight lager. The sky, clear and cloudless, had all the promise of a fine late summer's day, although just over the horizon there was an unusual reddish-purple tinge to the first morning light.

The Second Day

The central and rearmost legions were still intermingled with much of the baggage train when the Seventeenth forged ahead into the valleys and hills of the Teutoburger Wald. Behind it unfolded a long and winding column. Varus' command moved smoothly and the march proved an easy one. The head of the column stepped and rolled its way nine miles into the closely forested highlands before taking a midday pause. The advance elements secured their frontage with a strong party of scouts and guards while the commander of the Seventeenth oversaw the construction of a small but effective forward trench system, dug by his pioneer elements.

Nearly all of the legionaries carried pioneering tools and camp equipment. While forward units built the parapets of the stopover positions, the remainder of their comrades guarded the work parties. Meanwhile, residual elements of the legion, including support troops and associated carts and wagons, slowly made their way into the clear area behind the front. The two remaining legions followed close behind.

Initial reports from the forward scouting parties told of nearly impenetrable forests to their front. There was no easy way to maneuver around the Berglands without a long and time-consuming detour on the northwest approach toward Arminius' last reported position. Much to the disappointment of Marcus—who was increasingly concerned about the obvious dangers posed by the close country through which they were moving—Varus decided to continue on the present line of march. The Romans disliked marching through the forested highlands in Germany and avoided such places at all costs. They preferred instead open country, where the legions had room to maneuver and, if necessary, fight in formations to which they had become accustomed. Hilly countryside favored those who held the woodland heights on either side of the deep ravines and valleys. Varus' legions were moving along the valley floor, and were thus in a potentially precarious position, one where a quick tactical deployment in an emergency would be nigh-on impossible. Varus had considered this, and against the advice given by both Marcus and the commander of the Seventeenth Legion, presented instead what he considered to be an inspired plan.

The forward reconnaissance cohort would continue leading the legions on the current line of march, but the flank scouts and guards, comprised mainly of German mercenaries, would push farther out from the main force. Supported by contingents of reserve support elements from the Eighteenth and Nineteenth Legions, they would advance on a parallel axis over the surrounding hills, three to five hundred yards from the central force moving through the valley floors. Varus' plan was a tactical maneuver routinely employed by commanders moving through close country. It extended all around protection and ensured early warning of threats from the flanks. It also allowed the Romans to have a force pre-positioned on the heights on either side to negate an enemy's advantage.

Varus believed deploying the German mercenaries on the nearby slopes and hilltops, with the reserve contingents available nearby should they be required, offered sufficient protection for the advancing legions. Such is fortune and the ways of man, for Varus' decision helped seal the fate of his legions. Indeed, his plan deployed Arminius' own first line of attack against the Romans on the best terrain possible. Arminius' original plan had been for the German auxiliaries and flank scouts (including the rear German mercenary quarter guards), at a prearranged signal, to leave their established march positions and disappear into the surrounding hillsides and Bergland. Once they were far enough away, they would form for battle and turn on their Roman masters, attacking from their flanks that only minutes earlier they had been protecting.

Though Marcus Aius did look upon the German auxiliaries as a threat, he was uneasy about the rapidly emerging change of circumstances, the alteration of the marching formation—and the signal lights that had cut short his sleep. His vigorously voiced objections, however, fell on deaf ears.

When the midday break ended, the legions took up the revised formation and the auxiliaries disappeared into the surrounding wooded slopes and hills. As the Seventeenth filed out from the temporary camp, snaking its way toward the north through the thickly wooded valleys, Marcus sent a message to the legion's commander, Gaius Numonius Vala. Marcus ordered him to drop his cavalry back from their current position in the central van of the marching troops and reposition them between the Eighteenth and the Nineteenth Legions bringing up the rear. Vala understood what Marcus wanted: the move would enable the riders to deploy freely on either side of the column should an enemy attack the front or flanks of the Seventeenth Legion. The redeployment would also remove the cavalry from the confusing mass of supply wagons and carts and hundreds of pack mules interspersed with the marching legionaries as they slowly made their way through the dark woodland glades and valleys of the Teutoburger Wald.

Though the move was flawlessly implemented, Marcus grew more frustrated with each passing minute. Despite his best efforts, the length of the column was increasing with each step. Intermingled with the whole were many thousands of women and children who had become an integral part of the life of the legions during the two years of their occupancy in the German province. Among them were wives, girlfriends, camp followers, slaves, servants—a huge elongated mass of humanity

and animals coursing a fitful journey with their soldiers to rescue
Arminius from his aggressors. Marcus shook his head as he viewed the
motley procession. It was a strung-out line of noncombatants and
marching legionaries—an army on the move with but little semblance of
marching order and discipline.

Several times that afternoon, the advance was forced to stop and fell
trees to clear a path through the difficult terrain. Sometimes bridges and
track ways had to be laid across sodden patches of the valley floor. It was
grueling work that slowed the column to a crawl. Before long, most of the
men were cursing the difficult march instead of contemplating the
dangers of an enemy attack while in such a vulnerable position. A Roman
army was trained to fight in an extended battle formation; marching in an
ill-disciplined arrangement, Varus' legions were virtually defenseless
and strung out for several miles.

Just as Gaius Vala was about to order his pioneers to establish an
overnight lager, the unthinkable happened. It took place not from the
front, where the soldiers of the Seventeenth Legion remained blissfully
unaware of what was transpiring, but on the flanks along the center and
rear of the lengthy snake-like column. There, German auxiliaries
received the order they had been waiting for: turn on the hated Romans.
And so began the debacle that in later years would be known as the
Varusschlacht *(The Varus Battle)*.

*   *   *

The first onslaught was as frightening in its speed as it was terrible in
its consequence. The flank guards of the Eighteenth Legion, deployed in
support of the German auxiliaries and flank scouts, were the first to go
under. They were completely surprised when a mass of auxiliaries,
accompanied by hundreds of painted tribesmen, washed over the
extended files of men making their way through the woodland trails
along the edges of the upper valley slopes. In the same way they had
overrun the outposts and observation forts, the Germans remained silent
as the grave as they threw themselves against the Romans. The heavy
silence triggered a terrifying instant of fear in the hearts of the
unsuspecting men of the Eighteenth, a shock that seized in their throats
and rendered them speechless. They fell by the score to arrows and
javelins, to hacking and stabbing swords that quickly slashed exposed

throats. The attack was so sudden and unexpected that most of the Romans barely had time to look up in amazement at the hordes of auxiliaries and tribesmen, their painted bodies flowing over the ridges and down the slopes like a mass of lemmings throwing themselves over the cliffs into the sea of humanity below. By the time they realized what was happening, they were dead.

The first hint those walking and marching in the formations through the lower valley received that something was seriously amiss were the short, sharp screams of the fatally wounded. Even so, it was too late for many hundreds of soldiers, women, and children to protect themselves from the murderous onslaught gathering about them like storm clouds in an angry winter sky. Screams of pain and cries for mercy mingled and spilled their way through the valley as the slaughter consumed everyone within striking distance. The nightmare of a thousand lives extinguished in but a handful of minutes shattered the peace and tranquility of the woodland glades. There was no mercy, no quarter.

Almost as fast as the Germans struck they were gone. In their wake they left complete disarray, confusion, and hundreds of corpses. The legionaries and civilians marching in advance of the portion of the column struck so swiftly were thrown into a near-panic, for the constricted terrain of the valley floor made turning about and deploying for battle nearly impossible. Those immediately behind had formed as best they could, unaware of exactly what had happened or why, for the enemy was no longer visible. Those marching near the end of the column in the Nineteenth Legion had also been attacked, though no one else knew it yet. Like a vulnerable worm, the drawn-out column had been cut in two near the middle, both ends wriggling and seeking answers as the bloody mess in the center of the body continued to throb with pain and disorientation. It was the first onslaught, but it was the worst possible event that could have befallen Varus' legions. The Romans were left with a foreboding sense of facing overwhelming odds, deployed in a valley in which there was no room to maneuver. Fear of the unknown gripped everyone with its icy fingers. A sense of hopelessness began seeping its way into the hearts of the legionaries. Whatever poise Varus' legions possessed they never recovered, their capacity to wage war effectively (and cleverly) neutralized.

Varus was beside himself with a mixture of rage and fear. He witnessed some of the carnage from his elevated position on the back of a horse, protected by his own Governor's Guard and soldiers of the Eighteenth Legion. He had watched, stunned, as the mass of German warriors—many recognized as his own auxiliaries—wreaked their bloody havoc. Somehow, Marcus had managed to move forward through the chaos to the point of contact. A few quick glances gauged the situation exactly, and the veteran barked out a series of commands to officers milling about nearby. When he caught sight of Gaius Vala pushing through the milling throng to join him, Marcus rode toward him.

"Gaius, form these men here," yelled Marcus, waving his drawn sword in a line facing one of the sloping wooded hillsides, "and here!" pointing in the opposite direction. The Tribune knew the soldiers were in good hands. A courier reined in next to him, shouting out a message he had carried from the rear of the column. Marcus nodded his thanks, sent the man back with a message of his own, and then kicked his mount toward Varus to ascertain his condition and ask for further orders.

He reached the Consul more quickly and easily than he expected. Thankfully, Varus was unwounded.

"Marcus!" Varus spoke the name as if a great burden had been lifted from his shoulders. "What in the name of the Gods is happening?"

"Sire," replied Marcus, his horse turning away from the consul, fighting its rider's commands. "We have been attacked on both flanks by German tribesmen." Marcus cleared his throat. "Just before I moved forward to join you I received a message from the commander of the Nineteenth Legion. The rear of the column has been savagely mauled. Our flank guards were not sufficient to prevent the surprise, sire."

"How serious was the attack? What are our losses?" inquired Varus.

"We have lost many, sire. The Nineteenth, nearly two centuries before the soldiers could turn and deploy to engage the enemy properly. I have asked for additional reports, but according to a courier, the commander of the Nineteenth believes he is being quartered by a large force of Germans, and he needs to break out into more open country to take up proper positions to engage the enemy. I think we should also turn the cavalry, now between us and the Nineteenth, and allow it to move out to the flanks and investigate the apparent loss of our auxiliary scouts and flank guards. It also appears the flank guards from the Eighteenth Legion have been lost."

As Marcus was finishing his initial report, Vala rode up next to him. He nodded his head to confirm the observation. "What is happening with our auxiliaries, Marcus?" asked Varus. There was a higher pitch to his voice than usual.

"I have great suspicions about their fate. They may well—almost certainly, I think—have changed their allegiance. I suggest our cavalry flank around to the rear of the column and take up a supporting role with the rear command of the Nineteenth."

Varus, too, was having difficulty controlling his mount, which was snorting and shaking its head in response to the dying screams of two fatally injured horses, shivering on the ground just a few yards away. One, a brown mare, was lying on her side with a large lance sticking out of the side of her chest. Try as she might, she was unable to close her jaws around the spear in an effort to bite at the source her pain. The other lay on his side, his lower left rear leg completely severed. The wound was bleeding profusely.

"Damn this!" exclaimed Varus. "What reports do we have from the Seventeenth? Are there any reports of attacks against the front of the column? Is it a full-scale attack?"

"We are yet unsure," answered Marcus. "But I believe it was a well-planned strike, sire, and heavily delivered. It was not a band of tribesmen looking for booty. No reports from the front, only from the middle and rear of the column. I think we have no time to waste. We must turn and face the enemy or risk more attacks like the one we just suffered."

"Even if there is a large enemy force to our rear, Marcus, I do not think we should spend time trying to turn about three legions to seek out an unknown force of Germans in these damnable woods and valleys!"

Before the Tribune could answer, a mounted messenger drew up from the direction of the Seventeenth Legion. He handed a sealed scroll to Marcus, who passed it to Varus. The Consul scanned the document. "A message from Arminius, Marcus. The tribes are growing in strength, but are in the main still fragmented into tribal pockets. He has information the Chauci are moving up from the southeast to join with them. He suggests we break for a stretch of open ground, not far forward from our current position at the head of the column, and establish an overnight lager." Varus smirked at this report and leaned closer to his executive officer. "What more proof do we need that my plans are the right ones?

Forget this wish to turn around. It is obvious we need to continue moving north to join up with Arminius. Let us get this mess quickly sorted and reinforce the link with the Seventeenth. We will continue the march the way I ordered. Inform the commander of the Nineteenth Legion to continue marching with an eye toward the south. If the Chauci are moving up behind us, it makes sense to push forward and regroup in the open ground to the north, and take up defensive positions there before we consider how to continue on and link up with Arminius."

Before Marcus could protest and reaffirm his tactical evaluations, another messenger rode up, this time from the southern end of the column where the officers of the Nineteenth Legion were still counting their dead and wounded.

Marcus heard the courier out and informed Varus of the new information. "Sire, as we earlier learned, the rear of the column has also been attacked, but now communications with our command of the Eighteenth and the Nineteenth are severed—for the moment. It would also appear our flank scouts have changed their allegiance, for many of the attackers were indeed our own allies." Marcus paused a moment and then renewed his request to turn the column around and deploy for battle as well as possible, given the constraints of the terrain.

"Damn it, man, I command this force!" Varus closed his mouth hard for a moment before continuing, more calmly now. "I respect your noble position and experience as a great commander and friend, Marcus Aius, but I have made my decision, and this latest report does no more than confirm my tactical appreciation of our situation. We must continue northward. The Chauci are obviously close on our heels, and we need to break out to open ground as the commander of the Seventeenth suggests, and regroup to fight on ground of our choosing. Make the orders now." Varus turned to the commander of his guard, a clear sign that he had finished with Marcus. "Centurion," he barked, "get our command on the march again, and get some real legionaries in front of us and on our flanks—particularly on our flanks. Let us be on our march quickly."

Finally, Varus turned to directly address Gaius Vala, who was still awaiting orders. "Commander, make all speed back to your legion, see that your flanks are protected, and let us march from these cursed woods."

At that moment a huge streak of lightning raced across the sky, tracing the length of the column. The blood drained from Varus' face.

Peals of thunder ushered in a driving rain that swept in from the west. The reddish sky of the early morning was a weather gauge a man disregarded at his own peril. Heavy sheets of rain drowned the Romans. It was as if a nightmare sent by the Gods had swallowed the legions whole. Varus shivered violently as the rain soaked every man, uniform, and piece of equipment, turning dry earth and the valley floor into muddy, boggy swamps within a few minutes. The spirits of the men sank lower as they tramped through the soggy ground. Rivulets of water, small at first but growing as the minutes passed, coursed down through the wooded slopes and came together in the lower valley floor, where the growing stream washed through the bloody gore littering the line of march of the Seventeenth, Eighteenth and Nineteenth Legions.

*   *   *

Cassius Dio wrote:

Meanwhile a violent downpour and storm developed, so that the column was strung out even further; this also caused the ground around the tree roots and the felled trunks to become slippery, making movement very dangerous, and the tops of the trees to break off and crash down upon them, causing mass confusion.

While the Romans were struggling against the elements, the barbarians suddenly surrounded them on all sides at once, stealing through the densest thickets, as they were familiar with the paths. At first they hurled their spears from a distance, but as nobody attacked them in return and many were wounded, the Germans closed in to a shorter range; for their part the Romans were not advancing in any regular formation, but were interspersed at random with the wagons and the non-combatants. This meant that they could not easily concentrate their strength at any point, and since they were everywhere over-whelmed by their opponents, they suffered casualties, and were quite unable to counterattack.

Accordingly, they pitched camp on the spot after taking possession of a suitable place, so far as one could be found on wooded and mountainous ground; afterwards they either

*burned or abandoned most of their wagons and everything
else that was not absolutely indispensable to them. . .*

*   *   *

*Varus, however, decided that if anything remained with him in the
column, it would be all his personal possessions and household
necessities, all the treasures and the gold and silver his legions had
gathered in their forays across the German heartlands. This huge
treasure was to remain with him to the end.*

1994–1995: Pondering Treasures Lost

I have always been fascinated with lost archaeological treasures, and
have been avidly reading everything written on the subject for many
years. Some have been buried for thousands of years; others are scattered
across the globe, littering ocean floors. Each awaits discovery. More than
anything else in all my years of research on such matters, the
archaeological and historical jigsaw puzzles of lost treasures fascinate
me.

In 1989 and 1990, with the dawning realization that Kalkriese was
indeed the actual site of the *Varusschlacht*, a germ of an idea began to
form in my mind. I discussed these thoughts often with Professor
Schlüter as I began fleshing out the picture of the final days of Varus and
his soldiers as they prepared for the worst, facing defeat from every
quarter. Carried with them were their worldly goods and possessions,
many of which had been obtained during their summer occupation of
Germany. What was to be done with these treasured possessions,
personal effects, jewelry, family heirlooms, etc., all about to be lost to the
enemy? What would they have done? What did they in fact do? Of even
more interest to me was how they handled the taxes and tithes (anything
of a precious nature other than the furs and skins) Varus had levied
against the German tribes and collected during his summer sojourn on the
Weser and in the lands surrounding it. Would they have simply given up
this significant treasure to the enemy?

Plunder was the essence of a German tribesman's incentive to fight
and wage war. The average warrior was not by any means a political

animal. Arminius dragged the tribes together to take on Varus with the promise of plunder and rich pickings after a successful battle. This and this alone, was the deciding factor in the coalescing of the tribes.

During this time period, a Roman nobleman—and there were many in Varus' immediate entourage and inner council of advisers, including senior officers and Varus himself—possessed many gifts and personal property. Though basic in concept—cutlery, dinner services, drinking goblets, personal items of toiletry, writing equipment—these possessions were often crafted from precious metals. Thus the column that stumbled its way through northern Germany included thousands of items of solid gold and silver, fine bronzes, exquisite ivories, black onyx figurines and even exquisite furniture. All that was precious would not have been discarded swiftly or easily. The thought of these personal accoutrements, combined with Varus' swollen treasure chests, heightened my interest in establishing Varus' probable line of march to destruction at Kalkriese.

From both a tactical and logical point of view, I have always argued that Varus had come up through the Teutoburger Wald from the southeast, drawn to his end by the clever and carefully crafted plans of Arminius. I do not believe Varus lived long enough to see Kalkriese, for his last lager position was some distance to the east. If this indeed was the case—and according to Cassius Dio's description of the sequence of events it seems virtually certain that it was—Varus not only prepared himself during his last night on earth, but probably ordered his personal chattels and Roman assets secured to prevent them from falling into the hands of the Germans. It would have been a logical thing to do; after all, his own personal Governor's Guard proved its loyalty by remaining behind to dispose of his body after he committed suicide. If these men tarried to carry out actions considered to be in his best interest after he was dead, then it is not difficult to imagine these same men could be trusted to follow Varus' wishes when he was alive by preparing and secreting (and probably burying) the legions' treasure chests before the Germans could overrun them. This thought has always intrigued me, especially as I walked and drove the probable course of Varus' last march.

I believe I now know what happened to Varus' treasure chests. I think I know where some of them are, and I think I know how they came to be there. Time will tell. I hope one day we can uncover these precious relics of a bygone age and reveal them in all their glory in the new

Kalkriese museum for everybody to see and admire. It would be a suitable final resting place for these treasures, for that is where the *Varusschlacht* came to its bloody conclusion, where history marked the end of the Varus legions.

The End of the Second Day

The endless day finally began drawing to a close. The rain continued sheeting its way to earth and the ground underfoot was by this time so waterlogged, the men and wagons could barely slog or roll their way forward. The advance elements of the Seventeenth Legion finally broke free from the oppressive woodland and poured out into the open to protect the forward pioneer elements tasked with erecting the earthen ramparts of the overnight lager. The legionaries strove to finish the outer circumference of the position as quickly as possible, their work hastened by the threat and fear of further attack. But by this time the soupy earth was nearly unmanageable, and the establishment of the redoubt took far longer than usual to erect. Once the basic confines of the lager were created, the fragmented sections of the Eighteenth and Nineteenth legions spent the next two hours struggling up from the wooded valley onto the elevated plateau. There they would spend the night.

During those hours the intensity of the enemy attacks along the extended Roman column had fallen off. Still, a number of minor but harassing and occasionally deadly forays from the woods against the exposed flanks continued. From the trees screamed a javelin or a spray of hissing arrows. Most missed their mark, but some struck unfortunates who struggled within the column of humanity as it ambled its way toward what it collectively prayed would be a safe haven. Much to everyone's relief, no further heavy attacks fell upon them.

That night, Marcus ordered the guards on the walls of the lager trebled. In his headquarters, Varus attempted to establish some form of command and control. His first action was to clarify the numbers of men and quantity of equipment that had been lost. By the time the sub-unit commanders answered the questions asked of them, the night was well advanced. Varus, Marcus Aius, and the three legion commanders, meanwhile, gathered in Varus' tent to plan their next move. The situation reports were not encouraging.

Only a few direct attacks had been launched against the flanks of the column—including skirmishes against the rear. The real losses had been suffered during the drawn-out aggression from the flanks—the hurled spears and flights of arrows launched from invisible hands. These hit and run tactics had taken an immense toll of both men and animals, including store-carrying mules and ox-drawn wagons. The loss of these essential stores and equipment, including food, was a severe blow. Much of the tentage was abandoned in the confusion, which exacerbated the effects of the cold and rainy weather and further depressed the spirits of the men. Varus' men were wet, cold, hungry, and frightened.

As the results of the roll-call poured in, it became abundantly clear that in the short space of a single day, the three legions and their auxiliary and echelon forces had lost an astonishing three thousand soldiers. This figure did not include civilian camp followers who had fallen by the hundreds, much to the dismay and sorrow of many legionaries who had close friends and loved ones among them. The news could not be contained and coursed quickly through the ranks like flames lick dry tinder. Morale fell further as the lager's occupants tried to settle down for the night.

The situation actually improved during the dark hours, though the reason behind it was not so readily reassuring. During the commanders' conference, Varus and his officers decided that the surrounding countryside, including the land to the northwest through which they were about to march, was not suitable for the large number of wagons and equipment that still formed part of the three-legion entourage. It took some time, but the commanders finally accepted the fact that the wagons, while invaluable to the column, were hindering their ability to deploy and fight as a disciplined army. The effort to protect them during the long bloody march was one of the primary reasons behind the high losses that had been suffered. Varus reluctantly agreed and ordered them burned.

The mass of fires lit the night sky, illuminating the outer edges of the lager perimeter. The warmth and light from the spreading conflagration restored somewhat the damp and flagging spirits of the men, who sat quietly and watched as roiling clouds of sparks and flames shot up into the night. The heavy rain had tapered off after nightfall into a light fitful drizzle before stopping altogether. In its wake was a heavy blanket of humidity. Trails of gently rising steam from drying kits and equipment surrounded hundreds of burning pyres of wagons and their contents. The smoke from the fires joined with the dank humid steam rising from the highlands of the Teutoburger Wald.

The Germans warriors were not inclined to throw themselves at the burning walls of the overnight lager. Instead, they kept the legionaries fitfully awake by launching a series of feints against the perimeter. From the surrounding woods, captured Roman soldiers—some already wounded, others not—could be heard screaming and pleading for their lives while they were tortured into eventual silence.

When the morning mists began to clear with the onset of first light, wisps of smoke were still curling slowly skyward from the smoldering embers of the burning wagons and carts. The Romans were trying to come to terms with their plight. Soldiers with gritty and sore eyes, deprived of any meaningful sleep, gazed upon the state of their surroundings. The men knew what the loss of the wagons and carts meant. Every legionary would now have to carry food and stores on top of his already heavy backpack of equipment. If they were to survive even for a few more days, food and water would become an increasingly important and critical resource. With minds still numb from yesterday's events, they responded lethargically when reveille sounded within the lager. Orders were quickly given, a hasty toilet and breakfast were undertaken, and officers were informed of how they would depart from the encampment.

It was only now that someone realized that in the confusion of the previous night, a large quantity of oats and hay had been consumed in the pyres of wagons and equipment. Although food stocks for the soldiers were sufficient for the next three or four days, there remained only one day's ration of fodder for the horses traveling with the column. It was a crippling state of affairs, and it would have a marked effect on their capacity to fight in the days ahead.

Once legions were reorganized, with adjustments made to specific cohorts to compensate for their losses, Varus and Marcus decided that the Seventeenth would continue to lead the column and provide flanking guards for the first half of the advancing body. The legion had suffered the fewest killed and wounded, east, and was well suited to the task. The Eighteenth and Nineteenth legions, which had experienced heavier losses, were ordered to link their commands but remain in the same marching order used the previous day. Marcus ordered their commanders to pay particular attention to their flanks, remain in contact with the Seventeenth Legion, and establish a strong rearguard force. The latter was particularly important and would make it possible for the legions to draw up the rear of their column into a strong defensive shell should the necessity arise. Marcus was worried that no gaps might develop in the protection surrounding the entire column and his orders to his subordinates reflected this concern: "You will see that a force of arms is facing outward on both flanks and to the rear throughout the day's march." Like an armor-plated woodlouse with a defensive shell all round—not unlike an enlarged testudo—the Romans formed up to deploy for the march northwest toward Arminius' last known position.

The Third Day

And so they continued their advance. They marched in better order that day. A collective sigh of relief could almost be heard when the men realized the country, while still wooded, was more open than the terrain over which they had just marched—at least during the first part of the day's advance. There were still harrying attacks from the flanks and against the rear of the column, but this time the enemy was often seen and the damage was not as great. Maintaining forward momentum was absolutely essential for the survival of the column. The result was growing frustration within the ranks, for the pace of the march did not allow for the men to deploy and counterattack when the Germans approached to within skirmishing distance. This decision, in turn, allowed the tribesmen to pick away at the flanks and rear at will before disappearing in the surrounding woods, only to reappear yet again at another point and repeat the process.

By the early afternoon, scouts from the Seventeenth Legion reported that the countryside to their front was thickening up. The Romans were slowly entering the woods and hills of the Wiehengebirge; the easy going of the more open country through which they had just passed was at an end. This news was sent back through the column, and via headquarters, down the line to the Eighteenth and Nineteenth legions trailing in the rear. The Seventeenth continued through the thickening woodlands. Defiles and valleys became more pronounced, the opportunities for ambush and attack more plentiful. Encouraged by the absence of the enemy, the soldiers plodded on, for there was no other route to follow.

The pace picked up slightly. Before long, it was harder for the men in the middle and rear of the column to keep well closed and prevent gaps from appearing in the line itself, and between the flanking guards protecting it.

With the main Roman body well into the Wiehengebirge, the Germans struck again without warning. The strikes consisted of a series of sharp attacks against the flank guards. Continuous flights of arrows and javelins rained down on the legionaries struggling to maintain the pace of the march and their own security against the missiles meant to kill them. It did not take long for gaps to appear between the flanking elements of the leading Seventeenth Legion and those trailing behind it. Not daring to stop and gather their forces to counterattack for fear of losing contact with their own command elements, the men marched on through a gauntlet of ambushes. Indeed, the attacks quickened the pace of the soldiers. When word of the harassing attacks and consequent problems reached Varus, who was riding behind the Seventeenth, he ordered the legion's commander to set a slower pace so that flanking guards under assault could better deal with the harassing Germans.

It was at this point Arminius put the next phase of his plan into effect. The Seventeenth was marching unopposed and did not yet know of the problems far to the rear. The order to slow down the advance had not yet reached the legion's commander. Those following moved quicker to maintain contact. Many men marching in the middle and rear of the column, however, where the attacks against the flanking guards were taking place, slowed their own step in order to support the outer perimeter with reinforcements. It was a delicate balancing act, for the column had to keep up a forward momentum and tight formation, and still offer some reasonable form of defense. In the rough terrain, the Romans were unable to perform both feats. The result was the opening of a gap between the Seventeenth Legion and Varus' headquarters, and between Varus' headquarters and the trailing Eighteenth and Nineteenth legions. In places, the column formed giant bottlenecks of congestions and chaos. At others, the column was but thinly manned and seriously overstretched. Communication in the close country and under these circumstances was difficult in the best of times, and these were not the best of times. Although Varus did not yet know it, his ability to command and control his men was quickly unraveling.

The Germans picked their points well. Where the Romans were stretched thin, they launched heavy attacks that overran the legion flanks and smashed into, and often through, the central column itself. These attacks were delivered both in front of, and behind, Varus' position in the line. Others issued hit-and-run strikes that killed and maimed on a smaller scale, but killed and maimed nonetheless. Still more Germans spent their time dropping trees across the line of march to impede and sap the energy of the Romans. Confusion coursed its way up and down the column as the hours slipped past and the shadows lengthened. And still the attacks continued.

Frustrated and more than a little frightened at the deteriorating state of affairs, Varus ordered Vala to form up his cavalry to charge and break up the next German attack should it occur in the vicinity of his headquarters. No charge took place, however. By this time, infantry, cavalry, and support elements had become so congested and intermingled along the narrow route that untangling them in some disciplined fashion for deployment against the enemy was impossible. The killing continued.

By this time it was almost dark, and the losses suffered in men and equipment were appalling. Of the three legions, cavalry, auxiliary forces (the majority of which had absconded to Arminius) and women and children, perhaps twenty-five thousand souls in all, there remained no more than fifteen thousand, including those sorely wounded and being carried by friends. The path followed by the legions through the hills and valleys was now littered with dead and dying, which in turn created bottlenecks of their own. Troops from the Eighteenth and Nineteenth legions had the worst of it, their way often blocked by the bodies of their comrades, dead horses and pack mules, freshly-cut trees, and mobs of demoralized troops and civilians.

Only the firm hand of Marcus Aius brought some semblance of control to the column. The officer was indefatigable, riding up and down the line yelling out commands, forming squads of flank guards, organizing relief parties to move trees, all the while encouraging the men to keep moving forward. When he came across a group of soldiers huddled together and unmoving, he reined in his mount and yelled down at them, "To stop is to die! Your orders are to move forward. Do so immediately!" When no one moved, he leaned over and slapped the side of his sword against the nearest man's back. "I will kill you where you stand, or you can do your duty and march!" The men began moving, but within a few minutes they were brought to a halt once more, the route utterly closed with a congealed mass of humanity milling about in front of them.

Marcus drew in his mount, pondered the situation for a few minutes, and settled upon a solution. He dispatched couriers with orders to both Vala and his horsemen, and the commander of the Nineteenth Legion, to leave the narrow route altogether by splitting their forces on either side and taking up the line followed by the flanking guards. Although it was difficult to get the men to understand what was expected of them, once they understood and moved off the track, the two legions—although still suffering under nearly continuous skirmishing attacks—advanced at a much quicker pace. Within a short time the gaps in the line had been closed and the tenuous links with the flanking guards of the Seventeenth Legion reestablished. The men were also better situated to fight back with some small success. The German warriors disappeared into the growing shadows.

Varus and his legions were still in desperate straits, for they had not been able to erect a proper march lager before darkness settled over them. The Seventeenth Legion remained nearly unbloodied, well-closed, and with a strong sense of order permeating its ranks. Its commander had taken up a strong position on one of the hills and maintained a circular defense throughout the long night. With only wet wood to burn, however, the observation fires were difficult to maintain. An extended force of infantry was established along the axis of the central column, as well as the parallel routes taken by the flank guards. With this protective barrier in place, the men of the Eighteenth and Nineteenth legions, including nearly all of Varus' headquarters staff, filed into the Seventeenth's defensive position throughout the night.

The soldiers pitched camp where they lay. Small groups of legionaries huddled together in pockets of defensive groups, lighting fires where they could. Damp, cold, fearful of their circumstances, the men began to doubt whether they would ever leave Germany. Death was ever-present, looking over the shoulder of every man. Morale, which was already low, slipped lower still. By the time Varus and Marcus Aius achieved some form of control and organization, dawn was breaking to the east.

The Fourth Day

Marcus turned away from the spreading light in the east with a heavy heart and stepped into the tent. He knew what the light would bring with it. Gathered before him were the commanders of the three legions and the cavalry leader Vala. Varus was not in attendance, deciding instead to remain in his bed and leave the tactical decisions in the hands of his executive officer. Varus looked ill and had withdrawn to the point where he no longer pretended to be in command of his legions. The losses and hardships suffered over the past few days weighed heavily upon him, for he felt the loss of each man. It was clear he no longer believed his legions would emerge on the other end of the endless tunnel within which they found themselves. Guilt is a heavy cloak, and Varus did not wear it well.

Marcus decided the best course of action was to break out to the southwest, down to the Lippe River and the support of the forts and legions stationed there. He knew in his heart that every messenger he had ordered to strike out for the Lippe and the Rhine had been discovered and cut down by the enemy. But continuing northwest toward Arminius' last reported position had become too perilous. For both logistical and tactical reasons, the march northwest was no longer possible.

"I want the Seventeenth to turn about and become the rear of the column," explained Marcus. "Gaius Vala, your cavalry will carry out a series of fast patrols of the land directly southwest of our current position and identify a march route to take us down to the Lippe. Your legion, together with that of the Nineteenth, will regroup and lead the advance to the river. Flank protection must be maintained at all times," continued Marcus, "and it must be impressed on the men that . . ."

Without warning, Varus stormed into the briefing. "Marcus! I have just received another message from Arminius," he exclaimed, waving a small parchment in the air. "I want to hear no further talk of running to the Lippe. If we can join forces with him, we will have the upper hand and strength to fight together to put down this bloody insurrection!"

Marcus could not hide his surprise at both the sudden interruption and the shrill tone of Varus' voice. "Sire, we cannot continue on this route, for . . ."

Varus cut his answer short. "We will not desert him, Marcus Aius! I am in command of these men, and you will carry out my orders. We will move to assist Arminius. Any move to the contrary will be viewed as an act of treason." Varus glared for a few seconds at Marcus and the gathered commanders through eyes reddened from lack of sleep.

"Yes, sire. Of course."

With that, Varus grunted in reply and stormed out of the briefing tent. A stunned silence lingered after he left. Marcus and the officers quietly absorbed the enormity of the order they had just heard. Marcus gathered himself, cleared his throat, and quietly said, "Gentlemen, the situation is clear. Varus has decided my plan is not to be put into effect. We are to continue to move forward as before, toward the last reported position of Arminius and his auxiliaries and cavalry, join forces with them, and attend to this insurrection from a position of supremacy to be established at some point in the near future."

Vala looked at Marcus as if to object, but Marcus waved his arm and cut him short. "I will not challenge orders given to me by my commander, but what I do say to you is this. Let us be about our business with the discipline and fortitude that has carried the names of the great Roman legions into history. We are desperately pressed in our forward deployment to the northwest, and yet that is where the Commander has ordered us to march, to aid Arminius." Marcus lowered his voice to a whisper. "Be especially on guard. I fear Arminius has his own agenda in these matters, and that he is no longer a friend."

Vala and the others nodded in agreement. They had obviously been thinking and discussing the same thing.

Marcus continued. "Keep good order. The Seventeenth will lead as before, and the Eighteenth and Nineteenth will now absorb the command headquarters element. I wish you all good fortune, a strong right arm, and success. You will be informed of any developments as they occur. When we come together again, gentlemen, let it be in the spirit of conquest and success. We owe these Germans much retribution for the loss of our comrades and women and children. I entrust you with the honor and reputation of the Eagles of Rome, the Eagles of the Seventeenth, Eighteenth and Nineteenth of Rome's finest legions."

And so the legions of Varus continued their advance. The fourth day was comparatively successful in terms of ground covered, although the Germans continued to inflict losses on the Romans, concentrating their attacks against the rear of the column rather than its flanks. The Seventeenth Legion, slogging ahead at the front of the column, continued unhindered in its advance.

Reorganized to a large degree, the soldiers marched armed with a new directive and inspiring words from their commanders: "Soldiers of Rome! Stand and die here in this forsaken land, or fight when necessary and press forward to the northwest and escape. Our mission is to pass through the Wiehengebirge northwest to the open Dieven Wiesen, to find Arminius and his auxiliaries. Take up the Eagles, and maintain good heart. We are not far from better ground, where we will turn the tables on our foe. For Augustus, for Rome! Go forward and take heart, for we have many lost comrades to avenge, and they seek your bloody vengeance upon their killers. May the grace of our gods and our Caesar accompany you, for it is with their support we will overcome these German peoples."

With these words, the three legions of Varus moved down toward the Kalkriese Berg and the passes at Ostercappeln.

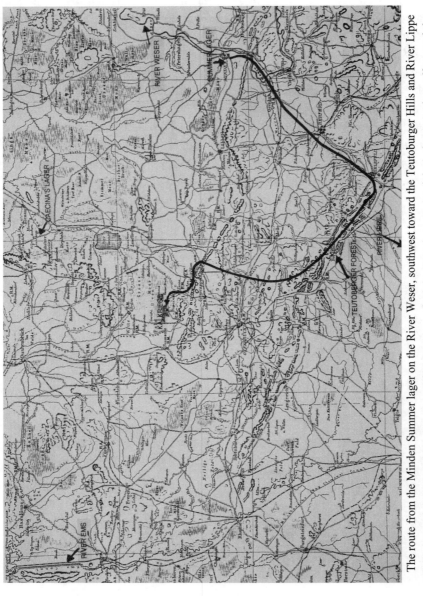

The route from the Minden Summer lager on the River Weser, southwest toward the Teutoburger Hills and River Lippe forts beyond, back to winter quarters. When Varus reached the Teutoburger, Arminius' plan went into effect, and the legions changed direction northwest up the line of the Teutoburger Hills toward the passes at Ostercappeln.

Chapter Nineteen

Varus' Last Lager at Felsenfeld

By midday the going once more became extremely difficult. Heavy rain and violent winds driving down on their positions made walking difficult, and more trees were found blocking the route. Utterly exhausted, the Romans finally could advance no farther, such was the ferocity of the storm. Such a cyclone of wind and rain had not been seen in Germany for many years, and made the normal late summer storms seem calm by comparison.[1]

The Germans continued with their skirmishing attacks. They did not suffer the many difficulties that beset the Roman column, for they were used to bad weather, were not encumbered with women and children, and knew what they were about. Although both sides spent much of their

[1] The heavy pounding storms that swept Germany and much of northern Europe in 1981, and again in 1984, may well have been an example of the conditions that prevailed at the time of the Varus battle.

*time slipping and sliding along the forest floor, the Germans firmly held
the upper hand.*

  Cassius Dio:

> *It was impossible for them [the Romans] to wield their weapons.
> They could not draw their bows nor hurl their javelins to any effect,
> nor even make use of their shields, which were completely sodden
> with rain. Their opponents, on the other hand, were for the most
> part lightly armed, and so could approach or retire without
> difficulty, and suffered far less from the weather. Beside this, the
> enemy's numbers had been greatly reinforced, since many of those
> who had first hesitated now joined the battle in the hope of taking
> plunder. Their increased numbers made it easy to encircle and
> strike down the Romans, whose ranks by contrast had shrunk, since
> they had lost many men in the earlier fighting.*

*   *   **

  *The commander of the Seventeenth Legion had established a
bridgehead of sorts around the front of the column as it straddled a deep
valley bordering on the verge of the Wiehengebirge ridge, now only a
short distance to the north of their position. Once he had re-secured his
flanks, for his legion was now the only effective force in strength
remaining of the Varus legions, he dispatched a force back around the
perimeter areas of the column to assist the beleaguered troops pinned
down in the valley floor, help clear trees and undergrowth, and put up a
protective shield around the central command core. These actions gave
some small relief to the trapped remnants of the Eighteenth and
Nineteenth legions, whose losses were alarmingly high. The Germans
drew off once more when they encountered this increase in resistance,
patient in their determination and conviction that they would win, no
matter how long it took. The ground and time were on their side. They
watched and they waited.*
  *Arminius was well pleased with the way the battle had progressed
thus far. Although the Germans had all the advantages of ambush and
withdrawal, they had still suffered losses of their own. He was content
however, for the Romans were still moving in the direction he needed
them to go, ever northwest. His men would stand off for a time and*

continue to coax the legions along with but minor skirmishing forays until he could herd them into the final ambush, the final killing field.

Arminius had planned his final series of ambushes in the main westerly pass at Ostercappeln, less than one mile from his camp at Krebsburg. It was an ideal bottleneck to trap the remnants of Varus' legions, and if necessary, another entrapment zone might follow around the Kalkriese Berg at Kalkriese itself. This location was the ultimate bottleneck—a tightly restricted path around a small projecting knoll lying on the northerly edge of the Berg, no more than fifty to one hundred yards wide, with the boggy black morass of the Dieven Wiesen squeezing the trail against the slope of the hills. Arminius, however, had made one small but important oversight. He had forgotten the tenacity and strength of Marcus Aius, his courage, and his leadership skills. He had also not taken into account that Vala still retained command of a fair proportion of the original force of cavalry, oversights that would have a marked effect on the outcome of the next twelve hours.

The command center of the legion column was still reasonably intact. The Consul's own personal guards surrounding and protecting Varus' entourage were hand-picked seasoned veterans of many past campaigns; some of the guards had served Varus for years. Hard as nails and just as mean if not meaner than any painted barbarian, they had savagely fought off any attacks made against the central core of the command cell.

Now in a more positive frame of mind after a short nap, Varus gathered Marcus and his commanders of the Seventeenth and Nineteenth legions for meeting. They were in deep conversation when Vala joined them in the tent.

"Ah, Vala—just the man I wish to see," began Varus. "I have decided, Commander, that we cannot survive this piecemeal onslaught in these cursed valleys and hills much longer. The commander of the Seventeenth has reported that the Wiehengebirge is not far to our front, and there are a number of passes we can use to gain the open ground to the north of the ridge line."

Vala looked at the faces around him. Marcus met his eyes with a grim look. He turned back to Varus. "What would you have me do, sire?"

"I need you to take a fast-moving mounted patrol—take all of the cavalry you can muster—and ride like the wind when you do it. I want a clean pass to get into the open ground. If these attacks on us are any

example of what lies ahead . . ." Varus' sentence drifted off into silence for a few seconds. "I still do not know how Arminius fares." He barely whispered the words.

Marcus slowly shook his head in dismay at this latest reference to Arminius, but Varus went on, "We have but one chance to make good and recover the situation. Get into the open ground, regroup, and then swing northwest toward the Ems, marching out from the northern edge of the ridge in the open ground where we can better defend our positions and recover the damned initiative. Marcus Aius will assume temporary command of your Eighteenth Legion. Order it now, but let the Seventeenth have your report first."

Before Vala could reply Varus turned to the commander of the Seventeenth. "On receipt of Commander Vala's report you are to act as quickly as you can. Take the clear pass and secure a battle lager position in the open ground as quickly as you can. Leave your flank protection in place and we will bring up the Eighteenth and Nineteenth legions into position as soon as you have gained and secured the ground." No one moved. "That is all." Varus was not seeking counsel or questions. He had issued his battle orders and expected them to be carried out. He dismissed the Orders Group and prepared for the next move forward. Marcus walked with Vala to attend the cavalry reconnaissance briefing, unable to remain in Varus' company and listen to more platitudes about the traitor Arminius. Marcus had long since given up on Varus' views that Arminius was still waiting for help from the legions somewhere to the northwest. As far as Marcus was concerned, Arminius was directly tied to, and probably leading, the battle against the legions. Even now, mused the Tribune, the German traitor was planning the next attack against them.

During the next hour, while the Germans held back from the outer protection afforded by the Seventeenth on the flanks of the Roman column, and the rain and winds were still lashing through the valleys and hills, Vala and his riders made their quick dash to the Wiehengebirge. It did not take him long to examine the ground at Ostercappeln, and in particular the passes to the east and west of the area leading away into the open ground to the north. He was about to move back from his vantage point when he saw a streak of color moving up from the valley and into the forests of the westerly pass. A stream of tribesmen, barely visible through the driving rain, was moving across the open ground. The pass to the west was not open. The eastern pass was the only route of escape into the open ground. The results of Vala's reconnaissance were swiftly issued down the chain of command. The Seventeenth pressed forward through the boggy valley floor, maintaining a flank guard at all times, through which the rest of the column progressed in its hasty move toward the open ground and a place called Schwagstorf.

Originally Marcus Aius believed the column should swing northwest after moving through the pass and press on immediately towards Vorden. But the more he thought about it, the more he realized Varus' order to establish an early overnight battle lager was well founded. By the time the Seventeenth began its advance through the eastern exit the day was drawing to a close. Exhaustion and desperation was carved deeply on every man's face—a clear indication that regrouping and establishing the reassuring walls of an overnight battle lager was an urgent first priority. With so many tired and wounded legionaries starting to sink under the strain of the last four days of intense hardship, of sleepless nights and days, it was decided to run for the highest ground on the other side of the feature slightly northwest of the pass, to a ground swell called Felsenfeld *(Felsen Field).*

And so the legions swarmed through the easterly pass onto this rising ground where the Seventeenth hastened to establish a tactical battle lager. Dying and wounded comrades were dragged and carried toward the new redoubt, and Roman spirits again lifted slightly as the rain and winds slowly dissipated. By early evening the hasty lager was up and the remnants of the three legions began pouring into the new position. Roman hearts took a little strength from the momentary relief of a stable and reasonably well protected environment.

*   *   *

Arminius was beside himself with rage. He had taken a well deserved break, a short sleep, and had given orders to be woken should events warrant it. The Roman breakthrough into the eastern pass and then around to the hill at Felsenfeld had been achieved so fast, however, that his own tribesmen had not recognized the flanking move by the Romans for what it was, believing instead that the easier of the two routes—the westerly pass—would be the natural continuing axis of the Roman line of march. And so Arminius was left to sleep. For once, the adverse weather conditions had assisted the legions by helping to conceal their flanking move through the pass. Before the Germans realized their error, still patiently waiting in their prepared ambush positions in the western pass by the Krebsburg, the Romans had secured their strong foothold on the high ground at Felsenfeld, where they erected their lager and dug extra ramparts with an alacrity similar to the frantic activity found in an overturned ants' nest.

Marcus breathed a sigh of relief as he watched the redoubt quickly take form. Through the misty rain that lingered after the heavy rain and lashing winds of the storm, he could see that Vala had chosen the ground well. The final traces of the day were now giving way to the twilight of the evening. In the distance he could just make out the distinct gap of the westerly Ostercappeln pass where, unbeknownst to him, Arminius' forces were preparing to move out from their unsuccessful ambush positions.

All Marcus knew at that time was that for some inexplicable reason they had been given a small respite. Finally, the unlucky sick and wounded could be attended to. The Greek doctor and the remnants of his medical team were soon at work, doing what they could to stem bleeding limbs and sew up split heads and severed muscles. But spare linen and cloths were in short supply, and they were unable to do much for the more seriously wounded men and women, who soon passed into oblivion.

Varus' survivors took stock of their plight. Besides the huge number of wounded requiring urgent medical attention, by far the most important and most disheartening logistical statistic was the loss of manpower. Out of a total strength of more than 20,000 legionaries, cavalry, and auxiliary forces—not counting Arminius' auxiliaries and scouts, who had changed their colors—and the many camp followers of women, children, and servants, there now remained perhaps 7,000 men under arms and a few hundred camp followers. Everyone else had been killed, lost in the forest, wounded and left behind, or had deserted.

They had lost some of the few wagons that had not been burned, and most of the pack mules had perished in the hills and valleys of the Teutoburger Wald. Of all their essential stores, there remained only a pitifully small amount of food and no fodder at all for the cavalry mounts. Varus' legions could not have been in a worse state. The remaining personal baggage of any note was Varus' massive accumulation of accoutrements and possessions, including the Consul's treasure gathered in for Augustus Caesar from the German tribes during the summer months.

Spirits and morale were at a low ebb. A great lethargy had fallen like a shroud over those who had survived the last four days of terror. Once inside the lager the men lolled about. Some fell down in a fitful stupor; others leaned against the parapets, their heads bowed onto the damp earthen walls wondering, sometimes aloud, how it had managed to come to this. Acute exhaustion was a common experience for Roman legionaries—and not just from combat. Life in a legion, with its often harsh discipline and demanding physical tasks, could wear a man out quickly. But these men were not merely tired but dispirited, desperate. Each fully recognized the disastrous plight they were in. They had been given a short respite, and for that they were thankful. But they also knew death was creeping closer each hour.

In his own camp, Arminius was doing the best he could to rectify the error that had allowed the Romans to swing around the Ostercappeln feature through the eastern pass. There had been a temporary saving of face for the Germans in the ambush positions after suffering the wrath of Arminius' rage. A lone detachment of Roman soldiers that had lost contact with the main column had inadvertently moved through the wrong pass. They suffered the onslaught of hundreds of swords and lances meant for a larger body of enemy. The small group, some 50 souls in all, fell as one, their bodies savagely desecrated and hacked to pieces in the bloody heat and rage of the German attack.

Arminius ordered out a large force around to the eastern flank, through the Ostercappeln feature and down the pass on the eastern side, to follow in the footsteps of the remaining Romans. Their task was to establish a barrier to prevent the Romans from breaking out of their newly established position to the east and making their way back to the lager at Minden. They were tasked with insuring that when the attacks against the Roman battle position began, the weight of the attack would come from the eastern flank, and so discourage the Romans from breaking back to the Weser.

Arminius surmised that Felsenfeld could possibly prove to be the end of the Varus legions, and he wanted to make sure his plan of entrapment sealed off any hope the Romans had of moving back to the relative safety of the summer lager. However, if he could not finish them off here, he *wanted them to move farther along the route of his choosing, to Kalkriese, the ultimate position for their final annihilation.*

*   *   *

The Romans, past masters at recovering from serious tactical setbacks, had not in their wildest dreams expected to be trapped in such a precarious position as they were in Germany. During Julius Caesar's major battle against the Gauls, when he was outnumbered three to one, the situation was never considered untenable. Even battling against those odds he had come through, the reputation of the legions forever enhanced. Now, however, the end of the once-omnipotent Romans occupying Germany loomed large.

As the hours of darkness settled over Felsenfeld the rains stopped. The respite from attack, safety of the lager, and end to the rain lifted spirits balancing on the brink of despair. Hope, small and barely flickering, danced anew within their minds. The guards were posted and the rolls called. Every name on the muster was spoken; few were left to answer. Marcus Aius walked the outposts, spoke to the guards, visited the sick and dying, and encouraged everyone he met to stand fast, to fight for their families, for Rome, for Augustus Caesar, and ultimately, for their very own lives. Instead of hopeless stares, Marcus was pleased to see the firm nodding of heads, even smiles. He walked back inside the lager and moved through the mass of humanity huddled inside. There was little order, as most of the men had simply dropped where they could, their shields next to them. But something had changed. More often than not, encouraging words of duty and firmness answered his call to arms. Perhaps, he thought as he approached another group of soldiers, just perhaps . . .

A chilling cry from beyond one of the lager walls pierced the solitude. Marcus jerked his head to the right in the direction of the scream just as it was cut short, strangled in mid-throat. It had come from one of the outposts! He rushed his way to the parapet and peered out into the darkness. The attack came in the form of a silent rush of tens of hundreds of shadows. The demons pitched in from every direction, coursing over the outposts without stopping to desecrate the soldiers they had slain in passing. Within seconds they had swarmed to the edge of the ditch around the lager, at speed and with an impetus that seemed impossible to withstand. Marcus screamed out the alarm, just as several others were also doing. He watched with incredulity as the Germans flung bundles of brushwood into the ditch to form small causeways over which they ran. With poles they scaled the ramparts. In the darkness, as they flowed up and over the defenses, they appeared as a wave of ghosts—evil, haunting, fatal. And not a one uttered a sound. With a whisk of metal, Marcus drew his sword and the Romans rose as one to meet the attackers. The silence was no more.

A mighty roar, like a sudden wall of sound, rose up to the sky as shields, swords, and bodies came together in a thunderous cacophony of killing. Screams and gasps of pain, cries of recognition and anger, and shouts of hatred and defiance in a score of languages and dialects filled the lager. No quarter was given, no quarter called. By simply standing and facing outward, and with only a few hasty commands, the Romans had formed a thick wall of soldiers. Marcus had run deep into the lager to get the men organized for defense, pulling together groups of soldiers into a reserve. As he was arranging them Varus suddenly appeared next to him, white-faced and open-mouthed, spinning in every direction as if unsure what to do next.

"Marcus!" He screamed. "How can we hold them back!"

"Sire," yelled back the Tribune, "we are tightly gathered and in good order. We will beat them back. Please leave the tactical arrangements to me." Without another word Varus vanished into the throng of gathering soldiers milling about in the middle of the lager.

Marcus turned away in disgust and looked at the men along the front line next to the parapets, each fighting behind his curved scutum, thrusting with a short sword into the recklessly exposed stomachs and chests of their enemies. One Roman pushed with his shield against a massive German as he bent to the right, reaching in and cutting with his blade, hamstringing his opponent. Unable to stand, the warrior fell to the ground where, with a single stroke to the throat, he expired. The Roman lifted his sword just in time to utter his own demonic scream as he thrust his blade deep into the mouth of a bellowing barbarian. The tip of the sword lodged for a few seconds in the thick bone of his skull. The victorious Legionaire yanked his gladius free and was turning to face another attacker when a javelin hurled from an invisible arm whistled through the chill night air and struck him down. As he crumbled to the ground, another nameless Roman waiting behind him stepped up to take his place. Within a few minutes, German and Roman bodies began piling atop one another, intertwined in death and dripping blood and entrails that made the ground a slippery, stinking morass of gore. Many soldiers on both sides lost their footing and, unable to recover quickly enough, fell to the ground and died as a result.

Deep in the distance a German horn sounded, strident and loud, calling forward fresh waves of shadows into the stalled attack. From the inner recesses of the redoubt a Roman horn answered the call, and , and a section of the reserve trotted out of the inner sanctum of the lager, doubling forward, pushing aside exhausted comrades to hurl themselves at the German foe, short swords stabbing at naked bellies, slipping into unprotected groins and stomachs. For the first time, Roman voices began to be clearly heard above the death struggle, shouting and screaming oaths at the foe.

"Forward the Seventeenth! Forward for Rome!"

The adrenaline and heat of battle drove them now, pumping the blood through their veins, some to be spilled in jets and spumes from severed arteries and limbs hacked from bodies that were dead before they hit the ground.

Marcus looked up to watch as a torch arced through the air over the ranks of fighting Romans and landed behind them. Another, and then several more along the lines followed. For a moment he was puzzled, but then he understood. The flames highlighted their alignment and revealed their weaknesses. Legionaires quickly extinguished the flames and the mindless as the merciless fighting continued.

By now, every yard of the ramparts, and some of the interior rim of the lager itself, was a reeling, roaring line of battle as the tribesmen continued pouring across the breastwork to be met by the grim Romans waiting within. How long this assault lasted nobody knew. Some estimated thirty minutes; others two hours—or longer. But when the attack finally ended, when the Germans finally realized they were not going to penetrate the ranks and overwhelm the defenders, they fell back into the night that had delivered them. There was a sagging of tired limbs, and for a short while an unbelievable hush descended over the fort. Even the wounded seemed to hold their breath, as if a cry of agony or plea for water might bring forth the demons a second time.

Marcus Aius leaned wearily against the upright supporting the main entrance position. His breath came in great painful gasps as his eyes settled upon Centurion Gaius Suebus, who had been fighting nearby without either man knowing of the other. Marcus smiled in a show of self-assurance. "We held them and drove them off! We must hold longer—they cannot have many more resources! Surely, in the name of all the gods, we cannot be fighting all the German tribes together?"

The Centurion's response was softly spoken. "We have lost so many men, Marcus. I cannot see how we can stand up to this relentless swamping of our position if they renew the attack. Look at how many these demons have thrown at us this time." He pointed his sword and drew it in a semi-circle around him to indicate the heaps of German dead and dying.

Marcus watched as his men moved among them, putting to the sword any survivors, silencing the groans and cries of the wounded enemy. When a fallen comrade was found alive, he was picked up by the teams of stretcher-bearers and medical assistants working their way through the morass of fallen bodies. The Romans had long since ceased their worthy practice of treating the enemy along with their own wounded and dying. The sword was now the lance that drew not the poison from the wounded body, but life itself—swift, merciless, unforgiving. The Greek surgeon moved swiftly about the battlefield, advising on who could be saved and who should be left to die.

"Organize your men here," ordered Marcus. "Man the wall heavily and prepare for another assault."

"Yes, sire," answered the Centurion. He stopped for a moment to look at Marcus. "How long can we hold out?"

Marcus shrugged his shoulders and exhaled. "With a bit of luck, a few days perhaps. Much depends on whether our runners have managed to escape through the enemy lines and drop down to the Lupia and Anreppen to seek reinforcements. We also have a problem which I shall have to address shortly. The commander of the Seventeenth has fallen, and other senior officers have been lost. Our commander is totally in despair at the treachery of Arminius; indeed, he refuses to believe it still! He fears for his honor, having lost so many from the three legions. I think he fears Arminius has special plans for him."

"I have heard talk of a breakout," began Gaius Suebus.

"It does not bear thinking about!" hissed Marcus, who went on to admit that there was talk in some quarters of such a move. "If we did such a thing, we would lose the last remnants of our command and control, *and the Germans would make short shrift of us. No, we must stand and fight together! Gaius, organize your men, count the bodies and take a roll-call. I must know how we fare. Send a runner to Commander Vala, for I need to speak with him soon."*

The Centurion braced himself erect and smartly saluted, his forearm striking across his chest in the recognized manner. *"At your order, it will be done, and you must look to your wounds too, sire; you have taken a nasty gash on your sword arm, and if there is anything we need it is the might of your attacks to aid us in our defense. I fear it will not be long before the enemy returns."*

Marcus looked at his arm with surprise. He did not even know he had been cut. The wound was a superficial slice, and had already clotted itself. He nodded in response. *"I must speak to the men. They have been brave and fearless, and they deserve much praise, for they have honored Rome with their courage. I did not think they would be so strong, so committed."*

He moved quickly away into the crowded space surrounding the ramparts. Marcus cut a commanding figure, his long muddy red cloak swirling about him as he forced a laugh and gave encouragement to his men. *"Well done, men! We will beat these cursed Germans, and just to show we are about our normal business here, let us have our early breakfast, and charge ourselves for the next sporting event!"* Even in the face of such adversity and despair, most of the men within earshot grinned at this jocularity. Here and there soldiers made rude and coarse remarks in reply, their tension lessening somewhat. They thanked their gods for a strong arm and steady nerves.

Marcus had not eaten since the previous morning and was feeling the nagging pains of hunger. He had too much to organize to stop and eat. The legions, with much of their command hierarchy dead, wounded, or missing, had to be pulled together, reorganized, and then briefed on the tasks that lay ahead. Parapets needed to be repaired; the dead needed to be cleared away; and order had to be pulled from the chaos. No one knew how long it would be before the unpredictable enemy struck again. At the very least, the wounded needed to be protected and cared for, and an issue of the meager remaining stocks of raisins and hard bread distributed to the troops. Marcus issued the orders. Having done as much as he could, he went off to meet Vala to verify the state of his forces, and then on to Varus' command post to submit his report. There was not *much more he could personally do in the van of the battle at the inner rim of the lager; a score of other pressing matters needed his attention.*

It was three hours before dawn when the next attack swept up against the lager. Somewhere a war horn sounded, and before the wild note had died away the tribesmen broke from cover, yelling like fiends out of Tartarus as they swarmed up through the bracken, heading for the broken ramparts the legionaries had not had time to fully repair. Tree trunks were used as ramps across the ditches, followed by firebrands that flashed and sparked as they were thrown into the midst of the defending Romans. Chaos reigned again. This time the Germans pressed their attacks against the eastern and southern flanks of the fort, while feints and skirmish-style tactics were used against the northern and western sides to pin the Romans defending there firmly in place.

They came on without respite, heedless of the Roman arrows and javelins that thinned their ranks with every step. Marcus, this time up closer to the front in the thick of the battle, saw a mounted warrior in the van of the attack—a wild figure in streaming robes that stamped him apart from the other attacking dervishes and half-naked warriors. The rider was whirling a firebrand in one hand and carrying a long, heavy flat-bladed sword, unlike the smaller swords carried by the others. His reins were clenched firmly between his teeth. Suddenly, in the light of his whirling torch, the wings on his plumed helmet, rising against the backdrop of the flickering lights and shadows, appeared to shine with a radiance of their own.

Marcus' heart skipped a beat and he found himself unable to tear his eyes away from the warrior's familiar face. Shaking his head with rage, he cast about for an archer. "Shoot that devil there!" he shouted, pointing at the mounted rider. "Kill that damned traitor!" The archer nodded vigorously. In one swift movement he drew an arrow from his quiver, seated it, bent the bow and sent the missile on its errand. The Roman auxiliaries were fine bowmen, but the arrow missed its mark by a few inches, passing through the wings of Arminius' helmet. The archer cursed and was reaching for another arrow when a large rock struck him square in the face. He fell backward, knocked unconscious. A comrade dragged him deeper into the lager. The mass of attackers, with a courage and fortitude that took no heed of losses, poured in over the dead lying heaped in the ditch. Screaming in their bloodthirsty tongue, the wave of warriors smashed up against the parapet and the hand-to-hand combat began anew.

Marcus yelled out for the men to stand strong and together as his eyes searched the enemy throng. The mounted chief was no where to be seen. Someone shouted his name and he had enough presence of mind to side-step a charging German swinging an axe. Hacking back across his body, his sword nearly severed the warrior's head from his thick neck. Marcus ran to a corner embankment and encouraged the archers massed there to continue their deadly task of loosing masses of arrows into the mass of seething bodies below them. The acrid smell of smoke, of blood and gore, of sweat and of fear drifted across the compound. As the battle settled down into one of attrition, a steady two-way stream of traffic took hold; reserves moved up to the ramparts and the wounded stumbled, crawled, or were dragged back away from them. There was no time to carry away the dead. Some were pulled down from the ramparts to make way for the living, but those that fell inside the lager were left as a natural barrier to the attacking Germans.

To the surprise of everyone trapped inside the fort, the second attack did not last as long as the first. After less than twenty minutes the enemy suddenly broke off and fell back, leaving their dead lying twisted among the trampled ferns and muddy ramparts. Another breathing space, another respite, another period of grace to ponder when and how the end would finally arrive.

For many the end had already arrived or was about to. As the night dragged on the Germans kept the pressure up, firing batches of arrows into the stronghold that impaled those unlucky enough to be on the receiving end. Screams from the newly wounded echoed around the earthen ramparts, and the Romans, peering through sore red eyes itchy with grit and smoke, were kept awake that night by regular banshee howls of Germans lurking beyond the lager's walls. Arminius had waged a brilliant campaign of terror designed to disorient and confuse the Romans, refuse them sleep, and ultimately carry them to the brink of despair—attack, withdraw, harass, attack, skirmish . . . kill.

Varus' command area was now a pathetic remnant of what it once had been. Deep inside the lager and beyond the range of any enemy arrow, his torches flickered low on the small spread of tentage, mimicking the morale of those who gazed into the dancing flames. Around Varus was his immediate entourage of senior commanders.

Marcus Aius and Gaius Vala were not present for they had not yet finished reorganizing the walls to resist another attack. The atmosphere in the marquee was oppressive, pervaded by a heavy swell of foreboding. Many officers looked into each other's eyes without speaking, believing the end of their existence had already been written. Others spoke in hushed tones as they discussed the enormity of the act they were about to commit.

It had been openly discussed, quietly and sensibly. The Germans were winning. Indeed they had already won. They would show no mercy to anyone unfortunate enough to be taken alive—especially officers. Many of these men had witnessed firsthand what the barbarian Germans had done to their own. During the first attack, many Legionaires had been pulled over the ramparts and whisked away into the night—alive. During the second attack, their tortured bodies had been thrown back over the ramparts. Their tongues had been cut out, their eyes gouged clean of their sockets, and their hands and feet severed and the stumps sealed in tar. They were still breathing and choking in pain for they could no longer speak. Their comrades had ended their suffering with a swift stroke of the sword. Others openly recalled how, during the move through the Teutoburger Wald, Roman corpses had been found still alive and nailed to trees in an effort to demoralize the living. Some were women. Many were children as young as five. Being taken alive, all the officers agreed, was not an option, for their deaths would be long, lingering, and a bloody retribution for their activities in the province.

Varus sat grimly silent, having finally succumbed to the realization that Arminius had drawn him upon the horns of defeat. For him, Arminius would reserve the most terrible of punishments.

And so the officers had reached an agreement and were about to set in motion a sequence of events that were irrevocable: suicide—not by a lone figure, but by them all. Each would select a trusted aide to assist them in their gruesome task; each would take himself into his private quarters where the assistant would stand near to deal a fatal strike should the pain and suffering of the Selbstmord *be too much to bear, or the strike poorly pushed home. Each officer knew how to deliver the fatal blow and played out the act in his mind over and over again, with teeth clenched and agony already written across a drawn face. First, the sword was placed with the point on the belly, facing upward, hands on the hilt, so when the blade was thrust its slice would move through the stomach and into the heart. Death was not instantaneous, but if properly done was nearly so. Many men, however, because of their fear of pain or for other reasons, hesitate at exactly the wrong moment, and so mismanage their deaths and end up torturing themselves beyond belief. A deep thrust into the stomach alone would usually kill, but only after an agonizingly long period of suffering.*

And so the need for a trusted aide. His role, should the officer fail to take his own life properly, was to relieve the agony, cut short the pain, and achieve the last wish of the man committing the final act of suicide—to depart this world and rise in the next. It was the act of a loyal and respected friend or trusted servant; someone who would stand by and deliver the final act of friendship.

The obvious question, however, remained unasked and unanswered: who would serve the man who served his master in suicide?

*   *   *

And so Varus, and all the senior officers, fearing that they would be either taken alive or slaughtered by their bitterest enemies – for they had already been sorely wounded – nerved themselves for the dreaded but unavoidable act, and took their own lives.

— *Cassius Dio*

The Death of Varus

While Marcus had been busy securing the lager for the next onslaught, Varus and his remaining entourage, the inner sanctum of noblemen and councilors, together with a few of his more senior commanders, made their final preparations for Selbstmord. *Some wrote final messages home to loved ones in Rome; how they would ever reach friendly hands they did not say. Varus could not bring himself to do the same. He was too depressed and distraught at the dishonor of what had become of his mighty army. The humiliating loss would stain his family name forever. His disgrace in the eyes of his Emperor, Augustus Caesar, was something he could not even imagine; no words he could write would ever make up for the insult to Rome and to Caesar. What would Caesar think and say when he learned the terrible news?*

Varus sighed and hung his head. He lifted his hands and cupped them over his ears to blot out the screams of the wounded. Suicide was his only honorable course of action.

His mind completely made up, Varus made his preparations quickly. He called for the Centurion of his personal guard and verbally issued his last will and testament. The treasure of the taxes and tithes, and all his own valued personal possessions, should be buried in their store chests within the immediate area of his command cell. The utmost secrecy was to be preserved as to the exact site where the chests were to be interred, and the Consul's Guard was sworn to preserve the final wishes of their commander. Once the task was complete and Varus was dead, his corpse was to be cremated as quickly as possible to prevent recognition by the despicable Germans, who would undoubtedly desecrate his remains if they could identify him. The thought of that was anathema to him. His remains would then be quickly buried.

When his own final preparations had been made, Varus' scattered thoughts fell for a moment upon the loyal Marcus Aius, who was even now encouraging the men and reorganizing the thinning defenses. "Marcus," he whispered softly to himself. "You were right all along. Why did I not heed your warnings or see what your eyes so clearly saw?" For Marcus there would be no final instructions, no words of thanks, no parting thoughts. Nothing.

And what of the men? Varus pondered on their fate for but a fleeting moment before saying aloud, "That is up to them to decide now."

"Sire?" asked the Centurion.

The distracted commander merely shook his head and waved a hand in reply. He lifted his short sword from the table and knelt on the floor, breathing deeply. Sweat beaded on his forehead and he wiped his brow with the back of his left hand. His vision blurred for a moment and he blinked several times. His hands were shaking. Gripping the hilt tightly he exhaled and pushed the point gently up against the soft paunch just below his ribcage. He turned and looked at his Centurion, who had already drawn his sword and was waiting within two feet of the kneeling Varus.

"You know what I expect."

"Yes, sire. It shall be done."

Without another word Varus fell forward on his sword. His motion was clumsy, his attempt weakly executed. The blade penetrated but two inches, not enough to do more than cause him to cry out in pain and spill blood down the weapon. Varus had known he would not be strong enough to end his own life quickly. Working on standing orders, the Centurion—even as Varus was falling onto the sword—stabbed down through the back of his neck and to swiftly end his life.

The deed was done.

* * *

With the death of Varus and most of his senior commanders, the legions lost nearly all of their command structure. Only a small handful of officers remained, including Marcus Aius and Gaius Vala, the sole remaining legion commander.

News of the suicide pact and Varus' demise traveled like a bolt of lightning through the lager. Marcus learned of the deed when Varus' Centurion executioner stopped the walking officers and told him the news.

"Sire," he began. "I have news from Commander Varus."

"Yes, yes, I have been busy here," Marcus brusquely replied. "I will be along very shortly."

"There is no need. Varus is dead."

Marcus pulled up short. "What?" His mouth fell open. "Dead? Are you certain? You have seen this with your own eyes?" When the Centurion nodded, Marcus asked, "How?"

"By his own hand, sire." He hesitated a moment. "And by mine—at his request." The soldier filled him in on all the details and named the other members of the suicide pact.

And then Marcus began to giggle. The chuckling was at first soft and quiet, but within a few seconds his entire body was shaking with the deep laughter of a man who was too tired and too hungry to do anything else except cry. The Centurion looked confused and shuffled his feet while the most respected warrior left inside the lager stood in the middle of the gore-splattered fort and laughed until he could laugh no longer.

"Now? When the men need to see and believe in good leadership, when the odds and the gods seem aligned against us, he takes the coward's way out?" He paused a moment and then corrected himself.

"They take the coward's path." The Centurion remained silent, as he must.

"I should have seen it coming." Marcus grabbed the Centurion by the shoulder and looked him in the eyes. *"There is work to be done. See that your men have eaten and rested as best as possible and prepare them with strong words and with courage in your eyes. We will see this through yet."*

The new commander of the legion remnants spun in the other direction and made haste to reach Varus' command tent. Two sentries ordered to block the door against anyone's entrance took one look at Marcus's sharp glare and parted to let him pass. He threw open the flap and entered without breaking stride. The Consul's Guard was busily going about their business, carrying out the bodies from the mass suicide and preparing to bury them in the immediate area of the command headquarters.

"By all the gods," muttered Marcus, as he slowly moved around the surreal activities, and tried to take in the enormity of the events. As he was digesting the scene, Vala silently drew up beside him.

"I have heard. I cannot believe it, and even as I gaze upon this scene, I am not sure I believe my eyes," he said. *"What madness is about that they should do this? Did they speak to you of their intentions, Marcus?"*

"No, never a word, never a whisper." The pair moved off to the side to let two guards carrying a bloody corpse pass. *"Where is the honor in this?"* continued Marcus. *"Where is the spirit of the man, where is his fortitude and his courage? You, I, all that remain of our legions, may well not survive this sorry state of affairs, but I will die cutting German flesh and bone as I go down, until I can do no more. I never thought I would ever see such a sight. Surely this must rank as one of the saddest moments in the history of Rome."*

Vala looked at Marcus to catch and hold his eye. *"I will never abandon you, Marcus. I will fight to the end with you and the men."*

As the men walked back to the front entrance, Marcus noticed the standard-bearers of the three legions had assembled, the golden Eagles firmly held on their wooden staffs. The bearer of the Eagle of the Seventeenth, Brutus Maximus, was known to them both from the march to the Teutoburger Wald from summer camp. Hanging from his waist was the battle mask Vala had given to him. On this night his face was white, and his hand trembled slightly. The Legionaires carrying the Eagles *remained at attention while the bodies were removed from the command area, their right arms crossed in a salute on breast armor; disciplined, erect, honorable, their bearing contrasted sharply with the disgraceful actions of Varus and his companions. Vala's heart swelled with an overwhelming sense of pride and honor as he watched the standard-bearer and carrier of his own Eagle, the Eighteenth, standing tall and steady at his banner staff.*

As Marcus' eyes took in the Eagle perched atop the Seventeenth's staff, he noticed it was beginning to wave slightly side to side. He lowered his gaze a few feet until it settled on Brutus, who was by this time shaking as if with a bad fever and deep chills. The shivers were consuming his body, and as he began to sag, Marcus moved as swiftly as a cat and took the weight of the standard in one hand, the bearer in his remaining arm. He lowered him slowly to a kneeling position and carefully eased the staff from his clammy hand that was still firmly gripped around the hasp of the lance.

Only then did Marcus notice that Brutus Maximus was not only cold, wet, and dog-tired, but wounded as well, and seriously. Blood was trickling down the inside of his left arm. The soldier groaned in pain as Marcus eased him down onto his back. His tunic was a mass of bloodstains from two sword slashes down the left side of his torso. Under normal circumstances, the wounds would not be fatal or render him utterly unfit. But these were anything but normal times, and the loss of blood, coupled with the general exhaustion, lack of food, and filthy conditions, had exacerbated his condition. Marcus staked the standard of the Seventeenth Eagle hard into the boggy ground and ordered the remaining pair of bearers to stand guard on all three Eagles. Two nearby Consul Guards were summoned from their duties to help him get Brutus Maximus into the entrance-way of the headquarters.

Vala stood over them both and watched as Marcus examined the wounds. Satisfied that the soldier was not in any immediate danger of dying, he stood up and removed his own long red cloak, the robe presented to him many years before by his father. He laid the garment around the shoulders and upper torso of the blood-soaked bearer-warrior, fastening it at the neck with a favorite bronze uniform clasp, which had also been presented to him by his father. Brutus, suddenly aware of his surroundings once again, came out of his stupor with a start, darting his eyes about in search of the Eagle that was his responsibility—the golden emblem of the Seventeenth Legion. When he did not immediately spot it, he began to panic at the apparent loss of the standard.

"Ease back, my friend, all is well. We have the Eagle here, protected," Marcus quickly reassured the wounded man. "You have been wounded, twice, and are sick with a fever. You need some rest, and then you may resume your honorable duties."

With the thick red cloak around him, Brutus Maximus was already feeling warmer. He nodded, almost embarrassed at the attention he had received from Marcus, and thanked him. Marcus decided to leave him with one of the Consul Guards. He had other more pressing matters that needed his wisdom and attention.

Marcus reached up and eased Vala outside the tent, motioning him to one side. A loud buzz of conversation had overtaken the lager. "By now, everyone inside this fort knows of the suicides and that Varus is dead. If we want to keep a fighting chance Vala, we need to act now to keep these men together. Otherwise, they will take it upon themselves to organize their own destiny, and in doing so, no one will survive."

A meeting of the handful of remaining senior officers was called, well away from Varus' command headquarters, to avoid having to craft a plan in that surreal and depressing atmosphere. Within a few minutes most of them had gathered. By this time some of the legionaries were arguing for a breakout attempt to the east, in an effort to try and reach the Weser. Many others vehemently disagreed. The main thrust of Arminius' attacks had been against the eastern and southern flanks of the lager, they insisted, so the best direction to move was northwest to Vorden and then to the Ems.

Some, including many of the wounded, thought their best hope was to remain in the lager and seek mercy from the Germans. As the officers listened to Marcus and he to them, each could hear the heated discussions about what course to follow. The Legionaires were almost beyond the point of control.

After listening to several of the most experienced officers and taking his own counsel, Marcus reached a decision. "Commander Vala," he began, "your riders' mounts have been without fodder and decent watering too long. I have decided we can no longer support the retention of our cavalry forces in this bloody mess. If we do not give them the freedom to forage independently out to the west, toward the Rhine, and do not extract them from our slower marching infantry, we will soon lose every horse and rider we have. We have but little maneuverability left as it is."

"What would you have me do, sire?" asked Vala.

"You will take your cavalry and break out to the west. Rather than ride into the morass of the Dieven, you may find a suitable route through the valleys and hills due west of here. You must get back to the Rhine lagers and warn our forces that the feared German uprising is at hand, and we must take swift action to increase the strength of the River Lupia forts." Marcus took a heavy breath and continued. "It is a tall order, Vala, but no other officer stands as good a chance of getting through the enemy lines as you."

The shock of the order was etched clearly on Vala's stunned face. "But sire, I am needed here, with you, with the men. . ."

Marcus reached over and he gripped his well-muscled forearm. "Vala, your task is critical to the outcome of this bloody mess. We must regroup and contain this uprising from the Rhine as fast as we can."

"But you are asking me to desert my legion at its hour of need." Vala was almost pleading now. "You are giving me and my riders a chance of escape—but my men here, in the lager . . ."

"The Eagle of the Eighteenth will remain here with the other standards. Your men of the Eighteenth have fought well and hard, but your command is no longer recognizable as a legionary force of arms. Your responsibilities are now raised far above those of us who will remain here."

With that, Marcus took Vala by the shoulders and drew him close in a rare public display of genuine affection. After a few seconds, he pushed him away when Vala began raising another objection. "No arguments, Vala! You will ride for Augustus Caesar, and you will ride to tell of Arminius' treachery. Go now—go with the blessing of our gods, and with luck you may come through and save the day for Rome."

Resigned to the order he had been given, Vala sighed and nodded in agreement. Marcus was right. It was critically important that word of the uprising and the defeat of Varus get back with all speed to the Rhine legions; Rome must know the German province was falling to pieces. It was his duty to see that the message got through. As he nodded, a tear formed in his eye and rolled down his dirt-stained cheek. "Farewell, Marcus. I will see you again on the Rhine." Neither man believed it.

Marcus watched Vala walk away and then turned back and faced the remaining officers. "All of you will gather up your remaining men— everyone who can move, including the walking wounded—and prepare them to break out from this position."

Which way shall we head, sire?" asked a Centurion from the Seventeenth Legion.

"On my order we will break for the northwest following the line of the Berglands on our southern flank. It is far too dangerous and distant to contemplate a move to the east back to our summer camp. The whole of the German province is rising up against Rome, led by Arminius, a man who knows our business and our order of battle." With his sword point Marcus traced the route in the muddy earth. "We must be prepared to battle march at full speed—"

He was abruptly interrupted by one of the senior Centurions of the three legions, Gaius Suebus, who a short while before had been with him at the ramparts. "Sire, forgive me breaking in, but I know that you can only move as fast as the slowest man. Leave the wounded and dying with me here in the redoubt. When you have gone I will send a message to the Germans telling them we wish to discuss terms for surrender. When we have some of their long-haired savages inside the lager to discuss the matter, we will keep them here in the time-honored fashion of Rome's finest, and we will fight the painted fiends where we stand. You must take the fittest, sire, and carry the three Eagles of Rome to safety. Even if those left here perish, the Eagles must not! Forgive me, sire, I felt the need to speak now—and forcefully."

Marcus stared at the Centurion for a few moments, and then sighed loudly. "Centurion, after all the disgrace of these last hours, my heart and spirits are lifted when I hear words such as yours. You speak in Rome's finest traditions, and I commend you. I also take heed of your advice. The fittest of our soldiers will come under my command to break out to the northwest. Those who are wounded and cannot make the speed we require will remain here to defend our sick and dying."

Marcus looked at each officer. Most nodded in agreement. A few looked troubled and said nothing.

"Gaius Suebus, you have the command, and you are now promoted in the field to the rank of Primus Pilus. One day, I hope, perhaps a long time from now, other men, other military men from far-off lands, will *recognize and remember your courage, and tell all of how you stayed with the sick and dying of the three legions. You do great honor to us all."*

A near-speechless Gaius Suebus bowed his head in thanks. "Sire."

"However," continued Marcus. "You must issue an immediate announcement that those who move with me will have a better chance than those who stay behind. There will be malingerers who believe that all is lost and wish also to stay here with the wounded for their own less honorable reasons. Go now with the knowledge that I have decided that your concern for the three Eagles must now be paramount in my considerations." Marcus now spoke to everyone present. "I will issue movement orders shortly. No one is to move anywhere without my orders to do so. I must speak to the commander of the Consul's Guard. Before I do, are there any questions?"

Suddenly, as one man, the assembled officers brought themselves to attention and saluted Marcus in the time-honored fashion. He was a leader they could trust, and would trust and follow to the end. The show of support humbled Marcus. He nodded his head gently and moved among them to offer his farewells to those whose fate was written on a different parchment than his own.

When words of encouragement and farewell had been spoken, Marcus left the tent and stood for a moment in the twilight of the early morning. As his eyes adjusted to the darkness, he noticed just a few yards away three men holding aloft the staffs of the three Eagles. As he approached he took note of the legionary standing at the far end of the line. It was Brutus Maximus, once again standing proudly and wearing Marcus' long red cloak, the hem of which nearly touched the ground. Marcus stood before him. Brutus was still shivering slightly, but had obviously recovered his composure and physical stamina quickly. When the soldier spotted him he straightened up as tall as possible.

"Sire. I await your command."

Marcus was quiet for a few seconds, as if trying the find the proper words. "I think our fate is entwined, you and I, Brutus Maximus," he nearly whispered. "Our similar looks make me suspect we have a common destiny. But now, the three Eagles . . . " Marcus turned to face the other two bearers and increased the volume of his voice. "The three Eagles of Rome must not be taken by these accursed Germans. Guard your emblems well, for the Emperor and Rome, fight through and keep the Eagles flying on our standards."

"Yes Sire!" shouted all three men in unison.

Thirty minutes later, Vala led his column of riders out of the lager due west to the hills and valleys of the Kalkriese Berg, toward Icker. Everyone listened until the sound of their hooves faded into the blackness and the night again grew still. The sick and dying of the three legions were selected and would remain behind in the battle lager under the brave Centurion Gaius Suebus.

Brutus Maximus moved forward with the other two standard-bearers to join the growing mass of soldiery assembling to break out of the lager with Marcus Aius. Still ill and weak, Brutus asked the standard-bearer of the Eighteenth Legion if he would like the honor of carrying the mask and helmet given to him by Vala. Although he wished to carry it himself, he had all he could do to simply hold aloft his Eagle. The weight and discomfort of the extra accoutrements bothered his wounds. Knowing that Brutus was in a weakened state, the bearer proudly accepted.

And so the remainder of Varus' three legions gathered their gear and prepared to march from the camp to their destiny—to Kalkriese. When the column began to march, Brutus slipped in the mud and fell to one knee, groaning aloud at the pain that racked through his body. With the help of a fellow soldier he regained his footing but failed to notice the loss of the few coins he had in his small leather purse, which was so damp and mildewed it was now literally falling to pieces. The face of Augustus Caesar was pushed into the mud of Felsenfeld by the weight of many hundreds of sandals, and would not see the light of day again for another two thousand years.

1995: Felsenfeld

Together with Wolfgang Schlüter, in 1995 I began a series of investigations of some of the land east of Kalkriese. It was from this direction the remnants of the Varus legions had marched before meeting their end. Wolfgang and I had long recognized the importance of aerial photographs, and although they did not always reveal obvious activities from past ages, on occasion they did.

The theory that the legions had established their final lager east of Kalkriese was not a new one. Schwagstorf was a key point on the map, and was (and still is), an important tactical position in the layout of the ground in that region. The passes to the southeast, and in particular the one to the south where the latter-day Krebsburg encampment, established during the Middle Ages, still nestles into the slopes of the Berg, can easily be seen from the heights of the hill at Felsenfeld. The hill is essentially an elongated escarpment with all-round vision, an ideal place to establish a secure defensive position. It undoubtedly played an important role in the affairs of ancient peoples thousands of years ago. Even now, in modern times, in the lee of the northwestern corner of the range, there exists a crossroads of seven routes that converge into a small carousel of a roundabout. Running down the eastern flank of this feature, Wolfgang had already identified the line of a long recessed wall in the ground, as revealed in a series of aerial photographs.

I obtained more aerial photographs of the area, and much to our mutual delight, the line running down the eastern flank was clearly visible. Felsenfeld remains, a "live" issue, crying out for more archaeological investigation when that great decider of the affairs of man—money—becomes available. My own investigations required no serious cash outlay, however, and I decided to concentrate on two key issues that beckoned me into the area.

The site of the German camp at the Krebsburg and earlier occupation of the Schnippenburg was obviously worthy of a complete investigative project of its own at some time in the future, but my interest at this point was identifying purely Roman activity. I have often referred back to the writings of Mommsen when needing further inspiration, and once again he proved an invaluable source of information. Mommsen's observations supported my premise that significant Roman activity had occurred in the area of the Ostercappeln passes:

"Of other things and goods of value which the legion carried with them, bronze goods must have fallen into the hands of the victors in a greater abundance than coins and money. Additionally it may be worth mentioning that, according to the message from Padre Kassman of Ostercappeln and Menadier, bronze horse brasses of probable Roman origin have been ploughed to the surface a long time ago at the edge of the previously untouched artificial hill at the forest above Ostercappeln in the region of Gut Krebsburg."

I had walked through the woods of the Schnippenburg in 1988 and 1995, looking over the ground that had comprised the early period encampment. By now, after so many centuries had passed, the visual evidence consisted of little more than a few indistinct ridges and ditches laid out in the woodland glades. Was this where Arminius had visited Thusnelda? Was this where he had slept for a short while and missed the flanking move of the Roman legions pouring through from the easterly pass to regroup and take up their positions on Felsenfeld? We will likely never know with certainty. I leave you, the reader, to judge for yourself, when you walk this battle-weary way and trudge through these very valleys; through the hills and slippery slopes of the Teutoburger Wald; through the passes at Ostercappeln and on to Felsenfeld. There, you will feel the sense of loss, the deep despair that was prevalent during those desperate times. The heavy sense of gloom only grows as you make your pilgrimage to Kalkriese, where the sounds of battle still echo down through the years.

If the legions had deployed any forces through the Ostercappeln passes, then perhaps some evidence of their passing remained. I intended to at least survey the fields in the pass, particularly those running down through the northerly edge on the rising dry ground. I spent twenty hours divided between two weekends walking the fields with my detector. I had almost reached the end of my second weekend of the planned survey, and was searching the final part of the field I believed was part of a logical route down through the pass, when I struck it lucky once more. During a period of two exciting hours I unearthed bronze coinage of Augustus Caesar. I was completely beside myself with excitement, and couldn't wait to show my finds to Wolfgang and the Kalkriese archaeological team.

These finds would eventually lead me out to the Felsenfeld. In truth, I have yet to conduct an intensive and meaningful investigation of what I consider to have been Varus' last position, for the demands of Kalkriese and other areas, both east and west of the epicenter of the last ambush position, have demanded every spare hour of my time. However, Felsenfeld has already revealed some of its secrets. On a high point of ground on the escarpment I pulled from the brown-gray soil Augustus' proud regal features and aquiline nose as revealed on his royal coinage. I carefully looked through the residue of earth still affixed to the coin and then made out what was a perfectly formed Roman As. I had found the first Roman copper coin ever recovered from that site. As I turned it over in my hand, the face of Augustus Caesar could be clearly seen. Yet another piece of the giant jigsaw puzzle of Varus' legions was now in place.

Vala's Last Ride

Once free of the lager Vala and his cavalrymen rode like the very wind, streaming across the open ground falling away from the western flank of the lager. Vala urged his mount forward at a tear-away gallop. Although the steed was feeling the deprivations of the last five days, it sensed the urgency of its master's loud cries of encouragement and flew across the broken countryside of dips and gentle valleys with a speed and grace that surprised its rider. The column thundered across the flat lands leading directly toward the defilade entrance into the Kalkriese Berg at Borgwedde some two miles ahead. They could barely make out the ground to their front, but they were riding for their very lives and the lives of their trapped comrades with the most important message any of them would ever carry: "The Germans are rising up in strength."

As the men broke free from the immediate siege area of the lager, painted German faces, startled and surprised by the suddenness of the move, scrambled out of the way of the mass of thundering, heaving horseflesh. Many were unable to escape the weight of horse and rider and were driven into the ground by the pounding hooves of scores of frightened and excited horses. As they rode through the line of enemy warriors, the Roman riders hacked and slashed with their swords. Several riders were struck by German missiles and fell to the ground—alive. No one stopped to help them. They were already beyond saving.

Vala rode as he had never ridden before. His men followed by instinct rather than by any form of tactical leadership, hardly able to focus any farther than the horses to the front and side. The dark heather and bracken streaked past Vala under his horse's thudding hooves, the long hair of its mane flowing back over his wrists and hands, and the wind sung past his ears. There rose in him the pure euphoria of speed, the surge of adrenaline quickening the pulse, exciting the very element of his being, the danger of the situation lost in the exhilaration of the moment.

They had to use all their skills of horsemanship to keep clear of hidden pitfalls, the hummocks and holes they could just begin to make out as the soft grey light of morning began marching across the eastern sky behind them. On and on they hurtled to their destiny, skirting several small tracks and stones converging at one point into a series of ancient graves, and then swerving on toward the larger trail that disappeared into and through the narrow valley to their immediate front. After fifteen minutes of hard riding, Vala suddenly realized they had completely broken free of the Germans surrounding the lager. Unable to see behind him, his view blocked by the trailing mass of cavalry, he eased his mount well to the left until he had a better view of his rear. As best as he could make out, they were not being followed. "By the Gods," he thought to himself, "we might actually have a chance!" For a few short moments he reflected on the remnants of the legions under Marcus, who by now were readying themselves to storm out on their own breakout attempt to the northwest. He clenched his teeth and wished them well, kicking his horse back ahead of the body of riders.

The riders had entered a narrow valley, known locally as Borgwedde, and were riding beside a trail running alongside a small rocky stream. The ground gradually sloped upward on their left. Out of the corner of his eye, and for but a split second, Vala saw a small recessed area with a large curiously-shaped rock. It flashed by so quickly he thought perhaps he had imagined it, but he could have sworn that standing on top of the large boulder was a man, or what resembled a man. The body was human but the head and shoulders were crowned with a stag's head and skins. Vala shook his head and discarded the vision as a flight of fancy. If he had had the time to compare notes with his men, he would have found that many had also seen the same strange figure standing ominously astride the stone watching the galloping Romans thunder past.

They rode hard through the woodland trails, which now climbed gently upward west through the Berglands. Through the leafy umbrella of the open woodland shimmered the grey streaks of dawn. As they broke over the top of a blind rise, the riders surged forward into a broad expanse of open country, a huge sprawling natural bowl that extended as far as their eyes could see. With the other riders behind him urging their mounts faster up and over the rise and into the bowl, Vala saw with painful clarity his destiny, and his heart filled with despair. The near rim of the bowl and each immediate flank was ringed with a mass of Germans, both mounted and dismounted. The Roman cavalrymen continued pushing up out of the woods jostling their comrades in front, pushing themselves ahead with the weight of their forward momentum.

They might have escaped even then if their way forward had been clear, but five hundred yards to their front was the battle camp of the German tribes at Icker. The Romans riding at the head of the column, realizing now what they were riding into, began shouting at one another and desperately trying to slow their frenzied mounts in an effort to stop the flow into the trap. Vala watched as hundreds of painted warriors poured out from the tents and lean-tos to take up positions, barring his line of advance. As the surge of men and horses ground to a halt behind him, Vala took stock of his situation and quickly reckoned the odds. More than two thousand tribesmen surrounded his force of no more than two hundred lightly-armed riders.

Vala turned his mount in a full circle until he again faced forward. Raising his voice to make sure most of the Germans could hear him, even if most would not understand him, he cried, "I see the odds favor us, men! There appears to be the handsome odds of only ten to one!"

At that, many of his men laughed out loud or yelled oaths at the enemy. They already knew they were dead, and so had relaxed in the face of their destiny.

"It is time we had this fight head-to-head!" yelled Vala. "These German dogs have hidden too long in the woods and hills, attacking us from the safety of the hillsides, hiding from the might of our arms. Killing women and children is hard work for them! Let's see if they can fight man to man!"

Vala was still talking when the German tribesmen began slowly striking their swords and lances against their shields, the staccato beat of the strikes slowly increasing in intensity until they became a crescendo of noise that drowned out his final words. And then the Germans began advancing from all sides, drawing the noose tighter as they moved forward. The room for maneuver was collapsing by the second.

With a loud shout, brandishing his sword aloft, Vala drove forward toward the advancing Germans, crying, "For Augustus, for Caesar, and for Rome!" Two hundred Roman throats took up the call. With that cry, Vala's cavalry became part of the history of the Varus battle and disappeared into the mists of time.

* * *

Vala's honor and intentions have been misrepresented by modern interpretations of his responsibilities. This misreading of the record has cast doubt on his integrity and the reasons for his breakout through the hills and wooded glades of Borgwedde, the Kalkriese Berg, and into Icker, where they fought, fell, and died . . . with honor.

The Storming of Varus' Last Lager

Gaius Suebus, now Primus Pilus, *slowly walked the perimeter of his new command. He had witnessed Vala's speedy departure from the lager straight up over the western walls of the encampment. The stream of men and horses flowed over the ramparts like a mass of deer on the move through the woods—bounding, even flying at times, a continuous surge. And then they were gone. Distant yells and shouts of surprise and rage echoed in the darkness, but within a few minutes these, too, were no more.*

Both Gaius and Marcus had worried that Vala's breakout might trigger an immediate attack against the lager. To their relief, the Germans remained at a distance. Marcus had waited a quarter-hour before deciding that if he did not move quickly, any window to escape might close for good. Without incident his Legionaires broke out cleanly over the northwestern corner of the lager. The enemy line was but thinly held at that point—almost too thinly held. What little fighting that occurred was over almost before it began. The Romans moved rapidly toward Vorden and the Ems, via Kalkriese, an unknown equation in the affairs of man, and the Romans.

Gaius Suebus never felt so alone as he walked across to the hospital tent that had been erected next to Varus' former headquarters. The Greek surgeon was busy working on one of the legionaries, sewing a severed arm muscle back on to its parent tendon. He looked up for an instant when Gaius drew up alongside the operating bench.

"How goes the war?" he inquired. Gaius could not help but hear the sarcasm dripping from his words. For a few moments he said nothing and simply watched as the Greek continued lacing the gut through the exposed flesh and drawing the open tissues together.

"I do not start wars, doctor," answered Gaius. "I just fight them, and you just repair the bodies of those who fight them, when and where you

can." The Greek merely grunted in reply and did not look up. "I respect your decision to stay," continued Gaius. "I hope the Germans will respect your services and station in life and spare you and those you treat."

At this the Greek looked up and chuckled softly. "Surely you jest, Gaius Suebus. You know what the Germans will do to us—all of us—once they get inside these walls." All of us. The words pounded inside the Centurion's ears.

Gaius sighed and placed his hand on the Greek's shoulder. "I have a more pressing matter to attend to. Before I do so, is there anything I can arrange or provide for you and the wounded? Soon enough, the wounded, dead, or dying may well be one and the same, but we must be seen going about our normal business, if only for the morale of the injured."

"No, I am content that we have done all we can in these sorry times and conditions. My only annoyance is that I have given my surgeon's bag to one of my chief medics accompanying Marcus Aius, and it holds a particular instrument I could have used here to good effect. However, I am sure their needs will be just as great as mine before this day is done." He stopped and looked up at Gaius. "I have nothing you need to concern yourself with. I'll continue here as long as I can. I hope the Gods watch out over you, friend." The Greek looked once to each side and then lowered his voice. "I shouldn't say this as a doctor, but give them all the might of your right arm, and take as many of those barbarian bastards as you can. Now go—I have work to do, as do you."

After speaking with the doctor, Gaius sent his personal messenger outside the lager to ask the Germans to discuss terms for surrender. His body was returned to the lager in pieces—with his head, arms, and legs severed and tied to his bloody torso with strips of cloth ripped from his cloak. Gaius had his answer. No quarter will be asked or offered.

The end came with a swift rush of figures storming the eastern and southern ramparts. Even though the walking wounded and less incapacitated legionaries were expecting the brunt of the attack to fall against them from those quarters, and had reinforced those ramparts, they were surprised by the massive flood of fresh Germans thrown against them. During the night, tens of hundreds of tribesmen had joined Arminius, including members of the Chatti and the Chauci, who had been drawing up behind the legions over the past two days as they had advanced through the Teutoburger Wald. Now they were part of Arminius' reinforced army. Many had joined for the prospect of plunder and booty. They would not be denied, and looked forward to leaping directly into Varus' lager to reap the harvest of their successful onslaught.

Arminius was not present to witness the final destruction of the lager. He had not been taken in by the ongoing defense of Varus' encampment by the remaining Romans stationed there. Indeed, he had already moved west with two-thirds of his army, some to the Kalkriese Berg itself, in the area of the Icker Bowl, and the rest down into the Kalkriese Pass to man the final ambush position. Here at Felsenfeld, Arminius had left specific instructions for the German chieftains to follow once they had overrun and secured Varus' encampment. Except for one man, everyone was to be put to the sword, for there was not time enough to properly torture prisoners. Except for Varus' personal possessions and treasure chests (which were to be guarded and transported to Arminius, without exception, as his personal victory spoils), any booty found could be kept. He had also demanded they ascertain whether Varus himself had escaped from the lager with the columns or had been killed inside the camp. If possible, he wanted Varus alive; he wanted revenge and he meant to have it.

After overrunning Felsenfeld, the warriors were to rush on to Kalkriese, but move slightly north of the immediate Berg feature and march west along the old narrow track that ran across the southern edge of the Dieven Wiesen, known locally as the Alte Heerstrasse. *Their mission was to ensure that any Romans lucky enough to escape from Felsenfeld should be dissuaded from breaking out to the north and be harried northwest into the final trap at Kalkriese. Arminius had not wasted his years with the Romans in the study of military tactics and deployment; his goal was to make sure every last Roman was put to the sword.*

The terrible slaughter in Varus' lager was like a scene from Dante's Inferno. *After the nightmare of the four days' march through the Teutoburger Wald, the wounded and dying Romans were once again sucked into the jaws of Hell. Indescribable horrors were inflicted upon them by the painted German tribesmen who ignored Arminius' orders about taking prisoners. Mercifully, death came swiftly for many of the*

Romans who went down fighting near the walls, a gladius in one hand, a heavy sodden shield in the other.

Gaius Suebus was fortunate enough to be among them. After killing and maiming more than a dozen of the enemy, his left arm was severed near the shoulder with a mighty swing of a crudely-fashioned, heavy German blade affixed to a long wooden handle. He had not seen it coming, and only figured out what had transpired when he spotted his shield on the ground, his arm still attached. His eyes blinked several times while he watched his own hand clench and unclench itself, while his brain tried to catch up to reality. With a loud scream of anger he swung around with his right sword arm in an effort to skewer his attacker, but his body was now out of balance and his aim wide of the mark. His thrust found only air, and he stumbled and fell to his knees. Though he felt only a numbing throb below his shoulder, the blood was pumping out of the stump in massive spurts as Germans gathered around him in a circle to laugh at his final plight.

Gaius forced himself to stand and face his enemies. Rome, he guessed, was off to his right, so he turned in a half-circle to smile in the direction of his Caesar.

"Give them all the might of your right arm, and take as many of those barbarian bastards as you can." The Greek doctor's final words rang in his ears. " . . . the might of your right arm . . ."

Gaius bent his right arm at the elbow and pulled back his wrist. With every remaining ounce of energy he possessed, he snapped his arm forward at the nearest German. His short sword sang as it cut through the air and impaled a shocked warrior in the throat. The blade severed his spinal column and came to rest with the point sticking several inches out of the back of his neck. Gaius drew pleasure in watching the hilt jiggle up and down several times before the warrior stumbled two steps toward him and collapsed.

Without warning, Gaius' peripheral vision began to narrow. A dizziness overcame him and the ground rushed up to meet him. Before his corpse splashed into the German mud, his enemies surrounding him heard Gaius Suebus laugh one final time.

For many others, the march into oblivion was horrendously slow-paced. Wounded and unable to fight back, they were taken alive. Unspeakable depravities were then committed upon their already pain-wracked bodies, and their screams and cries were lost on the cold morning air, in the early morning light of that day in September in 9 AD.

One of the German chieftains, tasked personally by Arminius to find the hated Varus, trotted through the encampment with a dozen warriors in search of the Roman commander. It only took them a few minutes to come upon the party of Consul Guards who had been given the duty of disposing of Varus' remains. They were attempting to burn his corpse with oil, but the wet conditions made it difficult and the torches did not provide enough heat to properly ignite the oil and the flesh. The guards were laboring to complete their gory task when the tribesmen fell upon them, cutting them down where they stood. After verifying the charred remains as Varus'—one of the soldiers broke down and revealed all he knew in the false hope it would save him—the Germans mutilated and despoiled the corpse, hacking off Varus' head and throwing it to one side.

One of the warriors, Segimundus, had other ideas. "I think Arminius would like this as a present; I will take the head of this coward and personally deliver it to him as a trophy of our victory."

"Do that," replied the senior chieftain, "but make haste. We have orders to make our way as fast as possible to Kalkriese to chase the remaining Roman pigs into Arminius' final position."

Within a short time it became obvious that there was but little to plunder within the stripped lager, a fact that did not please the warriors. Varus' personal possessions and chests of treasure were nowhere to be found, and the few Romans remaining had nearly nothing in the way of personal property. The booty, they concluded, must still be with the Romans running now to Kalkriese.

By the time the sun broke above the eastern horizon, of the three Varus legions and supporting auxilary troops, only Marcus Aius and his remaining six or seven thousand legionaries were still alive.

*   *   *

I stood on the heights at Felsenfeld, looking out across the broad expanse of ground running away to the southwestern pass of Ostercappeln and the site of the Krebsburg. As the evening drew to a close, I felt a great sense of loss and of sadness. I had these selfsame feelings of sorrow and emotion whenever I stood in the glades of the knoll at Kalkriese, and in one area in particular of the Dieven Wiesen, though I have never been able to establish a reason for the feelings that particular site stirred within me. But Felsenfeld produced waves of emotion that picked away at my senses. I heard the pleas and cries for mercy that rose from the ground around me, the cacophony and bedlam of a thousand voices engaged in heated battle.

For those who sense such things, the noise still rises across the centuries, from the very mists of a time long gone by.

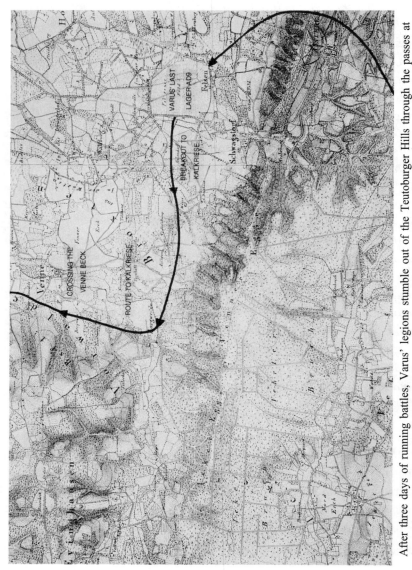

After three days of running battles, Varus' legions stumble out of the Teutoburger Hills through the passes at Ostercappeln to regroup at Felsenfield, where the final battle lager was erected, and where Varus took his own life. The remnants of the legions break out toward the Kalkriese Pass.

Chapter Twenty

Kalkriese: The Last Eagle

"Keep moving . . . don't look back and don't think of anything but steadily marching forward," urged Marcus Aius as he rode up and down the extended but swiftly-moving column of legionaries. He and his remaining senior officers, each mounted, worked hard to keep the soldiers in a close formation as they stumbled and stamped their way farther from the deadly lager.

Marcus reined in his horse and sat for a moment watching part of the column tramp past. Their breakout just before dawn had been easier than he expected, the fighting lighter, and the march route well within their exhausted capabilities. The heavy mist, however, draped the landscape and made it difficult to see more than a hundred yards in any direction. Still, so far, so good. But what would the flank and rear scouts report? His favorite reconnaissance officer answered that question just moments later when he cantered his tired mount into view and edged it up to his own.

"Ah, you have come, and sooner than I expected," said Marcus. *"What do you have for me?"*

"Sire, as far as we can tell, the Germans are not pressing either our flanks or our rear. My men have pushed out through the fog in all directions, and have not been able to make contact with the heathens."

Marcus eyed him keenly and listened to every word. The scout reeked exhaustion, but his eyes glowed with nervous energy. Everyone was bone-tired—and yet exhilarated by the emotional high of their apparent escape. His news surprised Marcus. *"How could it be this easy?"* he wondered in a whisper to no one but himself. Had the move truly taken Arminius by surprise?

"Very good. Now, ride deeply for the rear and double-check again for me. Find me and report each hour. I fear it is from that quarter we shall be struck, if at all."

"Yes sire," answered the breathless rider as he set his heels and rode away. Marcus turned and watched as the struggling soldiers plodded on, one step at a time.

The march was not the disciplined force of arms Marcus would have liked. Still, all things considered, the fact that they were marching at all was little short of a miracle. During the initial flight from the lager, the soldiers had been allowed to spread out across a much wider front than normal. Otherwise, the tail of the column would have remained in the lager too long and been severed from the body. Once safely away, however, Marcus and his officers pushed and prodded the men to come together in a more tightly-organized march formation which, under the circumstances, ended up as a loose alignment six or eight men wide.

Security and speed were foremost in his mind. The forward elements of the column efficiently cleared the ground ahead, and the three Eagles were well protected in the center of the column. The rear almost took care of itself, for the men operating there knew the danger and required little urging to maintain a secure, tightly-grouped unit. Each man at the tail knew that, sooner or later, the Germans would be after them to snap at their heels and pick away at the escaping Romans.

As they covered the dips and wells of the undulating countryside, the early morning sun was well up. They marched alongside the Berglands, still visible on the left southern flank, with the boggy moor of the Dieven Wiesen beginning 1,000 yards distant on the northern side. For the first hour of the march the vanguard had some degree of flexibility in its *selection of the ground traversed. But as the minutes passed, the marching slowly became more difficult. The land between the hills to the left and the moor to the right began to narrow, and in stretches the route became nearly impassable, broken by black-water swamps and sucking bogs. Only a handful of carts and ox-drawn wagons were with the column, but deep ruts and muddy hollows had slowed them to a crawl.*

Gradually the column slowed to a halt, prompting Marcus to kick his horse along the edge of the cursing soldiers toward the van. A trusted Centurion was already moving back to meet him.

"What is the hold up?" Marcus demanded.

"Sire, as you know the ground has grown progressively more difficult for us, but there appears to be a dry pass west of our position."

Marcus pondered the words. "How wide is the pass?"

"It is difficult to say with precision, sir, but it appears to be quite narrow," answered the officer. "There is no other route to pursue, for directly ahead the land is too swampy for passage. Our only other option . . . would be to turn back and seek out another route."

Marcus sighed aloud at this. The only alternative to the narrow pass to their west was long gone. What had appeared to be a sound east–west route had been spotted shortly after they broke out, but that was now well behind them. Reversing the column was not a viable option. He looked about him, noting how the morning mist was beginning to thin.

"Continue on, Centurion," ordered Marcus. "Pay particular attention to what is ahead of the column and on the flanks, and let us pass through as quickly as possible."

With that, the Romans marched into the pass, bound for a place called Kalkriese.

Into the Mists of Time

The success of the breakout from Varus' lager by Marcus Aius' remnants of the three legions was based more on luck than tactical judgment. The majority of the Germans on the eastern side of the lager had no immediate knowledge of the Roman escape, while those deployed west of the fort, though very much aware of the possibility of such a move, had been distracted by Vala's cavalry column, which had broken out over the western wall. Further clouding the matter was the doomed emissary dispatched through the southern rampart by Gaius Suebus only moments after Marcus' force left the northwest corner of the lager.

This combination of events gave Marcus the breathing space he needed to get the majority of his men well away from the close confines of the lager before the Germans began their final onslaught against the position. By the time Gaius Suebus and his small band of brave but woefully inadequate soldiers met the onslaught of German swords and lances, Marcus had trotted his command more than a mile from the escarpment of Felsenfeld, moving in a generally west to northwest direction.

The route was relatively unknown to the Romans, who had always endeavored to use the more northerly east–west concourse of the highways or "Old Ways," which ran farther north of the outer extremities of the Wiehengebirge and Kalkriese Berg across the bottom of the Great Moor, or even the route above it, which used the many established Holzmoorwege *(wooden track ways) that crossed the wetlands of the Great Moor. The latter route existed even before the Romans had imposed themselves on the affairs of the north German tribes.*

Marcus now had little option but to follow the obvious and direct line around the northern flanks of the Kalkriese Berg, though he still wished to remain some distance from the obvious threat that the hills and valleys of the Berglands presented. As long as he was on firm and fairly level ground, his soldiers would have some chance to maintain discipline and counter an attack from the open moorland. The column held at most 7,000 legionaries, a handful of wagons and support pack animals, the left-over remnants from the burning of stores and equipment during the second night of the battle, and a very small mounted division of cavalry and scouts.

Marcus sat his horse and looked into the eyes of those who still had the energy or desire to meet his glance. The men were again moving, and the going was relatively good again, the stretches of bogs and swamps now mostly behind them. Bloody, wounded, tired beyond belief, the men were driven now only by man's keenest instinct—survival. And so the solders beholden to the Eagles of the Seventeenth, Eighteenth and Nineteenth Legions of Rome made their way to their last arraignment.

As the head of the column approached the narrow defile, some of the less cautious suddenly found themselves wallowing about in black muddy

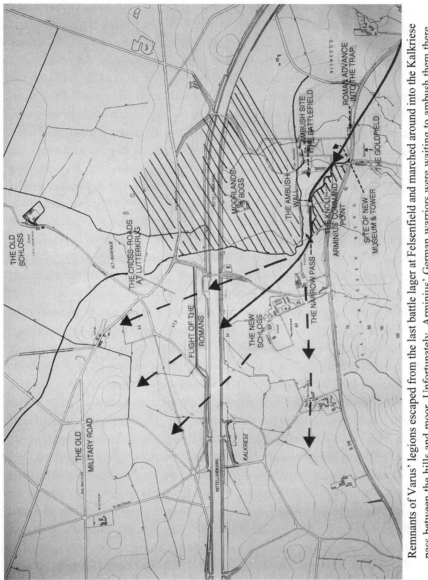

Remnants of Varus' legions escaped from the last battle lager at Felsenfield and marched around into the Kalkriese pass between the hills and moor. Unfortunately, Arminius' German warriors were waiting to ambush them there. Only a handful of legionaries managed to escape the trap and make their way west from the *Varusschlacht*.

pools and concealed holes full of sucking, tangled weeds. They had unwittingly stumbled into the morass of a peat bog. As the unlucky cursed and fell about in the clinging mess, those moving up from behind followed the leaders directly into the unsafe ground of the moor. The powerful press of humanity pushed the lead elements deeper into the swampy ground and made it impossible for them to either withdraw from the bog or maneuver onto the safer side of the approach through the pass. Officers on horseback were not immune to the wayward throng and were likewise carried into the bog, where the animals began snorting and whinnying in fright, bucking and heaving to escape the treacherous ground. The troubled animals and shouts of warning from those trapped in the swamp eventually carried back to those still on firm ground. Once the slipping and sliding in the morass along the edge of the Dieven Wiesen was recognized for what it was, those that were able veered away to the left, toward a path that would take them closer to the lee side of the Berg, which was now no more than a few hundred yards from their left flank.

It was at this point of the march that some of the more observant of the advancing legionaries noticed, through the haze of the morning mists, a banked feature running along the flank of the hill. The earthen form was as if the very contours of the Berg had been raised as they ran around the small knoll on the northern extremity of the Kalkriese Berg. It was then the threat that had been pounding all morning inside every Roman's heart made its sudden unwelcome appearance; the screams and words of warning coursed through the ranks like a bolt of lightening: masses of painted German tribesmen were pushing up against the rear.

Marcus was riding a few hundred yards behind the leading elements. Around him was a small command cell, led by a compact collection of standard party guards surrounding the three Eagles bobbing proudly above their heads. The golden symbols glinted each time a ray of the early day's sunlight broke through the slowly thinning morning mists.

From his mounted position he had watched with dismay as the leading troops hit the boggy ground. As those behind crushed up against the others, the whole pushing deeper in the swamp, a deep-seated apprehension swept over Marcus. The march was falling to pieces on the worst ground imaginable. He dispatched several riders to direct the men to push hard to the left around many hundreds of men now struggling in the sucking mud and weeds. He kicked his own horse forward and helped guide the throngs of men left.

"Sire, I think the men are finally moving as we wish," explained a mounted officer, "but it is hard to tell with this fog. Many though are stuck fast in the swamp and I fear scores have been trampled into the bog."

"Damn these accursed mists," Marcus swore aloud, "they seem heavier now than ever. Come, ride with me. We must do what we can to keep these men moving through this pass."

The men rode their horses forward until they neared the advance of the left flank, urging the men to continue marching without delay. Marcus leaned forward and stared deeply into the steamy vapor. Something had caught his eye, but the swirling mists had blocked his view. When the fog lifted a few moments later he saw it again.

"What in the name of the Gods is that?" he asked, pointing his right hand toward the outline of the curious banked earthen feature.

"What is what, sire?" answered the officer, straining to follow his superior's gaze. When Marcus did not respond, he repeated the question. He was about to do so a third time when he realized Marcus had pulled his mount to a complete stop. The officer did likewise and turned back to look at the Tribune.

Marcus' eyes and mouth were wide as if in awe of what he beheld. "That is a raised embankment!"

"Sire, what is wrong?" he asked with an urgency fitting the moment.

And then Marcus knew. He saw it all evolving in the snap of a finger. He realized the importance of the wall, the pass, the bog, and chaos inside the narrow zone. And he also knew it was too late to alter what was already taking place . . .

*   *   *

Arminius stood quietly 50 yards behind the ambush wall that ran around the northern extremities of the lone knoll. He had ordered the position prepared late on the previous day, after he had taken control of his violent mood that had erupted when the Varus legions had swung through the eastern of the two passes at Ostercappeln. That line of march had bypassed his planned ambush and allowed the Romans to establish themselves in their lager on the heights at Felsenfeld. He kicked himself for assuming the Romans had lost their will or determination to fight as a unit—even after the grievous losses they had suffered. The night attacks on the fort had proven they were still able to defend themselves. This final ambush at Kalkriese was designed to accomplish their utter destruction, and it was planned to perfection.

Arminius watched as several warriors closer to the wall fidgeted with their spears, anxious to be the first to heave it into the enemy when the order arrived to do so. "Not yet, my brave warriors," Arminius whispered. He turned to a Cherusci elder standing on his right. "I have told them many times. Any man who spoils this attack will suffer a thousand burns and cuts before I take his head. They must be still and be quiet. The Romans are drawing near."

The Cherusci nodded in agreement. "They know what is expected, Arminius. They know your orders and will execute them perfectly."

Arminius was suddenly nervous and not fully convinced. "Pass the word again," he said, fearing that the trap would be sprung too soon. "The first flight of javelins and arrows must only be released on my signal. After that, the first wave of warriors, and I mean the first wave only, is to move through the wall gates and hit the near flank of the Romans as hard as they can. Are we clear on this?"

"Very clear, Arminius," answered the elder, "but I will pass your order again just to ensure the word has been taken in by even the most stupid dolt. How much longer do you think it will be?"

"You will just have time to insure the message is passed yet again before they are among us. I suggest you move swiftly. I already smell Roman blood, and I have scores to settle."

As the elder moved away and sent his runners about their business, Arminius studied the layout of the ambush and ran the entire plan through his mind one last time. Around the flowing contours of the knoll that formed the extremity of the Kalkriese Berg he had erected a series of interlocking earthen walls up to six feet in height. Most of the wall was covered with heavy turf and disguised throughout its length— particularly on the leading concourse facing northeast. It was difficult to make them out at any distance, and the morning fog only served to better camouflage the work. The walls were designed to take the brunt of the Romans as they forged their way through the bottleneck between the ambush walls and the boggy moorland. By the time they reached the walls, or at least Arminius planned it this way, the legions would be harassed from the rear by Chauci and Chatti warriors, who had detached a large force of tribesmen from Varus' lager to follow up the Roman column that had broken out to the northwest. Ultimately, the Romans would have no choice but to flow into the jaws of death waiting for them at this bottleneck in Kalkriese.

About every 50 yards, the Germans had opened a disguised break in the ambush walls to allow their warriors to sweep through and attack the Romans from the firm ground of the southern flank. The openings were staggered purposefully to provide the Germans with a reasonable degree of protection as they moved in and out of the pass whenever they chose, but were built in such a way as to prevent the Romans any meaningful understanding of the scope and size of the enemy arrayed against them. Thus, painted warriors could appear at will in any force of numbers, or withdraw to strike out again from another gate 50 yards away. The building of the walls had not been without its own drama. The high water table in the area created a pool of muddy water that had quickly accumulated at the inner base of each rampart. Hasty ditches had been dug to drain away the excess water before the pools completely eroded the base of each wall. It had been a near thing, for there was little time to get it right before the remnants of the Varus legions arrived.

While the Chauci and Chatti pressing hard against the rear of the Roman column, driving it forward, the narrowing of the pass between the heavy walls on one side and the swamp on the other would steadily squeeze the mass of Romans pressing ahead through the bottleneck. According to Arminius' plan, thousands of enemy soldiers would be compressed into a narrow strip of ground where they would be unable to deploy into any meaningful tactical formation, and thus unable to defend themselves in a concerted effort. At that point, the Germans would pick them off at will. The morass of the peat bog on the north was for all practical purposes impassable; on the left was the thick earthen wall manned by hundreds of javelin-throwing and arrow-shooting warriors; behind the Roman mass were the organized Chauci and Chatti warriors. The few Romans who managed to break through the bottleneck to the west and northwest could be brought down piecemeal as, and when, the German tribesmen decided.

Arminius was satisfied that he had done everything possible to achieve success. Now he waited impatiently to launch his trap. He would, of course, join his fellow countrymen in close support and combat should the situation so require, but he knew it was best to retain command and control of the battle as it developed. "I have you now," he whispered to himself with a smile on his face. "I have you where I want you, Varus—and you, Marcus Aius, with your superior ways. We shall see the end of you both this day."

Kalkriese

Before Marcus could answer the officer's question, shouts from the rear of the column reached his ears: the Germans were attacking in force there! Although Marcus could not have known it, the German attack was delivered from two angles, one directly full-on from the eastern end, and the other a foraging attack from the northeast. Together, they pushed the remnants of the legions farther into the Kalkriese ambush. Through the clearing patches of mist Marcus could already see how the men behind him were pressing forward. Fear was written across their faces as each tried in his own desperate way to avoid being the slowest man in the herd. The head and body of the column, without a choice in the matter, were mercilessly pressed into the bottleneck. The rush of humanity, anxiously striving to get away from the immediate threat in their rear, turned a reasonably well-ordered column of marching legionaries into a surging mass of bodies.

Before he could take any action to stop it, Marcus and his command elements found themselves carried along in a tightly-packed mass of men, horses, pack mules, and wagons, unable to move to one side or another. Like a flowing river, the current moved only in one direction: into the bottleneck. Marcus could still see the three Eagles in the midst of the standard guard force waving back and forth 50 yards to his front. The rear would have to take care of itself, he thought. The battle he might affect would be to the front, and he had to get as many men as possible through the pass. Marcus kicked his horse in and pushed his way ahead of the men, who did the best they could to avoid being trampled under his horse's hooves.

He was still some distance away when he realized that one of the standard-bearers was wearing the battle mask Vala had presented on the march from the summer camp a week earlier. The donning of the mask struck him as odd for a few seconds, until he realized the battle had already begun on his left front. To his horror, missiles of every variety were now raining down on the unprotected Roman host.

* * *

Arminius stood unmoving on the knoll, concealed from Roman eyes by the trees and undergrowth in front of him. When the surge of Roman legionaries finally flooded into the ambush position, he yelled out one word: "Now!"

A buzzing swathe of arrows and spears soared into the sky and arced over the wall, dropping like a deadly metal rain into the seething mass of Romans. The devastation was terrifying. Nearly fifty percent of the soldiers forming the advance of the Roman column were brought down, either killed or wounded, by this downpour of projectiles from the left flank.

"Now!" shouted Arminius again.

A mass of painted warriors poured out of the disguised doorways along the ambush walls, throwing themselves against the trapped legionaries, stabbing with swords and spears into their tired Roman bodies. Others, with axes held above their heads, hacked away, one blow after another, at the dazed and confused humanity screaming to their front. After five days without sound sleep, with but little food, and surrounded by constant death, the Romans buckled under the sudden lethal attack. Resistance was almost non-existent as they surged one way and then the other in a frightened effort to evade the spectacle confronting them.

"Form a testudo around the Eagles!" Marcus screamed as he watched attacking tribesmen cut their way within 30 yards of the standard-bearer party. His call was quickly followed up by the lone remaining horn blower, whose strident trumpet notes broke above the din. The sharp call seemed to inspire the men around the banners whose shields, though wet and heavy, were thrown upward and forward to establish a blocking defensive wall around the precious Eagles. Though well executed, the maneuver did little good. There were simply not enough men with serviceable shields to form an all-round interlocking defense. Many of the shields had been so wet for so long they were falling to pieces. The result was that many of the shields that were raised proved ineffective in the mêlée of close-combat fighting.

As Marcus struggled to protect the banners, the Germans surged forward into the Roman column, slicing through sodden wood and leather, hacking away arms and heads, and screaming their war chants at the top of their lungs. If nothing was done to slow down the intensity of the onslaught, Marcus quickly realized they would effectively be encircled on three fronts, leaving only the boggy moor as the only avenue of escape. He urged his mount through the cacophony of sound and bodies in an effort to reach the banners, crying out, "On me, men of the legions, on me to save the Eagles for Rome!" Holding his sword high in the air, ready to hack down the nearest tribesman he encountered, Marcus pushed his nervous horse onward toward the threatened Eagles. His encouragement brought a resounding response from the legionaries immediately around him, and together they pushed forward through the mob to reach the embattled standard-bearer party.

Nearly encircled, the standard guard was waging a bitter hand-to-hand combat. Cries of "Go for the belly, thrust for the belly!" could be heard within the ranks as Roman short swords stabbed forward in search of German flesh. Stab. Hack. Maim. Kill. But the lethal power of the Roman gladius—the world's foremost killing weapon—was only effective when combined with the weight of a Roman shield. The tough weathered metal boss on the front of the shield was pushed forward into the enemy and lifted slightly to expose the gut of the foe, which allowed for parrying thrusts while simultaneously skewering the enemy at close range. Without enough serviceable shields, the men did not stand a chance.

The masked standard-bearer was the first of the three standard bearers to be brought down. A javelin flying over the sweating bloody sea of humanity dropped on its course and sank into his chest. The spear had been thrown by so strong an arm that its shaft slid through his body and knocked him rearward, exiting from his lower back to impale him into the soft ground. He remained frozen in this awkward angle still clutching the staff of the Eagle. As life passed from his body his corpse slipped to its knees and the helmeted head dropped forward onto his chest.

Marcus had almost reached the scene when he saw the Eagle fall toward the ground, where it vanished from his sight. "An Eagle is down! An Eagle is down!" he shouted with all his might. "Push through to the Eagles, men, push on! Push on!" By this time the mass of humanity was so tightly compressed that plowing through the few final yards to the standard-bearer party was virtually impossible.

Unable to influence events just beyond his reach, Marcus watched in horror as the Germans cut their way through the thin wall of guards on one side and opened a path into the inner circle where the standards awaited. Into the breach rushed a massive tribesman with an axe in both hands held above his head. Locked in his eyesight was the frightening mask affixed to the helmet of the kneeling figure. The standard-bearer was dead, but neither the tribesman nor Marcus realized it. Unable to turn away, the Tribune watched as the German brought the blade sharply down and with a single swing that decapitated the kneeling figure. Marcus cursed in his exasperation at the bloody end suffered by the sick and already wounded Brutus Maximus. The young man's head, still adorned with the mask and helmet presented by Vala, rolled away into the blood and gore underfoot; his torso remained impaled and unmoving. The staff of the standard remained braided between his nerveless fingers, its weight resting against the corpse's right shoulder.

Even before the head stopped rolling, a Roman lining the inside of the small circle of guards turned around and hacked the axe-wielding German across the back with his sword, severing his spine a few inches above his waist. The swing dropped the flopping, and now uncontrollable, body into the blood-spattered soil. A final downward thrust through the German's open mouth and out the back of his head ended his agony. Without thinking, the legionary left his waving gladius in place and tore the standard out of the bearer's lifeless fingers, holding it erect once more so that others could see the Eagle flying high.

It was a fatal mistake, though a violent death would surely have found him eventually regardless of what he had done. A German archer, watching developments from the safety of the walled ambush redoubt, notched another arrow, took careful aim, and let it fly. The bolt hit the legionary full in the throat. He fell to the ground like a pole-axed steer, taking the standard down with him.

By this time several tribesmen had been killed trying to enter the inner circle, but another soon forced his way inside, his attention drawn like a magnet to the fallen Eagle lying just a few feet away. The warrior bent down, clutched the shaft in his free hand, and raised it aloft with a blood-curdling howl of glee. He was holding a Roman standard! His joy was to be short-lived, however, for Marcus had finally managed to urge his mount through a small sliver of space and reach the rear ranks of the standard party. With a cry of rage, he hacked down and struck the triumphant German directly between the neck and the shoulder. The blow was delivered with such tremendous force that the blade carved through the muscle and tendons supporting his head, and then through the bones deep down into the chest cavity. The suddenness and severity of the blow froze the German for a second or two as he tried to understand what had befallen him. The Eagle dropped from his grasp and tumbled forward. Marcus lurched out and grasped the haft of the standard, nearly unhorsing himself in the process. Holding it with one hand, he sheathed his sword with the other.

"The Seventeenth is still ours! Rally to the Eagles, for Rome and Augustus Caesar!" he cried. With that he held the standard higher. The hot breath of an arrow caressed his cheek. "Fight hard! Push back, soldiers of Rome!" Spotting two of his officers immediately behind him, he leaned in their direction and shouted, "Commanders! We cannot go forward here! Turn the men about and withdraw in fighting groups!" A javelin, well-aimed by an invisible hand, flew true and would have struck him in his left side had he not spotted it at the last moment and leaned forward against his horse's neck just enough to let it pass. The officers nodded in his direction to signal their understanding, and began doing what little they could to implement the near impossible orders.

Try as he might, Marcus could not gain control of the situation and execute a tactical fighting withdrawal. Behind him surged thousands of legionaries, blocking completely any movement in that direction. One end of the Roman line of march was blocked by the Germans at the point of ambush, and the other, striving to escape the harassing attacks following up the rear, pushed forward into the mêlée near the walls. The result was complete and utter confusion.

Arminius had been intensively studying the Roman debacle with a burning pride for the manner in which it was unfolding. He was particularly drawn to the events surrounding the standard-bearer party. When he spotted the mounted officer riding into the group from the rear, he ran forward and grabbed an archer by the shoulders, lowering his mouth within a few inches of his ear to yell, "Get that officer on the horse near the Roman Eagles! Bring him down and you will be rewarded after this battle with the greatest of honors!"

Flattered by the attention of Arminius, the archer nervously pulled out an arrow, seated it, and released his bow string. The arrow looked as if it passed through his head entirely, so close to his face did it fly. Even Arminius was stunned when the officer failed to fall. "Damn!" he shouted as the archer drew another arrow. Arminius grabbed a javelin from the hands of another warrior and took two steps forward, heaving it with all his might. The officer turned and looked in his direction as he let the spear fly, leaning forward just in time to avoid the razor-sharp tip.

"The man is blessed by the Gods!" roared Arminius. "I will have him yet!"

As Arminius was crying out for another javelin, the archer sent a second arrow on its journey. If Marcus had remained stationary just a moment longer, he would have been killed then and there. Fate, however, had already written him a different end. As he twisted in the saddle to make sure the other two Eagles were still safe, the arrow struck him in the upper left arm, smashing through muscle but only scraping bone until it finally came to a rest against his body armor. An inch higher and it would have missed his armor and continued into his chest cavity. The searing pain burned its way into his shoulder and upper torso as the effects of the arrow took hold. His head sagged with the enormous shock and pain of the strike and he nearly fell from his horse.

Arminius thrust a fist into the air as a victory signal and placed his other hand on the archer's shoulder. "You have done well, we shall talk again soon. Lay your next arrows as true and we will soon be finished with Varus' mighty legions!" Believing the mounted officer had suffered a fatal wound, Arminius turned away to attend to other pressing tasks that required his immediate attention.

As Marcus sagged on his mount the Eagle tipped forward. Unable to hold the heavy shaft, it slipped from his fingers and dropped beside his mount into the muck and blood-soaked ground, while his horse nervously reared and balked among the closely-packed bodies fighting and screaming around it. Through pain-filled eyes Marcus spotted the two remaining standard-bearers five yards away, their Eagles still held proudly aloft. As his eyes settled on them he recognized his own long red cloak hanging from one of the men. He lifted his gaze to the standard-bearer's face only to discover it was Brutus Maximus! The young man was not only alive, but still proudly holding the Eagle of the Seventeenth above his head. What Marcus was never to learn was that another of the standard-bearers had offered to carry the heavy helmeted mask in an effort to lessen the wounded bearer's burden.

Thoroughly confused, Marcus scoured the ground in an effort to ascertain the identity of the decapitated bearer of the fallen Eagle and determine which Eagle he had picked up and dropped. Because of the mud, gore, hundreds of shifting feet, and general battle chaos, however, finding the fallen standard was by now virtually impossible. Looking down at the torn soil from the back of a twisting horse sent waves of nausea coursing through him. Marcus lifted his head, closed his eyes, and willed the dizziness to pass. When he opened them, he saw that several more warriors had penetrated the guard's circle in an effort to steal away the remaining banners. He urged his steed forward toward Brutus Maximus and the rallying point of the battle: the remaining two Eagles of the Varus legions.

Marcus's large horse cut through the mass of struggling bodies like a ship's prow slicing through a turbulent sea. One of the Germans, in a seemingly suicidal move, threw himself at the packed mass of Romans fighting close by Marcus, hacking and stabbing in a frenzy of aggression. Although stabbed and cut several times by Roman blades, he somehow managed to reach Marcus' horse and, with a cry of triumph, savagely hacked at its hindquarters with his sword. With one final blow he half-severed the beast's left hind leg before he fell to the ground under a rain of deadly blows. Marcus' stallion let loose a terrifying scream of pain and fear heard above the din of the battle. When it attempted to rear, pulling up its front legs, its wounded hind limb buckled under the weight, tumbling horse and rider to the ground.

Marcus was thrown over his mount's left hindquarters and landed squarely on his back. The horse narrowly missed him as it crashed down on his right, breaking the neck of a Roman soldier unable to move aside. It took Marcus several seconds to collect his wits and his wind amidst the nightmarish chaos swirling above him. All he could see was a sea of legs and lower bodies, a continuous mass of movement, ebbing and flowing, stamping the bloody earth and undergrowth around him. With his left arm still pumping with pain, he reached across his body with his right hand and, firmly gripping the exposed shaft of the arrow, snapped it off. The action sent new shock waves of excruciating agony shooting through his shoulder and arm and he cried out in pain.

Marcus had always been physically powerful and blessed with a cast iron will that matched his strength and determination. Still, he was grateful when a strong hand grasped him under his good right arm and dragged him to his feet, aided then by another carefully holding his injured side. Two of the standard's guards were assisting him, holding him half-erect as they dragged and pulled the wounded officer through the mass of troops encircling the Eagles, to a position where he could fully take in the desperate plight of the legions.

Taking stock of the situation, Marcus noticed Brutus Maximus a handful of yards away, standing firm and resolute with the Eagle of the Seventeenth flying high above him. Of the other Eagle, there was no sign. "Where is the second Eagle?" Marcus gasped as loud as he could, still not aware of the identity of the first bearer who had fallen to the javelin and decapitating cut.

"They likely have it, sire," replied one of the guards, shouting directly into Marcus' ear to make sure he could be heard above the din of the battle. "We could do nothing to prevent it. A sudden flight of dozens of javelins and scores of arrows took down so many of the guard that we were lucky to regroup to protect the Seventeenth Eagle. We did not even see the Nineteenth Eagle fall, nor see the Germans take it. I believe you saw the standard fall, sire."

So the first standard to hit the ground was the Eighteenth Eagle, thought Marcus. "I did not just see the loss of it, Centurion. I am the man who lost it to these accursed dogs! I do not intend to lose the last vestige of our honor—the Eagle of the Seventeenth!" Marcus could barely hear his own voice even as he screamed the words.

"Sire!" The Centurion was now nearly screaming to be heard above the bedlam. "We have fought as well as we are able, but we can no longer mount any meaningful counterattack, nor hold our ground here. They are picking us off like the flies on a sow's belly, and we cannot withdraw! I fear—."

His final words were cut off mid-sentence when a German lance transfixed the Centurion straight through his armor, exploding his chain mail into hundreds of flying silver links that fell into the mud like a myriad of disappearing fireflies, shattering his breastbone and ribcage and tearing onward into his chest cavity, striking hard against his lower backbone and severing the spinal column in the process. The fatally wounded officer looked into Marcus' eyes and coughed a spume of blood *from a ruptured lung as if he intended to continue the conversation. He died immediately thereafter and fell backward against the packed mass of the legionaries gathered around the surviving Eagle.*

Marcus wiped away the blood and mucus from his face with his good right hand, the results of the Centurion's last attempt to finish his verbal briefing. Before him was the gallant figure of Brutus Maximus, still clothed in Marcus' own broad red cloak of office, still holding his Seventeenth Eagle aloft. Marcus staggered across the short divide separating them. As he approached the standard-bearer, the final duty he had been spared to perform suddenly became clear to him.

It was apparent now that all was lost. It was now only a matter of time before the Germans completely overran the few Romans left to fight. The face of Brutus Maximus loomed before him, so much like his own in many ways, and Marcus saw his life and his dreams rush by in a kaleidoscope of instantaneous impressions: Rome, his loves, his wife, his family, his loyalties to his Caesar . . . He shook his head in overriding fury at his moment of weakness. What was he thinking? He thrust his self-pity to one side. He understood what fate had in store for him, and he was glad he had been part of this moment.

The Germans had prepared well, he had to give them that much. Besides the obvious assembly of resources of men and arms, Arminius had followed the principles of warfare and turned them into a fine art. Anything that could be used as an effective means to put an end to the Roman legions was worthy of consideration and implementation, and even the basic commodities of warfare, the stones and the slingshot, were part of his impressive ordnance of weaponry lined up against the might of the Roman fighting machine. He had learned his lessons well over the years of his stewardship as a Roman knight, and was now putting that art to extremely effective use.

Arminius, meanwhile, knowing the battle of annihilation was almost won, had moved closer to the wall. To one of his tactical officers he yelled, "Pull our men back a short distance, particularly away from the guards surrounding the Eagle. Make ready the stones—but no slingshots! Our warriors are too close. I want to take the last of the Eagles. Without their Eagle rallying point, the Romans are lost and we will finally have won the battle. Quickly, be about it, man," he urged the junior commander, "and wait for my signal before the stones are thrown!" The message was quickly passed.

Steadying himself to the task before him, Marcus drew his sword anew and trudged forward closer to the fighting. Were his eyes and ears mistaken, or was a reprieve underway? The onslaught by the dismounted Germans seemed to be waning; most were withdrawing completely toward the wall and even disappearing behind it. Had they exhausted themselves? For the shortest of moments Marcus' spirits lifted and he thought perhaps, just perhaps, there was a chance to turn the tide of battle in their favor. But it became abundantly clear what was happening when a cloud of missiles, stones, and other projectiles soared from behind the ambush walls, darkening the sky with their shadows and mass before descending into the concentrated Romans with a crippling effect.

The large stones struck exposed heads and limbs. Many Romans had lost their helmets, which would have afforded at least some protection. Such is the nature of man that a great many soldiers looked up at the swarm of flying missiles floating in on the crest of the morning sunlight above them, only to plunge suddenly with devastating results. The heavy stones gouged into human flesh and bone, split heads, crunched bones, smashed sword arms raised to defend and shelter cowering bodies, and snapped wrists like twigs underfoot. Weapons, just seconds earlier held in powerful grips, dropped from damaged fingers.

Marcus was one of the lucky few to avoid the fresh onslaught. Brutus Maximus was not as fortunate. One of the largest stones struck the bearer of the Seventeenth Eagle full in the upper right side of his face. The two-pound missile broke his cheekbone and nose and caved in his right temple, squeezing his eye from its socket in a small spray of mucus and blood. His jaw, once so proud and square, was fractured in a number of places, his top set of teeth fragmented, and his tongue nearly cut in two. The fact he survived such a blow was incredible. More astounding was that Brutus Maximus, though on his knees as if praying with his final few breaths, retained the Seventeenth Eagle aloft, though the shock of the impact had caused him to drop his sword. His empty hand clawed the heavens in supplication, as if to beseech someone to take his standard and secrete it to a safe haven far away from that terrible place.

Though Brutus could no longer see and was rapidly falling into a shocked stupor, he could feel strong hands easing him onto his side as he made out the authoritative voice of Marcus Aius in his ear. "We are brothers, you and I, Brutus Maximus, and I tell you now that your Eagle will fly high in the minds of men." Seeing Brutus' eyes beginning to cloud, Marcus yelled the final words, shaking him gently as if to will him to hear these final words. "Brutus! I will not let these savages take it from us. This Eagle may never see the light of day again, but at least it will not be used to ridicule Rome in our defeat on this day! . . . I relieve you of your honorable task, Brutus Maximus, and one day I will reveal to all how your bravery and courage was a shining example of how men should behave in battle."

With that, Marcus staggered to his feet and broke off the Eagle from the top of the stave. He looked down upon his fatally wounded comrade with both pity and pride. "You are a true and courageous man. Your Eagle is now with me, so rest yourself." Brutus heard none of these words for he was already unconscious.

Marcus thrust the golden emblem into the inner part of his tunic and looked about in an effort to determine the best way to escape the milling horde of fighters. He marveled once more at Arminius' brilliance. The German had steered the legions into a carefully laid ambush on a scale previously unknown in the annals of warfare. Once the trap was sprung, there was no way for the Romans to regain control of the wedge of the remnants pouring into the pass at Kalkriese because there was no room to move in any direction—save to the west and northwest through the bottleneck, where only death awaited. The only other avenue from this man-made hell was through the Dieven Wiesen, the boggy swamp directly north. Marcus knew that an escape in that direction could only end one way and he wanted none of that.

Dodging another rock that was followed up quickly by a hissing javelin, he drew his sword and began hacking his way through a jagged line of Germans and Romans struggling to the death in front of the ambush walls. Other men pushed behind him. Tucking his head down as another stone projectile knocked his helmet away, and with the Eagle clutched tightly inside his tunic, he fought step by bloody step forward toward the exit of the Kalkriese bottleneck and his appointment with destiny. An enemy appeared before him; Marcus thrust and cut him down. Another on his right swung in his direction with a sword, but the blow was wide and Marcus ducked and stabbed him in his soft stomach, pushing him away with his good shoulder. A fellow Roman fell against his wounded left arm, triggering a sharp ripple of pain that pulsated to his fingertips and throbbed at his temples. Bloody, wounded, gasping for breath and exhausted beyond all reason, he had one final mission to fulfill before he could fall into the arms of eternal rest.

*   *   *

And Florus wrote: *As for the standards and Eagles, the barbarians possess two to this day; the third Eagle was wrenched from its pole, before it could fall into the hands of the enemy, by the standard-bearer, who, carrying it concealed in the folds around his belt, secreted himself in the blood-stained marsh.*

*   *   *

Arminius was forever in the thick of the bloody business of the mass slaughter. Some 7,000 legionaries had surged into the walled ambush site at Kalkriese; after less than two hours of hard fighting, perhaps 1,000 remained who were still capable of standing and fighting. Each sought an exit from the overpowering surge of Germanic warriors who continued to slash and stab into the shrinking Roman masses. These groups of legionaries often moved as one, easing their way en masse around the walls and through the bottleneck as stumbling, struggling bodies of desperate men. For others, temporary relief was found fighting behind earthworks of the dead, whose corpses were stacked so high against the leading edge of the ambush wall that the Germans could no longer cleanly engage those taking shelter beyond the macabre rampart. None of these men had any real chance of survival and they knew it, but they vowed both to themselves and aloud that they would take many of the bloodthirsty enemy with them before they expired.

On the other side of the feature, around the far side of the wooded knoll, occasional flashes of reds and browns could be seen: scattered legionaries running—escaping through the Engpass *(the Kalkriese bottleneck), flowing down the rise toward the old road running west by northwest through the foot of the moor 1,500 yards away. Between the rise and the old road there was the moorland, with its mass of 0s and treacherous swamps interspersed with odd patches of solid grass and fern-covered ground. For every legionary who made good time in his initial escape down from the pass, another fell prey to the bog, his flight slowing to a nightmarish slow-motion series of steps, each becoming progressively slower and more ponderous until exhaustion or an enemy's javelin or arrow cut him down.*

After long and hard fighting, the solitary Romans breaking through the bottleneck opened into a small trickle of fleeing figures that a few minutes later become a stream of several hundred Romans flowing down from the terrifying debacle of butchery and mayhem behind them. The knowledge that no quarter would be given, nor mercy shown, lent speed to their flight and energized tired legs and bodies driven by fear as they fled from the Varusschlacht.

*   *   *

During the spring and summer I maintained my search efforts in the large fields and even moved across the canal into the area some 500 yards short of the crossways.

Slowly but surely, an identifiable pattern began to emerge from my coin and artifact finds. Lines began appearing linking the road running east–west around the Kalkriese Berg, and behind me through the knoll, to the military road also running east–west about 1,500 yards away to the northwest. The picture was somewhat reminiscent of a large starburst, with the stars all bursting out in one direction. There was every indication that a large contingent of people had splayed out from the area at the apex to the field and the knoll, fanning out in a 90-degree arc north and northwest down to the crossways, the military road, and the lands beyond, as if fleeing from some as yet unknown horror. . . .

*   *   *

Only a tiny sliver of those legionaries who somehow managed to fight their way clear of the ambush and squirm out into the fields and moorlands to the northwest ever made their way back to the Rhine to recount the terrible defeat that had befallen Varus' legions. Some of the fleeing Romans successfully reached the old east-west road some 1,500 yards distant and so made good their escape. The vast majority of those fortunate enough to push through the bottleneck were chased to exhaustion by whooping and screaming tribesmen intent on their final slaughter. Small pockets found themselves trapped in the many boggy pools of sucking mud and waterlogged meadows, their escape attempt at

an end. Utterly out of options, they turned and fought, transfixed in the
quicksand of the morass that was the Dieven Wiesen.

Summer, 1996

In the early summer of 1996, I was searching a more central area of Kalkriese. It was part of an elongated piece of land that had originally been a stretch of waterlogged moor before modern farming had drained away much of the excess damp from the soil. Both Professor Schlüter and I had often discussed the strange anomaly that continuously revealed itself in the artifacts graph of the Kalkriese area: many of the more intensive artifact sites were on land that had once been predominantly wet. Some of the more interesting finds Klaus Fehrs made over the years as he walked up and down the Kalkriese fields were centered on these sites. For some inexplicable reason, neither he nor I had ever settled on a search survey of this particular field set in the middle of Kalkriese.

I spent one weekend surveying the entire northern side, which had originally been submerged in bog for all these many hundreds of years. I quartered the field and over two days examined every inch of ground. To my dismay and utter surprise, not a single artifact was uncovered. How could this be? Not one coin or man-made remnant in such a promising area—the central path of the escaping Roman flight from the ambush site? No reasonable answer was forthcoming. There were other considerations and other fields beckoning me, and I put the matter behind me and went on to other sites, continuing my search farther to the west.

A few weeks later an excited Wolfgang telephoned to tell me about the most amazing find that had ever been made in central Kalkriese. By some accounts, it was one of the most important archaeological discoveries in Northern European history. It was easily as important, and perhaps more so, than the parade mask or any of the other artifacts we had unearthed during the previous nine years. Klaus had uncovered the major part of a sword scabbard embossed with solid silver retaining loops, a central core mount of black onyx in type, inlaid in the Greek style, with the figure of a Grecian lady with long bound hair and long flowing robes. A sword in such a scabbard could only have been worn by a Roman of high nobility and status—a high-ranking senior officer of the legions and perhaps even one of the three legion commanders. No officer would have donned the blade if he believed he was about to engage in battle—such was the intrinsic value of such a sword and scabbard. Almost certainly its owner had no knowledge of the events to come in the year 9 AD of the *Varusschlacht*.

The Last Eagle

A bare-headed Marcus Aius nearly stumbled and fell in surprise when he suddenly found he had killed and maimed his way through the wall of Germans holding the far side of the bottleneck. Beyond, open space beckoned. Although he had not known it, fighting behind him was a tightly-knit group of Romans who, surging forward in his bloody wake, burst out with him from the ambush position.

He willed himself to break into a trot, licking his feverish swollen lips as he winced at the pain wracking his weakening body. Blood was trickling freely down his forehead from a nasty gash in his scalp and his tunic was a mess, splattered with the blood and tissue of a score of men, Roman and German alike. The enemy arrow was still embedded in his upper left arm, the arrowhead nicking and tugging away at his tunic where it had emerged beneath his armpit. Each time he moved his arm the pain returned, triggering sickening waves of nausea. Bile rose up from his throat and spilled over his parched lips, the acid burning his throat and mouth, for he had no saliva to wash the liquid away. Through his agonizing haze and sweat-filled eyes Marcus took in the fields and moorlands spreading out from the knoll. It offered a confusing picture of legionaries swarming away from his position, intermingled with German tribesmen slashing and stabbing them in the back as they fled. Screams of mercy fell on deaf ears.

The majority of his fellow soldiers who had managed to escape the bottleneck were fleeing in a northwesterly direction, down through the slope of the moor that fell away from the Kalkriese Berg. A few were running in a more general westerly direction, apparently avoiding altogether the large number of Germans chasing the Romans into the boggy moor. As he was digesting the scene before him, he realized he was being swept along with the pack of soldiers gathered about him. If he did not extract himself from them soon, they would suffer the fate of those being brought down by the screaming German tribesmen.

As much as he wished to stand and fight, to die alongside his men, he knew he had to continue with his mission to rescue the Eagle of the Seventeenth Legion. He was the only one left who could make sure it did not fly above Arminius' victory posts. He also knew the odds of a complete escape were slim, especially in his physical condition. In that case, he would see that the Eagle disappeared with him into the bogs of the Great Moor, never to be seen again.

Once he decided on his course of action, Marcus threw himself sideways against the press of bodies around him and kept moving left across the path of the main surge of soldiers until, with a final shove, he fell forward out of the main stream of running legionaries. Once he did so, he found himself face to face with a huge grinning German warrior, his sword poised to strike him down.

As he raised his sword to ward off the blow about to fall, the Eagle came tumbling loose from his tunic. With his wounded arm he attempted to re-secure the standard before it fell to the ground. The German's eyes widened with surprise and disbelief and he hesitated before delivering his blow. Marcus knew enough of the dialect he spoke to understand his outburst: "An Eagle!" he screamed "He has a golden Ea—"

As he was shouting the alarm, Marcus changed his sword angle from a defensive block to a forward thrust and pushed the blade straight into the exposed stomach of the German, twisting it to slice apart his intestines with a scream of pleasure of his own. The tribesman's eyes again widened, this time in shock. Marcus pulled the sword free and cut a sweeping forehand blow across the throat of his enemy to prevent any further cries. Gasping for breath, Marcus stopped only long enough to stuff the Eagle firmly inside his tunic before stumbling west, veering away from the path taken by his fellow Romans. Although it was the height of summer, the ground lying at the foot of the Kalkriese Berg was still wet from underground springs and waters from the boggy moor to the north.

From the apex at the exit point of the ambush, Arminius stood with one of his men and watched as the lone Roman officer broke free across the open ground, splashing through the meadows and patches of moor. Plumes of water broke upward as he moved away to the west. The warrior standing at his shoulder was anxious to get into the fight, and had been pleading with Arminius to release him to join the battle, which was now obviously won. Arminius was about to order him to chase after the obviously wounded man, but when he looked down at the mass of fleeing Romans moving away to the northwest in front of him, he decided instead to release him to chase down easier pickings. With a yell and a flourish of his long sword, the warrior set off into the mêlée of running figures, seeking out as many as he could to satisfy his insatiable appetite for Roman blood.

Despite his handicaps, Marcus made fairly good time and managed to put approximately 1,000 yards between himself and the knoll, which was now nearly out of his sight. Looking over his left shoulder he let out a gasp of despair. A large force of mounted Germans was pouring out of the woods from the Kalkriese Berg itself only 400 yards from his position. Without thinking he threw himself forward into a waterlogged patch of ground, sliding into the wet undergrowth and hoping to the gods he had not been seen. He lay there for a few moments trying to catch his breath, half expecting to hear the heavy clumping hooves of enemy war horses approaching his prone position. Another wave of nausea poured over him; the searing pain from freshly opened wounds hammered away at his senses. Rubbing his eyes and furrowed brow, he slowly raised his head to seek out the pursuing German cavalry.

To his surprise, the mounted warriors were galloping toward the confused mass of Romans and Germans pouring out of the ambush bottleneck. They were about to place the cork firmly into the bottle and seal up the hundreds of men left of Varus' legions trapped in the Kalkriese Engpass. The lone figure of Marcus Aius was not worth chasing.

Marcus tried crawling but, unable to withstand the pain in his torso and arm, staggered to his feet and changed direction slightly away from the Berg to his left. He would move off in essentially the same direction as his legionaries, but on a far-removed parallel course. By this time he was beginning to experience difficulty distinguishing illusion from reality. He knew that somehow he was still on his feet, and he could feel the warm mid-morning sun on his back. The sudden appearance of Germans running alongside forced him to stop and stab at phantoms. He watched them fall, bleed, and die. And he kept trotting. Had he just killed another enemy or was he imagining combat? When he heard Varus shout his name and unspeakable obscenities, Marcus realized with certainty he was losing his grip on reality.

During the next hour he fell to the ground more times than he could count. Each time he would lay still for a minute or two, raking in deep rasping gulps of air as he sought to retain his senses and slow his pounding heart. The last time he was unable to rise. The black water was seeping up against his body and beginning to engulf him. He so desperately wished to lie there and never rise again, for he both knew and felt his life's blood draining away with every yard of ground he covered. He was near the end. There would be no escape. There would be no Eagle safely returned to Rome, and he would never see his beloved wife or Rome again. But if he died here someone would surely find him—and the golden standard. He tried to rise but fell back into the shallow water. He blinked away tears of self-pity as they pricked at his eyes.

"No!" he whispered through clenched teeth. "If Rome cannot have the Eagle, then neither will the traitor Arminius!" He dragged himself back into a kneeling position in the bog. He remained there a while longer, his dripping and muddy head hanging forward against his chest as he gathered enough strength to will himself up. He began to strip himself of all his remaining accoutrements: uniform fittings, belts, money pouch full of denarii and a few golden aureii – anything that would lessen the load on the last stage of his flight. His fingers paused when he reached his scabbard. The precious and beautiful housing had long held his beloved sword. Both had been presented to him by his father so many years before when he entered the service of Rome in the officer corps of the legions. The scabbard was a wonderful piece of artistry, embellished with sets of engraved figures in silver and gold, the loop-securing mounts in solid silver, with a central mount of a Greek-styled pendant of black onyx inlaid with a Grecian-style female figure set in pale ivory, her long hair and flowing robes so very much like the picture of his wife he always kept in the forefront of his mind.

He unbuckled the heirloom and held it out in front of him. This time he was unable to hold back the tears as they filled his eyes and spilled down his blood-stained cheeks. He gently kissed the small ivory inlay, murmuring as he held the beautiful scabbard, "I hope one day you will see the light of the sky once more, for you are far too beautiful to be lost forever . . . Farewell, sweet memories, farewell, my love." And with that, he set the piece into the water and pressed it firmly into the boggy black water.

After making sure the Eagle of the Seventeenth Legion was firmly seated inside his tunic, he struggled to his feet and took a step forward. Another followed, and then another, and soon he was steadily stepping and slipping west again. To his relief, the ground became firmer as he gained the area surrounding the old road running through from the east. When the wind was just so, he could occasionally hear screams from the last acts of the drama he had somehow managed to survive—if only for a while longer. Distant intermittent flashes of color danced through the undergrowth and trees north of his position as he cut through the center of the place called Kalkriese.

He stumbled upon what was to be his final resting place, tumbling down through a patch of heavy clinging undergrowth. The spot was in the middle of a small forested area less than two miles from the site of the ambush position. Before him was a small lake. The bluish-gray water was serene, surrounded by trees interspersed with small glades. A kingfisher ignored his appearance and plunged into the cold waters in search of an elusive breakfast.

The tranquil waters, so cool and inviting, calmed him. He eased his aching tortured body into the gentle caress of the shallow water and watched as the kingfisher soared into the air, a small fish wriggling in its clenched beak. A smile broke upon his chiseled, weathered face as a warm sense of peace washed over him, a wonderful feeling of déjà vu and serenity. The deprivations and horrors of the last days fell away, replaced by a contentment he had never before experienced. His sword slipped from his grasp and disappeared beneath the surface. He slowly eased his way deeper into the water. A brilliant stream of sunlight danced on the surface just beyond his reach. Below the surface was a vision of home, of family, of friends, and of loved ones; of Rome. He watched as his wife smiled at him, called out his name, and opened her arms to embrace him. He took another step toward her, moving deeper into the cool clear water.

As the water came up over his chest Marcus stepped off the lake shelf and disappeared beneath the surface, held tightly within the arms of his family. The added weight of the Seventeenth Eagle of Rome lodged securely within his tunic carried him slowly to his watery grave. The mass of roots and weeds cloaking the floor of the lake welcomed him as if to bed, gently wrapping themselves around his mortal body, holding the soldier and the Seventeenth Eagle of Rome in their firm yet gentle grasp. His spirit left his tired frame even before he felt any sense of drowning.

And so Marcus Aius faded from the affairs of man and disappeared into history along with the other men of the Seventeenth, Eighteenth, and Nineteenth Legions of Rome.

The Hermann (Arminius) statue in Detmold, Germany. *Clunn*

Aftermath

From the Mists of Time to the Present

When the dust settled and the last man of the Varus legions had been put to the sword or captured, Arminius and his warriors celebrated their victory with days of feasting. Their gluttony was punctuated with the ritual torturing of several hundred especially unfortunate Romans, most of whom were probably already wounded before their capture. When there was no one left to kill the Germans left Kalkriese. In their wake was one of the most dreadful battlefields the world had ever witnessed. Strewn along many miles and across many days were literally tens of thousands of dead men, women, and children. The Romans were left where they fell, for the Germans were not about to expend time and energy properly disposing of the enemy dead.

The battle's final day around the Kalkriese bottleneck left a scene no pen or brush could faithfully describe. The corpses of thousands of Roman soldiers, singly and in small groups, littered the ground. Along the eastern and northern reaches of the earthen ambush wall a new form had arisen. The new structure was composed almost entirely of human flesh—a huge mass of torn bodies stacked several high and many more wide stretching for a distance that must have staggered eyewitnesses. Affixed as ornaments around the site were dismembered bodies that had been tortured; others had been left stretched out on racks and gibbets, and Roman heads remained affixed to the trees around the pits and scenes of barbarity. It was a scene of such unspeakable butchery and horror that even the writers of that bloody era had difficulty describing the full depths of man's inhumanity to man that occurred at Kalkriese in September of 9 AD.

Writing more than a century after the event,Publius Annius Florus penned these words in an effort to describe what had taken place:

> Never was there slaughter crueler than took place there in the marshes and woods, never were more intolerable insults inflicted by barbarians, especially those directed against the legal pleaders. They put out the eyes of some of them and cut off the hands of others; they sewed up the mouth of one of them after first cutting out his tongue, which one of the barbarians held in his hand, exclaiming, "At last, you viper, you have ceased to hiss."

The stink of blood and gore pervaded the air about Kalkriese for weeks.

*   *   *

Rome took the Varus defeat hard, for it was indeed a significant military setback. Cassius Dio left a lengthy account of the events that unfolded after news of the slaughter of Varus and his men reached the ears of the empire's capital:

> At the time when Augustus learned of the disaster which had befallen Varus, he rent his clothes, according to some reports, and was overcome with grief. His feelings were not only of sorrow for the soldiers who had perished, but of fear for the provinces of Germany and Gaul, above all because he expected that the enemy would invade Italy and even attack Rome itself. There were no able-bodied citizens of any fighting capacity left in reserve, and the allied forces, such as were of any value, had suffered heavy losses. However, he made such preparations as he could in the circumstances.

When no men of military age proved willing to be conscripted, he made them draw lots. Through this arrangement, every fifth man under thirty-five was deprived of his property and his civil rights, together with every tenth man of those beyond that age. Finally, since even then a great many men would not respond, he had a number put to death. He then selected by lot as many as possible from those who had already completed their military service and from the freedmen, and after enrolling them in the army, ordered them with all speed to the province of Germany to join Tiberius. At this time there were many Gauls and Germans living in Rome; some served in the Praetorian Guard, others resided there for various reasons. Augustus feared that these might start an uprising, and so dispatched those who were serving in his bodyguard to various islands, and ordered those who were unarmed to leave the capital.

Cassius Dio continued:

These were the actions that he took at that time, during which none of the usual observations were carried out, nor were the festivals celebrated. Later, when he received news that some of the soldiers had been saved, that the province of Germany was garrisoned and that the enemy had not ventured to advance even to the Rhine, his fears subsided and he paused to review the situation. It struck him that for such a great and overwhelming calamity to have taken place, the wrath of some divinity must have been incurred; besides, the portent which had been observed both before the defeat and afterwards made him inclined to suspect that some superhuman agency was at work. The Temple of Mars in the field of that name had been struck by lightning; many locusts had flown into the very city and had been devoured by swallows; the peaks of the Alps had appeared to collapse upon one another and to send up three columns of fire; the sky was lit with flashes in many places and showers of comets appeared at one and at the same time; spears appeared to fly through the air from the north and to fall in the direction of the Roman camps; bees formed their honeycombs about the altars in the camps; a statue of Victory which stood in the province of Germany facing the enemy's territory had been turned around so as to face Italy; finally there was an occasion when fighting broke out around the Legion standards in the Roman camps; the soldiers had thought that the barbarians had attacked them, but this proved to be a false alarm.

*   *   *

After the battle and the celebrations that followed, Arminius and the Germans seized all the Roman fortresses along the Rhine but one, that at Aliso on the eastern side of the river. They were unable to capture the stronghold because they did not understand the complexities and science behind siege warfare.[1] The Romans also employed a large number of archers, whose arrows repeatedly checked their enemy's attacks and inflicted heavy losses upon them. The delay in dealing with this final position was perhaps the primary reason why the Germans neither crossed the Rhine nor invaded Gaul.

Arminius soon learned the Romans had stationed a garrison at the Rhine and that a general named Tiberius was approaching with a formidable army. That was enough to convince most of the German tribes to withdraw from the fort; the detachment left behind removed itself to a safe distance so as not to suffer losses from sudden sorties of the garrison. Eventually, the Romans trapped inside Aliso escaped to the Rhine, and for a time the Germans and Romans remained locked in a stalemate with the broad Rhine separating them. Tiberius had little inclination to cross into the wilds of Germania, and Arminius' warriors had little stomach and no logistical wherewithal to launch a sustained invasion of Gaul.

While Tiberius was protecting Rome from behind the Rhine, the popularity of Augustus' great-nephew Germanicus increased. The emperor ordered his great-nephew to regain the initiative in Germany. In 13 AD, four years after the Varus legions had succumbed to the barbarian hordes, Germanicus crossed the Rhine with a strong army and invaded Germany. Retribution for the defeat of the Varus Legions and the obvious insult to Rome drove the offensive.

Cautious lest his army suffer a similar disaster, however, Germanicus did not move too deeply beyond the Rhine. As a result, he was unable to come to grips with the German enemy in any meaningful way, and thus did not fight and win any pitched battles or subdue any rebellious tribe. The Romans remained east of the Rhine until late autumn, celebrated the

---

[1] This implied that Arminius was not necessarily engaged in this part of the German insurrection, as he undoubtedly had the Roman expertise and knowledge to enable him to instruct his men in the necessary tactical aspects of containment of an established, well defended position

birthday of Emperor Augustus by holding a horserace supervised by the Centurions, and quietly returned to the left bank.

The passive presence of the Romans changed radically over the next four years when Germanicus launched a series of expeditions that led to direct confrontations with Arminius and his Germans. After the first year of seizing ground directly across the Rhine and up into the central axis of the Lippe, Germanicus concentrated his forces for a march on the central German plains and the tribes within.

"In the next year," wrote Tacitus,

> . . . when the consuls were Drusus and Gaius Norbanus, a Triumph was decreed to Germanicus. The war, however, was not over. Its next stage was a sudden raid on the Chatti in early spring. But he was planning a large-scale summer campaign against the major enemy, the Cherusci. It was hoped that their allegiance was split between Arminius and Segestes. These two leaders stood respectively for treachery and goodwill to Rome. Arminius was Germany's trouble-maker. Segestes had often warned Publius Quinctilius Varus that rebellion was planned. At the feast which immediately preceded the rising Segestes had advised Varus to arrest Arminius and the other chiefs, and also himself, on the grounds that their removal would immobilise their accomplices and Varus could then take his time in sorting out the guilty from the innocent. However, Varus was destined to fall to Arminius. Segestes had been forced into war by the unanimous feeling of the Cherusci. But relations between the two Germans were still bad. Domestic ill-feeling contributed because Segestes' daughter, engaged to another man, was stolen by Arminius. The girl's father and husband detested each other. The marriage relationship, which brings friends closer, increased the bitterness of these two enemies.

For his offensive against the Chatti, Germanicus transferred four brigades (according to Tacitus) to Aulus Caecina Severus as well as 5,000 auxiliaries and some German emergency troops levied from west of the Rhine. Germanicus kept the same number of Roman troops for his own use and twice as many auxiliaries and moved out against the Chatti. Although he left behind a force to construct roads and bridges to make sure when he returned during the rainy season his men could still march, a rare drought dried the land and made the ingress and egress of the lands east of the Rhine easier than expected.

Tacitus wrote of the results of this movement:

> Germanicus completely surprised the Chatti. Helpless women, children, and old people were at once slaughtered or captured. The younger men swam across the River Eder and tried to prevent the Romans from building a bridge. But they were driven back by missiles and arrows. An unsuccessful attempt was made by the tribesmen to come to terms. Then there were some desertions to the Roman side. But the majority evacuated their towns and villages, dispersed and took to the woods. Germanicus burnt their capital, Mattium, and, ravaging the open country, started back for the Rhine. The enemy did not dare to harass the rearguard, as they are fond of doing when they have retreated for strategic purposes rather than in panic.

Although the Cherusci naturally wished to aid the Chatti, Caecina's aggressive movements kept the enemy separated while he methodically defeated the Marsi. Thereafter, a special commission sought out the Romans to appeal for the liberation of Segestes, who was under siege by hostile German warriors operating under Arminius. Segestes' own son, Segimundus, was a member of the group. Knowing Segestes was friendly to Rome, Germanicus moved quickly and successfully to free Segestes and many of his relatives. "These included women of high rank, among whom was Segestes' daughter, the wife of Arminius," wrote Tacitus. "She was temperamentally closer to her husband than to her father. From her came no appeals, no submissive tears; she stood still, her hands clasped inside her robe, staring down at her pregnant body. The party brought with them trophies from Varus' disaster, many of them distributed on that occasion as loot to those who were now surrendering."

Tacitus left the best account of how Segestes responded:

> And then there was Segestes himself, a huge figure, fearlessly aware he had been a good ally. "This is not the first day I have been a true friend to Rome," he is recorded to have said. "Ever since the divine Augustus made me a Roman citizen, my choice of friends and enemies has been guided by your advantage. My motive has not been hatred of my people—for traitors are distasteful even to the side they join—but the belief that Roman and German interests are the same, and that peace is better than war. That is why I denounced to your former commander Varus the man who broke the treaty with you—Arminius, the robber of my daughter!"

"But Varus indolently put me off. I lost faith in due processes of law, and begged him to arrest Arminius, and his partisans—and myself. May that night confirm my story—I wish I had not survived it! What followed is matter for mourning rather than excuses. But I did imprison Arminius; and his supporters have imprisoned me. And now, at my first meeting with you, I tell you I favour the old not the new – peace, not trouble. I am not after rewards; I want to clear myself of double-dealing. And if the Germans prefer remorse to suicide, I am a fitting agent. For my son's youthful misdeeds I ask pardon. My daughter, I admit, was brought here by force. It is for you to say which shall count the more, the son she is bearing to Arminius, or the fact that I am her father."

Germanicus promised safety to Segestes' children and relations, and a home in Gaul for himself. Then Germanicus withdrew his forces, allowing himself to be hailed as victor on Tiberius' initiative. A son was born to Arminius' wife; he was brought up at Ravenna.

Tacitus continued:

The news of Segestes' submission and good reception pleased those who did not want fighting, and distressed those who did. Arminius' violent nature was only enhanced by his wife's abduction and the prospect of servitude for their unborn child. He made a rapid tour of the Cherusci, demanding war against Segestes and Germanicus. These were some of his savage taunts: "What a fine father! What a glorious commander of a valiant army, whose united strength has kidnapped one helpless woman! I, on the other hand, have annihilated three divisions and their commanders. My fighting has been open, not treacherous—and it has been against armed men and not pregnant women. The groves of Germany still display the Roman Eagles and standards which I hung there in honour of the gods of our fathers.

"Let Segestes live on the conquered bank, and make his son a Roman priest again. With this warning before them Germany will never tolerate Roman rods, axes, and robes between Rhine and Elbe. Other countries, unacquainted with Roman rule, have not known its impositions or its punishments. We have known them—and got rid of them! Augustus, now deified, and his "chosen" Tiberius have gone away frustrated. There is nothing to fear in an inexperienced youth and a mutinous army. If you prefer your country, your parents, and the old ways to settlement under tyrants abroad, then do not follow Segestes to shameful slavery—follow Arminius to glory and freedom!"

Besides the Cherusci, the tribes around responded to his call. It also won over Arminius' uncle, Inguiomerus, long respected by the Romans. This increased Germanicus' alarm. To create a diversion and break the force of the expected blow, he sent Caecina with forty regular battalions through the territory of the Bructeri to the river Ems, while cavalry under Pedo Albinovanus crossed the Frisian borderland. Germanicus himself sailed with four brigades across the lakes. When infantry, horse, and fleet affected a junction on the Ems, a contingent of auxiliaries offered by the Chauci was incorporated into the army. A flying column under Lucius Stertinius, sent by Germanicus against the Bructeri when they started burning their possessions, discovered the Eagle of the Nineteenth Legion that had been lost with Varus. The army ravaged the countryside between the Ems and the Lippe, marching to the extremity of Bructeran territory.

In 15 AD during one of the expeditions to defeat Arminius, Germanicus marched his army to Kalkriese to find the site of Varus' defeat. Tacitus again reflected on the demise of the Varus Legions once more:

Now they were near the Teutoburgian Wood, in which the remains of Varus and his three divisions were said to be lying unburied. Germanicus conceived a desire to pay his last respects to these men and their general. Every soldier with him was overcome with pity when he thought of his relations and friends and reflected on the hazards of war and human life. Caecina was sent ahead to reconnoitre the dark woods and build bridges and causeways on the treacherous surface of the sodden marshland. Then the army made its way over the tragic sites. The scene lived up to its horrible associations. Varus' extensive first camp, with its broad extent and headquarters marked out, testified to the whole army's labours. Then a half-ruined breastwork and shallow ditch showed where the last pathetic remnant had gathered. On the open ground were whitening bones, scattered where men had fled, heaped up where they had stood and fought back. Fragments of spears and of horses' limbs lay there – also human heads, fastened to tree-trunks. In groves nearby were the outlandish altars at which the Germans had massacred the Roman colonels and senior company-commanders.

Survivors of the catastrophe, who had escaped from the battle or from captivity, pointed out where the generals had fallen, and where the Eagles were captured. They showed where Varus received his first wound, and where he died by his own unhappy hand. And they told of the platform from which Arminius had spoken and of his arrogant insults to the Eagles and standards—and of all the gibbets and pits for the prisoners.

So, six years after the slaughter, a living Roman army had come to bury the dead men's bones of three whole divisions. No one knew if the remains he was burying belonged to a stranger or a comrade. But in their bitter distress, and rising fury against the enemy, they looked on them all as friends and blood-brothers. Germanicus shared in the general grief, and laid the first turf of the funeral-mound as a heartfelt tribute to the dead. Thereby he earned Tiberius' disapproval. Perhaps this was because the emperor interpreted every action of Germanicus unfavourably. Or he may have felt that the sight of the unburied dead would make the army too respectful of its enemies and reluctant to fight – nor should a commander belonging to the antique priesthood of the Augurs have handled objects belonging to the dead.

Battlefield Finds in Kalkriese

In late 1994, Professor Schlüter's field team, joined now by an archaeologist new to the group, Dr. Joachim Harnecker, sliced through a section of the main battlefield on the eastern side of the main site. There, they uncovered a huge mass of bones, both human and animal. They were not just an accumulation of bones en masse from men who had died where they had fallen. Rather, these bones had been carefully placed into a pit from the side, turfs gently laid over them, and then the remains of horses laid over that. The whole was then further covered over. It was the leading edge of a massive burial site. Since that first cut through the grave, the remains of many Roman soldiers have been removed from the ground and sealed in molds of plaster of Paris, thereafter to be carefully examined by Professor Schlüter's team of experts.

I had long looked upon this section of the Varus field as a potentially productive archaeological area. Once the ambush walls had been identified and their established line around the hill verified, I advocated that the main German attack was launched on the leading eastern edge of the point of ambush, where the large force of incoming Romans was compressed into the narrow defile of the *Engpass*. If true, this was also where the majority of Roman losses would have been suffered, the bodies left to rot by Arminius. Six years later Germanicus had marched to the site and discovered a massive unburied graveyard. He would not have taken the trouble to move the skeletal remains any great distance, and so would have established the burial site on the field of battle—near the ambush wall and reportedly the site where the Eagles of the Eighteenth and Nineteenth legions had been finally lost to Arminius.

I was promptly informed of the discovery of human remains and recall visiting the Information Center at Kalkriese, which has grown from being a small tourist enclave to a major archaeological institute. The original farmhouse and outbuildings had been taken over by civil authorities of the Landschaftsverband and the Denkmalpflege and converted into offices and research and restoration laboratories. Behind the Information Center was a small room that held a profusion of large white moulds, each holding the remains of many who had fallen in the 9 AD battle. I still vividly remember going into the room the first time. It was an emotional moment, for no reason I now care to mention. But entering the room was nothing compared to visiting the open grave itself. Susanne Wilbers-Rost showed me the moulds and we discussed them in detail before walking to the excavations taking place on the site of the grave. The pits were covered by a series of large waterproof canopies to protect the dig site and its precious contents.

I stood off to one side of the wide trench and absorbed the enormity and incredible importance of the find site. I walked up to the knoll and looked down upon the ambush site—from which place Arminius commanded his forces and where he had his prisoners tortured after the battle. It was no more than two hundred yards away from the burial pits. I once again visited Felsenfeld and walked over the site of the last battle camp erected by Varus' command. I felt their presence, heard their shouts and cries, the bedlam of battle, the screams of desperate and wounded and dying men; an overpowering sense of sadness washed over me. Although I knew my quest for the lost Varus Legions would continue for many more years to come—during which I intended to seek out the truth behind the writings of Tacitus and Cassius Dio and seek the other places where Arminius and the Romans had confronted each other—here and now at Kalkriese I felt, for reasons inexplicable, that I had finally come home.

*   *   *

The pure archaeological work at Kalkriese progressed in a series of leaps and bounds as the archaeologists sought to answer the myriad of questions still surrounding the site and the bloody battle that had been fought there. Beginning in 1995, resident archaeologists Suzanne Wilbers-Rust and Joachim Harnecker worked to expand their understanding of the core areas of the field. Suzanne's expertise as the expert responsible for the central fields covered the ambush positions, and Joachim Harnecker's interests concentrated more on the archaeological explorations of the lands and ground features to the west and east. In particular his work focused on the eastern side, the direction from which the Legions had advanced from Felsenfeld, Varus' last Battle Lager, and then on into the narrowing gap of the Kalkriese Pass.

Explorations of the eastern approaches and a number of the high banked contour lines of the Berglands lying just on the western side of the small town of Venne indicated marked evidence of activity on the rise, where Joachim's exploratory digs had produced several finds, some of gold and a small number of bronze. It was as if a small party of observers had stayed there, possibly to oversee the Legions' line of march as they forged their way toward the west around the Bergland feature.

A short distance away, but closer to Venne, explorations with metal detectors produced a relatively large quantity of copper coins, but only on one side of the valley floor. The coins may mark the site of a forced crossing of the stream and boggy area, where a hasty wooden footway had been erected for the legionaries to clamber up the other side. Had some of them dropped some of their coins while negotiating the slippery slope? The men who lost these coins were still fleeing for their very lives after three days of deprivation and battle, running westward toward safer territory and friendly forces, away from the horror of Varus' last Lager, where Varus and so many of their officers had committed suicide. The lost coinage at this small crossing point helped enhance the picture of flight by thousands of sorely pressed and demoralized Roman soldiers who, though they could not have known it, were fleeing to their ultimate demise at the Kalkriese Gap.

The work progressed in areas in and around the central field, and each year produced still more fascinating revelations. My own interests turned to other matters. After having found this tragic place—in actuality a giant cemetery—my curiosity got the better of me. I was more than willing to leave the difficult archaeological work to others more qualified than I and set out again on my own to seek out the other parts of this saga of the Roman incursions into northern Germany. Of particular interest to me was the life and times of Arminius, or Hermann the Cherusker, as he is better known. I maintained a deep interest with developments in Kalkriese and a very close relationship with the administration and archaeological teams, but I could not shake loose my desire to explore fields yet unfound.

It was time to take stock of all that had transpired during the preceding years: my first discoveries of coins in 1987 had been followed by two important years of work that created the base plate for the archaeological digs that transpired under the expert guidance of Professor Schlüter in late 1989. The handful of years that followed were a blur of travel: from the Rivers Lippe and Rhine, out to the Weser, and back down to the Roman Lagers on the Lippe—those uncovered and those still waiting to be found, including Aliso, the last bastion of Roman activity after the Varus Battle before it too finally fell. When I arrived back in Germany from my short tour of duty in England in 1993, initially to Berlin until 1994, then down to Düsseldorf until 1996, I found I still had a great desire to go out once again and look for all those other places of Roman antiquity that had been lost in the mists of time.

During this time I established many valuable contacts with other historians and budding archaeologists and adventurers like myself. I became involved with a number of research projects, most arranged during spare time work supporting other archaeological institutes and museums throughout northern Germany. Two people became guiding lights in these new forays of mine. One was a business man from Berlin by the name of Wolfgang Prauss, whose key interests supported my own fascination with the lost site of the Aliso Battle Lager on the Lippe; the other was Willy Dräger, an important member of the Archaeological Institute in Hannover whose main interest was Roman history and associated German sites. By the time the century turned I was involved in any number of truly exciting searches and investigations, some of which are still being conducted: from the Rhine and the authorities responsible for the rebuilt Roman Town of Xanten, to the River Lippe and the Museum at Haltern and Dr. Kuhlborn at the Institute in Münster, to Hannover and Dr. Gebers and Dr. Cosack of the Archaeological Institute there. They were and still remain halcyon days. Each year produces more pieces into the jigsaw puzzle of those times long forgotten.

The lost lager of Aliso, where the last remnants of the Roman forces in Germania gathered up after the Varus Battle before making their escape to the Rhine and safety, is a source of constant argument and debate within the German archaeological community. My own investigations, back by the support of the Rhine Institute, have led me to believe the site is close to the town of Drevenack bordering on the now dry riverbed of the Lippe in that area. Both aerial and ground survey maps lend credence to my theory. My finds of Roman denarius on the 30-yard elevations of the old Lippe river banks in that area also lend weight to the existence of a Roman area of activity there, either a port or camp not dissimilar to that found at Haltern, or the camp of Aliso itself. And so the search continues . . .

The search continues for the lines of march during the German Wars taken by the Roman legions across the plains from the Rivers Ems to the Weser. It was there battle after pitched battle took place between Arminius and Germanicus. Those same lines of march also saw Caecina take his legion under Germanicus to visit the last sites of the Varus Battle as described by Tacitus in his Historical Annals. The search is still ongoing to discover where Germanicus forged his new army across the broad expanse of the north German plain from the River Ems through to the submerged wooden roads and moor crossings to the site of his march lager and camp, now affectionately known as "Caecina's Lager." It is possible this site is near present-day Diepholz. Caecina's route down to Felsenfeld and into the same morass and Bergland around the Kalkrieseberg and into the Kalkriese Gap, where the remnants of the Varus Legions had traipsed and met their end some six years before, also awaits discovery.

With the support of Willy Dräger and his team of associates and archaeological experts, my discoveries at Diepholz have now firmly established that the site was very much an area of Roman activity, though more investigations are necessary to uncover all of its silent secrets of days long past.

The fascination of the silver bars and the suggested site of a Roman port on the River Weser, north of Varus' summer camp at Minden, still beckons. So does the site of the silver treasure at the Galgenberg near Hildesheim, which was likely part of the plunder Arminius gathered from the Varus battle; the secret of where the rest of the treasure resides died with Arminius when he was taken down by members of his own family in 21 AD. Willy, his team, and I have already made a serious survey of the area. We are confident that more of these large chests of booty are buried deep in and around the Galgenberg woods—especially since several large Roman keys have been unearthed on the Varus/Kalkriese battlefield. Only time will tell. Our first hole in the ground has been dug, but the signals are still too deep—even after digging down three yards. At this time, the ground and the area does not allow us to introduce deeper excavating machinery. New dig plans are underway.

Kalkriese: The Work Continues

Similarly fascinating work continues in Kalkriese. Suzanne's and Joachim's archaeological work goes on; my friend, Professor Wolfgang Schlüter, has now finally retired after years of dedicated work on the project, and now spends much of his time as a grandfather. In 1995, more of the rampart ambush wall, complete with drainage ditch and two additional burial pits, were discovered. The latter held only a few human bones and some fine artifacts, including a Roman spear shaft (*Lanzenschuh*). In other pits were several fascinating finds: two small bronze dolphins and a snaffle bow (*Trensenbügel*), several animal bones (possibly mules), and a human lower jaw sat below a plume holder.

The year 1996 brought more revelations. Only a handful of Roman artifacts were recovered, and then Suzanne extended the area around the first excavations and discovered yet another pit, this one slightly smaller than the others. More single bones were found here, including animal bones, and most telling of all, a single human skull.....

A complete overview of the Kalkriese Project site was undertaken in 1997. Its purpose was to set the goals of future excavations and ensure that the thousands of artifacts were being properly stored and analyzed. It was also important to ascertain what those finds meant in terms of interpreting the entire battlefield. Preparations were now underway for the construction of the new battlefield museum and tower. Clearing the immediate area of the foundations for those structures consumed considerable time and labor. The following year (1998) produced more single Roman finds, but none from the actual battle site itself. With this shortfall in finds, additional exploratory digs were made in the central areas of the battlefield, where the wall and line of the ramparts were further established to the east of the main ambush position. More Roman finds were recovered on the northern (Roman) side of the wall.

The chief prospector, Klaus Fehrs, had also been busy. During his forays into the surrounding areas (including the central sites), he had recovered a number of exciting artifacts. Among them was a helmet pintle, silver mountings for a gladius sword scabbard, and part of a cingulum. Later, he also unearthed a "Skyphos" receptacle handle, also in silver, and an Aureus, a brilliant rare gold coin.

Time continued to slip past. By 1999, work had progressed eastward into the construction area of the museum and tower buildings. A few Roman weapons and many pieces of militaria were recovered. These suggested the fight had started in that vicinity, but no further ramparts were uncovered there. At the eastern end of the ambush walls, about 100 yards from the museum site, the unearthed line of curved ramparts straightened suddenly as it ran into the western reaches of the battlefield. A ditch was found at the front of parts of this wall, the result of the removal of the earth to erect the earthen barrier. Other wonderful finds were made in this area, including an ornate buckle and clasp and a fascinating revelation that literally peered out of the excavations as it was uncovered: a glass eye. Additional digging revealed bronze Roman instruments, a sickle, a wooden shaft (*Deichsel*), and the bow frame of a helmet.

These investigations made the real history of the Varus Battle come alive once more. In the last section of the ambush wall area was discovered yet another pit, the fifth of its type. Apart from a number of animal bones, two human skulls were found, one of which had suffered a cleaving fracture caused by a sword blade. The find immediately brought to mind what Tacitus had written: "Then a half-ruined breastwork and shallow ditch showed where the last pathetic remnant had gathered. On the open ground were whitening bones, scattered where men had fled, heaped up where they had stood and fought back. Fragments of spears and of horses' limbs lay there—also human heads . . ."

Prospecting on the western side of the main killing field, the Oberesch, resulted in yet more wondrous finds. These included several bronze plate fragments, two bells, parts and pieces of swords, a horse's harness, and the superb (and amazing) find of a small personal bronze wine sieve, tucked away in a pocket of limestone under the wall. These finds, the result of Fisher metal detectors and digs, prompted yet more excavations of the wall—particularly along the western edge, where the small but deeply running Beck waterway had acted as a natural backstop to the end of the ramparts. As the ramparts were uncovered it became obvious that this part of the wall had not only been covered in grass turf, but also limestone on the outer (forward) side. Along the wall were found many small bronze plate fragments as well as an axe, a tent peg, and an ornate bronze weight. On the reverse of the rampart, the skeleton of an almost complete mule with an iron snaffle or bit was unearthed. It looked as though the animal had suffered a blow on the back of the neck after it had jumped over the wall from the Roman side. Further excavations in the area revealed the rampart had been damaged by the removal of some of the limestone, and more Roman bronze artifacts were found, including yet another glass eye!

As the year turned into 2001, the investigations of the line of the walled rampart required additional cuts back into the woods on the brow of the hill, where Arminius had commanded his tribesmen to such awe-inspiring effect. Regrettably, over the years following the battle the material of the wall had slowly slipped away, and so investigations of the wine sieve and the earth in which it had lain were inconclusive. However, more single Roman finds, including yet a third glass eye, were found. After the livid pictures the finds along the area at the end of the wall had conjured up—"where the last remnants of the Legion had gathered up to fight to the last man," Tacitus reminded us—the remains of two entire Roman mules were discovered. Following the diagonal line of the wall also proved rewarding. Roman artifacts found here included well preserved cheek flaps and the straps of a Roman helmet.

The excavations continued to excite all concerned and unearth one revelation after another. In 2002 and 2003, the digs were enlarged to seek the ever extending limits of the rampart wall to the eastern side of the field. Further work was being done in the center of the wall near the spot where the altar and burial pit of bones had been discovered all those years ago in 1994.

The new museum, tower, and battlefield park opened in March 2002. Presided over by Lower Saxony's Minister President, Sigmar Gabriel, the opening ceremonies were attended by more than 1,000 dignitaries and invited guests, including everyone who had been, or continued to be, involved in the site since its discovery. In less than three years, more than 250,000 people have travelled from all over the world to see the place where Varus' legions met their end. And they still come in ever-larger numbers—even during the winter months.

My own investigations continued apace. The questions raised by the Diepholz "Caecina's Lager" project have prompted me to look at the whole approach line into the area from the east, Felsenfeld, and the village of Schwagstorf itself. I surmised that Germanicus' legion under Caecina camped in the area as it settled in to recover and bury the skeletons and remains of Varus' legions in 15 AD. I had always carefully searched using various grids and paid special attention to semi-walled oblong features that may have been such hasty encampments. After Klaus' discovery of copper coins near the stream at Venne on the western side of the waterway, I concentrated my own surveys farther east. One particular rectangle, partially raised and banked on two sides, caught my attention. It was a natural bound from Klaus' finds to or from that site, so I had made a series of grid surveys of my own. My search uncovered a bronze animal figure, the top half shank of a wild boar with a small (missing) loop stanchion on the bottom bevel. It was later identified by experts as the top mounting figurine set on top of the bone handle of a Roman dagger or hunting knife. Close by was a beautiful denarius of Augustus Caesar, with Caius and Lucius Caesar on the reverse. Investigations have yet to prove the site as that of a camp, but the finds prove Roman activity, and are consistent with other finds coming to light throughout the Kalkriese area.

*   *   *

From Tacitus:

> I find from the writings of contemporary Senators that a letter was read in the Senate from a Chieftain of the Chatti named Adgandestrius, offering to kill Arminius if poison were sent him for the job. The reported answer was that Romans take vengeance on their enemies, not by underhand tricks, but by open force of arms. By this elevated sentiment Tiberius invited comparison with generals of old who had forbidden, and disclosed, the plan to poison King Pyrrhus. However, the Roman evacuation of Germany and the fall of Marobodus had induced Arminius to aim at Kingship. But his freedom loving compatriots forcibly resisted. The fortunes of the

fight fluctuated, but finally Arminius succumbed to treachery from his relations.

He was unmistakably the liberator of Germany, Challenger of Rome - not in its infancy, like kings and commanders before him, but at the height of its power - he had fought undecided battles, and never lost a war. He had ruled for twelve of his thirty seven years. To this day the tribes sing of him. Yet Greek historians ignore him, reserving their admiration for Greece.

We Romans, too, underestimate him, since in our devotion to antiquity we neglect modern history.

*   *   *

Nearly 2,000 years after the death of Arminius, Major General J.F.C. Fuller included the Teutoburg Battle in his influential book Decisive Battles of the Western World. There, the general attempted to calculate the incalculable: "Had Germany been for four centuries thoroughly Romanised, one culture, not two would have dominated the western world. There would have been no Franco-German problem, no Charlemagne, no Louis XIV, no Napoleon, no Kaiser Wilhelm II, and no Hitler. . ."

*   *   *

Kalkriese has much to offer those who possess the interest and imagination to see and feel the heritage of years long gone by. Today, you can walk the routes, visit the sites, and feel the atmosphere of the special places I have come to know so well. For those who wish to truly experience the final hours of the Varusschlacht as Arminius may well have seen it, I suggest a walk into the woods up the knoll at Kalkriese to the apex of the hill. The chilling site is just 300 yards from the new Information Center and some 75 yards from the main road.

Once you set foot on the right spot, you will be able to see through the trees across the ambush toward the northeastern corner of the field. This is the same view Arminius had. From this point he could see both his men in hiding and beyond the ambush walls, where the Romans unwittingly approached from the east; he could see the ground directly to the north and through cuts in the trees see out and down to the northwest to the killing fields beyond. This is where Arminius stood when he destroyed thousands of Roman soldiers in a single morning—and where he would have celebrated his victory afterward. This is the very place where he likely imprisoned and tortured the Romans unlucky enough to have been captured alive.

And if you stand and listen carefully on this spot you will hear . . . nothing. Kalkriese is a very peaceful and somber place, a testament to, and a graveyard for, the thousands of Romans who perished and the two Eagles that were captured at the Varusschlacht of 9 AD. And it is where I still seek the golden Eagle of the Seventeenth Legion in my continuing quest for the lost legions of Varus.

A Major in the Background: The Following Years

I took up the appointment of Director of the Museum and Park Kalkriese in November, 2000. My first meeting with Major Clunn took place in the first days of that month. I had naturally heard a lot about him before our meeting. He was the man who discovered the Roman battlefield at Kalkriese, the unique site of the *Varusschlacht* (Varus Battle), and much had been written about him concerning his discovery and subsequent work that comprises the project at the battlefield. I also knew Major Clunn's early finds of Roman coins, and later lead sling shot in the battlefield area, were not the only work with which he had been involved since he began working with the Osnabruck Archaeological authorities under the management of Prof Dr Schluter, beginning now some 17 years ago in 1987.

Throughout the ensuing years, Major Clunn has strongly supported the various activities linked to the archaeological work in Kalkriese, and has been an avid supporter in so many ways in promoting the site to and for the benefit of the German public. He followed the official traveling displays of selected artifacts across the length and breadth of Germany, from Berlin to Hamburg and to Hannover, and many other large cities, including the site of Hermann's statue at Detmold. His presence lent support to Prof Schluter and the project. Major Clunn also committed himself to a series of his own extensive presentations and lectures, journeying as far away as Vienna, Austria. All of his efforts have resulted in his completion of this now famous book "Auf der Suche nach der Verlorenen Legionen" (originally transcribed from the English version as "In Quest of the Lost Legions"). For his work in both Anglo-German relations, and the direct support he gave and continued to give to Project Kalkriese, he was honored by Her Majesty, Queen Elizabeth II, with the award of the MBE in 1996. The following year, he received the Order of Merit from the Landkreis Osnabruck, and in 1998 was presented with the German Medal of Honor from Landrat Hugo, President of the Landschaftsverband for Osnabrucker Land County.

One can understand my curiosity was more than aroused at meeting him in person, as I really did not know what to expect. I was pleasantly surprised and absolutely delighted. From the outset it was readily apparent that Major Clunn shared my own enthusiasm and positive outlook on the historical values and archaeological realizations that had transformed Kalkriese into one of the most important sites relating to German national beginnings and origins. His enthusiasm in wishing to assist in any way that might continue to promote this incredible archaeological site was extremely infectious.

What I did not realise at the time was that not only was he actively seeking to support and widen the public interest in Kalkriese through his own personal lectures and efforts elsewhere in Germany, but was also making serious efforts to widen the scope and promotion of those aspirations through both the future distribution of his book and the tourist possibilities yet to be sourced in other countries, both near and far. In addition to Germany, his expertise has been utilized and featured in documentary films, TV programs, and magazine articles in Holland, Sweden, France, Denmark, Austria, Australia, and Canada, to name but a few, and now, most importantly, in the United States.

From our first discussions in 2000 until the present, I have grown to appreciate Major Clunn's unswerving efforts to promote Kalkriese. He does so not for his own benefit necessarily, for he does not actively seek self-aggrandizement for his own purposes. Indeed, on many occasions he has to be encouraged to make public appearances that might focus upon his own personal efforts. His participation is for the good of the common cause. His ideas for marketing, promotion, and tourism remain at a constant pitch, and it is true to say that his own personal efforts in linking promotions with the American public are now coming to fruition.

I have followed these activities with avid interest, for he has clearly outlined the potential for a tourist linkage, a triangular concept of interest between Kalkriese (the site of the battle), Detmold (the site of Hermann's statue), and the small town of New Ulm in Minnesota, USA. Under Presidential decree a few years ago, this small town was declared the new center for German-American cultural affairs, having in the heart of the town's population a passionate desire to maintain links with their German forefathers, who in 1897 also had a desire to mark their German heritage with the erection of a large bronze statue of their own of Herman the Cherusker, the warrior chieftain who defeated the Varus Roman Legions all those years ago in 9 AD. Unbeknownst to many, some 35% of the American population is of German descent, the highest proportion of any section of the American community. The statue itself has been refurbished and was re-erected in October 2004. A small container of earth taken from the battlefield at Kalkriese was placed in the base of the statue.

I might add that that what I have described here is just a small part of Major Clunn's activities surrounding the Roman-German historical and archaeological aspects of his interests. In the years following the publication of the first edition of his book, he maintained a drive (some might describe it as obsessive) to answer many of the leading questions that have been thrown up surrounding the events of the Roman occupation of Germany, particularly during the period of the Varus Battle. His interests and activities have encompassed work and general support to Museum institutions in Munster, Rhineland, including the archaeological authorities in Xanten, where he still continues to search for the possible location of the missing Roman Lager of Aliso, possibly on the River Lippe. Notwithstanding his permanent interest in establishing the battle lines of the Varus Legions leading to the battlefield at Kalkriese, for the last few years Major Clunn has been making successful forays into the pursuit of other Roman areas of activity with the Museum and Denkmal authorities in Hannover, linked with the archaeologists there under the resident archaeologist Dr. Gebers and his great friend, historian, and project researcher, Willy Drager. In conjunction with the authorities in Hannover, his efforts to establish the possible movement sites of the Roman Legions under Germanicus during the years following the Varus Battle have produced fresh evidence in the Diepholz area, some distance north of Kalkriese. Indeed, evidence there suggests the Germanicus Legions might well have lagered there on their way toward one of the many engagements they had with the German tribes under Hermann during that time. His additional discoveries of Roman silver coinage closely matching the coinage found in Kalkriese suggest the site has historical relevance to the Varus period.

Since the opening of the "new" Museum and Park at Kalkriese in March 2002 under my Directorship, we have had many high ranking dignitaries and celebrities visit the battlefield. All of them have met Major Clunn and have expressed their enthusiasm and support for what we seek to achieve here in Kalkriese.

I, too, greatly enjoy and value his friendship, enthusiasm, and devotion to the Kalkriese Project. Most of all, I appreciate his support and positive commitment to making Kalkriese a shining light in terms of German historical and cultural affairs, and the recognition he has garnered of the archaeological importance of Kalkriese on the international and world stage.

Herrn Christian Jaletzke
Director, Museum and Park Kalkriese

The Hermann the Cherusker (Arminius) Monument
in New Ulm, Minnesota. *Photo courtesy of Rick Apitz*

Afterword

The Varus Battle and its Impact on America

The discovery of the historic battle site at Kalkriese by British amateur archeologist Major Tony Clunn, MBE (who was made a Member of the Order of the British Empire by Queen Elizabeth II for his efforts[1]), was nothing less than sensational. Unearthing a world-changing battle site where Hermann (Arminius) defeated three Roman Legions in 9 AD refocused attention on German national origins. Two millennia after the Kalkriese battle, the name and legend of Hermann the Cheruscan has gained new recognition as a symbol of the German peoples' cultural unity.

---

[1] In recognition of Major Clunn's discoveries and subsequent support to ongoing archaeological works in Germany, in 1997 the German authorities awarded him the first recipient of the Certificate of Merit, now an annual award for Meritorious Service to the German Community. This was followed in 1999 by the prestigious award of the German Medal of Honor.

The legend-turned-symbol was transferred to the new world by immigrants. Within a century after the erection of a Hermann Monument in New Ulm, Minnesota, the memorial was placed on the national register of historical places in the United States. The 106th Congress of the United States broadened the impact by designating the Hermann Monument at New Ulm to be an official symbol of all citizens of German heritage. How did this happen?

The Sons of Hermann

Since 1806, when Napoleon declared the collapse of the German Empire in Central Europe, German folk have been immigrating to America in waves. The American frontier west of the Alleghenies beckoned farmers and German idealists to a life of freedom unknown in their homeland. Unfortunately, many experienced firsthand the resentment that local people felt toward new immigrants.

Acts of violence against these German immigrants led directly to the founding of a German national society. In 1840, George Heiner from New York City suggested starting an organization to cultivate understanding of his people. The name "Hermann" was chosen as a symbol of German culture because it gave the new society identity and unity. On June 21, 1840, the first chapter of the Sons of Hermann was constituted in New York.

By 1848, the March Revolutions in Central Europe, led by patriots in search of constitutional democratic government, caused the American Sons of Hermann to celebrate with special nationalistic flair. The American society became known as the Order of the Sons of Hermann, and its ranks grew rapidly. By its 21st national convention in 1897, representatives of the 500 chapters of the Order were able to gather west of the Mississippi River in the prairie town of New Ulm, Minnesota, for the dedication of a Hermann Monument.

The Memorial

A Hermann memorial on American soil was the dream of artist and architect Julius Berndt (1832-1916). Berndt was uniquely qualified to create a smaller version of the memorial erected n Detmold, Germany.

An emigrant from Silesia at age 20, Berndt brought artistic skills and ideas from his homeland to the New World.

As a young man in Chicago, he was elected secretary of the Chicago Land Association, a partnership of recent German immigrants who desired to homestead on the frontier. In 1854, the Land Association selected land along the Minnesota River, thirteen miles from hunting grounds reserved for the Dakota Indians. Two years later, the Chicago Land Association united with a colonization association of the Turner Society of North American to give the settlement financial stability. The original half-dozen frame homes multiplied rapidly into a respectable village. But the outbreak of the Dakota Conflict during the nation's Civil War upset the peace and friendship between settlers and the Dakota (Sioux) nation. Two attacks on New Ulm in August of 1862 destroyed the homes, but defenders saved the town.

The town was rebuilt, and the talents of Julius Berndt—architect, building inspector for Brown County, and entrepreneur—were again put to productive use. In 1882, Berndt became the first president of the New Ulm chapter of the Order of the Sons of Hermann. He had already drawn up plans for a Hermann monument to be set on a scenic vantage point overlooking the city.

Hermann on the American Prairie

Berndt first broached the prospect of a memorial in 1881 at a national convention of the Sons of Hermann in Chicago. Four years later, he placed specific plans before the national convention. The New Ulm proposal was adopted. At the next convention, the national secretary announced: "Every German should be proud to erect such a memorial. But until now, unfortunately, only $10.50 has been collected for this purpose." The estimated cost to erect the monument was $20,000.00. Despite a seeming lack of enthusiasm for a monument on the prairie, Berndt was commissioned in 1887 to secure materials for it and oversee construction.

The New Ulm chapter of the Sons of Hermann purchased two acres west of the city. An appeal for funds went out within the national order. A contract to fashion the Hermann statue from Berndt's blueprints was let with the W. H. Mullins Company of Salem, Ohio. The company specialized in classical statuary and animal figures, but also listed among its credits the copper roofing of the Library of Congress in Washington, D.C. Responsibility for the statue was assigned to German-born sculptor, Alphonso Pelzer. He advertised as part of the Pelzer Brothers' sculptor studio "for works of art in wood, stone, and metal, monuments, figures, and ornaments." His primary claim to fame was the creation of several statues of President Abraham Lincoln.

Hermann proved to be a special challenge. Twenty-tons of clay were used to make the model. It measured almost 33 feet from sword tip to toe and weighed more than 4,000 pounds. On completion, Hermann was probably the largest and most striking figure of its kind made in the United States, second only in size and similar craftsmanship to the magnificent Statue of Liberty in New York harbor.

Dedication rites for the Hermann Monument were set for the last Saturday in September, 1897. Following an address by the national president of the Sons of Hermann, and the transfer of official documents by the building committee, the statue was unveiled. Hermann's home on the prairie was secured.

A National Symbol

The fortune of the Hermann Monument changed quickly in the 20th century. The Order of the Sons of Hermann declined rapidly as a result of World War I. When the local chapter disbanded after the war, the Hermann memorial entered the public domain. The city of New Ulm was given charge of the monument and the park. In 1973, the memorial was placed in the National Register of Historic places. As a follow-up to the 100th anniversary of the completed monument in 1997, the Hermann memorial received a special honor: The 106th Congress of the United States designated the Hermann Monument at New Ulm to be an official symbol of all citizens of German heritage.

Arnold J. Koelpin
January 2005

Aquilifer: Bearer of a legion Eagle and standard. Senior Signifer.

Auxiliaries (Auxilia): From the third century BC, Rome had increasingly recruited cavalry and light infantry (or men for specialist roles). Augustus established a permanent auxiliary army that probably numbered more than 100,000 (cf. 150,000 regulars = legionaries). Units were named after the place they were formed. Auxiliaries were not Roman citizens, but were commanded by citizens, sometimes of native origin. Many auxiliaries were recruited from within lands the Romans had taken over establishing their empire. Because of the weakness of the Roman cavalry (citizens), auxiliaries supplied three times the number of horsemen.

Centurion: In modern idiom, this was the rank equivalent to a company commander, although the number of men under command of any of the sixty-odd centurions in a legion varied between eighty and one thousand men, depending on his status and authority.

Cimber (or "furor Teutonicus"): Used by the Romans to describe the ferocious German tribesmen.

Consuls: The highest officials of the state and Senate. The Emperor usually took pains to show outward deference to the consulate. Tenure was normally annual, but as time passed replacements became more frequent, so as to spread the honor more widely. Except for Egypt, the governorships of the most important provinces were reserved for ex-consuls.

Cornicen: A military trumpeter, or horn blower.

Galley: A warship propelled by oars.

Gaul: Modern-day France.

Governors: There were two primary types of governors: A Pro-Consul, who governed "senatorial" provinces, elected by the Senate without imperial intervention; and the *Legatus* (imperial governor) of an imperial province, who was the Emperor's direct subordinate and commander of an army.

Groma: A surveying instrument.

Holzmoorwege: Old wooden causeways built across the wet moorlands of the north German plains. They were later used by the Romans, who rebuilt some and established other new causeways.

Knights (order of): The Roman *equites, equester ordo*. In the later Republic, this order comprised a powerful class of financial interests outside the Senate, and were often opposed to that governing body. Augustus reformed the order. Athough it still remained outside the Senate (and included the families of ex-slaves), it provided holders of many important and administrative posts. Members of this class were regarded as the patrons of young imperial princes, whom they named "Princes of Youth," the youth being knights under thirty-five (and senators' sons under twenty-five) who maintained the ancient cavalry origins of the order. Centurions also became knights on retirement from the army.

Lager: A fortified Roman encampment.

Legion: For purposes of translation, a Roman legion may be regarded as a brigade when its regular (citizen) troops, roughly 5,000 infantry and 120 cavalry, are alone considered. If thought of in conjunction with the auxiliary troops that often united under the same command during operations in the field, a legion may be considered a division. In early imperial times, the *Praefectus Castrorum*, the normal commander of a legion, sometimes represented more than one division, in which case he became corps chief of staff, or in effect, the second in command of the corps or army led by a governor or consul.

Legionary: A Roman soldier.

Onager: A single-armed stone-throwing machine similar to a catapault.

Optio: A Centurion's second in command.

Pilum, Pila: The heavy javelin of the legionaries.

Primus Pilus: The highest ranking centurion in a legion.

Principia: Headquarters building in a camp or *Lager*.

Scutum: A Roman shield.

Signifer: A standard-bearer.

Testudo: A square military formation hidden behind a shelter of battle shields resembling the carapace of a tortoise.

Tribunes: Staff officers under the command of a consul.

Borgwedde: A small rural community set in a valley of the Kalkriese Berg hills, through which a small stream runs. The area has a number of Stone-Age monuments, including the *Teufels Back Trog* (Devil's Baking Trough). Borgwedde was known as the *Borg am Heiligen Hain*, which roughly translated means Hill at the Holy Grove. At the apex of the hill, about one thousand yards due south, lies one of the largest Stone-Age graves ever found, some seventy-five yards in length. A large Sunteil Stone was erected at the eastern end. It is known as the *Teufels Stein* (Devil's Stone). This is on the hill of The Holy Grove.

Danube River: Ister in 9 AD.

Detmold: The site of Hermannsdenkmal (the statue of Arminius), once thought to have been the site of his victory over the Varus legions.

Dieven Wiesen: A huge expanse of moorland north of the Kalkriese Berg that was very wet in ancient days.

Elbe River: Suebi in 9 AD.

Ems River: Amafuis in 9 AD.

Engter: The next village west of Kalkriese. A key north–south pass through the Kalkriese Berg.

Felddungel: A small deep lake lying in woodland at the western extremities of Kalkriese.

Fisse-Niewedde Senke: The strip of land lying slightly east between the Kalkriese Berg and the Dieven Wiesen, site of the *Varusschlacht* (Varus battle).

Hildesheim: Site of the Hildesheim Roman silver treasure found on October 17, 1868.

Hunte River: Unsingis in 9 AD.

Icker: A small rural village area sitting in a large bowl in the middle of the Kalkriese Berg, due south of Kalkriese.

Idistaviso: The site of the battle between Arminius and Germanicus on the Weser, possibly south of Minden, or between Rinteln and Hameln.

Kalkriese: A small rural village area between the edge of the Kalkriese Berg and the Dieven Wiesen to the north.

Kalkriese Berg: The hill formation due north of Osnabrück ending at Kalkriese with the start of the Dieven Wiesen.

Krebsburg: A small hill where old German settlements had been established. Situated on the end of the Schnippenburg, part of the Kalkriese Berg.

Lippischer Wald: Renamed the Teutoburger Wald.

Lippe River: Lupia in 9 AD.

Mattium: Southwest of Kassel.

Ostercappeln: The town lying at the western end of the Wiehengebirge, near Schwagstorf. Just to the east lies the pass adjacent to the Krebsburg, the first feature of the Kalkriese Berg.

Rhine River: Rhine in 9 AD, the major geographic feature that delineated the eastern edge of the Roman Empire in Northern Europe.

Schwagstorf: The next village east of Venne.

Teutoburger Wald: A long line of hills and deep valleys centered on a ridgeline, stretching from the general area of Detmold in a northwesterly direction, which falls away into a series of open forested areas to the south and east of Osnabrück.

Venne: The next village east of Kalkriese.

Weser River: Visurgis in 9 AD.

Wiehengebirge Ridge: This feature extends from the lands east of Minden in a fairly straight line westward and ends at Ostercappeln, where the Kalkriese hills begin. The Weser splits this feature in two at Minden at the *Porta Westfalica*, a gap in the ridge.

Early

Publius (or Gaius) Cornelius Tacitus. Born in or about 56 AD, (possibly 57 AD). He may have survived Emperor Trajan, who died in 117 AD. Tacitus was a Senator from 81-96 AD, Consul of Anatolia (Asia) in 97 AD, and Governor fifteen years later. His short monographs, the life of Agricola and Germania, appeared within a short time of each other in about 98 AD. Of his major historical works, the *Histories* set forth the life of the Roman Emperors from Nero's death in 68 AD to 96 AD (the last year in the reign of Domitian (although only 68–69 have been found). The *Annals* were intended to cover the years 4-68 AD, a period of great significance. Unfortunately, part of Book V and all of Books VII–X are missing, and Book XVI breaks off in 66 AD. Tacitus was a friend and teacher of Pliny the Younger. In 77 AD he married the daughter of Agricola, the Governor in Britain from 78-85 AD, but he never mentioned her name. Tacitus is generally considered to be more reliable than either Cassius or Suetonius. He died circa 120 AD.

Cassius Dio. Greek Historian. Born in Bithynia 163 AD. Pro-consul in Africa under Alexander Severus and Governor of the Province of Dalmatia and Upper Pannonien (twice Consul). Cassius wrote perhaps eighty books on Rome's history: only Books XXXVI–LX (36 to 60) have been located. These deal mainly with the period from the Second Mithridatic War (69 BC) to the reign of Claudius (46 AD), and have survived virtually intact. Cassius died in 235 AD.

Lucius Annaeus Florus. Born 75 AD, probably in Africa. A resident of Rome. After travels in Spain, Florus returned to Rome and wrote a brief summary of Roman history (especially its wars) in two books to show the greatness and the decline of Roman morals. His work was based chiefly on Livy. He completed works to the reign of Augustus (31 BC–14 AD), although he probably intended to carry his writing through to his own time. Florus died circa 140 AD.

Flavius Vegetius. Lived circa 400 AD. He wrote a detailed account of recruitment and training for the Roman army, in which he tried to show how efficient the old system of training had been. His writings were only realized from a very late source, but much of what he wrote is still studied by modern-day commanders during their staff officer training. His description of a "testudo" (a solid square military formation hidden behind shields resembling a tortoise) can be considered a very early forerunner of the basic principle of the development of the battle tank now engaged in modern-day warfare.

Later Historians

Theodor Mommsen. German historian born in 1817. Mommsen's primary interest was Roman law, but the Varus battle fascinated him. When he learned about the coin finds in Kalkriese through find collections listed by H. Hartmann and P. Hofer, he ordered the Numismatician of the Royal Academy of Science in Berlin, *Königliche Academie der Wissenschaften zu Berlin*, J. Menadier, to go directly to Kalkriese in order to locate and collect all the information on Roman coin finds in and around that area, and to register the existing coins. Mommsen was awarded the Nobel Prize for Literature in 1903 for his multi-volume *History of Rome*, the same year he died.

Justus Möser. Born in Osnabrück on December, 14, 1720. He studied in Jena and Göttingen from 1740 to 1742, was *advocatus patriae* in Osnabrück in 1747 as well as "syndicus of the knighthood," and worked in a high-ranking position for the county government from 1761 to 1783. Möser believed the Varus battle had taken place at the Angivarien Wall near Damme, about eight miles northeast of Barenau. He had been to *Schloss Barenau* and had obviously taken down notes during his stay there. He died on January 8, 1794.

Hermann Hartmann. Born on March 22, 1826, in Ankum. Hartmann, who became Councillor of Sanitation, attended the Grammar School *Ratsgymnasium* in Osnabrück from 1840 to 1845, and studied medicine in Heidelberg, Göttingen, Würzbürg, Berlin, and Vienna. In 1850, he settled in Lintorf-Barkhausen (twelve miles from Kalkriese) to work as a general practitioner country doctor. Many of the reports and essays printed in the *Osnabrücker Mitteilungen* and other local magazines are based on Hartmann's historical and cultural studies and research. His book *Bilder aus Westfalen (Pictures from Westfalia)*, published in 1870, describes myths and legends, public and family celebrations of festivities, local traditions, superstitions, national history, and the cultural history of Osnabrück and Westfalia. Hartmann collected local legends and published the book *Sagenschatz Westfalens (Westfalia's Treasure of Legends)* in 1883, and a collection of poems. He died on January 26, 1901, in Lintorf.

Sequence of Events

27 BC—Birth of Augustus Caesar.

12 BC—Drusus carries out foraging action to the Weser.

11 BC —Drusus invades Germany east of the Rhine River, and later advances to the Elbe.

9 BC—Drusus fights four successive campaigns in Germany before dying on his return journey from the Elbe.

6–2 BC—Tiberius commands an expedition to the Elbe.

AD 4–6—Tiberius engaged in fighting in Germany.

AD 7—Varus appointed Governor of Germany.

AD 9—Defeat of the Varus legions (The *Varusschlacht*).

AD 10—Tiberius engaged in campaigns against the Germans after the defeat of the Varus legions.

AD 14—Death of Augustus Caesar. Tiberius appointed Emperor.

AD 15—Germanicus visits the site of the *Varusschlacht*. Also attacks and annihilates the Chatti tribe and destroys their capital at Mattium.

AD 16—Battle of Idistaviso (near Hameln on the Weser) between Germanicus and Arminius, who commands the Cherusker, Chatten, Brukterer, and Marser tribes. Outcome indecisive.

AD 19—Fighting between Arminius and Marobodus. Although the outcome was indecisive, Marobodus lost much of his power. Arminius' end was also nearing. A chieftain of the Chatti Tribe, Adgandestrius, made an offer to the Romans to poison Arminius, but it was not accepted. Death of Germanicus.

AD 21—Death of Arminius.

AD 37—Death of Tiberius.

The Roman Forts/Lager
(not all have been confirmed)

Tulifurdum: Minden: Varus' summer camp on the west bank of the Weser.

Castra Civitas: Hoxter/Corvey on the Weser.

Castra Vindecima: Brakel in Weserland.

Castra Decima: Neuenheerse in the Teutoburger Wald.

Castra Nona Neuenbeken/Benhausen in the Teutoburger Wald.

Castra Octa: Anreppen. By Paderborn on the Lippe.

Castra Septima: Kappel on the Lippe.

Castra Sexta: Lippborg on the Lippe.

Castra Ovinta: Kentrop on the Lippe.

Castra Ovarta: Oberaden on the Lippe.

Castra Trenta: Datteln on the Lippe.

Castra Secunda: Haltern on the Lippe.

Castra Prima: Holsterhausen on the Lippe.

Castra Aliso: Location unknown. Possibly at the western end of the Lippe across the Rhine from Xanten, or due northeast toward Osnabrück (and Kalkriese).

Castra Vetera: Xanten. By Wesel on the Rhine opposite the mouth of the Lippe.

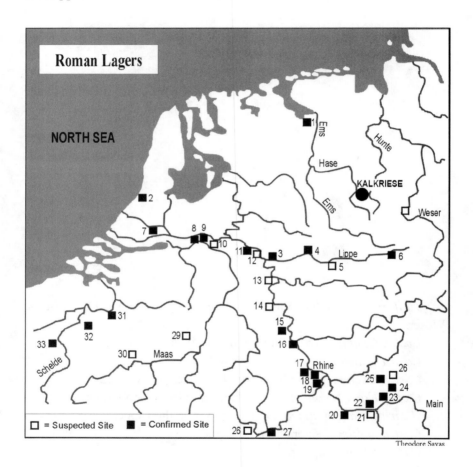

Theodore Savas

Bibliography

Berger, Frank und Stoess, Christian, *Die Fundmünzen der Römischen Zeit in Deutschland*, Abteilungen VII, Niedersachsen und Bremen, Band 1–3.

——. Band 4–9.

Bokemeir, Rolf, *Varus starb im Teotoburger Wald. Eine Antwort auf Kalkriese*, Kulturinstitut für interdisziplinäre Kultuforschung e.V. (Bettendorf/ Rheinland-Pfalz) 1996.

Brown, Anthony, *Fieldwork for Archaeologists and Historians*. BT Batsford Ltd, 1987.

Cassius Dio, *The Roman History*, "The Reign of Augustus. Penguin Classics, 1987.

Forster, E. S., *Lucius Annaeus Florus. Epitome of Roman History*. Loeb Classical Library.

Franzius, Georgia, *Aspekte römisch-germanischer Beziehungen in der Frühen Kaiserzeit*. 1995.

Vortragsreihe zur Sonderaustellung "Kalkriese–Römer im Osnabrücker Land." Osnabrück, 1993.

Hartmann, H., *Grössere Funde von Römermünzen im Landdrosteibezirk Osnabrück in der Provinz Hannover*. Monatsschr. Gesch. Westdeutschland 6, 1880, pp. 512–521.

Kühlborn, Johann Sebastian, *Germanien habe ich Befriedet*, Westfälisches Museum for Archaeology – Amt für Bodendenkmalpflege, 1995.

Mommsen, Theodore, 'Die Örtlichkeit der Varusschlacht', in *Sitzungsberichte der Preussischen Akademie der Wissenschaften*, 1885, 63pp (*Gesammelte Schriften 4* [Berlin, 1906] 200pp.)

Möser, Justus, *Osnabrückische Geschichte*, Allgemeine Einleitung (1768) 186f. 89, satzgleich mit Osnabrückische Geschichte, Teil I (1780), 3 Abschnitt, 159f. 15.

——, Justus, *Sämtliche Werke*, Band 2, Hist.-krit. Ausgabe in 14 Bänden, hrsg Akad. Wiss. Göttingen (Oldenburg, Hamburg, 1981), 123.

Peddie, John, *Invasion: The Roman Conquest of Britain*. Alan Sutton Publishing Ltd., 1987.

——, John, *The Roman War Machine*. Alan Sutton Publishing Ltd., 1994.

Schlüter, Wolfgang, *Archäologische Zeugnisse zur Varusschlacht? Die Untersuchungen in der Kalkrieser-Niewedder Senke bei Osnabrück*, Mit Beitragen von F. Berger, G. Franzius, J. Lienemann, A. Rost, E. Tolksdorf Lienemann, R. Wiegels, S. Wilbers-Rost, Germania 70, 1992, 307ff .

——, Wolfgang, *Kalkriese – Römer in Osnabrücker Land*. Rasch Verlag, Bramsche, 1993.

——, *Kalkriese – Römer im Osnabrücker Land. Archäologische Forschungen zur Varusschlacht*, Mit Beitragen von F. Berger, H. Buck, U Dieckmann, G. Franzius, J. Lienemann, J. Pape, R. Pott, A. Rost, R Stupperich, R. Wiegels, S. Wilbers-Rost, Bramsche, 1994.

——, *Osnabrücker Mitteilungen*, Band 88–1982.

——, *Römer im Osnabrücker Land, Die archäologischen Untersuchungen in der Kalkrieser-Niewedder Senke*. Mit Beitragen von F. Berger, G. Franzius, P. Glüsing, R. Wiegels, S. Wilbers-Rost. Schriftenreihe Kulturregion Osnabrück des Landschaftsverbandes, Osnabrück e.V., Band 4. Bramsche, 1991.

Schnurbein, Siegmar von, *Die Römer in Haltern*, Münster, Westfalen, 1979.

Seaby, H. A., *Roman Silver Coins, Vol. 1*, "The Republic of Augustus," 1978. Seaby Publications Ltd, London.

Tacitus, *The Annals of Imperial Rome*. Penguin Classics, 1956.

INDEX